The Structure of Society

The Structure of Society

BY MARION J. LEVY, JR.

PRINCETON, NEW JERSEY

PRINCETON UNIVERSITY PRESS

1952

TO

JOY C. LEVY

WHO HAS CONTRIBUTED
CRITICALLY,
SUBSTANTIVELY, AND
PATIENTLY

PREFACE

This volume is presented as a first and tentative step in a rather long range program of comparative social analysis. Briefly stated this program envisages work in four stages. This first volume is an attempt to construct from present knowledge of empirical materials on different societies a general conceptual scheme and theoretical system for beginning the comparative analysis of societies. The second stage of the program will involve the submission of the system of analysis thus obtained to careful and rigorous testing by attempts to analyze several societies that are apparently widely different from one another. When the materials from these studies are in hand, two further steps will remain: first there will be the comparative analysis of the materials so obtained; and second, there will be the revision and general reevaluation of the system of analysis in terms of the problems encountered in the attempts to apply it.

The reference above to the tentative nature of this volume cannot be emphasized too strongly. It was in the effort to accent this that the decision was made to publish the material in its present format rather than in a letterpress edition between "hard covers." The reader, it is hoped, will be constantly aware of the extremely elementary stage of development of the task that is barely begun here. References to gaps in and problems of the analysis appear throughout the text. The volume ends without any orthodox concluding chapter. It ends where it does because at that point I had no more to say than what had already been said. It certainly does not end there because

vii

anything approaching a definitive treatment of the subject
has been realized. When the specific studies contemplated
above have been completed, the group concerned with those
studies will have in hand the basis for a revision of the
analytical apparatus that rests on attempts to grapple
systematically with empirical phenomena. Without such
studies, revision would have to depend on further essentially "arm chair" work. The point of diminishing returns
for that sort of work has already arrived in my judgment
and in terms of my own present resources. It goes without
saying that no definitive treatment of the task begun here
will ever be completed. Conceptual schemes and theoretical systems applicable to empirical phenomena never finally solve the scientific problems of a field. If successful, they accomplish at most progressively more tenable
approximations to theoretical systems that are empirically
as well as logically closed. Actual achievement of such
closure would mean, of course, final and complete empirical knowledge, which is perhaps always a utopian but certainly never an actual goal of science.

The present volume contains the initial and tentative
system of analysis proposed for the program. It attempts
to reach the following goals:

1. It attempts to erect a conceptual scheme for
structural-functional analysis in general, and to define
with some precision those concepts of structure and function that promise to be most fruitful for this type of
analysis. Social scientists agree in general that mathematical analysis has not yet been shown to be generally
fruitful for most problems in social science at the present
stage of development. Whether this is due largely to
failures of the social scientists to provide the mathematicians with sufficiently developed models so that the
question of mathematical analysis could be raised, or to
failures of mathematical systems readily adapted to such
models to develop, or to some combination of the two, need

not detain us here. For the present at least the less
precise verbal forms of structural-functional analysis
seem to offer one of the more fruitful approaches for the
treatment of many problems in the social field just as in
the biological field. Progress in these attempts may even
facilitate progress toward the application of mathematical
analysis in these spheres. There exists, however, no systematic attempt to erect a conceptual scheme for structural-functional analysis and little discussion of systematic procedure in terms of such a scheme of analysis.
From the discussion of these problems two ends have been
sought: first, there has been an attempt to clarify some
of the concepts and procedures already widely used on an
implicit (i.e., the so-called "common sense") basis;
second, there has been an attempt to devise a method whereby the relative levels of generalization of statements
about social phenomena may be determined systematically.

2. The remainder of the volume attempts to apply the
concepts of structural-functional analysis so developed to
the problem of uniformities in social systems. The type
of social system on which attention is focused is that of
a "society." "Society" in this sense is a social system
such that all other social systems are either subcategories
of some particular society or of the interrelationships
between two or more societies. The question asked is substantially: "Are there general patterns that may be shown
to exist in all societies?" If these can be shown to
exist in any society, analysis can be carried systematically to lower levels of generalization, seeking similar,
though less general, uniformities in more and more specific types of societies. In order to implement this aim,
the following steps are taken in the volume:

a. A working definition for the term "society" is
proposed. This definition is such that: (1) it has an empirical referent, or is at least sufficiently explicit so
that the question may be tested; and (2) it is relevant

for the comparative analysis of social phenomena. There
is discussion at some length of why the concept is defined
as it is and the part played by the concept so defined in
the analysis that is attempted.

      b. There is an attempt to derive and indicate the
procedure of derivation of the functional requisites of
any society, i.e., of those conditions that must be present if a unit such as that defined as a society is to
exist within the range of variation possible for such
units.

      c. There is an attempt to derive and indicate the
procedure of derivation of the structural requisites of
any society, i.e., of the patterns of action such that the
conditions that result from action in terms of these patterns are the conditions necessary if the unit (society)
is to exist within the range of variation possible for
such units. In the derivation of the functional requisites of any society the question asked is: "Can anything
be shown as to what must be done if any example of the
type of unit concerned is to exist?" In the derivation of
the structural requisites of a unit the question is asked:
"Can anything be shown as to how what must be done, must
be done, if such a unit is to exist?"

      d. There is an attempt in part to indicate interre-
lationships among the structural requisites so derived.

      e. There is a further development of concepts already
in use for the analysis of different aspects of any relationship.

      f. There is an attempt explicitly both in general
terms and by means of examples to indicate how these different concepts may be used for comparative analysis.

      g. Finally, throughout the conceptual and theoreti-
cal development there is an effort to indicate systematic
procedures whereby errors in studies made in these terms
may be detected, thus leading to necessary revisions and
additions.

The volume thus presents in an initial and tentative form a system for the analysis of any society and a method of procedure whereby segments of such a unit may be analyzed and related to the whole. The system of analysis presented has not been assembled on a purely deductive basis. The "empirical" basis of what has been presented is the result both of past study drawing on general experience in this field and an attempt to grapple with numerous specific empirical problems in the field. It remains true, however, that even though the system has not been worked out as a "chess game," the tentative character of its present form inheres precisely in the fact that there exists no systematic body of empirical research in terms of the scheme. Such a body of empirical research is required if one is to be able to state with any degree of reliability to what extent the concepts suggested are useful and the theories advanced are more or less well confirmed. The next step in the program of this work is the task of determining by empirical research in what respects, if any, the system of analysis tentatively developed on a highly abstract level can be shown to offer useful concepts and relatively tenable theories. To ascertain the utilities, as well as the limitations and conceptual defects of the system in its present form, it is planned to test the system in a series of studies of societies that are widely different from one another. These individual studies would focus respectively on the United States, Russia, Ch'ing Dynasty and/or Republican China, Pre-Restoration and/or Post-Restoration Japan, Modern France, Modern England and/or Modern Germany, and at least one nonliterate society. These particular societies have been included in accordance with two criteria in addition to criteria suggested above: first, they represent radically different stages and types of industrialization, and hence their analysis separately and comparatively should throw major light on one of the major social problems of our

times; second, systematic scientific knowledge of these
societies is currently strategic for a whole range of
other social problems and for the development of a scientific knowledge of social phenomena in general.

In order to accomplish these objectives, a project
was presented to the Princeton University Research Committee for its consideration. The proposal called for a
group of men selected on the following bases: they would
form a group small enough for easy communication and large
enough to cover the comparative range sought; they would
already have specialized knowledge of the societies concerned; they would in general be familiar with the type of
analysis attempted; they would revise or add to the concepts suggested when the concepts proved ill-adapted or
insufficient, and refute or add to the theories proposed
when the theories were contradicted by the empirical materials; above all, they would not permit the target scheme
of analysis to become a "jail" for research rather than an
aid to it.

On the basis of this proposal the Committee made a
grant to permit the holding of two initial seminars. The
members of those seminars were as follows: David F. Aberle,
visiting associate professor (anthropology), Johns Hopkins
University; Alex Inkeles, lecturer (sociology), Harvard
University; David Landes, Society of Fellows (history),
Harvard University; John Pelzel, assistant professor
(anthropology), Harvard University; John Sawyer, assistant
professor (economic history), Harvard University; Francis
X. Sutton, assistant professor (sociology), Harvard University; and myself.[1]

The two seminars were held in April and October 1951

_____

1. Professor Bernard Barber of Smith College (sociology) participated in the first of the two meetings.
Professor Pelzel was unable to attend the first and Professor Sawyer was unable to attend the second.

and were devoted to criticism and discussion of the material in the present volume and the project proposed in
terms of it. At the end of the second meeting the members
agreed to further participation in the studies proposed in
the project if it could be realized. Their participation
would, of course, be within the limits set by current commitments or others necessarily entered into while seeking
to realize the project as a whole. For the present this
is where the matter stands.

The decision to publish the present volume was made
because a task of this sort and the empirical studies connected with it need all of the help they can get in the
form of criticism from scholars in the fields directly and
indirectly concerned. In this respect the useful distinction of criticism is not that between "destructive" and
"constructive" criticism but rather that between tenable
and untenable criticism. Tenable "destructive" criticism
can not fail to have its constructive side. Even if the
constructive side is confined to narrowing by elimination
the immense number of possible alternative paths toward
the goal, it will be no small accomplishment in a field so
unexplored, in so young and undeveloped a science as this.
Tenable "constructive" criticism will likewise have its
destructive side in the elimination of the erroneous, the
less precise, and the more nearly fruitless hypotheses.
Tenable criticism of whatever sort is always useful scientifically and, so far as this project is concerned, is
always welcome. Both my colleagues and I seek such criticism because it will place at our disposal intellectual
resources far beyond that of any restricted working group.

The question of acknowledgments is a thorny one in
such a work as this. The work draws on the general intellectual resources of its day and specifically on those of
the social sciences. Relatively few works have been cited
bibliographically because relatively few points have consciously been taken specifically and directly from other

sources. One can not very well cite a whole intellectual
climate. The reader will be well aware of the extent to
which this work has been influenced by the writings of
such past figures as Emile Durkheim, Vilfredo Pareto, Max
Weber, and Thorstein Veblen and by the writings of such
more or less contemporary figures as Kingsley Davis,
Robert K. Merton, Bronislaw Malinowski, Wilbert Moore,
Talcott Parsons, Pitirim A. Sorokin, R. H. Tawney, William
I. Thomas, and Florian Znaniecki.

A special indebtedness is owed, however, to Talcott
Parsons. The work grew out of concerns stimulated and
encouraged by him and by his work. This work was not done
in consultation with him, and it has taken many turns with
which I am sure he would not agree. He is certainly not
to blame for its shortcomings. Still its indebtedness to
him will be obvious enough to the reader, particularly
with regard to the distinction of the uses of concepts and
theories, the concern with systems of phenomena, and the
interrelationship of different aspects of social phenomena.

The work owes much of its initiation to the members
of a private seminar held at Harvard in the summer of 1947.
That seminar consisted of David F. Aberle, Albert K. Cohen,
Arthur K. Davis, Francis X. Sutton, and myself. At that
seminar the definition of the concept of society and the
list of functional requisites that form the bases for the
present work were produced. Both appear here somewhat
modified from the form in which they were worked out there
and published jointly in Ethics (Vol. 60, No. 2), but I am
indebted to the members of that seminar for their help
that summer. I am also in their debt and that of the
journal Ethics for permission to use and adapt that material freely.

My colleagues on the proposed project for the comparative analysis of social structure have been of considerable help by virtue of critical suggestions both
prior to and during the seminars we have already held.

The seminar suggestions themselves arrived too late to be incorporated in the present work. Further help by criticism was given by many scholars both at Princeton and elsewhere in the fields of anthropology, economics, history, law, political science, sociology and the like to whom the work was shown in rough draft. Among these were Professors Bernard Barber, William J. Baumol, Gerald Breese, Arthur K. Davis, Kingsley Davis, Josiah W. Goode, Donald Hager., Duncan MacRae, Myres S. McDougal, Wilbert Moore, Robert Palmer, Talcott Parsons, Gardner Patterson, Harold Sprout, Robert Redfield, Samuel Stouffer, and John Useem. A debt is also owed to the intellectual community outside of these fields at Princeton where epistemologists, biologists, physicists, and mathematicians stand unusually ready to help their colleagues in social science. From these latter fields I am chiefly indebted to John T. Bonner, Robert Bush, William Feller, William P. Jacobs, Marston Morse, Paul Oppenheim, Colin S. Pittendrigh, Rubby Sherr, John Tukey, and Hermann Weyl, none of whom is responsible for my misunderstandings of his fields or my own. My immediate colleagues in the social sciences and in history have been most patient, helpful, and understanding as have my students, both graduate and undergraduate, who have helped me in ways which defy identification.

Funds to provide partial relief from teaching, to finance two seminars for the project on comparative analysis of social structure, to aid in manuscript preparation, and to support the research in other ways have come liberally from the Princeton University Research Committee. The encouragement of this committee has not been limited to financial aid. Its members have been available for all sorts of advice and criticism of research and research planning. The personal value to me of the help provided through this channel has been enormous.

Finally three of my students have been of special assistance in the preparation of this manuscript for pub-

lication.   They are Mr. David Apter, Mr. G. Phillips Hanna
and Mr. Stanley Udy.   Mr. Udy has been particularly inde-
fatigable and thorough in his work on the index for this
volume.   Mr. Hanna has performed a corresponding service
in his preparation of the expanded table of contents.

Gratitude is due to the <u>American Sociological Review</u>
for permission to use material printed there and to the
Harvard University Press for permission to adapt material
from a book of mine previously published by them.

Marion J. Levy, Jr.

Princeton, New Jersey
March 1952

C O N T E N T S

THE STRUCTURE OF SOCIETY

C H A P T E R   I

INTRODUCTION

A. STATEMENT OF THE PROBLEM

As has been stated in the preface, this volume is presented as a first step in a long-range program of comparative social analysis. The total program is not aimed
solely at a series of analyses of different societies;[1]
it also seeks, in its present tentative form, to utilize
present knowledge of empirical materials on different societies in order to create a general conceptual scheme for
the comparative analysis of societies, and a theoretical
system[2] of general relevance to the structure and functioning of societies. Its revision, subsequent to the completion of the empirical studies included in the program, will
utilize the materials so obtained to modify and revise
those concepts and theories. It is obvious, of course,
that such a goal is one to be approximated but not one to
be achieved, for the same reasons that one never expects
to achieve final conceptual schemes and theoretical systems
in any empirical science. It is also necessary to admit

---

1. The concept "society" as used here is defined in
Chapter III, which is devoted to the definition of that
concept and a discussion of its derivation and use.

2. The distinction between conceptual schemes and
theoretical systems is discussed below in Chapter V,
pp. 226-237. It is discussed there rather than here in
order that illustrations in terms of concepts and theories
employed in this work may be used.

at the outset that such an attempt to approach the goal
may be doomed to failure in this field. The decision to go
ahead with the attempt rests on two foundations: first, a
faith that such an approach can be made, and second, the
absence of any convincing evidence or unshakable methodological arguments to the contrary. If such an attempt does
succeed in moving toward the goal sought, work in terms of
the conceptual scheme will progressively diminish four
general problems that plague comparative analysis: (a) a
consistent set of general concepts for the analysis of societies; (b) the identification of the various levels of
generalization involved in the use of comparative materials;
(c) the development of a theoretical system for the structure of societies; and (d) the use of a generalized system
of theory on comparative materials to facilitate further
theoretical development.

     (a) If one seeks to do comparative analysis on em-
pirical materials currently available, one is beset by the
persistent problem of the consistent use of concepts even
on the most general levels of analysis. The Cross Cultural
Survey at Yale University is certainly the most ambitious
and useful tool yet developed in social science for these
purposes, but it is limited by the nature of its raw material. Many social scientists are not in the habit of defining their major concepts at all, leaving the comparative
analyst only internal evidence to guide him in their use.
Many who do define them do not use their concepts consistently. Finally, comparative analysis is often frustrated
by the fact that the implicit or explicit concepts used for
similar purposes may have quite different referents in the
case of work on different societies by different or even
the same scholars. There is no call in what has been said
here to alter one's data to fit one's concepts. "Magic"
may be, and commonly is, of different types in different
societies, but if no general concept of "magic" exists of
which these types may be more specific subcategories, then
comparative analysis is reduced, to that extent, to an in-

tuitive rather than a scientific basis. This is a major
reason for pleading the cause of general concepts. And
their generality must be insisted upon. If the term "family" is defined as a concrete membership unit consisting of
father, mother, and nonadult children, then that unit is
identical in composition for all societies in which it is
found (although if one uses this definition there are societies in which it will not be found). Many empirical
differences will be lost sight of by such a concept, and
in many cases attention will be focused on a unit that,
from the point of view of actors in the society concerned,
is not a focus of attention. If, on the other hand, the
"family" is defined as "the smallest kinship unit on a membership basis that is treated as a unit for generalized
purposes by other parts of the society and other parts of
the kinship structure,"[3] whatever the shortcomings of the
definition may be in other respects, it makes possible the
notation of many of these differences without loss of com-
parability on a highly general level. Specific cases may
take the form of multilineal conjugal families in one society, patriarchal, patrilineal, and patrilocal ones in
another, and so forth. A conceptual scheme for general
comparative analysis must seek to erect systematically concepts that will retain general comparative implications and
yet provide leeway at lower levels of generalization for
adjustment to differences in the data. This type of concept has proved useful in all of the natural sciences (e.g.,
atom, nucleus, metabolism, skeleton, etc.) and, insofar as
developed, has also proved useful in the social sciences[4]
(e.g., clans, nations, role differentiation, universalism,

---

3. This definition cited as an example is taken from
M. J. Levy, Jr., The Family Revolution in Modern China,
Harvard, Cambridge, 1949, p. 5. (This book will be referred to subsequently as M. J. Levy, Jr., Family Revolution.)

4. G. P. Murdock, Social Structure, Macmillan, New
York, 1949, is an excellent recent example of this sort of
work.

social system, rationality, magic, etc.).

(b) Even if the concepts used in comparative materials on different societies are generalized concepts and
have explicitly or implicitly been defined in a manner
identical for the problem in hand, there remains the problem of whether or not the statements about the phenomena
in the different societies are on the same or different
levels of generalization. It is essential for comparative
purposes to know if, for example, the phenomena in one
case apply to all the individuals in the society and only
to a selected group in the other. It is hoped that the
scheme for analysis tentatively developed here will make
it easier (if not inevitable) to discover similarities or
differences in levels of generalization of materials being
examined for comparative purposes.

(c) It is hoped that some success will be achieved
in the attempt to devise in some detail the structural requisites of _any_ society. The concept of society used here
is explicitly defined in the body of the work. It is hoped
that the referent of that concept is roughly similar to its
general use by social scientists. Even if this is not the
case, it is hoped that there will be numerous empirical
referents of that concept as used here. If progress is
made here toward this objective, it should make possible
far more systematic analyses of societies (or other phenomena) than are being made currently. When analyses of
societies (or other phenomena) are made, they are made in
terms of either explicitly or implicitly (or some combination of the two) developed conceptual schemes. It is the
general tenet of this work that, except for the occasional
man of genius like Freud, a researcher is far less likely
to have trouble with concepts if his concepts are made as
explicit as possible. At least he can tell where his concepts are illsuited to the data on this basis. Moreover,
the explicit development of concepts is one of the basic
general methodological tenets of all science.

If these explicit concepts have empirical referents,

and if they are interrelated in the form of tenable theories, then it is possible to have a systematic test for
whether or not relevant material about a particular society
has been overlooked. The explicit development of concepts
for, and theories about, the structural requisites of any
society[5] will designate certain general types of patterns
that must be present in all societies (if the societies are
to persist), however much the specific forms may differ.
Furthermore, the attempt to be explicit in these respects
will make more explicit the attention to those elements in
analysis that are left residual. This should focus continual attention on the revision of the conceptual scheme
and theoretical system in the direction of greater adequacy.
Finally, as will be pointed out below,[6] such a procedure
will make more explicit the sources of difficulty in using
such analysis. Failure to discover material on a pattern
designated as a "structural requisite of any society" will
lie in one of three (or some combination of the three)
sources: (a) a failure in observation; (b) a theoretical
failure, i.e. a pattern called a "structural requisite of
any society" does not in fact have such a character; or
(c) the unit being analyzed may not actually conform to the
definition of a society. It can be seen from these three
sources of error, and from the discussion of the methods
used here, that this approach does not seek to impose a
ready-made conceptual scheme and theoretical system willy-
nilly upon the data, regardless of whether or not the
method of analysis is suited to that data.

(d) Finally, if such a systematic approach proves to
be useful, it should, both on its most general level and on
more specific levels, aid in the use of comparative materials for the systematic discovery of theories about empiri-

---

5. The concept of "structural requisites" and the
role played by this concept is discussed in detail below
in Chapter II, pp. 34-43 and 62-71.
6. See Chapter II, pp. 46-55 and 68-71.

cal phenomena. The method should facilitate this process
because the clustering of specific types of patterns (e.g.,
Are predominantly universalistic relationships likely also
to be predominantly functionally specific and rational
ones?) cannot well be overlooked if the general categories
of which these are specific subcategories can be generally
applied to the analysis of widely different societies.

B. THE CONCEPT OF SOCIAL ACTION

It is a basic tenet of this work that all of the social sciences are concerned with the analysis of the same
general data. These data have to do with <u>social action</u>.
The different scholars in this general field may approach
many different problems from many different points of view,
but the general source of data for them all is identical.
The economists may focus attention on the allocation of
goods and services, the political scientists on the allocation of power and responsibility, the criminologist on
"social deviants," the urban sociologists on the structure
and functioning of "cities," and so forth, but all of these
represent differing abstractions about what will be defined
as social action in this volume. The interest of the social scientist is not unrelated to the interests of other
scientists. At least in terms of levels of generalization,
this relation can be set forth without undue difficulty.

The most general level of analysis of empirical phenomena is that of physics. Any phenomenon that can be
placed in the "time-space" frame of reference is subject
for consideration in that field. The so-called biological
sciences separate from all the mass of empirical phenomena
those that can be described as "living." The biological
sciences study the possible variations of living matter
within the limits set by physicochemical considerations.
The social sciences are concerned with a specific range of
"living" phenomena, i.e., social action. At present the
social scientists are largely concerned with a certain

possible range of variations of the members of one particular species, homo sapiens.

  1. The definition of the concept of social action

    Ordinarily the social scientist is not interested in
all possible ranges of variation of these phenomena. He
is concerned with that range of possible variation within
the limits set on the one hand by human heredity in the
strict biological sense, and on the other by the nonhuman
environment. These limitations are comprised of biological
factors and the interrelationships of such factors with
"nonliving" empirical phenomena. The concept of social
action is residually defined for the purposes of this work
as all action (i.e., operation, including in that term mere
persistence) by individuals of a given species that (1) is
explicable or analyzable in empirical[7] terms, and (2) cannot be explained or analyzed adequately[8] for the purposes

----

    7. This does not, of course, exclude the empirical
significance of "belief" in nonempirical factors. Thus
"gods" as they are generally conceived by men are nonempirical factors. An empirical scientist qua scientist can
take only an agnostic position on substantive questions
about such factors. At the same time, human belief or
faith in such entities is an empirical phenomenon. Furthermore, there is ample empirical evidence to indicate
that a difference in such beliefs in nonempirical factors
does account at least in part for some empirical differences in other respects. The attitude and actions of many
devout Protestants and Hindus differ markedly in the matter of social mobility, and these differences are at least
in part affected by their differing beliefs in nonempiri-
cals. Social scientists are very much concerned with empirical observations of this order even though they involve, at least from the point of view of the actor, nonempirical considerations; nor does such concern by the social
scientists violate the empirical scientific character of
their work.
    8. An explanation of a given action is considered
"adequately explained or analyzed" for present purposes if,
on the level of generalization under consideration, one can
demonstrate why it is as encountered and is not otherwise.

intended in terms of the factors of the heredity of that
species and its environment, exclusive of other members of
that species.

The social scientists as a whole have been overwhelmingly concerned with the members of one particular species,
homo sapiens. Often social action is spoken of as though
it were confined to that species. Social action as defined
here is not so confined. Human social action is merely one
special case of social action in general -- the special
case concerned with those actions of humans (homo sapiens)
that (1) are explicable and analyzable in empirical terms,
and (2) cannot be explained and analyzed adequately for the
purposes intended in terms of the factors of human heredity
and nonhuman environment.[9] These two sets of factors de-

---

9. Notice of the position of human social action as
a special case of social action in general is important if
the concept is to be used as defined here. There may well
be action phenomena associated with species other than
homo sapiens that share this same emergent property here
defined residually. Insofar as this is so, there will be
a social action sphere of analysis for such species. In
all probability such spheres may be demonstrated for other
mammalian species, and the work of Prof. T. C. Schneirla
on the army ants (e.g., "Levels in the Psychological
Capacities of Animals," Philosophy for the Future [ed. by
R. W. Sellars, V. J. McGill, and M. Ferber], Macmillan,
New York, 1949; "Ant Learning as a Problem in Comparative
Psychology," Twentieth Century Psychology [ed. by
P. L. Harriman, et.al.], Philosophical Library, New York,
1945; "Problems in the Biopsychology of Social Organization," Jour. of Abnormal Soc. Psych., Vol. 41, No. 4 [Oct.
1946], pp. 385-402; "Social Organization in Insects as
Related to Individual Function," Psychol. Rev., Vol. 48,
No. 6 [Nov. 1941], pp. 465-486; etc.) would seem to indicate such a range with regard to that species. Most of
the definitions of social action in use, either explicitly
or implicitly, would seem also to have such counterparts
among species other than homo sapiens, or at least one may
say that the contrary has not been demonstrated. There is,
of course, every reason to believe that the range of possible variations of this sort is considerably more narrow
in other species having it than in homo sapiens, but this
constitutes a difference of degree, not kind.

The concern here, as in most social science, is with
human social action, however, and the shorter term, social
action, will be used throughout this work with that specific case in mind unless otherwise noted.

termine the limits of possible variation of social action, but at least at the present stage of development of the biological and physicochemical sciences, they are not sufficient to locate points within those limits, just as physicochemical factors in the present stage of development of knowledge are not sufficient in and of themselves to locate all the specific points within the range of variation open to "living" phenomena.

It has been noted that social action is defined residually for present purposes. This is done deliberately in the belief that the residual definition used here is just as useful and much less troublesome than many of the positive definitions usually employed. The residual definition used will involve certain imprecisions. Most notably there is the question, discussed immediately below, of uncertainty as to the location of these limits. But here the definition becomes no more or less precise than the present state of knowledge in the physicochemical and biological sciences, whereas the positive definitions depend, in large, upon the far less precise developments in the social sciences themselves. That is to say, the identification of any given action as social or nonsocial as here defined involves the question of whether it can or can not be explained adequately for the purposes in hand by means of physicochemical and/or biological theories at their present stage of development. The usual more positive identification of social action depends on the measurement of social factors themselves, and these latter are certainly, on the whole, less precisely developed than the former. For example, Max Weber defines social action in the following terms: "Action is social insofar as, by virtue of the subjective meaning attached to it by the acting individual (or individuals), it takes account of the behavior of others and is thereby oriented in its course."[10] The

---

10. Max Weber, The Theory of Social and Economic Organization, [trans. by A. M. Henderson and Talcott Parsons], Oxford, New York, 1947, p. 88.

techniques for ascertaining the existence of "subjective meaning," assuming that term to be empirically defined, let alone the determination of its context, leave much to be desired. In the judgment of the author it leaves more than is left by one's ability to discover the present stage of relevant physicochemical and/or biological knowledge. There is, of course, no definitively "correct" position on this question. The matter is perhaps best judged by the extent to which flaws in the general theories developed can be avoided by the use of a concept of social action differently defined. The position taken here on this question is stated explicitly in order to facilitate this type of correction. Any positive, more fruitful, and more precise definition of the concept will be freely substituted for its present one.

2. The limits of variation

The definition of social action proposed here affords a basis for differentiating the subject matter of the social from that of the natural sciences. Though residual, it is precise in the sense that those phenomena for which adequate explanations exist in physicochemical and/or biological terms can be determined for any given stage of development of knowledge in those fields. Thus, if the limits of possible variation (human heredity and nonhuman environment for present purposes) are conceived as forming the perimeter of a figure[11] (as illustrated below), then

---

11. The figure used is a so-called "free form." It is not used with any intention of playing consciously or unconsciously upon its peculiar mathematical properties except insofar as they are involved in the following two points which the figure is intended to illustrate graphically: (1) the possibility of any phenomena falling within or without the limits, for which purpose any figure having an inside and an outside might have been used, and (2) the impossibility of one of the two limiting factors, either the heredity or nonspecies environment of any species, having implications for the existence of that species without

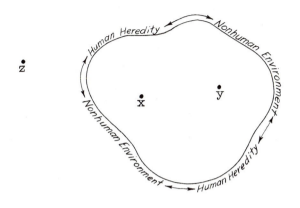

the area encloses the area of social action. Why a given
act falls at point x as opposed to point y can not be explained solely in terms of the limits of such possible
variation. If the action falls at point z, it can be so
explained on the level of generality given. Furthermore,
in the case of the example used, the question of explaining
why the action can or can not occur at point z as opposed
to point x or y or some other point within the limits may
also be capable of explanation solely in terms of the limits. Examples may be given of these points. One may, at
the present stage of development, explain some reflex actions completely in terms of these limits; they fall outside the figure (or on its perimeter, which comes to the
same thing for present purposes). One may also explain,
in terms of these limits, why the probability of a human
infant's survival without the aid of other humans for a

---

the other limiting factor being involved. The whole futil-
ity of the general "heredity vs. environment" controversy
is involved in the second point. It is quite impossible to
answer the question, "What are the implications of such and
such a genetically determined trait in a given animal?"
without specifying explicitly or implicitly some environment for it.

prolonged period following birth is extremely low, if not
zero. One can not explain in terms of such limits, however,
why the infants in one society are cared for differently
than are those in another, or why the infants in a given
society are clothed in one particular fashion and not another.

It would be amiss not to indicate that, whatever the
advantages of such an approach may be, it raises problems
for the social scientists that may be as great as those
eliminated. These difficulties may be classified under two
major headings: (a) ignorance, and (b) variation.

a. <u>Ignorance about the limits</u>. This difficulty is
inherent in the fact that final knowledge has not been
reached and is not to be expected even with regard to those
aspects of the nonsocial sciences that are relevant for the
social sciences. In addition to this "ultimate" difficulty, there is the fact that work in the nonsocial sciences
is in a very elementary stage of development in many of its
aspects most relevant for social science. It is difficult
to locate these limits save in extreme examples. Thus,
one may easily give an adequate explanation in terms of
these limits of the fact that, without mechanical aids, it
is out of the question that there be a society of persons
dwelling on the ocean floor, or one located in Antarctica
in which only bathing suits are worn. Similarly, one can
explain in terms of these limits man's inability to fly
without mechanical aids. These examples are deliberately
more extreme than the ones previously used in order to insist on the magnitude of the problem. In this work considerably more relevant and less extreme use of these limits is made, but there is a genuine sense in which our
ignorance, particularly of human heredity, in many less
extreme but highly relevant instances leaves room for argument that is not conducted merely for its own sake.

Frank recognition of this source of difficulty is not
a counsel of despair, although it would be dangerous to

ignore it. Much of this work is based on the premise that,
even with limited and imperfect knowledge of the exact nature and location of these limits, considerable use can be
made of them for the development of knowledge in the social
field. Frank consideration of this difficulty has another
advantage. It suggests a systematic basis of interdisciplinary cooperation among those scientists primarily concerned with the analysis of social phenomena and the nonsocial scientists in general (but particularly of those
nonsocial scientists interested in the implications of
their work for the understanding of social phenomena).
This cooperation lies in a systematic attempt to analyze
those factors setting limits. One of the major problems
faced by social scientists, for example, is the fact that
little is known about the range of variation or the specific factors that are determined by human heredity. Something
is known about blood groups, hair forms, skin color, morphological features, and the like. Some attempts have been
made to link morphological features (some of which are
supposedly and very probably determined genetically in
considerable part) and "personality traits." But the former knowledge so far is of a quite restricted range of
usefulness, and the latter is most questionable at just
those points at which the genetic determination of "personality" is alleged whether explicitly or implicitly.[12]
The fact that so little is known about this area of problems should serve only as an incentive to further work.
To the degree that these limits are incompletely known,
there will always be an element of indeterminancy about
social science because of the uncertain line that will

---

12. The contributions of Prof. W. H. Sheldon and his
followers are perhaps the most noteworthy in this field.
Whether or not he and his coworkers can definitively establish such connections, his work has already proved most
fruitful and stimulating in many directions. If he can establish such a connection definitively and meaningfully, he
will have cracked through a major scientific frontier.

exist between those factors generally having the form of limiting constants for any specific problem and the general variables involved in the analysis of the systems concerned. With differences in degree, most notable ones perhaps, the situation of the biological sciences as well as many others is not otherwise in this respect.

　　　b. Variation of the limits. Quite apart from the uncertainties imposed by inadequate knowledge, it is quite clear that, whatever else may be said of these limits, they are not immutable limits on levels strategic for social analysis. The sources of variation are of at least two sorts: firstly, variation may result from factors adequately explicable solely in terms of nonsocial factors (i.e., in terms of the factors of human heredity and nonhuman environment); secondly, the variations in the limits set may be explicable, at least in part, in terms of the results of social action. In both these categories of variation more seems to be known about changes in the limits set by nonhuman environment, but this would seem to be a result of the relative stages of development of knowledge about human heredity and the nonhuman environment.

　　　In the first category of variations fall such changes as viable mutations independent of social factors and, quite obviously, a whole range of geographic changes. As far as is known, earthquakes of major proportions, many climatic changes, and the like can not, with presently available technologies, be produced by men. Such changes, though they arise from nonsocial causes, may, and often do, alter the possible range of variation of social action by changing the limits of such action. The accuracy with which such changes can be identified varies, of course, with the state of empirical knowledge about such factors, but the accuracy with which the implications of such changes can be judged will vary with the state of development of the empirical conceptual scheme and theoretical system applying to social action.

The second order of variations is, in a sense, more complex and difficult than the first. Here the concept of "technology" in the usual sense of the term enters the discussion by way of illustration. There may be limits of possible social variation set by the factors of human heredity and nonhuman environment that can not conceivably be affected by man's social action, but in this day of rapidly and dramatically changing technology, few men would care to state what those limits are, and it is more doubtful whether any such positions could be proved. Furthermore, it is not possible, for the present at least, to account adequately for the stage of development of technology solely in terms of human heredity and nonhuman environment. There has not, it is true, been any notable conscious modification of human heredity limits by man so far,[13] but so obvious have been the alterations in the implications of the limits set by the factors of the nonhuman environment that no general discussion of a particular set of such limits would be undertaken today by competent scientists without some specific reference to, and explicit statement of, some particular state of the "industrial arts." It is quite obvious to all that the implications of terrain conditions, for example, vary enormously in relation to those societies using only human power, those having domesticated pack animals, and those having developed concrete roads and internal combustion engines.

Societies may vary enormously in the degree to which the activity of the people involved in them tends to keep these limits (or at least their implications) in a constant state of flux. "Modern industrial society," in the loose

---

13. Nevertheless, it remains an open question as to whether or not social patterns such as endogamy, exogamy, incest taboos, and perhaps many other types of patterns have so affected the "gene pool" of some populations as to change the limits of variation in relevant respects.

sense of that concept, is an extreme case of mutability in this regard. Thus it is precisely in the analysis of "modern industrial societies" that it is most difficult to gain a precise knowledge of these limits of variation. But the same problem in a somewhat simplified form is present even in the societies that are most sedentary in these respects.

The difficulties involved in the precise determination of the limits of possible variation of social phenomena do not preclude work in this field. They are mentioned for two reasons: on the one hand, to indicate a major focus of cross-disciplinary cooperation on the part of "social" and "natural" scientists,[14] and on the other, to present explicitly a major source of difficulty in the advance of social analysis. A great deal of social analysis in the past has tended to reduce all social explanation to the factors of human heredity and nonhuman environment or to ignore these factors altogether.[15] At the present stage of development of the "natural" and "social" sciences, these factors can not be the sole categories of explanation, can not be ignored in such explanations, and enter these explanations in the explicit consideration of the limits of possible variation with due concern being given

---

14. The increasing concern with the development of "social biology" is an example of this type of cooperation. In this field the concern is not, as so often has been the case in the past, with the biologistic determination of action, but with the limits set on such action by biological factors alone and the ways in which the distribution or composition of the biological factors themselves may be affected by social action directly oriented to such changes (most notably, technology) or by social action which has such results without self-conscious orientation to them.

15. See Talcott Parsons, The Structure of Social Action, McGraw-Hill, New York, 1937, pp. 43-86, for a discussion of the positivistic and idealistic theories of action. (This book will be referred to subsequently as Talcott Parsons, Structure.)

to the relation of particular social patterns or actions
and the exact locus of those limits.

Consideration of the limits set by human heredity and
nonhuman environment in the fashion suggested here, and
applied throughout the volume, avoids two sorts of difficulties that have plagued the role of these concepts in
social science. It does not avoid or give definitive answers to the genuine problems that gave rise to these
difficulties, but it is hoped that it provides an approach
in terms of which such solutions are possible. First, it
does not fall into the heredity vs. environment controversy. Seen from the point of view taken here, it is
meaningless to ask what factors are caused by either heredity or environment when one is considered in isolation
from the other. The requirement that infants be cared for
by noninfants if they are to survive is not explicable
solely in terms of either heredity or environment, but only
in terms of some combination of the two. Human heredity
could remain unchanged and this requirement could be
negated if the nonhuman environment were different in certain respects and vice versa. The implications of a change
in either heredity or environment for the range of possible
variation of social action can never be explored without
assuming or discovering whether or not the other factor
remained constant in relevant respects. Second, it avoids
the fallacies of explaining everything in terms of these
limits or ignoring them altogether. The limits are always
relevant at least in determining why certain other conceivable alternatives to a given action are impossible.
They are cast in the role of <u>necessary but not sufficient</u>
determinants of a given social action. They always explain
something, but they never explain all about a social action
insofar as the development of scientific knowledge about
these limits does not eliminate all possibility of a range
of variation set by them.

C. THREE GENERALIZED APPROACHES TO THE STUDY
OF SOCIAL PHENOMENA

On the most general level of analysis of social phenomena three approaches have been distinguished. Work of
a highly generalized nature with regard to both conceptual
schemes and theoretical systems is currently being carried
forward from all three points of view. Still other approaches may be forthcoming, but for the present these
three would seem to characterize the most highly generalized developments in the field. The three approaches are
directed to the questions, "What concepts can be used and
what theories can be derived about (1) any social action?
(2) any social system? and (3) any society?"

Work on any social action is in one sense the most
general type of work possible in the social field. It is
concerned with the most general determinants of location
of particular acts within the limits set by human heredity
and nonhuman environment. In work on this level, the actual "mechanisms" or processes of interrelations between the
nonsocial limits of variation and social factors are a
major focus of interest. So are questions of the social
factors themselves. Many approaches to parts of this problem are currently being developed and pursued. Students
of psychoanalysis, psychiatry, learning theory, and many
others have contributed and continue to contribute to this
line of development. In one way or another scholars in the
field of social science and the background of social literature from which it sprang have been concerned explicitly
or implicitly with these problems. In the United States
the names of men like Cooley and Mead immediately come to
mind. Among sociologists, as that term is generally used,
Parsons has probably been the most prominent recent figure
in this connection. His work first attacked this problem
in terms of a "means-ends" scheme and then shifted to an
"actor-situation" scheme. Only recently, in collaboration
with several colleagues, Parsons has prepared for publica-

tion a volume that attempts to attack this question systematically and thoroughly.[16]

The general theory of social action must seek concepts
and theories applicable in differing degrees and combinations to the most diverse acts -- to acts that, initially
at least, share in common only their inexplicability in
terms of the limits of human heredity and nonhuman environment. It represents, perhaps, the most formidable scientific task in the entire social field. Many problems can
no doubt be treated by making assumptions with regard to
this type of analysis, but the systematic development of
tenable analyses about any social action can not fail to
have far-reaching consequences for all the other work in
the social field. "Motivation," for example, is one major
category of phenomena that such developments will have to
elucidate. "Motivation" is presumably involved in such
diverse actions as the care of one's children, a speech on
foreign policy, applications for jobs, etc. Many problems
can be treated by simply pointing to the fact that people
are "motivated" to do given things, but greater understanding of the process is vital to the development of
knowledge about the wider potentialities of such phenomena.

Work on any social system is hardly less formidable as
an intellectual task. A social system is defined for present purposes, following Parsons' work, as any "system of
social action involving a plurality of interacting individuals."[17] A system may be defined for present purposes

---

16. The final published version of this work has been
under preparation at the same time as the present one, and
hence use of its findings has not been made here.

17. Talcott Parsons, Essays in Sociological Theory
Pure and Applied, The Free Press, Glencoe, Ill., 1949, p. 6.
(This book will be referred to subsequently as Talcott
Parsons, Essays.)

I. INTRODUCTION

as any patterned[18] collection of elements. The term "society" as it will be used in this volume is one particular type of social system, but it is only one of an infinite (or at least a very large) number of conceivable types. A monastery, Mr. Smith's family, two friends meeting on the street, a crowd, the United Nations Organization, are other examples chosen at will. Approach to social analysis from the point of view of any social system raises the question, "What can be said about the character or operation of any membership unit?" Its relationship to the approach of any social action is intimate, but the two are by no means identical. The analysis of the processes of action as they affect the individual is in a sense background material for the analysis of any social system. The social action approach uncovers and explains the broadest potentialities

---

18. A note on the term random is required here. It has been used in two senses, often confused. One use is in a technical sense, when the term is applied to a situation in which, for example, it is as probable that a given particle will be at one point in a given space as at another. In this sense a quite definite pattern is involved. On the other hand, it has been used to inject what would amount to a pure element of chaos in empirical phenomena. It has been used to refer to a variable as completely undetermined and unpredictable. It is one of the metaphysical assumptions of science that such elements do not influence empirical systems. If it were not, such elements, insofar as they were interrelated with other parts of the system, would of course make the entire system undetermined and unpredictable on high or low levels of generalization. Often variables about whose variation there is no adequate knowledge have been spoken of in this sense, but this is a dangerous procedure because of its implications for the system.

In this volume the term random will ordinarily be used in its technical sense. If the second sense is intended, it will be put in quotation marks. Thus, a "patterned collection of elements" is a non-"random" one in this sense. Its ordering principle may be no more detailed or revealing than that of randomness in the technical sense. It is a collection, in other words, about which some more or less tenable generalizations can be made, even if the generalization does not extend beyond the type of collection involved.

in the social field. The analysis of systems of action
proceeds to narrow the possibilities by focusing attention
on the question of the implications of membership or participation in a system.

The intimacy of the two approaches is not to be under-
estimated, however, because it is a simple matter to show
that in the complete absence of any systems of social
action, no social action of any sort could or would take
place. This theorem (an implication of the two definitions
if they in fact have empirical referents) is explicable in
terms of the factors of human heredity and nonhuman environment. Even if one assumes the possibility of accounting
for a human birth in the absence of any social system, one
certainly can not account for the survival of any human
infant without such elements. The care of infants by
others, usually adults, is necessary if the infant is to
survive. Even the action of an adult isolated from all
other individuals involves social systems of some sort
since it is not possible to explain his actions under such
circumstances without involving patterns inculcated through
social systems.

Every volume and paper in the field of social science
is of course concerned with social systems in some manner,
but explicit systematic scientific attempts to explore the
question of social systems on their most general level have
not been numerous. Scholars have been more concerned with
social systems of one or more particular types such as
crowds, schools, governments, business firms, families,
etc. Again, Parsons' work emerges as the most recent
large-scale effort in this respect,[19] but like the other
recent work of Parsons and his colleagues, scholars in this

----

19. This work, like the work of Parsons previously
mentioned (see Note 16 above) has been under preparation
at the same time as the present one, and hence use of its
findings has not been made here.

field have not yet had time to evaluate it in detail.

Work on _any_ society is a third possible approach to the field of social phenomena. As the term society is defined here,[20] it is a particular and peculiar type of social system. It is a particular type in that it is one among many possible types. As such, remarks about any society are on a lower level of generalization than remarks about any social system. Since a society, as defined here, is a system of social action, its analysis is also on a lower level of generalization in many respects than is the analysis of any social action. It is a peculiar type of social system in that all social systems other than societies are to be found either as parts or subcategories of one specific society or as the result of the interrelationship between two or more societies. This state of affairs is not true by definition; it is stated as an hypothesis. Given the concept as defined here, whether or not one can find a specific case of a social system other than a society but not a subcategory of a given society or the result of the interrelation of two or more societies is an empirical question. Some of the relevance of such a work as the present volume will rest, however, upon this proposition, and to the extent that exceptions to it are produced, some of the hope for the relevance of this work must be abandoned.

To the extent that a society is a peculiar type of social system in the respect stated above, it is a strategic unit for general social analysis. Analysis in terms of such a unit should throw into relief relationships among other types of social systems, and this in turn should have its relevance for social action. The peculiar status of the concept of society as used here is not a unique one in scientific work. In the field of biology, which would seem to share a large number of methodological

---

20. See p. 113.

problems with the social sciences,[21] the concept "organism" has an analogous position. In biology the analogy to the three approaches differentiated here in the social field would be approaches to (1) any "life," (2) any "living system," and (3) any "organism" as those concepts are often used. Furthermore, in biology, as in social science, it has not been common for these three approaches to be differentiated, nor has work in the field confined itself characteristically to one approach or the other.

It is not the contention of the present volume that work should be confined to one or another of these three approaches at any one time. Work that mixes them may be quite fruitful and valid. It is the contention, however, that some work that attempts to focus on one of these approaches at a time may also be fruitful and may elucidate problems that might otherwise be ignored. The intimate relations between the first two approaches has already been suggested. The relation between either or both of them and the third is no less intimate insofar as the hypothesis about the peculiarity of the relationship of societies to other social systems can be maintained. All social action involves social systems, and no social system can exist in the absence of social action. All social systems are coterminous with, or parts of, a society (or societies) and no society could exist in the absence of social action. At the same time, social factors, as such, are by no means the only elements that enter explanations in the social realm. The "biological factors" of human heredity and nonhuman environment are relevant to all three approaches. They can no more be eliminated from such analysis than they can be made, at the present stage of knowledge, the sole significant variables for adequate analysis in that realm.

---

21. Most notably, those involved in the use of the concepts of function and structure: see Chapter II below.

D. THE CHOICE OF THE "SOCIETY" APPROACH

The approach used here is the third one. It has been
selected for several explicit reasons and perhaps for
several implicit ones as well. It has been selected in
preference to the social action approach because of personal limitations of knowledge on the part of the writer. It
has been selected in preference to both the first and
second approaches because substantial efforts of a systematic character are currently being made along both those
lines by Parsons and his colleagues as well as by others.[22]
These reasons are not the major ones, however. The major
ones have to do with the nature of the unit society as
defined here. In the first place, it is a unit that seems
to the writer at least to be better adapted to the particular form of structural-functional analysis used here. That
form is analysis in terms of structural and functional
requisites.[23] It seems at least superficially that analysis of this sort is simpler and easier with regard to any
society than with regard to either any social action or any
social system because there are more elements in common on
the most general level in instances of the one case than of
the other two. The constant features of social action boil
down to its original residual definition. The constant
features of any social system are hardly more specific.
Work from these two points of view must proceed almost at
once to lower levels of generalization in order to derive
theories. The nature of the units of analysis do not "hold
still" sufficiently for work to go forward at the present
stage of development unless one takes not any social action

---

22. e.g., studies in learning theory at both Yale
University and Harvard University, theoretical reconstruc-
tions in the fields of psychiatry and psychoanalysis by
such scholars as Sullivan, Dollard, Horney, etc.

23. See Chapter II for a discussion of these concepts, structural-functional analysis in general and the
"requisite" form of this analysis in particular.

or social system but some specific forms of either or both.
At the present stage of knowledge only the vaguest generalizations can be made to hold true for all of the following:
any monastery, any society, and any university; or for any
learning action, any cooperative action, or any emotional
display. The referent of the term society is more specifically tied down on the most general level than is the
referent of the other two concepts. It is in this sense
that work on the most general level with regard to societies is "easier" than work on the other two. It is easier
in the same sense in which it is generally easier to find
out the requirements of one particular factory in New
Jersey than those of any factory in New Jersey. At the
same time, unlike the factory example, the unit, society,
is sufficiently general as a concept for one's findings to
have a broad empirical application. Work on the other two
approaches has of course even broader empirical applications, but here the researcher in theory is faced with a
choice of a unit sufficiently specific so that he feels he
can work with it, and sufficiently general so that he feels
such work to be valuable for the development of theory.

Another major reason for the present choice lies in
the peculiar nature of a society relative to other social
systems -- in the hypothesis that all others are either
subcategories of one or more societies. To the extent that
this is true, some of the general relevance of work from
the society approach is discovered. The general work on
any society involves the interrelations of many other types
of social systems. Further, to the extent that the requisites of any society can be established, the requisites
of other specific social systems are easier to establish as
something less than and/or different from those for a society. This point is explored tentatively later in the
volume when more of the substantive material has been
developed.[24]

---

24. See below, pp. 216-221.

For the present let it suffice to say that, if one can
develop a general framework within which any other social
system or any social action must fit, it should be relevant
for specific problems relative to these other approaches.

A final word may be added about these three approaches.
Each attempts to analyze the same data from different
points of view. The data are social actions and their
resultants. It is a faith, perhaps a naive one, that the
problems in the third approach are somewhat simpler than
in the first two, although they are very great in any case.
If the phrasing of the general problem of social analysis
and the reasoning about it advanced here are tenable, however, work on these three different approaches must always
be mutually relevant. They do not analyze and explain
different data but merely take different starting points
in the treatment of the same data. Thus, it would seem to
follow that work from these three different starting points
must dovetail if mistakes have not been made. If statements in terms of the theory of social action, the theory
of social systems, or the theory of societies are mutually
contradictory, there has been an error made in one or some
combinations of the theories. Work from these different
points of view promises, therefore, not only mutual fructi-
fication, but also mutual checks for error. In the long
run, development of the conceptual schemes and theoretical
systems of all three may make possible the development of
a single unified body of knowledge in this field. As such,
however, it will have to be a body unified through verifiable empirical findings and not solely by logical manipulations if the work is to be kept a performance in empirical rather than formal science.

C H A P T E R   II

GENERAL METHODS AND GENERAL CONCEPTS

A. STRUCTURAL-FUNCTIONAL METHOD IN GENERAL[1]

Structural-functional analysis is not something new
in either the social or the natural sciences. It has a
pedigree that stretches indefinitely far back in both
fields. The only "new" aspect of it is its formidable new
name, "structural-functional analysis." Simply speaking,
it consists of nothing more complicated than phrasing empirical questions in one of the following several forms or
some combination of them: (1) What observable uniformities
(or patterns) may be discovered in the phenomena studied?
(2) What conditions (empirical state of affairs) may be
discovered? or, (3) When process (or action) may be discovered to take place in terms of observable uniformities,
what resultant conditions may be discovered? The first
question asks what structures are involved. The second
asks what functions[2] have resulted (or have been performed).

---

1. The reader will find the specific definitions of
the concepts of structure and function and their subcategories used in this Section (A) and in Section B that
follows set forth in detail in Section C of this chapter.
If the meaning of these concepts is unclear in these first
two sections, reference may be made to the defining passages in Section C by consulting the index.

2. The term "function" is used throughout the volume
in a specific sense. It is not to be confused with the
use of this term to denote a special kind of resultant
state of affairs, i.e., one that makes for adaptation or

And the third asks what functions result when operation takes place in terms of given structures. As will be seen below in Section C there are many special forms of these three questions that are useful and necessary for the extraction of information about different types of problems (e.g., the possibility of adjustment in a system, its normative content, its "necessary" features, the degree of "planning" or "consciousness" involved, etc.), but all of these are variants of these three basic questions or some combination of them.

When one leaves off more or less pure description and becomes interested in the statement of generalized aspects of empirical phenomena, statements of these types are always involved. The matter is complicated, however, by the fact that some of the more "advanced" sciences, most notably physics and its derivatives, have had considerable "success" in the application of mathematical techniques to the development of their theories. Such applications have been "successful" in the sense that they not only have made possible a precision of statement of theories that exceeds what is generally possible or at least practicable in verbal terms, but they have also made possible the simultaneous statement of extremely complex interrelations among relevant variables and constants. At the present stage of development such applications have been extremely limited in the so-called "life" sciences such as biology and the social sciences. The spectacular results for theoretical development of the application of mathematical treatment to empirical phenomena argue that it is useful to discuss this matter briefly in a volume aimed at general theoretical development in the "life" sciences.

The term <u>mathematical analysis</u> as used here refers to the application of mathematical treatment to empirical

---

adjustment. See Section C below for the distinction between the concept of "function" and "eufunction" and the basis for the distinction.

phenomena. In the methodological discussions of social
science mathematical analysis has generally been defined
by analogy, and the analogy used has often been the field
of classical mechanics in physics. This procedure presents
certain difficulties. Mathematicians are by no means
agreed in their optimism or pessimism about the development
of mathematical analysis in the "life" sciences, but there
seems to be a rather high degree of agreement among them
that the type of mathematics that proved so fruitful in the
development of classical mechanics, i.e., the calculus and
its derivatives, will probably not prove the most fruitful
line of development in these other spheres. Mathematical
analysis in the sense of the term used here has been lightly defined for the author by one outstanding mathematician
as a technique that, once a problem has been defined, permits manipulation of the concepts involved without further
reference to their content. The results of these manipulations can be checked against the relevant data. If the
data bear out the conclusions reached, the particular
mathematical techniques involved have proved useful in that
context. This definition, though lightly offered, turns
out to be rather satisfying. It is perhaps as useful a way
to put the matter as any. A great deal is involved in it,
however. Mathematics itself is widely referred to as a
"formal science" or as a "formal discipline" by those who
object to the use of the term "science" in this connection
altogether. Mathematical theories and results are not
concerned with any question of empirical content. The
interest lies in invariant aspects or properties or relationships that can be proved regardless of empirical content. One disproves pure mathematical theories not by
discovering an empirical exception to them but by finding
a flaw in the reasoning involved.

The application of mathematics to an empirical discipline always presupposes the development of a model for the
phenomena concerned. A model in this sense is a generalized description of the system of phenomena concerned -- a

description that states the component parts of the system
and at least some of their interrelationships. Given an
explicit model of the phenomena concerned, it is possible
to seek help from the mathematicians. Presented with a
model, experts in mathematical techniques may be able to
decide that the application of existing mathematical techniques is likely to be useful. This is largely a question
of determining: (1) whether existing mathematical models
(i.e., models devoid of empirical content) are sufficiently
similar in form to the empirical models to suggest that
trial applications will be fruitful, and (2) whether the
constants and variables in the empirical model can be so
stated ("measurement" is one form of statement) as to permit of meaningful mathematical manipulation. If the
mathematicians decide that no mathematical models exist
that seem promising in these respects, they may be able to
devise ones that will, or to raise stimulating questions
about the further revisions of the empirical model.

It can not be emphasized too strongly, while on the
question of models, that these models must not be reified.
Such models are not "real" in the sense that they exist,
or even reflect empirical phenomena with very detailed
accuracy. They are simply ways of ordering abstractions
about empirical phenomena in such a manner that it is
possible to erect systems of theory about the phenomena.
The "payoff" on a model is positive to the degree to which
theories erected in terms of it can be relatively well
confirmed if it is an empirical model, or proved if it is
a mathematical model. The molecule is a useful model in
natural science. It is quite conceivable that the purposes
it serves might equally well or better be served by another.
If another arises that is sufficiently more fruitful to
justify the tremendous labor of restatement of theories
that would be involved, the molecule will almost certainly
be replaced as a model. The precedent for this in scientific method is well established. The model of the atom
as an irreducible particle is gone forever, and probably no

physicist of note today would accept models of subatomic or "elementary" particles as irreducible minima unless no alternative procedure were possible.

The "unreality" of models need not appall the social scientists any more than it appalls the natural scientists. It is the reification of models that is a source of trouble. The most rarefied and abstract models may prove to be extremely useful. No terrestrial falling body in fact conforms to Newtonian theories[3] (assuming for a moment their confirmation as unaltered by later theoretical developments in respects relevant here), but the theory, $s = 1/2\ gt^2$, is none the less useful. When results deviate from its predictions, it diverts attention to factors other than "g" or "t" or "s," and when relevant factors other than these three and their relations to these three are known, it gives a determinate solution or at least a solution that is determinate to the degree that the other factors are accurately known. More than this is not to be expected of models, but those who reject them for these limitations must, if they place any value on consistency, reconcile themselves to the rejection of all science.

So far the mathematicians conceive of four types of mathematical models with a possible relevance to empirical science. Three of these have had applications already. The usefulness of the fourth and the possibility of an indefinite number of other types is a question for the future.[4] The first is the most familiar. This is a model

---

3. The term "theory" is sometimes used to identify what has here been referred to as a "system of theory." Scholars unaccustomed to the way the term is used here may avoid confusion by consulting pp. 226-237 (esp. pp. 230-235) for a detailed discussion of the manner in which the term is used here, after which they may, of course, wish to convert the discussion here into the vocabulary to which they are more accustomed.

4. The author is deeply indebted to Prof. John Tukey in particular and several of the mathematicians and physicists at Princeton in general for aid in the present statement on mathematical analysis. They can not, of course, be held responsible for any inadequacies in the present statement.

that is quantitative and deterministic. Classical mechanics with its application of the calculus is the famous
example. The second is quantitative and probabilistic and
has had applications in the statistical mechanics and in
the field of genetics. The third is qualitative and
deterministic and has been used in the application of
Boolean algebra to problems of complicated relay circuits.
The fourth is a qualitative and probabilistic one for which
no clear-cut applications seem to exist, and in fact the
mathematics involved here is only in a speculative stage.

Detailed discussion of these general types of models
would be out of place here. Speculation among mathematicians would suggest the second and third types as those
most likely to be fruitful in the biological and social
sciences, but this question will have its answer in the
future if mathematical analysis in these fields proves
useful in the long run, and there is no certainty even
about this latter question. In any case the more general
forms of theoretical statement of which mathematical analysis is a specific form, i.e., structural-functional statement as defined here, can not be ignored. Forms of it
other than the mathematical forms must be used before the
requisites of mathematization are at hand. This is most
striking in the poorly developed sciences, but it is
present at the frontiers of even the most highly developed
sciences. There is always a nonmathematical phase at the
frontier of theoretical development (as distinguished from
the elaboration of present theory) if only in the brief
stage of statement that certain new empirical insights must
be fed into the models themselves.

Most of the present work in the field of scientific
social analysis is being carried on at the stages that are
at most preparatory for mathematical analysis. This is
certainly true of the present attempt at construction of a
model of any society. When greater success than has at
present been achieved in model building is available, the
peculiar virtues of mathematization may be available also.

The relatively precise exhaustion of the logical implications of the general interrelationships involved in a
mathematical model that is theoretically useful, and
similar exhaustion of the logical implications in an individual case insofar as that case conforms to the model
will be possible in the social as in the natural sciences
if that stage is reached. If it is not, the less precise
or logically exhaustive results of general structural-
functional analysis may still be judged on their own merits
apart from this other desirable goal.

In seeking such goals one must not be misled by a
confusion of mathematical analysis with highly developed
statistical techniques. It is possible to confirm or dis-
confirm theories that can not be mathematically stated by
the use of quite sophisticated statistical techniques.
These latter divert attention to the design of experiments
and the question of the significance of data, but they do
not constitute mathematical analysis in the sense of the
term here. The application of statistical techniques may
be a help in the direction of mathematical analysis, however, if those who use such techniques understand their
mathematical basis. Every statistical procedure implies a
model that can be made mathematically explicit. The choice
among alternative statistical techniques should, from the
methodological point of view, involve some careful speculation as to whether or not the models in the statistics
have anything in common with models that are relevant in
terms of the data. One may, for example, extract significant results by assuming that it is meaningful to represent
two variables in terms of Cartesian coordinates, but if
such an assumption has no meaningful empirical referent,
results based upon it may be quite misleading. Sophisticated use of statistical techniques, however, by focusing
attention on the structure of the models involved should
sharpen development of the theoretical systems concerned,
with all the implications that such development may carry.

B. STRUCTURAL-FUNCTIONAL REQUISITE ANALYSIS

1. Introduction

Although structural-functional analysis is nothing new
or startling, it has sometimes been difficult to see the
standard elements involved in it. As Professor Merton has
pointed out, the term "function" has been used in many
senses[5], and it may be added that the definitions of the
term "function," and that of "structure" too, have as often
as not been left to context. It has sometimes been difficult, therefore, to ascertain which of several forms, or
which combinations of several forms, of structural-
functional analysis was being applied. There are many
possible forms and combinations of forms of such analysis.
For some purposes one form is useful; for others another
or some combination serves best. The primary orientation
of this volume is to a particular form with other types
used when relevant. The primary orientation here is to
"structural-functional requisite" analysis. This section
of the present chapter will be devoted to a general discussion of that method. The following section is devoted
to an attempt to define in detail some of the more generally useful concepts of structure and function and indicate
their special applications.

2. Structural-functional requisite procedure

The first step in "structural-functional requisite"
procedure is the definition of the concrete unit to which
the analysis is to be applied. The definition itself is
arbitrary in the sense that "the specific denotations of
any given term are not determined by previous usage or any

---

5. R. K. Merton, <u>Social Theory and Social Structure</u>,
The Free Press, Glencoe, Illinois, 1949, pp. 21-81. (This
book will be referred to subsequently as R. K. Merton,
<u>Social Theory</u>.)

authority other than the person using the term."[6] If the
concept of a particular unit is to be a useful one[7] for
empirical scientific purposes, it must of course have an
empirical referent, that is to say there must be concrete
empirical phenomena or aspects of concrete phenomena which,
whatever the level of abstraction involved, the criteria of
the definition presumably identify. Whether a given definition proves to be useful or not is another matter,[8] but
scientific analysis, or any other for that matter, proceeds
in terms of concepts that are either explicitly or implicitly defined. If they are explicitly defined, it is
presumably easier to decide how to alter them to improve
their usefulness when that question arises. Explicit definitions also minimize the element of surprise and confusion over the implications of concepts when they are
manipulated.

The units concerned are _concrete_ in the sense that
they identify cases of models such that examples of these
models are at least in theory capable of physical separation from other models of similar types. Thus, even in
theory, one can not physically separate the volume and the
mass of a molecule.[9] In the social field concepts such as
"family," "society," "business firm," etc., whether defined
as groups of individuals or systems of action involving
groups of individuals, are concrete units in this sense.
In the social field, aspects of social phenomena that are

---

6. For a brief discussion of the problem of defini-
tion in scientific systems see M. J. Levy, Jr., "Some
Basic Methodological Difficulties in Social Science,"
Philos. of Sci., Vol. 17, No. 4 (Oct. 1950), pp. 291-294.

7. i.e., fruitful for the development of scientific
theories.

8. See the general discussion of the distinction
between concepts and theories below, pp. 226-237.

9. This matter is taken up below in this chapter.
See pp. 88-100 on the distinction between concrete and
analytical structures.

only analytically separable are also to be distinguished.
The "economic" and "political" aspects of action, as those
terms are used here,[10] are examples of such aspects since
it is not even possible in theory that an allocation of
power and responsibility take place without the simultaneous involvement of some allocation of goods and services and vice versa. The same sort of distinction between
concrete units and analytically distinguished aspects of
phenomena is applicable in the field of biology as well as
in physics and the social sciences. In biology the concepts of concrete units are such as that of an "organism,"
a "cell," a "root," etc. Analytically distinguishable
aspects are such patterns as define "assimilation," "respiration," etc. Here again the application of this procedure
in the social sciences is no departure from extremely
well-recognized scientific procedure.

As used here, the concrete units concerned will in all
cases be systems of social action involving a plurality of
individuals. The models produced will presumably, then,
refer to or identify membership[11] units of various sorts.
These units will not be defined as a collection of individuals of a given species but rather as the system of
action that identifies such a collection and that does not
"exist" (i.e., is not empirically observable) in the complete absence of the plurality involved. Once a unit of
this sort has been at least tentatively defined, the next
step in the analysis may be taken. If such a unit has an

---

10. See below pp. 89-90, 330-336, and also Chapters
IX and X.

11. The term "membership" may for the moment be left
to its usual connotations. It is discussed in a more precise fashion below (see pp. 122-127.) It goes without
saying, of course, that in the case of some membership
units the matter of determining who is and who is not a
member is much easier than in others. This distinction
corresponds to a rather obvious empirical variation. The
membership of the Phi Beta Kappa Society is, for example,
much more easily determined than is the membership of,
say, the Catholic Church.

empirical referent (i.e., if there is a range of empirical
phenomena in the analysis of which it may be used as a
model[12]), it is possible to raise the question of the
setting of the unit. The term setting as used here refers
to the factors that determine, either exactly or on a
probability basis, the maximum range of possible variation
in the patterns that characterize the unit. Human society
is the type of unit with which this study is concerned,
and the setting in this case consists of the factors of
human heredity and nonhuman environment when the most
general considerations relating to any human society are
sought. The setting factors of an American university
would be quite different, of course, but at least in theory
it is possible to determine the factors setting the maximum range of variation of any unit if the unit is defined
and if there are empirical referents for such units. In
practice it may be extremely difficult to locate such
limits. Some of the difficulties involved in these respects have been illustrated above[13] relative to the setting in the present study. Nevertheless, given the unit
under consideration, the location of these limits is not
arbitrary in the sense that the choice of the unit is. If,
for example, one studies family units or ant societies,
there are factors that set limits such that action falling
outside these limits is adequately explicable without
reference to these units, and action falling within these
limits is only explicable with some reference to these
limits though that reference will not suffice for an adequate explanation of the phenomena.

Whatever the setting of a particular unit may be, two
considerations mentioned above[14] must always be kept in

---

12. And of course its usefulness as a model will depend upon the validity of the theoretical formulations
that result from its use.

13. See above, pp. 12-17.

14. See pp. 16-17.

mind. First, one must avoid interpretation based on the attribution of exclusive importance to a single element of the setting. The relationship here is one of interdependence. The sterility of the heredity vs. environment controversy is a classic case of this kind of difficulty. The lesson to be learned from this experience should not be ignored in the use of different concepts that enter similarly into the theoretical system employed. Thus, if one assumes for the moment that the setting factors for modern U.S. society are the heredity of members of U.S. society, the nonhuman environment of that society, and the human non-U.S. environment of the society, one may not attribute greater or lesser relevance to one of the three as opposed to the others unless it is possible to show that the others are relatively constant or irrelevant to the question in hand. But this demonstration is no more than a demonstration that the original statement of the setting was more general than was necessary and could have been narrowed down in the first place. Investigations of this sort are fruitful for scientific purposes only if they have such a result and hence, methodologically speaking, should be oriented to such a result with, of course, due objectivity as to whether such a result is achieved.

Second, the place of the concept of a "setting" in scientific analysis is such that the setting factors may not be used as adequate explanations of the phenomena of which they are supposedly setting factors, nor can they be ignored in such explanations. Here again the discussion of heredity and environment in Chapter I is a case in point, but the same case would hold true for any other setting factors. If they are adequate to explain the phenomena, there is no range of variation set by them. If they are irrelevant to the phenomena, whatever else may set the range of variation for the unit and level under consideration, the irrelevant factors do not.

The difficulty in locating the setting factors exactly

is a persistent source of difficulty that will never be absent as long as this approach is used on empirical phenomena. If one could devise a unit with an empirical referent and determine its limits of possible variation exactly, the exact implications of the presence of such a unit in such a setting could be deduced to the extent that the unit was precisely defined, and final knowledge on this score would be achieved. But final knowledge is a utopian goal rather than an actual one in science. Here, as in the case of models, one must settle for what is scientifically useful, whatever its drawbacks, rather than refuse to proceed until perfection is achieved at each stage. The insistence on perfection in empirical science would stop all work at the first stage. The test of usefulness of any given stage is its relevance to the development of confirmable theories at other stages, and the scientific ideal is always to increase this usefulness. As has been stated above, there are severe limitations on the present knowledge of the setting used in the present study, the factors of human heredity and nonhuman environment. Despite those limitations it is possible to use what seems to be reasonably well established to increase present knowledge of social phenomena.

Having chosen a unit tentatively and determined tentatively the setting of that unit, it is possible to proceed to the implications of the existence of such a unit in such a setting. Here at least two sorts of questions may be asked usefully. First, what conditions must be present if such a unit is to exist in such a setting, or more simply, what must be done if such a unit is to exist in such a setting? The answer or answers to this question establishes the functional requisites of the unit. Second, what observable uniformities (or patterns) of action must exist such that operation in terms of them will result in the functional requisites? Or more simply, how must what must be done, be done? The answer or answers to this second question establishes the structural requisites[15] of the unit.

The functional requisites of a given unit are no more arbitrary than is the setting of a unit. They are not derived by definition but are rather the minimal implications of the existence of such a unit in its setting. The setting is not a matter of definition either but something for empirical discovery. Moreover it may be and usually is subject to empirical change.[16] Certainly this is true of species heredity and nonspecies environment as limiting factors. The functional requisites of a unit may be different if the definition of the unit remains unchanged but the setting of the unit changes. The functional requisites of a unit do not define the unit nor does the definition of the unit decide the functional requisite question. Their relationship is empirical and not merely a formal logical one. Errors in fact as well as errors in deduction will destroy the position of an alleged functional requisite of any society. If, for example, human heredity and nonhuman environment turn out not to be the setting for any "society" as that term is defined here, the list of functional requisites tentatively suggested here will have lost an important part of its basis. The same will be true if, though the factors mentioned comprise the setting, the facts alleged about them (e.g., that it is understandable in terms of human heredity and nonhuman environment that human infants cannot survive if deprived of all human contact and care at birth) turn out to be empirically untenable.

The insistence on the nonarbitrary elements in both the settings and functional requisites is of some importance

-----

15. The definitions of these two concepts, functional and structural requisites, and a discussion of them appear at greater length later in this chapter. See pp. 62-76.

16. See above, pp. 14-17.

because failure to recognize this and its implications involves certain methodological difficulties. It is not
uncommon to find analyses of this general sort that start
by seeking the functional requisites of a unit that is
left undefined, i.e., a unit that is defined only implicitly. The setting of the unit is also left implicit. A list
of necessary conditions is then somehow assembled for a
unit that is undefined in a setting that is not discovered.
There is a temptation then to use the list obtained to
define the unit. This, of course, reduces the functional
requisites of the system to the arbitrary status of definitions in scientific systems and is a thoroughly circular
system of definition. More importantly, perhaps, it
reduces the derivation of functional requisites to a much
more haphazard procedure than is necessary. The derivation
of functional requisites always involves a unit and a setting for that unit. The unit may be either explicitly or
implicitly defined, and the setting may be explicitly or
implicitly discovered or hypothesized. Systematic and
precise procedure is certainly furthered by explicitness
in both respects. Finally, explicitness and the avoidance
of circularity serves another end in this connection. The
statement that such and such conditions are functional
requisites of a given type of unit in its setting is an
empirical theory. It is a generalized statement about
empirical phenomena, and it contains variables. As in the
case of all empirical scientific statements, it is at least
conceivably falsifiable and may in fact be more or less
well confirmed or disconfirmed. Since the question of
error in this connection is always relevant, explicitness
becomes more important. When difficulties arise, it is
easier to check the derivation of functional requisites to
the degree that the factors involved in their derivation
are explicitly rather than implicitly stated.

　　If there exists a specific empirical referent for any
particular type of unit, then the particular set of functional requisites is in theory at least finite under any

given system of classification. That is to say that while one may choose an indefinite number of different systems of classification, or even subdivide the parts of any given system indefinitely, the possible list of functional requisites on any one level of any one system is a finite one. This would seem to follow from the fact that one is dealing with an empirical unit in an empirical setting. For such a unit to exist, a definite list of empirical conditions must have been met. It would seem implicit in the concept "infinite" as used in mathematics that no infinite list of requisite conditions can be fulfilled by a finite unit, although the conditions fulfilled may be subject to an infinity of different classifications and subdivisions.

Although the functional requisites of a given unit are both subject to empirical determination and form a finite list, it does not follow that any particular list will be definitive. Absolute definitiveness in this as in all scientific endeavors is a goal to be sought but not to be attained. In social science as in other sciences the use of residual categories or imprecisions of assumptions and analysis make up the gap between the goal and the achieved. From the methodological point of view it is important to realize this and be ready at any time to make alterations that will tend to narrow this gap in any particular formulation of functional requisites. Whenever different formulations of the list can be shown to be more useful and more tenable, the old list must be changed.

The functional requisites, if known, can be used to discover the structural requisites of the unit. If one knows what conditions must be met for the unit to exist in its setting, one may then seek the patterns of action or operation that must exist if the action or operation in terms of the patterns is to produce the requisite conditions. The structural requisites of a unit when known give the minimal parts or aspects of a unit that must be present; the functional requisites give the minimum results of operation of such a unit. From this point on, more detailed

theories of both interrelationships of parts and sources
of "integration" and "malintegration" may be developed.

Structural-functional requisite analysis consists then
of the following procedure: (1) The selection of a unit
that (a) is presumably relevant to the problem to be
studied, and (b) has an empirical referent; (2) the discovery within more or less useful approximations of the
explicit empirical limits of possible variation of the
unit; (3) the discovery and explicit statement of the minimal conditions implicit in the existence of such a unit in
such a setting; (4) the discovery of the patterns in terms
of which operation must take place if those minimal conditions are to be produced.

3. Distinction between requisites and prerequisites

The concepts of structural and functional "requisites"
and "prerequisites" will be taken up later in this chapter,[17] but a short discussion of the distinction is in order here to avoid a frequent source of confusion. The term
"prerequisite" has frequently been applied to the concept
that appears here as the term "requisite" with various mod-
ifiers.[18] The question of structural-functional requisites
casts no light on the problem of any preceding state of
the unit concerned. It merely seeks to answer the question
of what is required in the situation under scrutiny without
reference to the time period before or after. As such the
results are "static" analysis, although the derivation of
the results involves "dynamic" analysis. The term "static"
is here used in precisely the same sense as in the field of
physics to apply to analysis in which the time factor is
not a relevant variable. It is not a substitute for

---

17. See pp. 71-76.

18. It has been so used by the author and some of
his colleagues. See D. F. Aberle, A. K. Cohen, A. K.
Davis, M. J. Levy, Jr., F. X. Sutton, "The Functional Prerequisites of a Society," Ethics, Vol. LX, No. 2 (Jan.
1950), pp. 100-111.

"dynamic" analysis (i.e., analysis in which the time variable is relevant) nor a preferable alternative to it. It
is neither better nor worse, scientifically speaking, than
dynamic analysis. Its theories are fruitful for dynamic
analysis and the reverse is also true.[19]

The problem of social change is a central problem for
social scientists as those of physical and biological
change are for physicists and biologists. For dynamic
analysis in the absence of mathematical techniques in both

---

19. In this connection some examples are in order.
These examples will involve terms taken up elsewhere in
the volume, and for the time being the tenability of the
illustrative theories is beside the point. The following
is an example of a static theory: the probability is high
that any relationship that emphasizes universalistic criteria of selection will also emphasize rational action in
terms of the relationship and a functionally specific definition of the relationship. The following is an example
of a dynamic theory: when the patterns of economic production in a society change in the direction of highly industrialized patterns (i.e., high multiplications of human
effort by means of tools and heavy reliance on inanimate
sources of power), the family patterns will change in the
direction of a multilineal conjugal family type (i.e., of
the sort in the modern United States) unless, of course,
family patterns of that type already existed. In the one
case, rates of change whether known or unknown are not
relevant; in the other, they are. But the static case is
relevant to dynamic theories. For example, if it is valid,
the following dynamic theory may be deduced: if, in a
relationship emphasizing particularistic selection, nonrational action, and functionally diffuse commitments, the
emphasis changes in the direction of universalistic criteria of selection, the probability is high that emphases
in the other respects will change in the direction of
rational and functionally specific emphases. Similarly
static theories may be deduced from valid dynamic ones.
If the dynamic theory used as an example is valid, then
one or both of the following static ones would seem to
hold: (1) family systems of other types than the one mentioned contain elements that are functionally incompatible
with highly industrialized systems of economic production,
or (2) highly industrialized systems of economic production contain elements that are functionally incompatible
with family systems of types other than that mentioned.
(Contrary to initial impressions these two theories are

biology and the social sciences (as well as others such as geology) the concepts of functional and structural prerequisites are useful. These concepts refer to the conditions and patterns that must preexist the presence of a particular unit in a particular setting. The relevance of static analysis emerges clearly, however. Change of any sort cannot be understood without two elements of static knowledge: (1) the basis from which change took or takes place, and (2) the state to which it goes. In the derivation of any dynamic theory such knowledge is either implicit or explicit. Thus, one cannot answer the question, "What was necessary to change France from its feudal to its modern state?" without knowledge of those two states. Similarly, to answer the question, "What changes must be made if China is to industrialize?" one must have at least some hypotheses about the nature of an industrialized China and some about "traditional" China. The structural-functional requisite approach permits of the establishment of minimal knowledge on any given level of analysis of such units, and hence sets the stage within which dynamic analysis may be carried out. There is, therefore, a sense in which some static analysis is logically prior to dynamic analysis, or is at least extremely helpful for it. Structural-functional requisite analysis is one systematic way to develop static theories that may have such uses.[20] It is for this reason that it is suggested explicitly in this volume. If its explicit application in the program of research mentioned in the preface proves fruitful, it is further suggested that its use be continued unless or until another method of analysis proves more fruitful.

---

not identical. The "proof" or confirmation of one does not necessarily "prove" or confirm the other.)

20. The use of structural-functional prerequisites may also develop dynamic analysis with corresponding uses for the development of static theories.

4. Limits of structural-functional requisite analysis

It must be kept in mind at all times that the use of functional and structural requisites gives a systematic approach only to minimal conditions and patterns. These conceptual tools cannot and do not in general tell one anything about the degree to which the conditions resultant from the operation of a given unit or the patterns of a given unit are in fact elaborated over and above such a minimum. In fact and in theory these tools could only give such results under one particular set of conditions, i.e., if the unit is defined by complete and exhaustive description. Under these conditions the minima and maxima are identical, and every conceivable pattern and condition of the unit are requisites of it.

In terms of structural-functional requisite analysis one attempts first to exhaust the minimal implications of the presence of the unit, as defined, in its setting. If the results are not sufficiently detailed, elaboration is pursued by lowering the level of generalization of the unit (i.e., by making its definition more specific), using the knowledge previously obtained to set further limits, and again deriving the requisites on the more specific level. For example, one may discover the structural requisites of any industrial society. This may not give one the kind of detail that is necessary for a desired level of understanding of United States society, but the information gained will be extremely useful in finding out the structural requisites of any industrial society that emphasizes heavy production. This more detailed knowledge will constitute a further approximation to the desired level. The process may, in theory at least, be continued to the lowest level of generalization possible.[21]

---

21. By the most generalized level, or the highest level of generalization, is meant that level of consideration most remote from any given empirical phenomena under discussion. Thus the consideration of the functional requisites of any society is on a higher level of generali-

This seeming restriction should not be startling. It
has its counterpart in all scientific theory. The so-called
law of falling bodies in physics does not tell one more
than certain minimal details about falling bodies under
given conditions. $s = 1/2 \ gt^2$ does not exhaust possible
detail even on bodies falling in a vacuum. About bodies
falling in terrestrial space it merely establishes one
element in their rate of fall or the distance covered. By
specifying further conditions (i.e., lowering the level of
generalization) and adding theories appropriate to those
conditions, a resultant more accurately in conformity with,
say, the actual case of knocking a lead weight from a tower
in a wind of a given velocity may be reached. In this
respect again, save for the absence of mathematical analysis, the most general methodological procedures in the less
advanced sciences do not differ from those in the most
advanced ones.

It is important that one realize the minimal nature of
this procedure lest one think that any given analysis in
these terms accomplishes more theoretically than it in fact
does. It is also important that one realize that there is
no genuine alternative in scientific procedure in this
respect. The problems raised by the abstraction element
inherent in scientific analysis no longer seem to disturb
the workers in the more advanced sciences. They recognize
either consciously or otherwise that their theories do not
in fact describe "empirical reality," whatever that may be,
but only give more or less useful approximations to

---

zation (i.e., refers to a more inclusive class) than consideration of those of any industrial society. The latter,
in turn, are on a more general level than are those of the
American form of industrial society. When a level is
reached such that going to a more specific level requires
the citing of a different type of unit, the lowest level
of generalization has been reached with regard to the
original unit. Conversely when a level of consideration
has been reached such that further generalization involves
a different unit, the highest level of generalization has
been reached relative to the original unit.

empirical conditions, whether those conditions be "real" or
only assumed to be real.[22]   In the social field the problem
remains, however, and there are many who phrase their
failure to understand this limitation of scientific method
by objecting to analysis that "takes the life out of the
material." There is an important truth in Pope's humanist
plaint that

> "Like following life thro' creatures you dissect,
> You lose it in the moment you detect."[23]

It is also important to realize that this is the inevitable
price of scientific theories. Leaving "the life in the
material" confines the work as closely as possible to the
purely descriptive level, often with the skillfully con-
trived, emotionally evocative qualities that differentiate
literature from science and gives the former, in part at
least, its contribution to a "fuller and more meaningful"
human existence. But it is the antithesis of the process
of abstraction and generalization that characterizes all
science.

There has been another tendency in the social field
that has caused difficulty on this score. The preoccupation in many branches of the discipline with therapy has
often focused overwhelming attention on the specific
details of an individual case with little regard for its
more general aspects. In the hands of unusually gifted
thinkers like Freud this does not prevent extremely useful
contributions usually derived and stated in terms of insight rather than systematic scientific analysis. In the
hands of less gifted workers it may result in ignoring
theories that in the long run might contribute materially

---

22. The ontological question as such lies outside
the realm of scientific analysis in the usual sense.

23. A. Pope, <u>Moral Essays</u>, Epistle I, lines 29-30.

to the understanding sought of the individual case.[24]
Almost no physical scientist today would try to predict
exactly where an individual molecule of water in an individual wave would hit a given beach at a given moment in
time. Almost any physical scientist would agree that
successive approximations to such detailed prediction are
more likely to arise from first acquiring a general knowledge of tide, wave, molecular phenomena, etc., and seeking
to narrow progressively the field of inquiry than from an
approach via the individual case itself. Work on the
individual case in all its richness of detail has often
proved invaluable in science, but only when the worker
himself or some other worker has used such knowledge for
its general rather than its detailed implications.

Increase of detailed knowledge by procedure from more
to less generalized levels has been a frequent development
in the history of science. But the history of science has
not been a one-way street in these respects. The accumulation of detailed knowledge, the extraction of its general
implications, and the use of those theories to establish
further detailed knowledge has been no less a part of the
history of science. In fact, the question of highly
generalized versus lowly generalized research as the main
factor in scientific development is a false question. It
is simply a matter of where one cuts the cake. Highly
generalized work is confirmed or disconfirmed by knowledge
gathered on lower levels of generalization (e.g., confirmation of one of Einstein's formulations by stellar observ-
ances), and what is more, such highly generalized work
usually directs attention to hitherto unsuspected sources

----

24. There is, of course, a rapidly growing body of
attempts at systematic scientific analysis relative to individual and group psychology. Certainly on the diagnos-
tic level some considerable degree of interobserver reliability is being reached. The danger cited here, however,
exists in spite of the work of many outstanding psycholo-
gists, psychiatrists, and psychoanalysts.

of more specific data and makes possible the use of those
data for the destruction or further refinement of the
original general work. Cutting the cake at another point
one observes that centuries of painstaking astronomical
observations -- work at an extremely low level of generalization as astronomy goes -- made possible the revolutionary
and much more highly generalized statements of Kepler and
Copernicus. These in turn greatly increased the accuracy
and scope of data-gathering in that field. The work in
this volume is not a plea for cutting the cake at one of
these points as opposed to the other. Reasonable students
of the history of science would no doubt agree that any
such policy of radical exclusion, whether of highly generalized or lowly generalized work, would prove ruinous in
any scientific field. The present volume does emphasize
procedure from more to less general levels of analysis.
Nevertheless, proposals to test the tentative results so
obtained at less general levels are vital to the work of
which this volume is a part. Popular impressions to the
contrary notwithstanding, relatively little rather than
much of social science has proceeded from this general
level.

Procedure from one level of generalization to another
in empirical science is _never_ a purely deductive procedure.
Procedure from higher to lower levels of generalization
always involves the addition of empirical materials that
are themselves subject to confirmation or disconfirmation.
After the additional material has been introduced one may
then deduce the special implications of this material for
the specific applicable formulation of relevant theories
derived on a more general level. For example, suppose one
takes as "known" the theory that some "family" system is
necessary if any "society" is to exist. The only implication that this has for lower levels of generalization (in
this case for specific types or cases of societies) is that
each must contain some sort of a "family" system. But to

the extent that one specifies a type or case of society, depending upon what empirical material is included in that specification one may be able to specify the type or case of family system involved or at least to eliminate certain possibilities. For example, given what is "known" of the functions of large scale patriarchal, patrilineal, and patrilocal family systems, what is "known" of the functional requisites of modern industry, and the theory taken as "known" above, when one changes levels from any society to any "modern industrial" society, the empirical data added by the referent of the term "modern industrial" and that of the specific type of family mentioned enables one to state that not only will there be a family system (insofar as a "modern industrial" society is a society and insofar as it is valid to hold that any society must have a family system if it is to exist), but also that the family system can or cannot be of the patriarchal, patrilineal, and patrilocal type (depending on whether the functions of that type are or are not compatible with the functional requisites of "modern industry"). But this procedure is far removed from "pure deduction" and involves at every turn materials that are at least in theory subject to empirical confirmation or disconfirmation.

Procedure from less to more general levels is just the opposite in the sense that it involves the progressive dropping of empirical material from the problem. Thus, if one examines a large number of different cases of the concept "society" and finds in everyone without exception a "family" system although these latter are extremely varied, then one may establish, subject to empirical disproof by the discovery of some subsequent exception, the theory that any society will (or even must) have some family system. But here too the process of deduction is not the only one involved. Methodologically the following factors containing elements other than deductions are involved: (1) there is a useful model of any society such

that all these specific societies are special cases of that
general class; (2) there is a useful model of any "family"
system such that all these varied "family" systems are
special cases of that general class; (3) since these two
general classes have empirical referents of which the
observed cases are special cases, and since one uniformity
observed in the material is the presence of a case of a
"family" system in every case of a "society," the theory
that any society will (or even must) have a family system
is proposed subject, as are all empirical scientific
theories, to continued confirmation or disproof by discovery of an empirical exception on the level of generalization on which the theory is proposed (e.g., the discovery
of any case of a social unit conforming to the definition
of a "society" but lacking any referent for the concept
"family"). Therefore, procedure in empirical science
either upward or downward in levels of generalization is
never a purely logical matter if more is to be learned from
the process than was previously known at the starting level.
Procedure from one level to another is subject to both
logical and empirical error.

At this point some word must be said about the grave
danger of teleology in this general type of analysis. One
of the besetting sins of, and sources of grave concern to,
those using the structural-functional requisite method
either explicitly or implicitly has been the ease with
which apparently objective arguments fall into justifica-
tions or rationalizations of the status quo or of some
particular program. The empirical existence of a particular phenomenon together with the parallel explanation of it
as a functional requisite of a given system serves as an
example of the pairing of verification and explanation.
This type of analysis and verification is quite acceptable
on general methodological grounds, but it is prone to the
fallacy of functional (or structural) teleology[25] unless

---

25. Professor P. A. Sorokin suggested the term functional teleogy for this methodological difficulty when the

great care is taken with it. The care required is often
given at the expense of an encumbered prose style, for it
involves a continuous reiteration of the general conditions
of the problem. Thus, it is methodologically acceptable
to state that a condition "x" is a functional requisite for
a unit (or system) "y" in the setting in which that unit
is found, for reasons a,b,c ..., and if that statement can
be verified, to deduce from it that in the presence of y
in such a setting, x is always to be found. It is not,
however, permissible to observe that the existence of a
given phenomenon "x" is the result of its being a functional requisite of the unit (or system) "y" in the setting in
which that unit is found. Its status as a functional requisite stands or falls on its necessity for the continued
operation, on the level of generality under consideration,
of the unit of which it is a feature in the setting in
which that unit is found. But its origin cannot be
explained in these terms. Even in cases in which the most
self-conscious planning takes place, the functional necessity of a condition is not an adequate explanation of its
presence. There must still be an explanation of the
"motivation" involved, the establishment of the condition,
etc. The fact that the probability is very high indeed
that human infants will not survive without care and attention in some form by human adults does not explain the
presence of such care and attention. It does, however,
permit the quite useful prediction that, whenever one finds
a situation in which human infants are surviving to maturity, he will very probably find patterns of care and
attention for the infants by adults in the system.

The existence of a functional requisite cannot be
assumed as necessary beyond the limits of the system concerned in that system's setting, nor can its existence be

---

matter was discussed with him some years ago. Structural
teleology would be the commission of the same error with
regard to patterns of operation as opposed to resultant
conditions.

considered preordained. In the case of social phenomena,
history is strewn with the relics of societies whose rise,
fall, reestablishment, and subsequent degeneration -- or
any portion of this process -- testify to the incorrectness
of a functional teleology, to the invalidity of maintaining
the necessary continued existence of any functional requisite in and of itself.

Thus, it is not permissible to say that a given process of allocation of duties in a business firm exists
because it is a functional requisite of that firm in its
setting -- that is teleogy, pure and simple, little if at
all different from the statement "legs were created to
wear pants and noses to bear spectacles." It is permissible to say that, if there is to be such a firm in such a
setting, there must be (or even in some cases that people
planned it so in order to have such a firm) a definite
allocation of duties, that in its absence the firm would
cease to function.

On the most general level of consideration of social
systems, it is easy to keep this factor in mind, but the
more specific the level, the greater is the tendency to
assume the necessity of some particular factor independent
of the system in connection with which it is found, or as
caused because it is a necessary condition of that system
in that system's setting. Such examples of functional
teleogy form the bases of many pseudoscientific discussions
of social change. For example, the continued existence of
the "traditional" Chinese family pattern, or some compromise form thereof, has often been explained and predicted
as a vital condition for the "Chinese way of life," although in fact that way of life has already begun to change
radically. This sort of analysis may lead an author to
ignore the facts that it is quite conceivable for a pattern
to persist after the system for which it may in part or
in toto have fulfilled a necessary condition has ceased
to exist, and that no social system has had its existence

proved inevitable or immutable.[26]

What has here been said of function may also be said of structure. There is a _structural_ teleology to match the functional one. But neither of these teleologies is inherent in structural-functional analysis in general or in any of its specific forms if they are used according to scientific methods. These difficulties are frequently fallen into by users of these methods, perhaps, and avoidance of them is no doubt difficult. The temptations are often disguised, and the results obtained by one who has been seduced may well be extremely satisfying. But these are all explanations and instances of human frailty and not of methodological inadequacy. Scientifically speaking, the method is not successfully attacked even though it is truthfully alleged that misuse of it (from a scientific point of view) is tempting, easy, and frequent.

C. SOME CONCEPTS OF STRUCTURAL-FUNCTIONAL ANALYSIS

1. Introduction: the general concepts of structure and function

Whatever their merits and demerits as scientifically useful concepts, few are more frequently encountered in both the biological and the social sciences than those of structure and function. In both of these fields somewhat similar difficulties are present with regard to these concepts though these difficulties are perhaps more noticeable or debilitating in the social than in the biological sciences. This, if true, may well be a reflection of their different stages of development. Professor Woodger in biology and Professor Merton in the social sciences[27] have

---

26. The above discussion of functional teleogy is, with slight modification, a reproduction of the same discussion in the author's book, _Family Revolution_, pp. 3-4.

27. See J. H. Woodger, _Biological Principles: A Critical Study_, Routledge and Kegan Paul Ltd., London, 1924, pp. 326-330, and R. K. Merton, _Social Theory_, pp. 22-27.

both pointed to the profusion of different referents given
to the term function. These different referents have for
the most part been left implicit in the social sciences at
least. The result has been somewhat chaotic.

Perhaps the major difficulty, next to that of having
no definitions of the concepts at all, has been the use of
a single term to cover several distinctly different referents. The difficulty has been most noteworthy with the
concept "function" with which such theoretical discussions
as exist in the literature have been largely preoccupied.
The concept "structure" has been to a far greater degree
left undiscussed, somewhat after the fashion of those who
sharpen the rotary blades of their lawnmowers and ignore
the stationary cutting edge. The term "function" has been
and may be quite usefully employed in several different
modifications of a general form of the concept. Two such
modifications, "functional requisites" and "functional prerequisites," have already been mentioned earlier in this
chapter. In order to prevent confusion, the term "function"
will be used for the most general form of the concept. All
of the various modifications of the concept will be subcategories of that general class. The same procedure will
be followed with the term "structure." The term function[28] is defined here as a condition, or state of affairs,
resultant from the operation (including in the term operation mere persistence) of a structure[29] through time.[30]

---

28. The term function, when used in the sense defined here, is not underlined following this definition.
Hereafter, when the term is used differently from its specific sense given here, it appears in quotation marks.

29. The term structure is considerably less controversial and difficult than is function. It is defined
below, but is left undefined for the moment since its
usual connotations and denotations cause no difficulty
here.

30. The phrase "through time" is in a genuine sense
redundant since a time factor is implicit in the term
operation. The redundant phrase is added to accent the
importance of this consideration.

It will be noted that this definition of function is
quite different from that use of the term "function" that
is paired with an opposite concept, dysfunction, although
the latter usage involves a particular modified form of
the usage here. A specific discussion of the paired terms,
"function" and dysfunction, is to be found in R. K. Merton's
work. For his purposes Merton states, "Functions are those
observed consequences which make for the adaptation or adjustment of a given system; and dysfunctions, those observed consequences which lessen the adaptation or adjustment of the system."[31] There is no intent here to quarrel
with Merton's usage. It would seem worthwhile, however,
to have a term for the class of which both Merton's
"function" and dysfunction are subclasses, particularly
since at least one other subclass (i.e., functional requisite) is used by Merton at least by inference, by many
other scientists (not only by social scientists but as a
minimum by the biological scientists among the natural
scientists), and by the present writer as well. There is
certainly no objection here to the use of the phrase,
"observed consequences," which is roughly if not precisely
coterminous with the phrase, "a condition, or state of
affairs, resultant from the operation ... of a structure."
It is, however, deemed useful here to indicate of what the
function is an "observed consequence." To avoid any confusion between the general concept (shorn of its adaptation,
adjustment, requisite, and other forms) and its subclasses,
the term function is reserved here for the general concept.

The term structure as used here means a pattern, i.e.,
an observable uniformity, of action or operation. The
general form of this concept is deliberately left in to
cover a wide range of possibilities from highly stable
uniformities to highly fleeting ones. This is done to
avoid the problem of classification of structures and

---

31. R. K. Merton, Social Theory, pp. 22-27.

nonstructures. The various qualifications of this term enter as specific subclasses of structure just as in the case of function. Any event may contain an element indicative of a structure insofar as it is considered with regard to its nonunique aspects or characteristics. Since the concern here is with social structure, it is the patterns of social action that are involved, but the concept is not limited to social applications. It has an identical and useful referent in biology whether explicit or implicit, and is useful in the model-building stage that precedes mathematical analysis in other fields as well.

It is in the structure of society and the interrelations between different kinds and parts of structures that much of the interest of scientific social analysis is centered. But the close interrelation between the concepts of function and structure emerges here. Structure, as defined here, refers to an aspect of empirical phenomena divorced from time. The patterns of action, qua patterns, do not exist as concrete objects in the same sense that sticks and stones do. The patterns of action in this sense are abstractions from concrete empirical phenomena, and they "exist" and are "empirically verifiable" in the same sense that the squareness of a box "exists" and is "empirically verifiable." What has been said here of patterns, qua patterns, does not apply to the patterns when they are in operation. Structures in operation are empirical in the same sense as sticks and stones.[32] In this sense the term structure in social science is no departure from the usage of the natural (including biological) sciences. The structure of atoms or amoebae is only a deduction or abstraction from the observation of concrete individuals of these two classes.[33] In the discussion of structures

---

32. See below, pp. 113-116.

33. When a biologist points to a portion of an organism and refers to it as "this structure," he is referring in shorthand fashion to "this particular exemplification of structure."

in operation,[34] i.e., in the empirical exemplifications of
structure, the concept of function plays its role. Parsons
puts the matter as follows:

> The logical type of generalized theoretical
> system under discussion may thus be called a
> "structural-functional system" as distinguished
> from an analytical system. It consists of the
> generalized categories necessary for an adequate
> description of states of an empirical system.
> On the one hand, it includes a system of struc-
> tural categories which must be logically adequate
> to give a determinate description of an empiri-
> cally possible, complete empirical system of the
> relevant class. One of the prime functions of
> system on this level is to insure completeness,
> to make it methodologically impossible to over-
> look anything important, and thus explicitly to
> describe all essential structural elements and
> relations of the system. For if this is not
> done implicit, uncriticized allegations about
> the missing elements will always play a part in
> determining conclusions and interpretations.
>
> On the other hand, such a system must also
> include a set of dynamic functional categories.
> These must articulate directly with the struc-
> tural categories -- they must describe processes
> by which these particular structures are main-
> tained or upset, the relations of the system to
> its environment are mediated. This aspect of the
> system must be complete in the same sense.[35]

---

34. Parsons observes of structure that, "It should
be noted that in machines the structure of the system does
not enter as a distinct theoretical element. For descriptive purposes, it is of course relevant for any given state
of the system but on the dynamic plane it dissolves into
process and interdependence. This calls attention to the
fact that structure and process are highly relative categories. Structure does not refer to any ontological stability in phenomena but only to a relative stability --
to sufficiently stable uniformities in the results of
underlying processes so that their constancy within certain
limits is a workable pragmatic assumption." See Talcott
Parsons, Essays, p. 22.

35. ibid., p. 23. It will be noted that in these
two paragraphs the term "functional" refers in different
contexts and different parts of the paragraphs (sometimes
without repetition of the word) to the terms function,
functional requisite, eufunction, and dysfunction. Despite

What has been said and quoted above may be amplified
as follows: If one is interested in the interrelationship
of different structures or the operation of a given structure,[36] the concept of function must enter the discussion.
In discussing such interrelationships some reference to
the condition or state of affairs resultant from the operation (including in the term operation mere persistence) of
a structure through time is always involved. Without the
concept of function, work on structure is confined to
static description and to that alone. In this connection
the importance of distinguishing the general concept from
its subcategories may be emphasized again. A given resultant condition used to link two structures in action or
describe one of them in process may be a requisite condition, an "adaptive" one, or a "maladaptive" one. It may
be some combination of the three[37] too, and often in a
given context in which it is unnecessary to distinguish
these three or their combinations, it is useful (and
imperative for the sake of consistency) to have the general
term distinct from its special forms.

The relation between function and structure in the
general sense may be put in another way following an
example used above relative to functional and structural
requisites. Functions refer to what is done, and structure
refers to how (including in the meaning of "how" the

---

this difficulty, the point made by the quotation of the
necessity of the two categories of structure and function
if process is to be described is well put.

36. The operation of a given structure generally implies interrelation with other structures since there can
be no operation in complete isolation save by an inclusive
unit such as a society.

37. The functional requisite is always to some degree
"adaptive" because in its absence the system concerned
would cease to persist, but a given function may at one and
the same time have both "adaptive" and "maladaptive" aspects. See the discussion of eufunction and dysfunction
below, pp. 76-83.

concept "by what") what is done is done. One refers to the
results of actions (or empirical phenomena in general),
and the other to the forms or patterns of action (or empirical phenomena in general). There may be and are of
course patterns of the results of actions. These too would
fall into the category of structure. Similarly, patterns
of action are themselves the results of the operation of
other patterns, and in this sense they are functions. This
consideration points to a special characteristic of the
referents of the concepts of function and structure. The
same empirical phenomenon may be an example of either a
function or a structure depending upon the point from which
it is viewed. Thus, the fact that "well-reared" children
in a given society (say Chinese society) are "polite" to
their elders is a function of a particular set of patterns
of child training. The existence of a particular set of
patterns of child training is a function of still other
patterns. The observable uniformity of "politeness" to
elders by "well-reared" children is a structure that in
turn produces certain conditions or functions when it
operates. The fact that the same phenomenon viewed from
different standpoints may be either a function or a structure does not make these two terms coterminous or useless.
Exactly the same situation exists with other concepts that
are quite useful for analysis. The concepts of intermediate ends and means are of the same sort. Intermediate ends
are means relative to other ends, and means are intermediate ends when viewed from an earlier point in the
means-ends chain. Still, from a single point of view the
means is not an end and vice versa. Furthermore, useful
results may be obtained by means of the distinction. For
example, what is a means from actor X's point of view may
be an end from actor Y's point of view, or what is an end
from actor X's short-run point of view may be a means from
his long-run point of view. In both cases the distinction
may make possible a tenable type of analysis that would
otherwise be impossible, e.g., judgment or comparison of

the rational or nonrational character of the action.[38]
<u>Production</u> and <u>consumption</u>, <u>power</u> and <u>responsibility</u>,
<u>oxidation</u> and <u>reduction</u> (given the electron definition of
those concepts), <u>cause</u> and <u>effect</u>, and <u>anabolism</u> and
<u>catabolism</u> are other examples from a variety of fields of
concepts of this sort.[39]   An interest in the results of
operation of a unit focuses attention on the concept of
function. An interest in the patterns of operation focuses attention on structure. An interest in the results
of operation of a unit and the implications of those
results focuses attention on both function and structure
since the implications that can be studied scientifically
lie in their effects on observable uniformities.

2.   The concepts of functional and structural requisites

As has been pointed out above in this chapter, the
concepts of functional and structural requisites are useful
in the discovery of the minimal implications of the existence of a unit of a given type in the empirical setting of
such a unit. A <u>functional requisite</u>, as that term is used
here, is a generalized condition necessary for the maintenance of the unit with which it is associated, given the
level of generalization of the definition of that unit and
the most general setting of such a unit. In seeking to
discover the functional requisites of a unit one seeks the
answer to the question, "What must be done to maintain the
system concerned in its setting on the level under consideration?" Determination of the functional requisites of a
system is reached by an examination of the minimal requirements set by the interrelationship of the particular system

---

38.   The terms <u>rational</u> and <u>nonrational</u> are defined
below; see pp. 242-244.

39.   The reader will notice the absence of examples
from the field of physics. There, the use of the plus and
minus signs in mathematical analysis obviate the necessity
of such a distinction in verbal terms.

concerned and its setting. Basically the test of any given
condition's status as a functional requisite of a system
is simple. A given condition is a functional requisite of
a system if its absence would result in (a) the total
dissolution of the unit, or (b) the change of one of the
structural aspects of the unit on the level under consideration. In the case of the most general or most inclusive
unit possible within a given range of variation[40] only the
first result need be cited, for any change in the structure
on the most general level of consideration dissolves the
unit. But the use of functional requisites as a tool is
not confined to the most general level. They may be used
on any level of generalization.[41] For example, one may
speak of the functional requisites of any society, but one
may also speak of the functional requisites of Chinese society. In the former case, failure to fulfill a functional
requisite leaves no society at all; in the latter case,
failure to fulfill a functional requisite may leave no
society at all or, perhaps, merely a different type of society.

Closely connected with the concept of a functional
requisite is the concept of a <u>structural requisite</u>. The
latter is less frequently mentioned explicitly than is the
former, but whether explicit or implicit, the two go hand
in hand. A <u>structural requisite</u>, as that term is used
here, is a pattern (or observable uniformity) of action
(or operation) necessary for the continued existence of
the unit with which it is associated given the level of
generalization of the definition of that unit and the most
general setting of such a unit. In seeking to discover
the structural requisites of a unit one seeks the answer

---

40. See above, pp. 22-24 for a discussion of the
peculiar status of society as in one sense the most general unit possible within its range of variation and in
another sense not.

41. See above, Note 21, p. 46 for consideration about
levels of generalization in this connection.

to the question, "In a given unit what patterns must be
present such that operation in terms of these patterns
will result in the functional requisites of the unit?"
The functional requisites of a unit are the answers to the
question, "Given a particular unit in such and such a setting what must be done if the system is to persist?" The
structural requisites are the answers to quite another
question. They answer the question, "How must what must
be done, if the unit as defined is to persist in its setting, be done?" In short form one answers the question,
"What must be done?" and the other, "How must what must be
done, be done?" It is in the answer to the second question
that much, if not most, of the interest of the social
scientist inheres when he is concerned with requisite
analysis. The pursuit of functional requisites is, analytically speaking, primarily, if not only, a means to an
end. The concept of functional requisites is not, generally, a focus of interest in and of itself. The end of
analysis is generally the patterns of action and not the
necessary conditions of action. The necessary conditions
are, however, a vital tool in the systematic treatment of
the patterns themselves.

The analytical usefulness of the concept of functional requisites lies in the fact that, once the list of
functional requisites of a unit has been worked out, there
exists a systematic method of ascertaining whether or not
in a given problem all of the minimally required structures
have been studied. For example, if relative to a given
unit say six functional requisites can be shown to exist,
and if, after all discussion of the social structures, one
or more (or parts of one or more) functional requisites
are not performed or met by one or some combination of
several of the structures discussed, then there exist some
serious lacunae in the treatment of the social structures,
unless the list of functional requisites can be shown to
be faulty or unless the unit concerned does not conform to

the definition of it that has been used. The concept of
functional requisites, however, plays another role that is
perhaps more helpful than serving as a check on whether or
not the coverage of social structures has been inclusive
enough. It directs attention to crucial problems for social structure and hence furnishes a starting point in the
search for and analysis of social structure.

In this process there are of course dangers. Rarely
in either the explicit or implicit use of structural-functional analysis has it been useful to construct a model
involving a one-to-one correspondence between structural
and functional requisites or even a one-to-one correspondence between structure and function in general.[42] A given
functional requisite is likely to be met by portions or
aspects of more than one structure in such studies as
exist. To the extent that this is true no direct transition is possible from functional requisites to structural
requisites. At the same time the structures of a unit,
however they may be differentiated, may and do have differing orientations and emphases, and in this respect the
careful consideration of functional requisites again
provides, as a minimum, fruitful suggestions as to the sort
of structure to look for.

One may recapitulate the so-called structural-functional requisite method of analysis as follows: the first
step is to define the unit of phenomena to be studied,

---

42. In the present study, for example, even when
analytic structures as opposed to concrete structures were
used, it proved more useful at least on a tentative basis
to use a model in which no such one-to-one correspondence
was involved. The impossibility of such a model in terms
of concrete structures is relatively clear. It is by no
means so clear for models in terms of analytic structures.
In this latter case the only defense of the procedure used
here is the greater usefulness of the present model on the
basis of tentative exploratory applications made by the
author. Definition of the concepts of analytic and concrete structure appear below, pp. 88-89. This difficulty
is taken up in more detail below, pp. 199-207.

i.e., the system concerned; second, one must discover the
factors setting the limits of possible variation of the
phenomena to be studied, i.e., the setting; third, one must
determine what general conditions must be met if the system
is to persist in its setting without structural change on
the level under consideration, i.e., the functional requisites of the unit -- the determination of the functional
requisites of the unit is the determination of the minimum
implications of the interrelationships between the factors
setting the limits of variation and the unit itself;
fourth, one uses the knowledge so obtained of what things
must be done to examine and determine systematically what
patterns must be present in the system as a minimum if the
unit is to persist in its setting without any structural
change on the level under consideration.

In using these concepts several factors must be kept
in mind. In the first place, nothing can be discovered
about the requisites, either functional or structural, of
any unit without knowledge of the referent of the unit.
Either an explicit or implicit definition of the unit is
always involved. In general, it would seem that explicit
definitions, however tentative, cause fewer difficulties
in these respects. With explicit definitions cases of
difficulty arising from relatively "useless" concepts are
far easier to run down. Furthermore, the process of discovery of the requisites is far easier to check when the
definitions are explicit. Preference for implicit definitions in science generally has all of the difficulties of
the "ostrich" procedure in any field.

Only in terms of the definition of the unit can its
setting be located. This does not mean that the setting
is part of the definition of the unit. The fact that all
known (or even expected) referents of the concept "dog"
are in fact found on a single planet (a portion of the
nondog environment of dogs) does not make location on this
planet a part of the definition of that term as it is

usually applied and any animal conforming to the usual
morphological definition of "dog" will be readily admitted
to the general class regardless of its location. On the
other hand, the setting factors for any "dog" are not
arbitrary in the sense that the definition of the term is.
They are in the general case dog heredity and nondog environment. In science failure to agree to such "rules of
the game" reduces all knowledge to the category of definitions (and hence to the arbitrary character of definitions
in scientific systems) or makes the definition of terms
irrelevant. Either alternative would radically alter the
general referent of the term science.

In the case of the requisite concepts one of the most
important factors to bear in mind about the definition of
a unit is its level of generalization. What is a structural requisite of an empirical unit considered on one
level of generalization is not necessarily a requisite of
the system considered on another level. The same is true
of functional requisites. For example, if United States
society is defined as the specific society existing today
within the continental boundaries generally understood for
the United States nation, then some patterns of private
ownership of the means of production may well be a structural requisite. If it is defined merely as a "modern
industrial" society within those continental limits, those
patterns are not structural requisites insofar as it is
empirically possible for a modern industrial society to
exist in that setting without patterns of private ownership
of the means of production. If that society is defined
simply as a society capable of existing within those geographical limits, even the patterns of mass production of
goods and services are not structural requisites. This is
not simply word magic or intellectual autoeroticism. The
distinction in levels has quite practical applications and
uses in science and applied science. For many therapeutic
purposes a veterinarian is interested in the general struc-

tures of any dog and any examples of certain types of dog
parasites. Treatment for worms varies with body weight of
dogs but breed differences as such matter little if at all.
The same is true of "distemper," dog encephalitis, etc.
But for the treatment of dog coats a more specific definition of the unit is relevant. For much of such therapy as
that it makes a difference whether the dog is an Airedale
or a collie or a basset hound, more factors than those of
any dog or any dog of a given weight are involved. In
this more specific case breed definitions become relevant
because of the specific differences of coats and skin conditions as among different breeds. Similar cases can be
found in any field in which empirical scientific analysis
is discovered, applied, or some combination of the two
whether those fields be physics, biology, social science,
medicine, bridge engineering, or whatever.

In dealing with strucutral-functional requisite analysis empirical error is always a possibility as in any
empirical scientific field. The findings in this field
are not simply matters of logical deduction from a set of
definitions. Systematic procedure in these terms is,
therefore, no guarantee against error. It does, however,
help in the location of errors. For example, suppose one
has discovered at least tentatively the structural requisites of a particular type of unit (e.g., any society);
then, in studying any specific case of a society, it is to
be expected that some specific patterns of a particular
structural requisite (e.g., "role differentiation" on the
basis of sex) will be found. Suppose, however, such patterns are not found. One of three (or some combination of
three) possible sources of error may exist. In the first
place, the patterns may not have come to light because of
faulty observation. In the second place, they may in fact
not be present, and the theory that they would be is invalid because, for example, some patterns of "role differentiation" on the basis of sex are not in fact structural

requisites of any society. Exploration of this source of
error involves exploration of the basis of the theory that
such patterns are structural requisites of any society.
This in turn involves a reexamination of the requisite
character of a certain function(s) on which the requisite
character of this structure is based. This in its turn
may involve a reexamination of the discovery of the functional requisites themselves, and hence a reexamination of
the minimal implications of the interrelation of the unit
as defined and its setting. This in turn may finally
raise the question of whether the setting factors used are
in fact the setting factors of the unit concerned. In the
third place, observation may have been correct and the
theory that the patterns are structural requisites of any
society may also have been correct, but the unit being
examined may not in fact be an example of the general class,
society. In this third case, although the theories connected with the model used have not been disproved, the
model has been shown at least to be less useful in this
respect for the kind of unit actually being examined than
it is for application to units of the type for which it
was designed. Furthermore, at least some of the respects
in which it is less useful have been developed.[43] Finally,
the error involved may be some combination of these three
difficulties. It cannot be overemphasized that in this as
in all primarily theoretical work, perhaps, the deepest
danger lies in permitting conceptual schemes and theoretical systems to become jails for empirical work. There is
never any basis in this type of analysis for disregarding
verifiable empirical factors on the level under consideration because they contradict theories or do not fit neatly
into the concepts. Under these conditions it is changes

---

43. This whole question of sources of error in the
use of this type of analysis is developed in both general
and specific cases throughout the volume.

in the concepts and the theories that are to be sought if there is to be scientific development.

Another difficulty that must be watched and avoided in the use of the requisite concepts is that of functional (or structural) teleology. Conditions or patterns can never be proved to exist because they are functional or structural requisites of a given unit. It is always possible that the units with which one connects them do not exist or, having existed, are currently (at the time of study) in the process of complete dissolution or change on the level of analysis under consideration. It is a tempting error in analysis, particularly given the current state of development of both theory and data collection in the social sciences. It is easy on the basis of superficial examination to classify a given unit as say a society and then to insist that patterns of role differentiation on the basis of sex must be present because they are a structural requisite of any society. This error is likely to be compounded with that of permitting one's conceptual scheme and theoretical system to become a "jail" for research -- of insisting that certain factors must be present because they are indicated theoretically without raising the question of possible invalidity of the theory in relevant respects. Structural and functional requisites of a unit do not <u>necessarily</u> "exist" in any empirical case. Their "existence" or "nonexistence" is dependent upon the "existence" or "nonexistence" of a particular sort of unit in a particular type of setting.

Finally another caution must be observed. Application of the requisite concepts tells one nothing of the question of origins of a unit or of its different aspects. The question of what "existed" when the requisites were present but the unit was not is meaningless in this procedure. These requisites have no "existence" apart from the "existence" of the unit which they are used to analyze and its particular setting. They are useful in the analysis of

questions of origin (i.e., questions involving change)
because knowledge of the functions and structures at a
starting and end point of a process give one the basis for
asking questions of interstitial states. They are useful
there because knowledge of them permits prerequisite analysis, but in and of themselves they give no answers to
such questions.

Within such limits of application as these, the requisite concepts may be extremely useful, focusing attention
as they do upon minimal unit requirements in a given setting. Failure to observe or recognize the methodological
limits of their application may more than vitiate their
usefulness.

3. The concepts of functional and
structural prerequisites

The concepts of functional and structural requisites
as noted above[44] are not in and of themselves oriented to
the question of change. But dynamic theories and problems
in dynamics are a central focus of interest in all scientific fields. There is probably a large body of opinion
to the effect that static theories and problems are
primarily useful for the light that can be shed thereby on
dynamics. Whatever one's position may be in this respect,
it cannot be denied that dynamic analysis has proved both
feasible and useful in scientific fields of all sorts. In
varying ways different concepts of structure and function
are useful in such analysis.

The concepts of <u>functional</u> and <u>structural prerequi-
sites</u> are analogues in a sense of the concepts of functional and structural requisites. The former direct attention
to the minimum requirements that must "preexist" for a unit
of a given type in its setting to come into being or to
change in particular ways. The term <u>functional prerequi-</u>

---

44. See pp. 43-45.

site may be defined as a function[45] that must preexist if a given unit in its setting is to come into being. The term structural prerequisite may be defined as a structure[46] that must "preexist" if a given unit in its setting is to come into being.

Discussion of the prerequisite concepts raises in general the question of change in empirical units. There is not space to go into this question in detail here. A few general remarks that set the problem for the present volume are all that will be attempted. Empirical units as that term is used here are structures in that they consist of observable uniformities of operation or action.[47] A unit is spoken of here as changed when its minimal features (structural requisites) are no longer the same on the level under consideration. Change of a unit may be one of three types of change. The unit may be totally destroyed. A totally destructive change is here defined as one that leaves no phenomena that are not at least in theory adequately explicable in terms of one or more of the setting factors of the most general class of the unit under consideration. Thus a meteor collision, or for that matter a war, that wiped out all human life in, say, the Trobriand Islands area would be a totally destructive change of the unit of Trobriand society. In this case physicochemical or biological theories (or social theories not relevant to the human species) would at least in theory suffice to explain the phenomena that remained. Such an event would not necessarily be totally destructive of units of geological or biological interest.[48]

---

45. See the definition of function above p. 56.

46. See the definition of structure above p. 57.

47. They are also concrete structures as that term is used here. See below, p. 88.

48. In theory, using this definition, totally destructive changes on the most general level of consideration could not occur in physics unless one speaks of the metaphysical question of the complete destruction of all

Secondly, the unit may be changed to one of a "different" type within the most general setting of the most general type of phenomena under consideration (i.e., general type changes). For example, a business organization may be taken over by a government, or a society may cease to be a society and become a subcategory of some other society by military conquest or by other means. In the field of biology, for example, some slime molds (e.g., Dictyostelium discoideum) start their life cycle as separate amoebae that operate (including reproduction) as separate amoebae and then congregate to form fruiting bodies from which some of the cells in spore form live on to renew the cycle.

Thirdly, the unit may change to another example of its original general type (i.e., specific type changes). For example, feudal French society may change to modern French society, or the family units of a society may change from patriarchal, patrilineal, patrilocal units to multilineal conjugal units. Classification of any given change into one of these three types ([1] totally destructive changes, [2] general type changes, and [3] specific type changes) obviously involves a determination of the level of generalization that is involved. What are totally destructive changes in terms of one level of consideration may be general type changes on another, and so forth. The distinction may, nevertheless, prove to be quite useful since, given any specific level of consideration, some factors may result in one of these types of changes and others in another. For example, given the most general level of social consideration, recent technological advances have posed a question not posed for humans in the past. It is at least in theory possible that the technology of war be totally destructive, i.e., wipe out all human social units

---

empirical phenomena. There is, of course, an unavoidable sense in which the ultimate limits of scientific concern are nonscientific questions, i.e., that science operates in terms of a definite set of nonempirical assumptions.

on this planet. In times of more "primitive" and "less
civilized" development the most thoroughgoing changes that
the application of the technology of war could reasonably
be expected to provide were changes in general and specific
types of social units. Under the circumstances factors
precipitating wars in the latter case do not in general
contain all the possibilities with regard to types of
change in social units that are presented by the former.

Two other concepts with regard to change may be added
here. The necessary but not sufficient, or the necessary
and sufficient "causes" of change, may be <u>internal</u> or <u>ex-
ternal</u> to the unit concerned. They are <u>internal</u> to the
unit if they are produced by the operation of that unit
itself. They are <u>external</u> if they are produced by the
operations of units other than the unit that changes.
There is, of course, the possibility that the "causes" of
change will be a combination of both external and internal
factors. Thus, many, if not most, of the factors changing
China from Yüan China to Ming China were internal ones.
Those currently changing China are in considerable part
external ones though many internal ones are also involved.

In any analysis of change three stages may be distinguished. The first is the stage from which change takes
place. For social analysis this may be termed the <u>initial
stage</u>. The second is the <u>transitional stage</u>, i.e., the
state of affairs during the period in which the change is
effectuated. Finally, one may distinguish the <u>resultant
stage</u>, i.e., the state of affairs at the completion of the
change. Obviously distinction of these stages is a question of how one chooses to state the problem under study.
Some statements of the problem will prove useful for analysis, and others will not. There seems to be no alternative
to this view of the problem since, empirically speaking,
some change always takes place if only that of increasing
age. No absolute initial, transitional, or resultant
stages can be discovered unless one makes what has so far

at least been a particular set of metaphysical assumptions.
These latter would have to be, first, an assumption of some
point as the ultimate origin of empirical process and,
second, an assumption of some point as the ultimate end.
This is possible in some spheres of interest (e.g., "creation day" and "judgment day" in many religious systems),
but such assumptions lie outside the scientific realm,
whatever may be believed of their "ultimate" truth or
falsity.

Thus, for some purposes it is useful to take the
France of Charlemagne as an initial stage and that of Louis
XIV as the resultant stage. For other purposes the France
of Louis XIV might usefully serve as the initial stage and
that of Napoleon as the resultant stage and so forth. In
scientific analysis of empirical process the chicken versus
the egg question is always a waste of time. If it proves
useful for the development of scientific theories, either
the egg or the chicken or both may be taken as the initial
stage.

In the study of change the selection of an initial and
a resultant stage is arbitrary in the same sense that the
selection of any problem for study is. That is to say it is
not scientifically more tenable to select one problem than
another.[49] But the relevance of these various stages to
the analysis of change is not arbitrary in any methodological sense. Without knowledge or hypotheses about two of
the three stages nothing can be said about the phenomenon
of change involved. Given knowledge or hypotheses about
the initial and resultant stages, it is possible to get answers about the state of affairs in the transitional stage.
Given only one of the two, this is impossible since one
cannot on that basis phrase the problem, i.e., one cannot
determine what change has taken place. Given knowledge or

----

49. The selection is not, of course, arbitrary in
the sense of having no cause or determining factors.

hypotheses about the initial and transitional stages, one
may make predictions about the resultant stage -- but again
not on the basis of knowledge or hypotheses about only one
of the two because the process of change cannot be determined on that basis. Finally, given knowledge or
hypotheses about the transitional and resultant stages,
one may at least develop a range of possibilities for the
initial stage but again, for similar reasons, not on the
basis of only one of the two.

At two of the stages of analysis of change requisite
analysis may be applied in order to gain the knowledge or
hypotheses necessary for the establishment of the third
stage. For the third stage the question of minimal
"preexisting" conditions or patterns, or the minimal implications of "preexisting" conditions or patterns may be
raised. In using functional and structural prerequisite
analysis many of the same limitations exist that exist for
requisite analysis. The eternal relevance of the level of
generality of treatment of the various stages is like that
of the relevance of the level of definition of the unit
for requisite analysis. The danger of teleology is identical with the different time factor included. Finally,
theories about the functional and structural prerequisites
of given types of units can no more legitimately be permitted to become a jail for social analysis than can those
of functional and structural requisites.

4. The concepts of eufunction and dysfunction and
   eustructure and dysstructure

These concepts are developed for use in relation to
problems of adjustment and maladjustment in units under
study. In one form or another such concepts have long been
used most notably in the biological and social sciences.
The term "function" in ordinary usage has as one of its

many referents what is here meant by the term <u>eufunction</u>.[50]
For example, the term "function" as defined by Merton[51] is
roughly equivalent with what is here called <u>eufunction</u>. The
term <u>dysfunction</u> in general use, and as defined by Merton,[52]
is roughly equivalent with the present use of the term.

Here <u>eufunction</u> is defined as a condition, or state
of affairs, that (1) results from the operation (including
in the term operation mere persistence) of a structure of
a given unit through time, and that (2) increases or maintains adaptation or adjustment of the unit <u>to the unit's
setting</u>, thus making for the persistence of the <u>unit as
defined</u> of which the structure concerned is a part or
aspect.[53] <u>Dysfunction</u> is defined as a condition, or state
of affairs, that (1) results from the operation (including
in the term operation mere persistence) of a structure of
a given unit through time, and that (2) lessens the adaptation or adjustment of the unit <u>to the unit's setting</u>, thus
making for a lack of persistence (i.e., a change in or
dissolution) of the <u>unit as defined</u> of which the structure
concerned is a part or aspect. The terms eufunctional and
dysfunctional may, of course, be applied to parts or
aspects of a given function. The phrase "unit as defined"

---

50. The use of the prefixes <u>eu</u> and <u>dys</u> in this connection is not without precedent, e.g., <u>eugenics</u> and <u>dys-
genics</u>, but tolerance must be begged of those whose sensitivity is jarred by the mixture of Greek and Latin roots.
They should feel perfectly free to replace these terms by
other symbols.

51. R. K. Merton, <u>Social Theory</u>, p. 50.

52. <u>ibid.</u>, p. 50.

53. Apart from the use of a different term for the
concept, the major departure of this definition from that
of Merton is the statement <u>of what</u> these conditions are a
result and <u>to what</u> the adjustment or adaptation takes
place.

is inserted because it is to the definition of the unit that one must turn to determine whether or not "adaptation or adjustment" making for the persistence or lack of persistence of the unit is taking place. Some care in these respects is necessary if terms such as eufunction and dysfunction (and their adjectival, adverbial, and verbal forms) are to be useful for scientific purposes. In rough terms a eufunction is a function that tends to preserve the unit as defined, and a dysfunction is one that tends to dissolve it, but all too often loose usage of these concepts results in use of eufunctional to refer to conditions making for "good" adaptations and of dysfunctional to refer to conditions making for "bad" adaptations. In such cases the unit concerned is often undefined or, if defined, has been ignored and/or replaced as a referent for this judgment by some ethical standard which may or may not inhere in the unit itself. Depending on how the American social system is defined many of the eufunctions discernible in its operations would be decried by all liberal social reformers, and many of the dysfunctions would be applauded. The important consideration is that for scientific work these judgments of good or bad must be kept out of analysis, and must not be permitted to creep back into the analysis because of failure to delineate concepts clearly enough to make the detection of such tendencies a relatively simple matter.

The misuse of the concepts of eufunction and dysfunction (or of their equivalents in general use, "function" and dysfunction) is an extremely serious matter. One of the most frequent accusations leveled against the self-conscious attempts to use the various forms of structural-functional analysis has been the charge that analysis in these terms has tended to develop into (or appears to develop into) a defense of the status quo or some other position. One of the major sources of this charge is the

teleological difficulty discussed above.[54] The other is
the implicit use of these two concepts as equivalents of
the terms "good" and "bad." Neither the teleological
difficulty nor this sort of injection of value judgments
into the analysis is inherent in this type of analysis.
The temptations and ease of unconscious commission are,
however, great in both cases. Both difficulties may be
avoided if the application and limits of the concepts are
understood and scrupulously observed. The value difficulty
like the teleological one is the result of misuse of the
concepts and method of analysis.

No condition or aspect of a condition is inherently
eufunctional or dysfunctional as those terms are used here.
The insistence, in the definition of the terms, on the
phrases "unit as defined" and "adaptation or adjustment of
the unit to the unit's setting" is essential here. Without
a statement of the unit concerned and its setting no judgment as to the eufunctional or dysfunctional character of
a condition can be made. The same condition that is
eufunctional from one such point of view may be dysfunctional from another. Thus, assuming for a moment that
Prince Ito and his colleagues were in fact responsible for
the "reforms" that changed Japan from its "feudal" Tokugawa
system to its "modern industrial national" system, the
acts of this group of men were in these respects dysfunctional for Tokugawa Japan and its remnants in its general
world setting and eufunctional from the point of view of
"modern industrial national" Japan in that setting. A
condition that is eufunctional from the point of view of a
family group in one setting may conceivably be dysfunctional from a single member's point of view in that or another
setting. Conditions that would be eufunctional for the
American Communist Party under present conditions would

---

54. See pp. 52-55.

undoubtedly be dysfunctional for modern United States society (if the latter is taken in its present form of
private ownership of many, if not most, of the means of
production), and so forth. Only reference to a particular
unit <u>as defined on a particular level and to its setting</u>
makes possible the classification of a condition or aspect
of a condition as eufunctional or dysfunctional.

 Even the classification of a condition or aspect of a
condition as eufunctional or dysfunctional tells one
nothing evaluative about it. It merely states an empirical
characteristic of it, namely, that it makes for, or lessens,
the adaptation or adjustment of the unit concerned to its
setting. These terms become evaluative only if either
explicitly or implicitly a value assumption is made to the
effect that it is "good" or "bad" (or "indifferent") for
the unit as defined to persist (or not) in its setting.
If one assumes that Tokugawa Japan <u>should</u> have been maintained, then, following the example above, the dysfunctional acts of Prince Ito and his colleagues were bad. If one
assumes that Tokugawa Japan <u>should not</u> have been maintained,
their dysfunctional acts were good. Similarly, if one
takes modern Japan as a unit and assumes it to be good,
their eufunctional acts relative to it were good. If one
assumes it bad, their eufunctional acts relative to it were
bad.

 In using the concepts of eufunction and dysfunction
it must always be remembered: (1) that determination of
classification in these terms depends on a statement of
the unit and its setting, and correspondingly that, given
variations in either level of generality of statement of
the unit and its setting or type of unit and setting,
classification in these terms may vary, and (2) classification of a condition (or aspect of a condition) in these
terms implies no evaluation unless some specific value
assumption about the maintenance of such a unit has been
introduced to the analysis. With these considerations kept

in mind the terms may be used for purely scientific purposes
without difficulty. Furthermore, by the explicit addition
of evaluations, the implications of such scientific analysis for social engineering may be discovered. For example,
if one knows scientifically what conditions are eufunctional and what ones are dysfunctional for the maintenance of
dope rings in the United States and, if one believes, as
it is generally held, that dope rings are "bad," then those
conditions eufunctional for the dope rings become conditions
to be eliminated. Those dysfunctional become conditions to
be encouraged, provided that elimination of the former and
encouragement of the latter are not more dysfunctional to
the United States than dope rings are and assuming that it
is "good" to maintain the United States.

The insistence here on departures from common usages
of terms like "function" is not made for sheer love of
complexity and change. The various concepts of function
and structure used here and their various subclasses have
distinct uses and referents. Confusion of them may cause
serious errors. Ordinarily, the concepts distinguished
here as functional requisites, eufunctions, and dysfunctions are more frequently useful than the general term
function of which they are subcategories. But apart from
the logical nicety involved in having a definition for the
general class of which the three terms are subcategories,
there is another justification for such distinctions. A
single "resultant condition" or "observable consequence"
may at one and the same time have one or more or some combination of such referents. It may be a functional requisite and have both eufunctional and dysfunctional aspects.
It may have both aspects and not be a requisite, and so
forth. The general term enables one to refer to the
condition without prejudice to these questions. Furthermore, the use of the term "functional" as the opposite of
dysfunctional may at least convey to some the idea that a
given condition is either one or the other and may not

combine the features of both.

The terms eustructure and dysstructure may be defined as follows: (1) eustructures are structures such that operation in terms of them result in eufunctions, and (2) dysstructures are structures[55] such that operation in terms of them results in dysfunctions. The adjectival forms, eustructural and dysstructural, following the pattern with regard to eufunctional and dysfunctional, may be applied to parts or aspects of a given structure. The principal usefulness of these concepts lies in their application in contexts in which structure rather than function is the center of interest. The cautions mentioned above with regard to the use of the concepts, eufunction and dysfunction, apply to these concepts equally.

The concepts of cufunction and dysfunction and eustructure and dysstructure focus on the question of the maintenance or lack of maintenance of a system. The requisite concepts focus on the question of what a system is like if it is maintained. The requisite concepts are useful primarily for static theories though dynamic analysis is involved in the discovery of the requisites of a given system in its setting. Like the prerequisite concepts, these adjustment concepts focus attention on dynamic interrelations -- on the implications of the operation of a particular structure or the presence of a particular structure or the presence of a particular function for the state of the system concerned at some future point in time. As such they (or their equivalents) have proved extremely useful in past scientific analysis in the social and biological fields. So often have they been used that the common usage of the term "structural-functional" analysis has probably referred more often to analysis in terms of the adjustment forms of the concepts of function

---

55. See above, p. 57 for the definition of the term structure.

and structure than to anything else. This has held true
despite the general confusion noted by Merton and others
about definition or lack of definition of these concepts.
The major concern in this volume is with static theories
of the functional and structural requisites of any society.
But the dynamic concepts proposed are useful in deriving
those theories, and those theories, if successfully developed, will make possible the more fruitful development
of dynamic analysis relying heavily on concepts such as
these.

5. Concepts of latent and manifest function
and structure

The use here of the qualifying terms, latent and manifest, in connection with the various concepts of function
and structure is an adaptation of these concepts as originally proposed by Merton many years ago and recently
published by him in a volume of essays.[56] These concepts
focus attention on the question of the degree and type of
intent of the actors in a social situation and on their
awareness of the implications and results of their acts.
Following Merton's usage a factor will be termed manifest
if it is "intended and recognized by the participants in
the system," and will be termed latent if it is "neither
intended nor recognized."[57] The application of these terms
is less limited here than in Merton's usage. In Merton's
usage only the concept here called eufunction has both
latent and manifest forms. In his usage dysfunction apparently has only a latent form, and of course the general
concept of function as used here does not exist at all
explicitly in his treatment. For purposes of example the
general concept of function may be used here. If, for

---

56. R. K. Merton, Social Theory, p. 51.
57. ibid.

example, an individual intends by saving five dollars a
day to be able at the end of a year to buy a new automobile, does so, and realizes that he has at the end of a
year -- that purchase is a manifest function of his action.
If, however, without intention or realization on his part
he thereby upsets his relations with his wife who regards
this action as an extravagance, then the consequent state
of their relations is a latent function of that action.
These examples are trivial, but far more important ones
come easily to mind. A high level of material output is a
manifest function of a modern industrial system of production. The nervous stresses and strains placed on individuals by participation in such systems of production and the
dysfunctions that may be produced thereby for the system
are latent functions of it.

The concepts, latent and manifest, may be applied to
any of the concepts of function and structure developed
here. Their most usual applications in the past have been
to the concepts here termed eufunction and dysfunction.
Such restriction is not necessary, and abandonment of it
provides useful concepts. The concept of manifest dysfunction is specifically included because it may well have a
special relevance for the analysis of certain types of
social change, i.e., planned social change of many sorts.
For example, the operation of many of the social patterns
inaugurated and fostered by the Japanese (especially, of
course, by their leaders) in the period preceding and
following the enthronement of the Emperor Meiji had results
that were manifestly dysfunctional to the system of which
they were a part (Tokugawa Japanese social structure),
though of course manifestly eufunctional, at least in many
respects, for the system that they sought to produce and
for the change to such a system. Failure to raise the
question of the possibility of manifest dysfunctions is
likely to preserve the frequent erroneous impression that
eufunctions are somehow identified with the "good" and

dysfunctions with the "bad,"[58] since the manifest pursuit of the "bad" is difficult for some to imagine. Great pains must be taken to prevent the subtle and unapprehended intrusion of value judgments into scientific analysis.

In using the concepts of eufunction and dysfunction and their structural analogues the necessity of stating both the system concerned and the setting implied has been stressed above.[59] In using the concepts of latent and manifest the action concerned and its results must be specified <u>but so must the actor or actors from whose standpoint it is being viewed</u>. What is a manifest function from the point of view of one actor in a system may be latent from the point of view of another. The different positions of actors in a given system and their implications for the system may be strikingly revealed by asking whether the manifest or latent functions of their acts coincide or conflict. Finally, it must be borne in mind that, just as a given function may have both eufunctional and dysfunctional aspects, a given function or eufunction or dysfunction, etc., may have both latent and manifest aspects.

As far as is known to the author, neither Merton nor others have generally applied these modifying concepts to the various forms of the structure concept. Nevertheless, after Merton's fruitful suggestion of them relative to the term function, their application to structure and its various subcategories is a simple and obvious step. It is certainly true that there are patterns of action that are intended and recognized by the participants therein and that there are those that are not. It is also true that many of the patterns intended and recognized often involve as concomitants patterns that are unintended and unrecog-

---

58. See above, pp. 78-81.
59. See pp. 78-81.

nized. Furthermore, the close connections between structure and function so often mentioned above would suggest
at least that concepts so useful as the manifest and latent
ones have proved to be in the one case would have corresponding uses in the other. They can and will be found of
considerable use for the general analysis of social structure and for its comparative analysis as well.[60] One of
the most useful applications that suggests itself immediately and obviously is in connection with the analysis of
social change, but even in static analysis such applications may be quite fruitful.

The application of the terms latent and manifest to
concepts of functional and structural requisites has not
shown itself to be particularly useful for the analysis
attempted here given its present stage of development.
The latent and manifest qualifications are useful for analysis in which the awareness or unawareness of the participants in a system is a crucial consideration. This is not
the case in the application of the requisite concepts at
their present stage of development. In this case the
emphasis is on the necessity of the condition or pattern
for the persistence of the system, and the primary use of
the requisite concepts is to make certain that no serious
lacunae exist (or at least to locate their existence) in
the delineation of social structure. Furthermore, all
functional (and structural) requisites are, at least in
major respects though not necessarily entirely, eufunctional (or eustructural). Therefore, insofar as consideration

---

60. The author has at any rate found the applications
of these terms to structure useful in the comparative analysis of material on China and Japan that is as yet unpublished. At least one other social scientist has explicitly used the suggested concepts, latent and manifest structure, in roughly their present form in his work. See
Arthur K. Davis, "Bureaucratic Patterns in the Navy Officer
Corps," Social Forces, Vol. 27, No.2, (Dec. 1948), pp. 143-
153.

of their latent and manifest qualities are concerned, they can be treated as manifest or latent eufunctions (or eu-structures) for the most part.[61]

Before leaving the concepts of latent and manifest a word should be said about their further extension. The present work has followed Merton's usage in emphasizing both intention and recognition in defining these concepts. At a further stage of development it may prove quite useful to draw a further distinction on these grounds. There are almost certainly empirical cases of functions and structures that are intended but unrecognized. Even more certainly there are those that are recognized but unintended. For present purposes these two categories may be identified as IUR (intended but unrecognized)-functions (or structures) and UIR (unintended but recognized)-functions (or structures) respectively. The former may prove to be useful concepts in treating certain "frustration" phenomena, most notably cases of so-called "compulsive striving." The latter may prove to be useful in the treatment of problems of reaction to unanticipated events such as windfall losses and gains, of "guilt feelings" and "remorse," etc. Still further development of the latent, manifest, IUR, and UIR concepts may take place in terms of

---

61. It is quite conceivable, however, that a given condition (or pattern) be at one and the same time necessary for the maintenance of a system and to some degree dysfunctional to it. For example, mass production in a highly industrialized society is necessary for its maintenance, but the processes involved may so upset the members as to "predispose" or "motivate" them to seek outlets in extremist highly authoritarian political faiths (e.g., fascisms and communisms) that may well prove to be incompatible with the maintenance of a highly industrialized society. Therefore, the dysfunctional (or dysstructural) aspects of functional (or structural) requisites probably should be explored in any given study. So far, however, exploration of such problems has proved sufficiently complex and difficult to preclude at the present stage of development any considerable attention to this point.

useful empirical distinctions among kinds and degrees of
intention and recognition on the part of the actor. At
the present stage of development of the present work, however, pursuit of these elaborations would be in the nature
of pure theoretical manipulation for its own sake, i.e.,
without specific problems of empirical analysis in mind.
Its future usefulness is, therefore, suggested but not
explored here.

6. Concepts of concrete and analytic structure

The distinction between <u>concrete</u> and <u>analytic</u> structure is oriented to the type of abstraction involved in
certain concepts useful for empirical analysis. <u>Concrete
structures</u> are defined as those patterns that define the
character of units that are at least in theory capable of
physical separation (in time and/or space) from other units
of the same sort. As the term will be applied for social
analysis it refers more specifically to the patterns that
define the character of membership units involved in social
action, i.e., units such that any given individual may be
classified as included or excluded (or some combination of
the two) from the unit. <u>Society</u> as that term will be used
here is a concrete structure in operation. Concrete structures other than societies are the patterns of action that
define the character of membership units within a given
society or those relating two or more societies. In this
sense the "family" as that term is often used is a concrete
structure; its patterns define a membership unit. So are
"business firms." The two may not be concretely separable
in the sense that one individual may at one and the same
time be a member of a "business firm" and a "family," but
nevertheless the social patterns characterizing the "business firm" concerned are not a part of the social patterns
characterizing the "family" concerned, however complex
their interrelationships may be (unless the firm is specifically and completely a "family" affair). Thus, it is

at least conceivable that all the members of Mr. X's
"family" be put into one room, all the members of, say,
the United States Steel Corporation be put into another,
and then, making the necessary selection, those individuals
who are members of both be put into a third.

Analytic structures are defined as patterned aspects
of action that are not even theoretically capable of concrete separation from other patterned aspects of action.
If one defines the economic aspect of action as having to
do with the allocation of goods and services and the political aspect of action as having to do with the allocation of power and responsibility, then the economic and
political patterns are analytic structures since there are
no concrete acts or systems that are totally devoid of
either economic or political aspects. Analytic structure
in the sense used here has its counterparts in the analytic
variables of other sciences. Some of the concrete particles studied by physics are spoken of as having both mass
and volume. By analytic abstraction it is possible to
discuss the one without the other, but a special type of
abstraction is involved in the process -- a type quite
different from that involved in proceeding from a low level
of generalization to a higher one.

The differences between concrete and analytic structure may be illustrated by reference to other scientific
fields. Atoms and molecules and cells and multicellular
organisms are concrete structures in the sense of the term
used here. The mass and volume of atoms and molecules and
the patterns of respiration and assimilation[62] of biologi-

---

62. By patterns of respiration and assimilation reference is made to how respiration and assimilation are
carried out. Respiration and assimilation are also used
to denote functions in biology, and there is an important
sense in which it is possible to have patterns of functions
(e.g., the interrelationships between different functions
or between one function performed at different times).
That is only one of the senses in which the phrase "pat-

cal organisms[63] are examples of analytic structures. Thus, in general, analytic structures cut clear across the whole of any given concrete structure, and concrete structures always involve parts of different analytic structures.

The distinction between concrete and analytic structure is particularly useful in attempts at systematic comparative analysis of social structures[64] in addition to its more general use. It is a distinct help in proceeding from one level of generalization to another, and the use of the distinction for these purposes is quite helpful in determining whether or not social structures in two different societies or in different parts of the same society are being treated on the same level and, if not, why not and what the difference in levels is.

By and large work in comparative analysis starts with concrete structures. This study in its attempt to develop general tools deals with the concrete structure, society. Comparative studies of this sort would start with specific societies. If this level of generality is not sought, the starting point is usually some concrete substructure of a society such as the "family" structure. Whatever level of generality may be the starting point for the analysis of concrete structures, there are two procedures, or some

---

terns of respiration and assimilation" is used here. It might be added here that patterns of functions always involve structural considerations at some points, and are in themselves analytic structures. See above, pp. 60-62, for the sense in which what are structures from one point of view are functions from another and vice versa.

63. "Biological" is specified here because of the frequency with which one meets the concept of social organism. The latter usage is perhaps serviceable for some purposes, but the loose analogy between concrete social structures and concrete biological structures has, perhaps, resulted in as many scientific difficulties as helpful insights.

64. Again the concern here is with social analysis, but the distinction has a similar usefulness in any field of comparative structural analysis.

combination of the two, possible for going to lower levels
of generalization. And of course when one seeks to compare
two structures not already analyzed, it is often in terms
of studying the lower levels of generalization of the
structures that their differences and similarities emerge.
One may proceed to lower levels of generalization by differentiating the concrete substructures which characterize
the structure concerned and proceeding systematically to
lower and lower levels of generalization by division and
subdivision of the concrete structures. For example,
assuming the United States as a nation conforms to the
definition of society to be used below, United States society could be subdivided into its "family" structure,
"governmental" structure, etc. And these structures could
again be subdivided into concrete substructures. How far
the subdivision could be carried would vary with the structure and the problem being studied. Its ultimate limit
would, of course, be the isolation of a concrete individual, though of course many concrete structures could not be
subdivided so far.

The second general method of procedure is to break
down the original concrete structure into its analytic
substructures. Thus, in the case of the unit mentioned
above one would delineate its economic substructure,
political substructure, etc.[65] This involves one in discussion not of different concrete parts of the original
structure but in the discussion of different aspects of
that structure. The distinction between the two procedures
is much like the difference between treating a cube by

---

65. Economic and political structures as defined
briefly above (see p. 89) are analytic structures. It is
also possible to distinguish "economic and political organizations" (i.e., predominantly economic and political
structures) as concrete structures. This distinction is
taken up below (see pp. 94-96). Care is required to avoid
confusion on this score however.

subdividing it into smaller solid segments as opposed to treating its different sides or its mass and volume.

The combination of the two is also possible, and at some point in the analysis is inevitable. It is impossible to treat a concrete structure simply by continued subdivision into other concrete structures. At some point in the treatment some consideration of the analytic structures is necessary, although of course it may be confined to treatment of the analytic structure solely insofar as it is involved in the concrete structure concerned. For example, a vital part of the analysis of "family" structure is a discussion of the ways in which goods and services and power and responsibility are allocated in the family. The combination is no less inevitable starting the other way round. One cannot differentiate levels of generality of analytic structure without some reference to concrete structure. For example, the structure of allocation of goods and services in the United States is more general than is the structure of allocation of goods and services of the United States "family" system, but this involves as a minimum the specification of the distinction between two concrete structures. Therefore one can only treat the analytic structures by showing the ways in which they enter particular concrete structures. For example, one treats the allocation of goods and services in the United States by showing the ways in which goods and services are allocated by "government" organizations, "families," "business firms," etc. The inevitability of the combination should not be surprising because the empirical acts studied are carried out by individuals or groups involved in concrete structures of which some of the patterns are only analytically distinguishable from one another.

When one is presented with statements about two different societies, it is relatively simple to determine whether they are both in terms of analytic or concrete structures or what combination of the two. If one is in

terms of concrete structure and the other in terms of analytic structure, it is immediately obvious that a difference in level (or at least type of level) is involved. If
the difference exists, the next step for comparative
purposes lies in determining the levels of generalization
involved when one is converted into concrete structural
terms or the other into analytic structural terms. If
both statements are in concrete structural terms or analytic structural terms, the similarity or difference in
levels of generality is to be found by proceeding systematically back to the most general level involved (i.e.,
the definition of the systems to be compared) assuming the
systems involved to be of the same level of generality.
If the systems are of different levels of generality, their
comparative status must be determined.[66]

It has been stated above on an impressionistic basis
that comparative analyses generally start with concrete
structures. It is not, however, inevitably so. The
starting point may well be analytic structures in which
case what has been said above must be modified, i.e., the
next level of generality involves the treatment of the way
in which the analytic structures are involved in concrete
structures. It may also be pointed out that, while the
examples given have proceeded from higher to lower levels
of generalization, the distinction is also useful for procedure in the reverse of this. If one starts with concrete
structures, one may ask of what more general concrete
structures are they components, or what general structures
do they exemplify. If one starts with analytic structures,
one may ask in what general concrete structure are they

---

66. In comparative analysis generally one is of necessity interested in the highest and lowest common levels
of generalization of the phenomena compared. Only in terms
of the location of some common level of generalization can
differences in levels of generalization be determined.

found or of what more general analytic structures are they
less general forms.

Thus, it may be said that this distinction is useful
for comparative analysis in two different respects. First,
with regard to the comparison of materials at hand it is a
useful tool for ascertaining similarities or the degree of
dissimilarities in levels of generalization concerned.
With regard to studies not yet made decision about the
pattern of procedure from one level to another in terms of
concrete and analytic structures will enable the student
to proceed systematically in the cases to be compared and
at least to avoid misunderstandings based on the unconscious comparison of things on different levels or different types of levels.

Second, it is by the study of the analytic structural
aspects of a given concrete structure that its interrelations with, and its similarities or dissimilarities to,
other concrete structures is highlighted. Conversely, it
is by the study of concrete structures that one sees the
ways in which different analytic patterns combine in an
empirical situation. For example, it is in terms of "role
differentiation" or economic patterns, or the like, that
some particular "family" structure is interrelated with
some particular "business firm," or comparison between the
two is done in terms of the different ways in which the
analytic structures are exemplified. Even if one attempts
to compare the two in terms of concrete substructures,
reference to analytic structure is involved. The reverse
is also true. If one attempts to compare the analytic
structure of allocation of goods and services with that of
power and responsibility, one does so in terms of reference
to concrete embodiments of these different aspects. For
example, one sees how goods and services and power and
responsibility are allocated within one or more such concrete structures as the "family," "business firms,"
"government" organizations, etc. The usefulness, in fact

the necessity, of using one type of structural reference
to elucidate the other results from the same general consideration mentioned above in another connection, i.e.,
because social analysis is an empirical study and its raw
data are concrete empirical acts, and because these acts
"are carried out by individuals or groups involved in concrete structures of which some of the patterns are only
analytically distinguishable from one another."

If one is to use the terms concrete structure and
analytic structure as proposed here, and if such structures
as the economic and political ones as defined here are to
be classified as analytic structures, it is necessary to
clarify the status of such structures as "business firms,"
"governmental" organizations, etc., which have in ordinary
parlance been called "economic or political structures"
(or "institutions"). These structures are certainly concrete structures in the sense of the term used here. As
much confusion results if one also refers to them as
"economic or political structures," since these have been
defined as analytic structures, the general solution to
this problem that is used here involves a consideration of
the primary orientation of a concrete structure. If the
primary orientation of a given concrete structure is to
the allocation of goods and services, it will be referred
to here as a <u>predominantly economic structure</u>. The structure of "role differentiation" as used here is also an
analytic structure. A concrete structure such as a "social
class," as that term is generally used, is predominantly
oriented to "role differentiation." <u>But predominantly
economic structures are not examples of economic structure
but rather are concrete structures in which a particular
type of analytic structure is most heavily emphasized</u>.

Obviously, in particular cases it may be extremely
difficult, if not impossible, to decide what analytically
distinguished patterns are primarily emphasized. In
"business firms" as they are understood in the capitalistic

portions of the industrialized West, the question is a
reasonably simple one, but it is not so simple if one takes
instead the firm of a "traditional" Chinese trader. In
many, if not most, concrete structures no one set of analytic patterns is easily discernible as receiving primary
emphasis. In these cases the patterns of differing emphases form one of the most important structural features of
the phenomena concerned. The relatively great frequency
of the mixed cases brings up one interesting point about
the relation between concrete and analytic structures and
the concept of function used here. It has been pointed
out above[67] that a general one to one correspondence
between structure and function is rare, if not impossible.
Nevertheless, depending on the classification of functions
used, a much closer correspondence between structure and
function is possible if the structures concerned are analytic structures. It is for this reason that the primary
orientation of a concrete structure to some particular
function may result in some confusion with analytic structures. Again, the attention given here to distinctions
such as that between predominantly economic structures and
economic structures may seem picayune, but from the point
of view of scientific rigor this is not the case. The
confusion of analytic and concrete structure is, methodologically speaking, a major source, if not the sole source,
of the fallacy of reification (or misplaced concreteness)
in social science. This is particularly clear in the case
of the field of economics, which has concerned itself with
a portion of social structure analytically separated
(usually implicitly rather than explicitly) from other
portions, subsequent to which this sphere has often been
treated as if it had been concretely differentiated. The
relevance of this confusion to the fallacy of reification
in social science should come as no surprise. The fallacy

---

67. See p. 65.

of reification is defined as treating as concrete an entity
that is analytically derived or defined. Since the major
concern of social science is with the description and
analysis of social patterns, and since these may be differentiated concretely or analytically, the confusion of the
two would obviously emerge as the major, if not the sole,
source of the fallacy of misplaced concreteness in this
field. Whether it be the sole such source or not, the fact
remains that real difficulty often arises in this connection. One may see this type of confusion in almost any social science work that attempts simple "causal analysis."
A combination of this difficulty and perhaps the most
strikingly grand scale implicit assumption of a one-to-one
correspondence between function and structure is fundamental to the whole scientific inadequacy and invalidity
of the theory of economic determinism.

A major caution in the use of concrete and analytic
structures follows from what has been said above. Changes
in concrete structures may be spoken of as causing changes
in other concrete structures. Thus, a change from relatively "nonindustrialized" predominantly economically oriented structures to "highly industrialized" ones may conceivably cause a change in the "family" system of a society
from one type to another, just as the acceleration of one
atom in a container may affect the movements of others.
On the other hand, analytic structures cannot be causally
related in that way. A change in mass does not cause a
change in volume. Both result from some concrete change
in the concrete unit of which they are aspects. Similarly,
changes in economic aspects do not cause changes in political aspects of social phenomena. Rather, concrete changes
in which the economic aspects are a major focus of attention cause concrete changes in which political aspects are
a major focus of attention. Patterns only analytically
distinguished from the same concrete phenomenon cannot
cause one another to do anything; both depend on the

maintenance or change of the concrete phenomenon of which they are aspects. These changes may, of course, leave one aspect constant while others are changed. Many of the arguments as to whether economic or political factors cause one another cease to be problems when one no longer attempts to use analytic distinctions as though they were concrete ones and vice versa.[68]

This limitation on the use of analytic structures for scientific analysis does not make them useless for such analysis. Analysis of the concrete structures, operation

---

68. A more detailed discussion of the concepts of economic structure and political structure as defined here is found below in Chapters IX, X, and XI. The sense in which these are analytic structures may briefly be pointed out here. There is, empirically speaking, no concrete act in which an allocation of power and responsibility is involved that does not involve some allocation of goods and services, even if the latter is only sufficient in terms of food, etc., to keep the power and responsibility holders alive. Similarly, no allocation of goods and services can take place without some simultaneous allocation of power and responsibility. When, for example, Mr. X gives Mr. Y a hundred dollars for a watch, the economic aspect is a pattern of exchange of money for a commodity. The political aspect as a minimum in this case is such that neither Mr. X nor Mr. Y simply grabs the other's "good" and runs. In the case of an armed robbery the power aspect is, perhaps, the most striking one of the phenomenon, but simultaneously with this exercise of power an allocation of goods takes place. Thus, one does not speak of the mass of a vase causing its volume and shape to fall to the floor and break; nor does one speak of the mass of a baseball causing this vase to fall to the floor and break. One does, however, speak of the impact of the moving baseball causing the vase to fall and break. In understanding such phenomena and making predictions about them, the concepts of mass, velocity, shape, volume, tensile strength, etc., of both the vase and the baseball are extremely useful. In fact, thus far no such theories can be constructed without them. The fact that one must be careful not to misuse isolated analytic distinctions in a causal sense does not destroy their usefulness for the development of empirical theories. The same is true of the use of analytic structures or their counterparts in all scientific fields.

in terms of which causes other concrete structures to
change, may well proceed most profitably in terms of the
analytically distinguished aspects of both concrete structures. Even were this not the case, however, analytic
structures would still have far-reaching applications for
the production of theories of predictive value. For
example, although the economic aspects of a phenomenon do
not cause the political ones to take a specific form, it
may well be that a given form of economic structure is only
compatible with one specific form of political structure
(or some limited range of variation). If this is the case,
discovery of the form of the economic structure makes
possible prediction of the political structure. Moreover,
under these circumstances a change that affects this economic structure in a given way will similarly affect the
political structure in a discoverable way. Thus, to the
extent that these analytically distinguished aspects can
be shown to have particular patterns that cluster with a
high degree of probability, they will have a definite
predictive value. For example, if one can discover the
analytic structural requisites of a highly industrialized
society, and if one knows the basis from which change takes
place, one can ascertain what types of changes will have to
take place in analytic structures for a given society to
industrialize. Similarly, in biology, since the mass of
nonaquatic organisms increases with the cube of their linear dimensions and the strength of the structures with the
square of their linear dimensions, given the setting factors, certain masses are incompatible with certain forms
of structures. An increase in those masses cannot take
place without a change in the form of the structures. This
does not mean that the change in mass causes the change in
form or vice versa. Both changes take place simultaneously,
if the result is viable, when certain concrete factors
operate on the genetic mechanism. Failure to observe these
cautions about the special uses of concrete and analytic

structures may result in the fallacy of reification or begged questioning or both. Realization of the special qualities of this distinction makes it possible to avoid such difficulties and facilitates the selection of concepts specially suited to given problems.

7. Concepts of microscopic and macroscopic as applied to the concepts of function and structure

These concepts are oriented to the relative level of generalization involved in analysis. These terms have appeared with increasing regularity in the recent writings of social scientists. Beyond vague references to smallness in the case of one and largeness in the case of the other, little in the way of explicit definition of them has appeared. These terms may be adapted to the concepts of function (e.g., microfunction and macrofunction) and structure (e.g., microstructure and macrostructure). The latter has been their more common adaptation. It must be emphasized that neither term has any absolute reference. These are strictly relative concepts. No structure is inherently microscopic or macroscopic. A given type of structure is so identified only in terms of some explicit comparison with another. Thus, the more inclusive one structure relative to another is, the more macroscopic or less microscopic it is _relative to that other_. The "family" structure of the United States is a microstructure relative to United States society as a whole. Vice versa, United States society as a whole is macrostructure relative to the "family" structure of the United States. That "family" structure is macrostructure relative to some other structures, and, conversely, that society may be microstructure relative to other structures (e.g., the United Nations Organization). The application of the prefixes, _micro_ and _macro_, is simply a shorthand device for indicating comparative levels of generality. To be useful the statement of at least two factors (i.e., the one characterized by one of these prefixes and the one relative to which it is so characterized) is always involved. Furthermore, these two factors must presumably have a relationship that is relevant to the analysis being pursued. Use of these prefixes without bearing these qualifications in mind may obscure rather than elucidate problems.

8. Concepts of institutions

These concepts along with the latent and manifest ones are the only general concepts so far discussed here that have a peculiar reference to human social phenomena. All the others have exact counterparts at least in such sciences as biology and often in physics and the like as well. The institutions concepts as they are developed here focus attention on the normative content of action just as the latent and manifest concepts focus attention on certain cognitive aspects of action. These concepts, in other words, focus attention on a distinction that has so far been unimportant in all of the sciences save the social sciences. This distinction is that between the phenomena as viewed by a scientific observer and the phenomena as viewed by a participant in the phenomena, i.e., the distinction between the point of view of the observer and the actor. This distinction may never be relevant in physics and chemistry and the like. It may, however, become relevant in some of the biological fields if instruments are developed to detect the point of view of the actor in "living" phenomena other than man, and if such a distinction in points of view can be shown to be meaningful for interpreting and understanding the actions of the members of these other species.

For the present, at least in the field of human phenomena, it certainly may make a difference in action whether given consequences are intended and recognized. It also may make a difference whether patterns judged to be "good" or "bad" or otherwise evaluated by the actors in

a situation are conformed to or not. The concepts of
institutions as developed here focuses on the questions of
evaluation, conformity, and reaction to conformity or
nonconformity. The consideration of these questions in the
past has produced some of the most important and useful
analyses of human social structure.

The most general form of these concepts oriented to
normative patterns and the problem of conformity is the
concept, institution. This concept is a focal point of
interest for the entire volume. The term institution as
used here will mean a particular type of normative pattern
that affects human action in terms of a social system. It
refers to those particular normative patterns (1) conformity with which is generally to be expected, and (2)
failure to conform with which is generally met with the
moral indignation of those individuals who are involved in
the same general social system and who are aware of the
failure. This is the sense of the term institution employed by Parsons some years ago.[69] This definition has
in it elements of indeterminacy that will be discussed
below, but it has been specifically chosen in preference
to Parsons' later modification of the term. A later
modification by Parsons that appeared in print in 1948
defined the concept as follows:

> To avoid misunderstanding it should be
> clearly stated what concept of institutions and
> correspondingly of institutionalization is being
> employed in this paper. A pattern governing ac-
> tion in a social system will be called "institu-
> tionalized" in so far as it defines the main modes
> of the legitimately expected behavior of the
> persons acting in the relevant social roles, and

---

69. See his essay entitled "The Motivation of Economic Activities," originally published in the Canadian
Jour. of Eco. and Polit. Sci., Vol. 6, No. 2, (May 1940),
pp. 187-203, and republished in his Essays, cited above.
This sense of the term was also used by Parsons in unpublished lectures of that period and earlier.

in so far as conformity with these expectations
is of strategic structural significance to the
social system. An institutional pattern is
thus a culture pattern [see below] to which a
certain structured complex of motivations and
social sanctions has become attached. It is
an _ideal_ pattern, but since conformity is legitimately expected it is not a "utopian" pattern.
An institution is a complex of such institutional
patterns which it is convenient to treat as a
structural unit in the social system.[70]

Parsons' later definition has not been used because
of the identification difficulty posed in the definition
by such terms as "main," "relevant," and "strategic." On
each of these scores classification of a given pattern as
an institution becomes a matter of individual judgment.
These aspects of indeterminacy in the definition appear in
addition to those in the earlier formulation. For the
purposes of the present work it is somewhat more convenient
and perhaps more systematic to minimize the difficulty of
identification of the referent of the general form of the
concept, concentrate all the indeterminacy involved in the
definition itself, and then get at the useful empirical
distinctions sought by Parsons by means of subsidiary
concepts.

In the definition used here the elements of indeterminacy lie in two quarters: (1) the degree to which conformity is "generally to be expected," and (2) the degree
to which failure in conformity is "met with moral indignation of those individuals who are involved in the system
and who are aware of the failure." There is, perhaps, a
double indeterminacy in the second respect in that different kinds of moral indignation may be involved as well
as differences in degree. These sources of indeterminacy

_____

70. "The Position of Sociological Theory," _Am._
Sociol. Rev., Vol. 13, No. 2 (April 1948), pp. 156-164
(esp. p. 159); later reprinted in _Essays_, pp. 3-16.

will be used here to permit of a difference of degree relative to the concept institution. This difference of degree
corresponds to an important empirical distinction of the
same order. A given normative pattern affecting human
action in terms of a social system will be considered more
or less well institutionalized to the degree to which conformity with the pattern is generally to be expected and
to the degree to which failure to conform with the pattern
is met by the moral indignation of those individuals who
are involved in the system and who are aware of the failure.
For the purposes of this work differences in degree having
to do with the first source of indeterminacy will be referred to as differences in the conformity aspects of the
institution or its institutionalization. Differences of
degree relating to the second source of indeterminacy will
be referred to as differences in the sanction aspects of
the institution or its institutionalization.[71]

An example may be used to illustrate these types of
differences of degree. In modern American society the
normative pattern of not passing red traffic lights and
that of not killing those who oppose one's views are both
institutions in the sense used here. There is a considerable difference in the degree of their institutionalization

---

71. The conformity aspect and the sanctions aspect
of institutions must not trap the unsuspecting into a confusion of statistically general patterns and institutions
or institutionalized patterns. All institutions are to
some degree statistically general patterns in any given
system, but not all statistically general patterns are institutionalized. Some statistically general patterns are
not normative ones (e.g., there are cognitive patterns,
affective patterns, etc.), and some normative patterns are
not institutionalized or are very little institutionalized
with regard to their conformity aspects, their sanction
aspects, or some combination of the two. Despite the importance of having clearly in mind the distinction between
statistically general patterns and institutions, the verification of the existence of institutions will, of course,
rest heavily upon the establishment of statistically defensible generalizations.

both with regard to the conformity aspects of institutionalization and its sanction aspects. It is, of course,
readily granted that statistical evidence is not advanced
here to prove this point, but sufficiently extreme examples
have been chosen, perhaps, to eliminate reasonable doubt
on this score. There is little question that a rather high
degree of conformity with both patterns is to be expected,
but there is also a considerable difference in the number
of people who drive through red lights and those who
literally murder their opponents in an argument. Cases of
both violations do occur, but even the most cavalier person with regard to these patterns seems to expect a generally high level of conformity with each. In relation to
the conformity aspects of institutionalization, the traffic
rule is less well institutionalized than the other. The
same is true for the sanction aspect. The moral indignation expressed relative to traffic violators of this sort
is sometimes both extreme and violent, but in general it
would probably be readily agreed that it is not of nearly
so great a degree as that relative to wanton murder of the
sort contemplated. It might, perhaps, be added that a
difference in the kind of sanction aspect may also be
involved. Distinction of this sort, however, would involve
as a minimum a systematically developed taxonomy of "emotions," and no attempt to develop the point further is
contemplated here. In the long run some development of
this point will almost undoubtedly be of great significance
in the study of social institutions.

Two other terms will be used here relative to the
term institution. One is the term <u>crucial</u>. This term has
been added to get at an aspect of institutions included by
Parsons in his later formulation of the definition. A
given institution will be called a <u>crucial institution</u> if
it is a structural requisite of the system in which it
appears. The other term will be used to get at a difference in degree. It is the term <u>strategic</u>. A given

institution is _more or less strategic_ to the extent that
(1) it is the institutionalized form of all or a portion
of a structural requisite, and (2) the pattern concerned
may (or may not) be altered without destroying the structural requisite involved. The first of these two aspects
of the strategic quality of an institution will be called
its _substantive aspect_, and the second will be called its
critical aspect. Again, examples are in order. The
normative pattern that employment in general, and occupational achievement in particular, should be judged on "universalistic" rather than "particularistic"[72] grounds is
a crucial institution for a "modern industrial" society[73]
insofar as it can be shown that without the institutionalization of this pattern to a high degree, both with regard
to its conformity and sanction aspects, modern industrial
society could not continue to operate. If one goes to the
most general level of consideration of societies, the most
generally defined institution affecting the allocation of
goods and services is a crucial institution. There can be
no society without some such normative pattern of allocation of goods and services. It must, however, always be
borne in mind that the question of the "cruciality" of a
given institution is never determinable without reference
to the specific level of generalization of the analysis.

The strategic aspect of institutions also hangs on
the level of generalization under consideration. The
normative patterns in modern United States society[74]

72. For definitions and discussion of these terms,
see below pp. 248-255.

73. For a brief discussion of its patterns of universalism in relation to industrialization, see M. J. Levy,
Jr., _Family Revolution_, Chaps. VIII and X.

74. The concept society is defined below in Chapter
III. The degree to which the United States as a legally
defined nation conforms to this definition is, of course,
not established here. A sufficient degree is assumed for
purposes of the example.

holding for the management of production on a business
footing for profit are more or less strategic both substantively and critically. They are to a high degree substantively strategic in that they form a major portion of the
crucial structures having to do with the allocation of
goods and services in our society. They are also relatively highly strategic in the critical sense. To the degree
that United States society is defined as a capitalistic
society, alterations in the normative pattern of private
ownership of the means of production in the direction of
government ownership will alter but not eliminate the
economic structural requisites of the society so defined.
They are not crucial institutions because some alterations
are possible without eliminating the structural requisites
concerned. If the level of generalization concerned is
changed to that of any industrial society, the degree to
which these patterns are critically strategic falls markedly since, at least in theory, an industrial society can be
maintained in which the institutions concerning the
allocation of goods and services are not of this private
ownership sort.

For further comparison the strategic quality of the
private ownership institutions in United States society
may be compared with that of brothers aiding one another
financially when no prior obligation interferes. The
latter is also an institutional pattern, but it is apparently far less strategic relative to the society both
substantively and critically than the other. It covers
only a very small portion of the patterns of economic
allocation in the society, and alterations in it would
have little or no effect on the level of generalization in
mind in the private ownership example. It might be added
that this normative pattern would appear to be considerably
less well institutionalized than the others both with
regard to the conformity and sanction aspects involved.

One additional qualification of the institution concept may be presented here, i.e., the concept of tradition. A tradition for present purposes is defined as an institution whose perpetuation is institutionalized.[75] An institution will be considered more or less traditional or more or less traditionalized to the extent that its perpetuation is institutionalized without regard to changes in the functional implications of its operations, whether these be eufunctional or dysfunctional implications. In this sense monogamous marriage in the United States would seem to be much more highly traditional and traditionalized than the pattern of driving on the right-hand side of the road. A tradition in this sense has a double institutionalization: (1) the pattern concerned is an institution, and (2) the perpetuation of the pattern is also an institution. The implications of this distinction are not difficult to illustrate. The institutionalization of rational action[76] in a given sphere of action, for example, makes the existence of traditions, in the sense intended here, in that sphere, precarious at best. To the extent that rational action is institutionalized, the perpetuation of institutions making for nonrational results are vulnerable. The possibilities of nonrational implications of tradition in this sense are too obvious to need examples here.

---

75. The term "traditional" in quotation marks is used to refer to a particular stage of Chinese society in many examples used in this volume. Factors referred to as characterizing "traditional" China are structures or functions characteristic of that society at the height of the Ch'ing Dynasty. Many of these patterns and conditions both antedated and postdated that period, but all of them existed at that period too. The present definition of the term traditional does not significantly contradict the special use of the term in quotations since the examples used in "traditional" China are almost without exception traditional in the sense intended here as well as in that special historical sense.

76. For the definition and discussion of rational and nonrational action, see below, pp. 240-248.

No doubt considerable further refinements and qualifications of the concept of institutions will be necessary
for the development of comparative social analysis. For
the present no more will be attempted than the minimal
conceptual scheme necessary for the rough first approximation analysis envisaged by studies in terms of the concepts
and theories developed in this volume.

D. SUMMARY

In what has gone before in this chapter there has
been a brief introductory discussion of structural-functional analysis in general followed by a discussion of the
specific form of that analysis (structural-functional requisite analysis) used in this volume. Subsequent to these
observations the principal general concepts in terms of
which materials will be treated have been outlined and
defined. For the present at least, it seems likely that
the main line of development in social science will involve
the use of the verbal forms of structural-functional method
rather than the methods of mathematical analysis. It is
to be hoped that the type of analysis attempted here may
in the long run eventuate in models that can be mathe-
matized. Until there are such models, however, one must
follow the lines that are most relevant for empirical
purposes and for the development of systematic theory. To
this end an attempt is made here to specify exactly what
is meant by the categories of structural-functional analysis that will be used, and to differentiate them in such a
way as to make them clear and precise and distinct from
one another. In the past, terms such as function and
structure have been used in many different ways and often
in different ways by a single author in a single passage.
In what has gone above some jargon has been added to the
field. If it serves to avoid some of this confusion and
aids in the construction of confirmable theories, the additional jargon may be considered justified, and if not, not.

From here the development of the volume will proceed systematically. First, there will be the definition of the principal unit of reference of this study, i.e., society, and a discussion of why the various aspects of that definition have been chosen. Second, there will be a discussion of the implications of the presence of such a unit in its setting. That is to say, the functional requisites of any society so defined will be developed as far as possible by the author. The final phrase of the preceding sentence must be stressed, for this sort of job is never finally and completely done, and one must always be well aware of the tentative character and difficulty of early attempts of this sort. Following this the general question of structural requisites both concrete and analytic will be discussed, and certain general relationship structures will be taken up. The structural requisites of any society will then be formulated, again tentatively, and the basis for classification of each item concerned will be treated.

C H A P T E R   III[1]

THE CONCEPT OF SOCIETY

The most inclusive structural unit involved in this study is that which will be called a society. In this sense the concept society is the most general concept of a concrete structure with which the study is concerned. Correspondingly, analysis of phenomena present in any society will be the most general level of analysis of the study. The central importance and peculiar character of the concept society has been briefly alluded to above,[2] and perhaps it is best to say no more on that score here.

It is the general objective of this work to derive and define systematically those concepts of most general use in the comparative analysis of institutions. Institutions in the sense intended here[3] are found as parts of a society or as the result of intersocietal relationships. This requires at the outset, then, an analysis of the general structural elements common to all societies, i.e., in the sense of the terms used here, the analysis of social

---

1. This chapter and the following one draw heavily on work undertaken by a private seminar at Harvard University in the summer of 1947. The members of the seminar were David F. Aberle, Albert K. Cohen, Arthur K. Davis, Marion J. Levy, Jr., and Francis X. Sutton. A report on the results of the seminar has been published as "The Functional Prerequisites of a Society," Ethics, Vol. LX, No. 2 (Jan. 1950), pp. 100-111. This material is sometimes incorporated as originally written and sometimes with considerable changes in these two chapters.

2. See pp. 22-24.

3. See above, pp. 101-109.

structure on the most general level. This analysis is to
be carried out in terms of the structural-functional requisite method, the concepts of which are for present
purposes defined above.[4]

In any effort of this sort considerable care must be
taken to make sure that the concepts employed have empirical referents. Failure in this respect would result in a
more or less a priori system of analysis, the results of
which would be "not conceivably falsifiable" and hence not
propositions of empirical science as that term is generally understood. Therefore, however general and abstract
the level of analysis may be here, there is never any
intentional abstraction from the empirical level altogether.

This brings up a second and closely related point.
The concept of society used here is defined on a general
level, but it does have an empirical content. Furthermore,
it is to be found and has its range of possible variation
in a setting that is also empirical, though treated only
in the most general terms, i.e., the limits set by the
heredity of a given species and its nonspecies' environment.
It is from the interrelationship of this abstractly but
empirically defined unit and its setting that the functional requisites of any society are derived. As has been
pointed out above the functional requisites of any given
unit consist exactly of the minimum implications of the
interrelationship of the unit concerned and its setting.[5]
The functional requisites of a society do not define a
society or vice versa. This point is of some importance
because failure to recognize it involves the methodological
difficulties referred to above.[6]

For use in the system of analysis attempted here the

---

4.   See Chapter II.
5.   See above, pp. 46-49.
6.   See pp. 40-41.

term <u>society</u> is defined as follows: a society is a system
of action in operation that (1) involves a plurality of
interacting individuals[7] of a given species (or group of
species) whose actions are primarily oriented to the system
concerned and who are recruited at least in part by the
sexual reproduction of members of the plurality involved,
(2) is at least in theory self-sufficient for the actions
of this plurality, and (3) is capable of existing longer
than the life span of an individual of the type (or types)
involved.

It is intended here to apply this concept in a human
context, and therefore the "given species" involved is
<u>homo sapiens</u> for present purposes. The specific designa-
tion of a species or combination of them has, however,
been left out of the definition because, although in other
species the range of phenomena involved is certainly more
limited than with regard to <u>homo sapiens</u>, and although it
has been fashionable among some sociologists and anthropologists to assume a sharp line of demarcation between
men and beasts in this respect,[8] to what extent phenomena
falling within this definition are to be found among the
"lower" animals (i.e., non-homo-sapiens) is by no means
precisely known. The possibility of a continuum of
development in these respects, albeit with a major difference of degree separating <u>homo sapiens</u> from any other
species, has by no means been definitely ruled out of
court. Nevertheless, what superficially at least seems to

----

7. The fact that the system is one "involving a plurality of interacting individuals" implies that it is "in
operation," but this phrase is included to emphasize the
point. The importance of this point will emerge in the
brief reference to the concept of culture below in this
chapter and at other points throughout the work.

8. At one time in the past a fashion set by quite
another group held that it was the appearance of the "soul"
at exactly the same line of demarcation that made all the
difference.

be a major difference in degree is advanced here as justification, however arbitrary, for the present preoccupation
with the homo sapiens variant of the concept.

A given society as defined here "exists" in the same
sense that a concrete empirical object such as a given
biological organism or a stick or a stone "exists."[9]   It
is true that in a sense a system of action qua system is
always an abstraction[10] or, perhaps more correctly, an
inference, from the concrete actions and interactions of
concrete individuals or groups of individuals -- that the
system involved consists of the uniformities observable in
these interrelations. But the same is true of a biological
organism or a stick or a stone or any other empirical phenomenon. It is perfectly true that one cannot see, touch,
taste, smell, or hear either directly or indirectly a
social norm such as the one which holds that one should
not drive an automobile at forty miles an hour through a
school zone. But one can observe such norms in operation.
One can observe what people in fact do and what they
refrain from doing, what they say and refrain from saying,
and so forth, and uniformities in such action can be
observed. Thus, while one can not observe the idea that
it is bad to speed in school zones, one can observe uniformities in the action of certain people in certain settings in this respect, or at least one can state uniformities that seem to conform to their action and enable one
to make predictions about it. For example, most of them
do not travel at forty miles an hour in such zones, most
of them say that to do so is bad, they or their representatives pass laws against it, arrest those who infringe the
laws, etc. This is not in essentials different from what

---

9. The ontological problem is not of interest here.
Whether the "existence" of empirical phenomena is "real"
or "imaginary" is beside the point for present purposes.

10. See above, pp. 58-59.

one observes in the case of a cell or a stick or a stone. In these cases, too, one observes certain uniformities in relationships. A given cell, for example, is not identical in its composition in all possible respects from one point in time to another, nor is it the idea "cell" that one observes. The same is true of a stick or a stone or, for that matter, of all other empirical phenomena.

It is true that some differences do exist between the empirical character of social systems as discussed here and the other empirical phenomena mentioned. All are subject to apprehension through some combination of touch, sight, taste, smell, and hearing,[11] but the specific combinations differ. "Touch," for example, is not a sense ordinarily involved in observations of social phenomena whereas it is in the other cases mentioned. One can touch a given exemplification of a cell or a stick whereas one

---

11. Or are indirectly apprehended by the use of instruments (e.g., electron microscope) in which the chain connecting the object observed and the observer can be clearly drawn, understood, and shown not to "distort" the phenomena or at least only to "distort" them in a definitely calculable fashion. In social science there are counterparts of such instruments. There are, for example, polling techniques of various sorts. The great difference between a polling technique and a microscope lies not in the basic pattern separating the observer from direct apprehension of the phenomena observed but rather in the fact that the chain relating the two is relatively simple and well established in the microscope case while it is not in the other. It is nevertheless interesting to bear in mind the fact that each new departure in instrumental techniques in the natural sciences carries with it a controversial period in which the reliability and characteristics of the instrument are explored. Many microscope techniques, particularly electron microscope techniques, are highly controversial today, and in some areas the uses of these instruments is much more in the nature of use to explore the instrument than to solve general problems. Furthermore, there is more than the instrument itself involved. The question of the preparation of material for observation raises serious questions in this field just as it does so patently in the case of a social science instrument such as polling.

cannot touch a given exemplification of a social system in operation, but the particular combination of observations involved in different empirical phenomena is subject to wide variation indeed, both of kind and degree. These are, however, differences on lower levels of generalization, not on the most general level involved.

The attention devoted to the point above may seem excessive, but it is not excessive for important methodological reasons. If social systems in operation have no such empirical status as that discussed here, all social analysis would have to be in terms of analytic structure as that term has been defined above.[12] All social science phenomena would fall in the category of such concepts as mass and volume. This is out of the question, however, for these concepts always involve concrete referents from which they are analytically abstracted and without such referents all social science discussion would have to be carried out in vacuo, empirically speaking; that is to say, social science would have to become either completely deductive after the fashion of mathematics or largely nonempirical after the fashion of any metaphysics, theology, and ethics.

With so much by way of introduction it is possible to turn to the concept of society itself. In the first place, something must be said of the identity and continuity of a society. The identity and continuity of a society always involves a set of actors or individuals, but it is in the persistence of a system of action in operation in which these individuals participate that the essence of the matter lies. The individual actors can be and inevitably are continuously changing. The membership, i.e., the individuals involved, is never constant by definition, for a statement about recruitment of new members is part of the definitions. Furthermore, empirical individuals being

---

12.   See p. 89.

mortal as they are, some individuals, given time, are bound to pass out of the picture by death[13] if by no other means. Thus, a society may survive and see a complete change of personnel although, of course, it cannot survive any and all possible changes. For example, the elimination of all individuals with college training in the United States at any one time would certainly result in radical changes in that society, if indeed it permitted any society whatever to survive, because of the extreme importance of professionally trained personnel for the operation of a "modern industrial" society. Chinese society has shown a remarkable flexibility with regard to certain types of personnel changes and a lack of it with regard to other types and nonetheless has, until recently at least, apparently been able to maintain many, if not most, of its basic structural patterns through some exceedingly thorough periods of foreign conquest.

There is another side to this question, however. A society may, and does characteristically, survive some changes in the personnel involved. It may, on the other hand, fail to survive in the face of an unchanged personnel or perhaps more accurately may fail to persist although personnel changes play no significant role in the failure. For example, a change in religious orientations, say the appearance of a charismatic leader such as Buddha or Jesus (or Hitler or Stalin for that matter), may change the type of society quite thoroughly. In fact, it might conceivably make any society at all impossible. Suppose, for example, a religious sect radically banning sexual relations should capture the imagination of the overwhelming majority of Japanese. If it persisted for a few decades, that society would disappear altogether.

---

13. They pass out as empirical individuals, but this may not end their social significance. The importance of ancestors in "traditional" China is a case in point.

As will be shown later on, some changes in membership
are of great importance for the existence and character of
any given society, but by no means all changes are so
relevant. On the other hand, the persistence, nonpersistence, or degree of change of the system of action in
operation is always the essence of the matter. If the
system of action remains the same, the society remains the
same. If the system of action disappears altogether, no
society exists. If the system of action changes, all sorts
of possibilities are open. Depending on the level of
definition of the society in question the changes may or
may not be of a type or magnitude to change the society
but not to prevent the continuation of some society. On
the other hand, the changes may make that society's continuation impossible, and the remnants of its membership
may be incorporated in other societies, and so forth.
History furnishes one with an enormous list of different
possibilities in this respect, and if most of man's activities had not in fact gone unrecorded, the list could, no
doubt, be expanded even more enormously. There are apparently cases of societies that have vanished leaving
only artifacts to mark their passing -- their members gone
one knows not where. There are societies which can trace
a pedigree of persistence and change through two thousand
years and more. There are also societies scattered to the
wind by a thousand circumstances, but with the track of
their remnants, both their patterns and their people, still
traceable.

A society as here defined does not exist of necessity,
nor is it impervious to change, but its major indicator is
the system of action involved. And in this connection
another point emerges. A society exists in a setting that
may be described most generally as the limits set by human
heredity and nonhuman environment, recognizing the elements
of indeterminacy involved in such a setting.[14] The per-

---

14. See above, pp. 12-17.

sistence of a society may be judged by the distinctness
maintained by human action within those limits. A society
does not exist, obviously, if there are no people to be
involved in a system of action. In this case the factor
of human heredity drops out, and the situation consists
only of the nonhuman environment. On the other hand, if
humans exist, but their actions are completely explicable
in terms of human heredity and nonhuman environment, then
no society exists either; or perhaps it would be better to
say that the concept would be of no significance since it
would contribute nothing to the understanding of human
action. If there are systems of action in operation, however, that are not explicable solely in terms of human
heredity and nonhuman environment, then a society or a
part of one has an empirical referent (i.e., "exists") and
will be relevant in the analysis of that action. Like the
concept of a living organism in biology, the persistence
of the unit here called society inheres in the fact that
it maintains the integrity of the unit, i.e., that the
most general aspects of the unit as defined remain unchanged.

The importance of the distinction between the unit
and its setting has other interesting implications. A
given society has, if one will, its ultimate limits of
variation set by the factors of human heredity and nonhuman
environment as discussed above, but many, if not most,
societies in world history have had interrelationships
with other societies that have limited still further the
possible range of variation of any one of the societies
concerned. Thus, the viability or persistence of any
conceivable society is limited by the factors of human
heredity and nonhuman environment, that is to say, the
most general possible setting or situation or limiting
factors for any human society. Any particular society may
and commonly does include some aspects of the human environment as a part of the conditions or setting or situation of the society. This leads once again to the question

of the level of generalization on which the unit is defined.
On the most general level, i.e., any society, the setting
is that of human heredity and nonhuman environment. On
lower levels of generalization those elements are never
absent from the setting, but human environmental elements
may and commonly do assume a larger and larger role. The
"almost completely isolated" society is less and less
possible in the present world, and even in the past it has
probably been more a source of fascination for myth makers
than it has been an actual phenomenon.

It has been noted above that it is not possible to
determine the functional requisites of a unit from the
unit alone but only from the combination of the unit and
its setting.[15] Implicit in this argument is, of course,
the proposition that the viability or persistence of the
unit is not determinable from the particular definition of
the particular unit concerned. It too can only be determined by studying the relation between the unit and its
setting. Again, an extreme case will be useful for purposes of example. Given the definition of society as used
here, the possibility of such a unit's existence would be
obviated if the nonhuman environment were to be such as to
prevent sexual reproduction by the membership of the unit.
Suppose, for example, an amount of radiation that would
sterilize but not kill humans persisted in the area in-
habited by the members of a society. Such a setting would
make the persistence of the unit as defined here an impossibility.

This point is of importance in the analysis of societies. In such analysis some setting is either explicit or
implicit. In making such elements of the analysis as the
setting and the unit explicit, it is important to limit
the level of generalization of definition to that practi-

---

15. The same may be said of the structural requisites.
See above, pp. 40-41.

cable for discovery of the knowledge sought. Failure to
do so will make the analysis so abstract as to be devoid
of the content sought, or so detailed as to be impossible
to handle. Suppose one takes as an example of this type
of problem two societies: one has had its membership wiped
out by some sudden catastrophe (unpredictable by the membership) such as an earthquake; the other has been assimilated by the members of some other group with which it has
had little or no previous contact. For many, if not most,
purposes of analysis of these two societies they can be
better studied by so defining the units and the settings
that the type of destruction posited does not represent a
failure to maintain the functional requisites of the societies, but rather represents a change in the limits of
variation of the societies, in the first case, a change in
the nonhuman environmental features, and in the second
case, a change in certain of the human environmental
features.

There is a flexibility involved in social analysis on
this score because the choice of units is in essence
arbitrary as long as the units are precisely defined, have
empirical referents, and the referents alleged are the
actual ones. It would probably not prove useful for any
social analysis to define a unit so that one of the functional requisites of the unit in its setting would be the
provisions necessary to offset any possible "natural"
catastrophe (i.e., catastrophic change in the limits set
by human heredity and nonhuman environment), and in fact,
given the present limits of human technology, it can be
shown that no unit so defined could in fact have an empirical referent. The second case mentioned above is another
matter, however. Depending on whether one was primarily
interested in studying that society as a unit prior to
assimilation or as a unit in process of change, different
approaches might be in order. Little light is likely to
be thrown on social phenomena by a study of why, for

example, Trobriand society might easily be wiped out by
the United States. On the other hand, a study of the
mutual structural vulnerability of the United States and
Russia would certainly be of great interest today. This
whole question is, however, a matter of degree about which
no hard and fast rules may be laid down for fear that, by
restricting the choice of problems, serious damage be done
to the field of scientific inquiry. It is sufficient to
point out the various factors involved so that students
will be aware of the possible range of choice and its
implications.

Four points in the definition of society may now be
singled out for separate treatment, following which some
further general implications of the unit as a whole in a
system of analysis such as this one will be discussed.
These four points have to do with: (1) the meaning of the
involvement of a plurality of interacting individuals in a
system of action, (2) the question of the recruitment, at
least partially, of the members by sexual reproduction of
previous or current members, (3) the theoretical (at least)
self-sufficiency of the system of action, and (4) the
question of duration of the system longer than the life
span of any single individual member.

(1) <u>The membership of the system</u>. The plurality of
interacting individuals who are involved in a system of
action of the type defined here, by virtue of the fact that
their action is primarily oriented to the system concerned,
will be called the members of a society. It is important
to keep in mind that the system of action in operation <u>is</u>
the society as the term is used here. A society in this
sense is not a group. The members of a society may and
commonly do vary in the degree to which they orient their
actions to the particular system of action concerned. They
may, and certainly today commonly do, either directly or
indirectly, orient their actions to more than one such system of action. For present purposes, however, any given

individual will be considered a member of that society in
terms of which his action is primarily oriented. The possibility of some individual achieving an exact balance in
these respects is perhaps conceivable, but the probability
of such a case is surely small. By primarily oriented is
meant that the action of the individual proceeds more in
terms of the structures in general, but of the highly
strategic and crucial institutions in particular, of one
such system than of any other.

Membership in a society is therefore a matter of degree. To the extent that a society member accepts and
orients his action without conflicts to the structures in
general, but particularly to the strategic and crucial
institutions, he is a more or less well integrated member
of that society as that term shall be used here. This is
an area in which differences of degree cannot be avoided
if the concepts used are to have empirical referents. One
may orient one's actions more or less to different social
systems. One may, however, also orient in different ways.
Acceptance of the structures and action in conformity with
them is one possibility, and, of course, there are at least
differing degrees of acceptance and probably different
kinds as well. One may also reject the structures and
deviate from them, and again there are differing degrees
and kinds involved. Both types of action may, however, be
oriented to the same system.

In the above respect another line of variation is also
of importance. This is one of social study's oldest and
most useful distinctions -- one which can no doubt trace
an authentic pedigree indefinitely far back into time. It
is the distinction between ideal and actual structures.
Many ideal structures of a given society may be of a sort
with which general conformity is not even expected, that
is to say, they are not institutionalized. These are utopian structures, i.e., the particular set of ideal structures which are not institutionalized though generally held

to be desirable in the highest degree.[16] But of those
which are institutionalized, few, if any, receive complete
conformity. The discrepancy between the institutionalized
ideal structures and their observed performance (i.e., the
actual structures) is by no means any simple indication of
lack of orientation to the institutionalized ideal structures. The discrepancy between the ideal and actual structures may even be great, and yet the orientation to the
ideal structures may be far-reaching. It is extremely
doubtful that the average murderer, for example, is completely neutral or nonoriented to the structures of his
society that cover the taking of human life. He may be
oriented to a different set of structures or even those of
another society, but ordinarily he is probably strongly oriented to the very structures he violates. So far-reaching
is this as a phenomenon that persons violating such structures as this one (e.g., theft, lying, etc.) with no particular apparent orientation to the structures, no "moral"
attitudes toward them, are sometimes classified as psycho-

---

16. Many utopian structures have a peculiar role in
social systems. In some cases, although the structure itself is not institutionalized, the structure of holding
such utopian structures to be "good" is institutionalized.
For example, the "love thy neighbor as thyself" structure
is a utopian structure in the United States. Conformity
and sanctions aspects are both extremely low if not nonexistent. But the structure of believing that utopian structure to be good is probably highly institutionalized. Such
structures play a larger role in social structure than a
mere basis for satire on the hypocrisy of man. It may well
be that, without the institutionalization of such structures
as unobtainable ideals, the institutionalization of many
less extreme structures could not be maintained. The example cited may be quite important in setting a framework
for the actual institutionalization of many structures concerned with the legitimate or illegitimate use of force.
Again, the all or none structure of "never tell a lie" is
utopian, but the indoctrination of generation after generation of children with the story of Washington and the cherry
tree may be a vital factor in explaining why the level of
lying is not even greater than is actually the case.

pathic personalities and are considered by many psychiatrists to be in a more or less hopeless category from the therapeutic point of view.

On the other hand, discrepancies between institutionalized ideal and actual structures may indicate relatively strong orientation to a different set of structures than that predominant in the society concerned. Toward the latter set there may be only such orientation as that necessary to cope with the general community's reaction to the different structures. This sort of situation often exists in, say, family structures among first generation immigrants to a new society who may have become more or less well-integrated members of their new society in other respects but not in this one. In the political aspect of action something of the same thing may be said of the faithful members of the communist and nazi systems of faith in the United States. In certain ways, at least, the discrepancies between their actual actions and the ideal actions generally held in the United States in these respects, is the result of, or indicates a genuine difference in, orientation. Their orientation to the more generally accepted structures may well be confined to the minimum necessary for their own personal continued operation.[17]

In the sense of membership used here an individual is ordinarily a member of only one society at a time. He may, however, be involved in more than one at any particular time. That is to say his actions may be oriented to more than one such system at any given time. This is peculiarly obvious today when most of the world's people are being more and more impressed by the interrelationship aspects of different societies rather than by their isolation,

---

17. In this particular case orientation is importantly channeled toward using the general structures for protection against attack because of their own deviant action.

although in this case their orientation to other societies is often through their orientation to one particular society. There are many other examples of this sort of thing, however. To the degree that China and the United States are different societies, Chinese of the more "traditional" type who reside in the United States are involved in both societies. The same is true of Americans resident in China. The involvement may be kept as slight as possible,[18] but it exists nonetheless.

A note of caution on the examples used is necessary here. Although "nations" have been used for sake of convenience here to illustrate societies, the legal concept of the nation is by no means coterminous with the definition of a society. Citizenship in the legal sense is not, therefore, the test of membership in a society. In the absence of a taxonomy of world societies, some "national" references are made for the sake of rough examples. It must be kept in mind, however, that the "national" references used bear only a rough correspondence to societies as defined here.

There is another point which must be made in connection with membership in a society. An individual from a given society x may in fact reside among the members of a quite different society y. He may do so over long periods and may conform to a high degree indeed to the structures of society y. To the degree that such conformity remains an expedient from his point of view and an expedient entered into in order to orient his actions in terms of society x, the individual remains in the terminology of this study a member of society x, or, if one will, a genuine member of society x and an expedient member of society y. To the degree, whether realized or not, that this conformity

---

18. Witness the Westerners who as far as possible maintained Western ways though long resident in China, and Chinese in the West who maintained Chinese structures.

ceases to be such an expedient, a shift takes place in his membership. The operational determination of such a case in any statistically acceptable sense may be extremely difficult; the general concept intended here, however, should be reasonably clear.

(2) The sexual recruitment of the system. The phrase of the definition of society that stipulates that its members be recruited at least in part by their own sexual reproduction is included in order to rule out certain empirical referents that might be possible in its absence. The members of the system, being mortal, must be replaced if the system is to continue its operation. The above phrase excludes all systems of action whose memberships[19] are, or might conceivably be, recruited solely by methods other than sexual reproduction. Such organizations as monasteries, clubs, cliques, crowds, and many others are thereby excluded. When the discussion turns to the functional and structural requisites of any society, this phrase in the definition in conjunction with the limits of the setting of the unit and other aspects of the definition has rather far-reaching consequences. For example, such a system obviously must involve members of both sexes whereas in the absence of such a phrase this inclusion would be by no means obvious or necessary. Such a system, for reasons to be discussed later, apparently must provide for some system of regulation of heterosexual contacts and also for some system of effectively integrating the new members

---

19. The definition of membership in a society has been given above. Membership in any system of action is defined as consisting of those individuals whose actions are primarily oriented to the structures involved in the system of action concerned in the respects specifically relevant to it. An individual may, of course, be a member in this sense of more than one system of action in a given sphere, if the systems of actions involved are not mutually incompatible, or of different systems in different spheres of action.

recruited by sexual reproduction. Quite different factors
would be involved if the recruitment of new members as
mature adults were a possibility by definition.

This phrase of the definition does not seem to exclude
from the category of societies such systems of action as
the Buddhist or Catholic churches.[20] These systems certainly do recruit their members at least in part by the
sexual reproduction of current members, but it is not a
matter of necessity that this be so, in theory at least.
On the other hand, it can be shown that this is a matter of
necessity, given other parts of the definition and the
setting of the unit for some, if not all, of the systems of
action that meet the criteria of a society.

The phrase does not exclude from the category systems
of action which recruit a portion of their membership by
means other than sexual reproduction; for example, by means
of immigration or conquest as those terms are generally
understood. There have no doubt been many systems of action conforming to the definition here which in fact have
recruited large numbers of members by methods other than
sexual reproduction. Some of these systems would be excluded on other grounds, but they are not excluded solely
on this one.

On the other hand, the phrase does exclude virtually
all systems of action that are completely exogamous. Systems of this sort, e.g., many family and village systems,
are generally parts of a society that covers in major part
a sufficient group of such units so that marriages can be
endogamous among the members of society, though not all of
them need to be of that character. Insofar as it is possible to maintain that, although marriage is exogamous, the
persons brought in become members before sexual reproduction takes place, many, if not all, such exogamous units

---

20. They are, however, excluded by other aspects of
the definition.

will be found to be excluded from the definition by virtue
of other aspects of it.[21]

In sum, there are two implications of this phrase of
the definition of society. In the first place, it must
have a bisexual membership if it is a human society.[22] In
the second place, recruitment must result at least in part
from the heterosexual activities of this membership. The
effect of the phrase is mainly exclusive. It excludes
several categories of systems as a minimum. It excludes
the following types: (1) systems with membership of a
single sex; (2) systems with membership of a bisexual
character but forbidding heterosexual contacts by the members; (3) systems with a bisexual membership among whom
heterosexual contacts are permitted, but which are not
necessarily recruited in part by such contacts. There are
many examples of all three types of systems, and some of
them are extremely inclusive and far-reaching in character.
They are not, however, of the generality of the systems
here conceived as societies.

(3) The theoretical self-sufficiency of the system.
The theoretical self-sufficiency of the system is perhaps
its most difficult aspect. There is a sense in which most
of the other aspects of the definition are only specific
clarifications of this one. The fullest implications of
this aspect of the definition and the setting of the unit
are developed insofar as possible in the sections devoted
to functional and structural requisites of any society.
In this section only clarification of it as an aspect of

---

21. e.g., that the system of action be in theory
self-sufficient for the actions of the members. See below
for the discussion of this criterion, pp. 129-134.

22. Insofar as certain other species of animals have
units otherwise conforming to the definition, the implications may be more complex than this -- for example, in the
case of certain insect populations.

the definition will be attempted.

A system of action in operation is in theory self-sufficient only if it is in theory capable of furnishing structures covering all of the functional requisites of the system. There are two immediate general implications of this definition: in the first place, the determination of self-sufficiency of a system depends upon the relation of the unit to the setting involved; in the second place, the degree to which self-sufficiency is approached and what is involved in the self-sufficiency vary with the definition of the unit under consideration and the level of generality of the definition.

The first of these implications should be obvious enough from the definition of self-sufficiency and what has been said about functional requisites. The kind of circular argument discussed above[23] is not involved in this procedure. The functional requisites of the system are not used to define the system and are not derived on the basis of an implicit definition of the system. Included in the definition is only the differentia specifica that this particular system must, without, in theory, dependence on other systems, be capable of providing structures to cover its functional requisites. It is true, of course, that the functional requisites of all existing systems are somehow being fulfilled (though not indefinitely into the future), but it is not by any means true that all these requisites are met by the system concerned. For example, it is a functional requisite for the existence of some such organization as, say, the "Junior Matrons' Service League of Galveston" that some structures exist in terms of which the members get sufficient food to stay alive and remain members, but that system itself does not furnish those structures. They are furnished by the society (or some portion of it) of which that club is itself a substructure.

---

23. See above, pp. 40-42.

Thus, the functional requisites of a society are not part of the definition of a society, but the provision of structures to meet the functional requisites of a society is a part of the definition.

The second implication of the point about self-sufficiency is, perhaps, less obvious. The system of action which is a society is by definition self-sufficient in the sense outlined above. In considering any particular empirical system, however, the degree to which self-sufficiency is approached will depend upon the unit chosen, i.e., upon its specific definition. Thus, a family system of the United States is not as self-sufficient as the system of action of United States society as a whole. Certain spheres of action, vital for the survival of the membership of United States society, are specifically cut off from the family system. For example, the overwhelming proportion of the production of goods and services in that society is not carried out in family terms, and without that production the family members themselves could not survive.

Further possibilities of variation in these respects become obvious if one contrasts the family system of "traditional" China with that of the United States. The family system of "traditional" China approaches self-sufficiency to a far higher degree than is the case with the family system in the United States. A far larger proportion of the allocation of goods and services (both their production and consumption) and of power and responsibility are carried out in family terms (i.e., are family oriented) in the Chinese case than in the other case. In the Chinese case the whole society is family oriented to a rather extraordinary degree whereas in the United States case the sphere of family oriented actions is restricted to an extraordinary degree. This does not mean, of course, that the type of family system in China is more important for Chinese society than that of the United States is for its society. Both are highly strategic, if not crucial, institutions in their respective societies, but their differing roles in their respective societies does go along with a different degree of self-sufficiency.

There is another type of example of the difference made by choice of a unit. If one chooses for purposes of example two such different units as a thoroughly isolated, "primitive," nonliterate society and a modern industrial society, on the most general level of consideration, they must both, if they are to conform to the definition of a society, be self-sufficient with regard to the functional requisites of any society. But if one then proceeds to less general levels of analysis to fill in the range of possible variation in the structures of the two societies, one finds that the range is quite different indeed. The industrial society must, for example, stress "universalistic" criteria for employment and "functionally specific"[24] relations. The primitive society need not and commonly does not do so. Furthermore, if one compares _any_ modern industrial society with its form present in the United States, one sees readily that the range of variation of structural possibilities in the latter is a restricted range within the range of possibilities of the former.

Something further must be said of the use of the self-sufficiency phrase. Here the subphrase "in theory" is important. The self-sufficiency phrase refers to self-sufficiency as a social system in operation and not to other types of self-sufficiency. The fact that the United States is not self-sufficient with regard to raw materials does not mean that it is not self-sufficient as a society. The degree of mutual interdependence of two countries engaged in international trade does not preclude either of them from classification as a society. The consideration that is significant here is whether or not the social system

24. See below, Chapter VI, for the definition of these terms.

includes structures necessary to obtain the goods required for its various purposes. One type of such structures is that in terms of which international trade is carried out. On the other hand, another is the type that covers, say, mining within the territory occupied by the members of a society. If the social system of the United States were unable to provide structures which permitted mining in the United States, or, if it were unable to provide structures which permitted the acquisition, either by peaceful trade or force, of necessary raw materials outside the United States, then, given the United States otherwise as it exists today, it would not be a society in the sense of the term used here.

On the other hand, the phrase "in theory" is introduced to indicate that the actual exercise of all the structures necessary for self-sufficiency is not the deciding factor for self-sufficiency either. If one assumes Occupied Japan to be a society in other respects, one may say that Japanese society is not in fact actually providing for many of the crucial institutions concerned with the allocation of power and responsibility in the society. In important respects the occupation authorities, i.e., for present practical purposes the United States forces, furnish these structures. These are structures which will be shown later to be requisites in some form or other for any society. Does this make Japan under occupation a subcategory of United States society? To the degree that Japan is in other respects a society, and to the degree that the Japanese system can provide such structures, structures that are, as it were, held in abeyance by the occupation, such a conclusion does not follow. On the other hand, should the occupation continue so long or in such a way as to render the Japanese system no longer capable of meeting the functional requisites involved, then, in terms of the definition used here, Japan would have ceased, at least temporarily, to be a distinct society.

Cases in which considerations of this sort are germane are not difficult to find. There is some real question, for example, as to whether or not the various Indian groups in the United States are distinct societies any longer. Has the Indian Service of the United States so replaced or taken over indigenous structures that the groups could no longer persist in the absence of the Indian Service?[25] The answer to this question has important implications for comparative statements about, say, the Navaho, from one period to another. If the answer to the question is "yes," then the Indian groups concerned are no longer distinct societies but are parts, however peripheral, of United States society regardless of the fact that many structural dissimilarities may exist between the Indian part of the system and other parts.

The exact determination of these matters, given the present instruments of social science, may be extremely difficult and complex and in some cases impossible. This state of the arts, however, is no reason for ignoring the matters. The more clearly such problems are stated, the greater is the likelihood that someone will devise more precise techniques for their determination. Furthermore, the difficulties that face the student in this realm do not alter the fact that such considerations lie at the heart of many problems of analysis. It is better from the point of view of future development in the field to be left with "more or less" statements about clearly defined problems than to ignore them altogether or leave their consideration implicit.

(4) _The duration of the system_. The duration phrase in the definition has been included to focus attention on systems that must be able to replace their membership and

---

25. This is not to be construed in any sense, positive or negative, as a criticism of either the ends or means of the Indian Service.

systems that in fact do so. It eliminates many highly
transitory systems which, however interesting they may be
for other purposes, would make work of the type attempted
here unnecessarily difficult. Another consideration is
also involved in the use of this phrase. Some temporal
span is implicit in all systems of the type discussed here.
The minimal span chosen here has been used because in conjunction with other parts of the definition it tends to
focus attention on units of the type frequently involved
in past uses of the term society. Some conformity with
ordinary usage is thereby preserved.

In this connection another consideration, which perhaps should have been mentioned above, emerges. The
variations of factors involved in the self-sufficiency of
a system have been discussed above. One addition may be
made to them here. The self-sufficiency of a system may
imply quite different things, even though the setting of
the system remains unchanged, if the duration element of
the system is markedly different. For example, the time
span used here requires that some effective socialization
process exist for the young of the members. This would
not necessarily be the case if the span were only a year.
This aspect of systems is well understood on a very practical level. Every executive understands that the problems
involved in setting up a "temporary" committee are very
different from those involved in setting up a "permanent"
committee. Certain factors are peculiarly subject to
variation in these respects. Notable among them are the
recruitment and indoctrination of personnel.

Attention must also be given to the fact that the
society is "capable of" this duration. Here one has reference of necessity to the relation of the unit to its setting. The fact that a volcanic eruption kills off all the
members of some Pacific Ocean society does not mean that
in the last ten years of its existence it was not a society.
The change of limits is relevant here. Similarly, a system

that may well be a society in one setting may not be in
another. For example, from the point of view of the actors
in one society another society may be part of the setting
of their society.[26] There have, no doubt, been many cases
of social systems capable of indefinite continuation as
societies if left alone that were incapable of doing so in
the face of aggressive or belligerent neighbors.

A society as defined here is in a sense an ideal type.
A given concrete social system is a society insofar as it
in fact conforms to the general model set up. A given social system may more or less approximate such conformity,
and often it will be extremely difficult to determine the
degree of approximation to classification as a society of
a given social system. At the present stage of development
of social science it may be better in some cases to make a
more or less arbitrary decision in this respect and proceed
with the analysis. If implications of the decision contradict the facts which later come to light, then the decision
must be altered. If contradictions do not appear, the
decision will either have been a valid one or at least one
more or less compatible to the type of analysis attempted.[27]

Difficulties in this respect increase, of course, as

---

26. This may be true from the point of view of an observer too.

27. The concern general in this essay for the definition of terms and the like must not be construed as indicative of a desire to make no move "till all is known and
then no move be needed." In social science as well as in
other spheres it often serves one's purpose well to "sin
bravely." The concern here is that one always be well
aware that, however pleasant or useful it may be, "sin is
sin." Without such "sinning" no scientific work would be
done, since it could not be begun until all was already
known. The advantage of "sinning bravely" lies in its
self-conscious aspect. Because of this, when trouble is
encountered in analysis, attention is almost immediately
drawn to the area of "self-conscious sin" as a possible
source of the difficulty. This is, of course, one of the
advantages of making one's concepts explicit.

one turns attention to the modern world. Particularly with regard to the industrialized areas, the interrelations are so numerous and complex as to make even hypothetical discussions of where one social system begins and ends, whether in theory it is self-sufficient even though not in fact, and the like, extremely discouraging. Nevertheless, one must face such problems or abandon such concepts altogether.

Without further refinement of the definition of society it is possible to turn to the question of the termination of a society and the closely related question of changes in a society. There are in general four conditions which, if realized, will terminate the existence of a society as here defined; that is to say, in the presence of any of the four conditions the system of action, though not necessarily in all cases the members involved, will cease to operate. These four conditions are: (a) the biological extinction or dispersion of the members, (b) the apathy of the members, (c) the war of all against all, and (d) the absorption of the society into another society.[28]

(a) The biological extinction or dispersion of the members. To arrive at this condition a society need not lose all its members, but need only suffer such losses as to render inoperative any one of its structural requisites. For some purposes analyses of such conditions may be made partially in terms of fertility, morbidity, and migration rates without reference to the highly complex factors underlying them. Analysis in these terms alone is not, however, sufficient to make the point. The further step of showing that a given morbidity rate, or fertility rate,

---

28. The treatment here of the four conditions terminating the existence of a society is taken nearly verbatim from the article cited above, "The Functional Prerequisites of a Society," Ethics, Vol. LX, No. 2 (Jan. 1950), pp. 100-111.

will make the operation of structural requisites impossible
must be made. In this connection one further point must
be noted. Catastrophic changes in the factors of heredity
or nonhuman environment might conceivably result in the
biological extinction or dispersion of the members of a
society. This situation would terminate the society no
less surely than would some changes or conditions of the
social structure. If, however, these changes in heredity
and/or the nonhuman environment were not socially determined or conditioned,[29] the termination of the society
concerned would be the result of nonsocial rather than
social factors.[30]

---

29. There will be more or less complex cases in this
respect. Should a meteor of sufficient size strike the
earth, future observers, whoever they might be, could
rightly conclude that the earth's societies were terminated
by factors explicable in strictly nonsocial terms, in this
case in physicochemical terms. In the case of a society
which persists in attempts to survive on the slopes of an
active volcano in the face of more or less damaging erup-
tions, a final thorough catastrophe has, certainly, its
social component.

30. For all the tautological character of this statement -- and it is tautological in appearance and fact --
it is necessary to make such a statement in this connection.
In the last few decades the social scientists have fought
a battle against those scholars who would reduce the exploration of all social phenomenon to the factors of heredity
and nonhuman environment, sic, the positivists. The battle
has been thoroughly won, but a few of the confraternity are
still too much embroiled to perceive the victory. They
fight on with an ever renewed vigor which has now carried
some of them to the point of maintaining in effect that not
only do these factors not determine human behavior but,
moreover, they do not affect it. For example, there are
those who not only maintain that heredity does not determine "intelligence," but further, that heredity has nothing
to do with it, that for example the social environment alone
is relevant. Some Marxist theory as well as others would
seem to fall into this category. At the present stage of
knowledge definitive proof of such positions is out of the
question. Here as in other respects the truth probably
lies in the middle somewhere: that is to say, that the
biological factors set limits within which variation takes
place.

(b) <u>Apathy of the members</u>. By apathy here is meant
the cessation of individual "motivation." This condition
affects some individuals in all societies, and large numbers in a few societies. There are reports of migrant
Polynesian laborers who have died of nostalgia, and it is
claimed that whole societies in Melanesia have withered
away from ennui. Carried far enough such absences of
"motivation" if widespread enough would result in the
physical extinction of the members involved, but before
this point could be reached the society might well have
perished. If apathy were sufficiently widespread to prevent the performance of some functional requisite of a
society, the change would take place. Such apathy might
be widespread, but it might also accomplish the same end,
though only a few persons were involved, if those persons
were strategically enough placed and sufficiently difficult
to replace.

(c) <u>The war of all against all</u>. This condition is
considered present if the members of an aggregate pursue
their ends by means selected only on the basis of instrumental efficiency. The actual mutual state of siege
envisioned by Hobbes need not be present, though certainly
life under the condition above would tend to be "solitary,
poor, nasty, brutish, and short." The choice of means
solely on the basis of instrumental efficiency might
conceivably result at times in cooperative combinations,
but these combinations would, by definition, be subject to
immediate dissolution if, for example, exploitation or
annihilation of part or all of the combination became (or
was thought to become) advantageous for any one member.
In such a situation a state of indeterminate flux rather
than a system of action would exist. The development of a
stable pecking-order, if such were possible, is similarly
antithetical to the idea of a society. Force is a sanction,
but never the essence of a society. A society based solely
on force would be a contradiction in terms if for no other

reason than that implicit in the classical question, Quis custodiet ipsos custodes? In theory, at least, in the absence of other restraints than force, it would not be possible to maintain any particular system of action let alone one "self-sufficient and capable of existing longer than the life span of an individual."

(d) The absorption of the society into another society. This condition is of quite another order than the three just discussed above. The three discussed above, if fully realized, would terminate any society whatever. Furthermore, it is not necessarily true that the three conditions above have in fact ever been realized. Certainly, a true war of all against all is rather more a useful concept than a state of affairs that has actually existed. But this fourth condition is another matter. What is involved here is the partial loss of identity and self-sufficiency of the system of action, but not necessarily the extinction of members. It is worth reemphasizing that a given society may at one time contain arrangements for maintaining its distinctness from other societies that form part of its situation, but that an alteration of that situation (the arrival of a numerically and technically superior group bent on conquest) may render these arrangements ineffective. In the terms used here it could not be maintained that the society thus absorbed had never been a society, but rather that in a changed situation it showed a relative inadequacy of one or more of its functional requisites that resulted in its absorption.

The more fully these four conditions are realized, the more indeterminate is the system of action, a condition also present when the rate of social change is very rapid. Hence, one may hypothesize that fluctuations in the vital indices, in apathy and in coercion are to some extent aspects of the rate of social change. In fact, revolutions (extreme social change) are characterized by increases in mortality, morbidity, apathy, force, and fraud. The faster

the change, the greater the stress, two manifestations of
which are force and apathy. Viewing coercion as a response
to stress should be useful in placing the discussion of the
role of force in social systems on a nonideological basis.

The conditions for the termination of any society are
useful in determining what are the functional requisites
(and consequently the structural requisites) of any society.
They are tools of analysis quite aside from whether in any
laboratory sense they can be brought into existence. They
constitute a device for relating the system of action
defined as society to its setting in the most general
sense. A given condition is a functional requisite of any
society if in its actual or hypothesized absence one of
these four conditions or some combination of them would
result.[31] The setting on the most general level is so
defined as to have empirical referents. The system of
action concerned and the conditions for its termination
have been similarly defined. If the function (or structure) under scrutiny as a requisite is similarly defined,
there is no reason why the argument about a condition's
status as a requisite should proceed in any but empirical
terms. There is no necessary a priori consideration at
this level of analysis. On the other hand, since the
argument will proceed in empirical terms, the possibility
of empirical error is involved in this as in any other
scientific analysis. With refinement and improvement of
the analysis the list of functional requisites so obtained
will, no doubt, have to be revised in light of new or
better marshaled empirical considerations. It will not,
however, be invalidated because the argument is nonempirical in character.

---

31. The fourth condition for termination is, of
course, on a less general level than the other three since
it does not apply to any conceivable society as here defined but merely to any society in contact with one or
more other societies.

The question of the termination of any society blends
by degrees into the question of changing societies. The
conditions for termination of a society have been set up
as an aid for the derivation of functional requisites for
any society -- for the most general level of analysis in
this respect. They may, however, be useful in considering
particular societies and particular problems of social
change within them. For example, it may be possible to
throw out certain possibilities of social change in a given
situation if it can be shown to result in the war of all
against all. Despite this possibility the usual analysis
of social change is not of such an all or none character.
Consideration of the all or none question is a device for
throwing light on the bare bones common to all of the
species under consideration. More often in actual problems
one is concerned with social change[32] of a less drastic
sort. One may be, for example, concerned with such questions as the extent of change in, say, French society
between the fifteenth and twentieth centuries. Is one
studying here one or several societies?

In the question of change from one society to another,
if the question of complete extinction is not at issue,
the level of definition of the society under concern is
always a factor of major significance for the analysis.
The basic structural features of fifteenth and twentieth
century France are certainly a world apart. If one defined
French society for rough illustrative purposes as that society predominant within the generally understood geographical boundaries, then one speaks of a single society that
has had a continuous existence although undergoing vast
changes, some evolutionary and some revolutionary. If one

---

32. Social change as the phrase is used here refers
to any alteration which occurs in a system of action of a
given species (human action in the case of concern here)
and which is not subject to explanation solely in terms of
heredity of that species and its nonspecies environment.
See above, pp. 72-76.

defines French society as a feudal society predominant in
some area in the fifteenth century, then it is a different
society from that present in France today. For some purposes of analysis the first approach is more useful, for
others the second. In both cases, of course, the same
changes have taken place. The first approach highlights
the progression of change itself, the dynamics of the phenomenon. The second highlights the comparison between the
two phenomena regardless of how the difference arose.

The point of this discussion lies in the following.
In this type of treatment one speaks of a single society
as long as no change has taken place in the range of possible variation of the structural requisites of the <u>unit</u>
<u>as defined</u>. If such a change has taken place, then a
different society has been brought into being, however
difficult it may be to pin its birth to a particular moment
in the passage of time.[33] The structural requisites of
French society in its more general definition above permits
of a range of variation which will cover all the changes
in the period mentioned. The introduction of the qualification "feudal" sharply narrows this range -- narrows it
in fact to such an extent that there is a difference in
kind between the unit as defined at the outset of the
period and the unit that existed in the area at later
periods, say, certainly from the French Revolution on.

These considerations must not be ignored lest the
analysis involved be seriously biased. Another example
may be mentioned. The structural requisites of any industrial society are more general than the structural requisites of the particular United States variant of industrial
society. Changes that would result in a new society, if

---

33. In the cases of evolutionary change the period
of transition may be of very long duration indeed. In the
case of revolutionary change the transition may be of relatively short duration. Compare, for example, the social
transitions of England for the past two or three centuries
with those of Germany or Japan.

the problem is considered from the second point of view, might not have this result from the first point of view. This whole problem is not a rarefied academic matter. It is a particularly pressing problem when social scientists tackle questions of major current social concern. It is of immediate significance, for example, in the consideration of one of the most discussed issues of the modern United States political scene e.g., the issue of whether continued or increased governmental regulation of the economy of the society will bring about the "fundamental" change of the society.

In concluding this chapter a few remarks may be made about the concept of culture in relation to the work in hand here. It is not necessary to bore the reader with another long listing of the various definitions of culture which have been attempted in the past. Any worker in the field is sufficiently familiar with the bewildering profusion in this respect. Culture has been so defined as to include not only all patterns of action but also artifacts -- all physical objects in any way altered by man. It has been discussed persistently as that element which differentiates humans from the other animals, and so has carried with it the faint whiff of the function performed for others by the concept soul.[34] There have been many other difficulties associated with the concept, and these difficulties have resulted in many brilliant and more or less fruitful discussions in virtually all of the different forms of publication in the field.

There is, however, one difficulty which above all others is a source of trouble here. The concept is virtually everywhere held to be a different one than that of society, but in few if any cases are the two defined in such a way as to be analytically distinct from one an-

---

34. See above, p. 113.

other.[35] In the general literature of social science these
terms sometimes seem to be used interchangeably, even
though they may have been differently defined, and what is
equally confusing, they sometimes are apparently intended
to denote different phenomena (or different aspects of
phenomena) although just where the difference lies is unclear. If the two terms are to be used to denote different
phenomena (or different aspects of phenomena), scientific
method requires that the test of difference be clearly
stated, and if they are to denote the same thing, in the
interest of clarity it might be well to dispense with one
or the other of the terms.

In discussion of these terms relative to human beings
there seems to be little disagreement that both society
and culture are concepts that are useful in the analysis
of human action, and therefore it follows that the referents of the concepts refer to different parts or aspects
of that action. Except for this starting point the distinction between culture and society used here may well
seem to have little in common with the general tradition.
Society has been defined above as a system of action in
operation that involves a plurality of interacting individuals of a given species (or group of species)....[36]
Culture, as the term will be used here, has the same level
of generality as the concept society. Just as other

---

35. The addition of the concept personality completes
a triumvirate of theoretical confusion. Much of what is
here said of the difficulties involved in the use of the
concepts society and culture may be expanded with appropriate permutations and combinations to cover all three.
It may well be some time before a general consensus is
reached on the most useful definitions of these three concepts (though there is little if any disagreement over the
usefulness of all three in some way or other), but the
time has certainly been reached for insistence that, tentatively at least, any particular scholar using the concepts
state what he means by them.

36. See above, p. 113.

systems of social action in operation are either subsystems
of a given society or the result of interrelationships between two or more societies, similar subsystems exist for
the phenomenon, culture, as the term is used here. But
these cultural subsystems are no more cultures than the
subsystems of a society are societies. They are subsystems
of a given culture or the subsystems resultant from the interrelationships of two or more cultures. Culture, as the
term will be used here, refers to the system of action of
a society considered apart from its involvement of a
"plurality of interacting individuals," apart from its
operation. The study of culture in this sense is not a
study of action but of the forms of action as forms. In
this sense the study of culture is possible apart from the
time variable[37] and is essentially static in nature.[38]   In
this sense of the terms, when one talks of a society no
longer empirically extant, one hypothetically reconstructs
it. Its culture has an "existence" which is no less nor
more real for the fact that the society of which it was an
aspect has ceased to exist. In this sense the artifacts
so often classified as parts of culture are not parts of
culture but are sources of evidence for culture. Shake-
speare's writings, an Alaskan totem pole, the Napoleonic
Code, Rembrandt's painting, a Beethoven quartet, the U.S.
Constitution, a statue by Polyclitus, etc., are not culture
but evidences of culture. They are sources of data about
the systems of action in which these things were produced.
Such sources of data may, if one likes, be called culture
objects.

---

37. This line of argument is close to, if not identical with, that of Parsons on this subject. See, for example, his discussion of culture as belonging to the
"realm of eternal objects," Structure, pp. 762 ff. Also
see Essays, pp. 8-10, 33, 40, and 279-280.

38. See above, pp. 43-45 for a discussion of the use
here of the terms static and dynamic.

From the point of view taken here the analysis of societies focuses on the analysis of action and is carried
out in terms of an action scheme. The analysis of culture
is an analysis of a system of action with reference to the
system or pattern elements rather than to the action elements. When no action "exists," no society "exists" though
the culture may. It is true, of course, that there is in
this sense no culture for which there has not at some time
"existed" a society. This view with regard to culture as
differentiated from society does not contradict some of
the elements approached by the large number of definitions
of culture in social science literature. It has relative
to it a place for the objects often included in the definition of the term. It preserves the "hereditary" aspect of
the concept: that is to say, culture in this sense has a
referent which is passed from one generation to another
with more or less modification. Changes in culture may be
noted and analyzed although the process of change itself
is an action phenomenon and hence analyzable in terms of
the society or societies in which it occurs. Thus, the
analysis of the differences between the Chinese language
in the T'ang and Ch'ing Dynasties is a cultural analysis,
but the analysis of the process of change involved is a
social analysis since the process of change is not explicable in other than action terms. Finally, this concept
of culture focuses on the patterns and forms of social
action, and this focus of interest has probably been present in most, if not all, of the various different concepts
of culture.

One final word is in order about the relation between
society and culture as those concepts are here defined.
Culture, in the sense used here, cannot "cause" anything.
However, it is true that, if one knows the culture of a
given society, one can say a great deal about the limits
of possible variation of action in the society and the
possibilities or probabilities of social change. One can-

not, however, speak of a change in culture bringing about
a change in action. Culture, as defined here, is only
analytically separable from a society. It is not concretely different. It is one particular aspect of the society
just as action is another. A changing culture is one
aspect of a changing society. The attribution of causal
efficacy to culture relative to society would beg the question of social change completely in the terms used, and it
is at least a subject for speculation as to whether this
has not sometimes been the case in the use of the concepts
in the past.

       The definition of culture suggested here may not prove
useful or may offend many who have used the term otherwise.
There is no plea here for its acceptance. There is, however, a plea that, if the term culture is not differentiated from the term society, one or the other be dropped.
There is also another plea. If it is differentiated from
the term society, certain rules should be observed. If
the two are conceived as different concrete units, then
they should be so identified as to make possible explicit
and precise determination of where the one begins and the
other ends, i.e., that one be able to distinguish their
referents precisely. Under these conditions the causal
implications of culture for society and vice versa can be
a subject for research. If they are differentiated analytically, as is the case here, then such causal use of
them cannot be made though they continue to share the usefulness mentioned above[39] of analytic distinctions for
predictive purposes. Whatever solution (or solutions) to
this problem may prove useful, the time has come for a
careful reexamination of these concepts unhindered, if
possible, by any traditional loyalty to words in and of
themselves.

----

       39. See pp. 96-100.

C H A P T E R   IV

THE FUNCTIONAL REQUISITES OF ANY SOCIETY

The term <u>functional requisite</u> has been defined in Chapter II of this book.[1] The term <u>society</u> has been defined,[2] and its definition has been discussed in Chapter III. In both of the above chapters the use of these concepts for the type of analysis intended here has been discussed. In brief, it may be said that a given function is a requisite of <u>any</u> society if in its absence the relationship between the unit under discussion and its setting in the most general terms (i.e., human heredity and nonhuman environment in this case) can be shown to be such that one (or some combination) of the four conditions for the termination of a society[3] would result. Such a result can be demonstrated clearly in some cases. Less clearly, but still convincingly, the nonfulfillment of certain other functions can be shown at least to foster one or more of the conditions negating a society. Here one is not concerned with the patterns of action in general and certainly not with specific patterns present in any specific society. Here one is concerned with general conditions. One is concerned with <u>what</u> conditions must exist if <u>any</u> society is to persist, not with how these conditions are carried out. It is necessary to state this explicitly to avoid

---

1. See p. 62.
2. See p. 113.
3. See above, pp. 137-140.

confusion. It is a functional requisite (or an aspect of different functional requisites), for example, that action in certain respects be patterned. But even in this case it is not the patterning of action but the necessary condition of patterning which is under scrutiny. Study of the patterns as patterns in operation comes under scrutiny in the subsequent chapters on structure.

For present purposes a list of ten functional requisites of any society has been devised. Before they are listed and before they are discussed and an attempt is made to establish their status as functional requisites, certain caveats about the tentative nature of this list should be reiterated. This list is not advanced as definitive either from the point of view of exhaustiveness or from the point of view of classification. The list has been made as exhaustive as is possible for present purposes and as useful as possible for the present analysis. An attempt has also been made to choose a particular classification of ten requisites in such a way as to make them analytically distinct from one another. Other students in this field may find other classifications more useful and exhaustive for the purposes sought, in which case their lists should by all means be substituted for this one. The various components of any such list should, however, be analytically distinct if canons of methodological elegance are to be observed.

The criterion of analytical distinctness does not, however, imply that these various functions are unrelated to, or independent of, one another. The various structural components of a society are interdependent and so are the functions. For example, if a society is to exist, its members must have food. They must also, to some extent, do different things at different times and even at the same time. Now, it is obvious that to do things (whether different or similar) people must be fed, and though it is less obvious, it can be shown that to have food different

people must have different roles to some extent. The two
conditions are certainly interdependent, but they are analytically distinct. Having food is precisely distinguishable in analytic terms from having different "roles." The
two, in this case, are not concretely separable any more
than having mass is concretely separable from having volume.
In the general use of functional requisites for analytical
purposes the attempt to be exhaustive and useful is generally made. Less attention, however, is generally paid to
the necessity of analytical distinctness. Analytical distinctness must be sought as well as exhaustiveness because
it contributes directly to the usefulness of the functional
requisite concepts. It is not necessary, however, to
sacrifice interrelatedness or interdependence for analytical distinctness, nor is it necessary to sacrifice analytical distinctness for interrelatedness or interdependence.

The list of functional requisites chosen is as
follows: (A) provision for an adequate physiological relationship to the setting and for sexual recruitment; (B)
role differentiation and role assignment; (C) communication;
(D) shared cognitive orientations; (E) a shared articulated
set of goals; (F) regulation of the choice of means; (G)
regulation of affective expression; (H) adequate socialization; (I) effective control of disruptive forms of
behavior; and (J) adequate institutionalization. General
students in the field will find nothing radical in this
list. Most, if not all, of the items included have been
included in previous lists of this sort by other authors
although this particular division as a whole is not to be
found elsewhere.

A. PROVISION FOR AN ADEQUATE PHYSIOLOGICAL RELATIONSHIP
TO THE SETTING AND FOR SEXUAL RECRUITMENT

This function has its primary reference to those
factors generally classified as the "biological needs" of

the members of a society. This includes adaptation to,
manipulation of, and alteration of the setting in such a
way as to (a) maintain a sufficient number and kind of the
members of the society at an adequate level of operation;
(b) deal with the implications of the setting for the
existence of the unit concerned in a manner that permits
of the biological persistence of the membership; and (c)
pattern heterosexual relationships to insure opportunities
and "motivation" for a sufficient rate of reproduction.
The matter may be clarified by examples of these three
points. The first alludes to the fact that the hereditary
character of man being what it is and the nonhuman environment being what it is, man's biological survival is not
explained by these factors alone. There may of course be
animals whose survival can be explained in these terms.
Some animals are apparently such that without the active
and current intervention of others of their kind they can
survive in their environment. This is not the case for
homo sapiens. A human infant completely abandoned by
humans at birth would undoubtedly perish.[4] The rate of
increasing coordination and control of the human infant
has its varying social components in any given society,
but there is a high level of helplessness involved that
can be explained in purely physiological terms. On the
other hand, the nonhuman environment concerned is such that
the food, shelter, and clothing necessary for the survival
of such an organism are not automatically forthcoming to
it. The case of the human infant is taken here because it
is obvious. At least with regard to the human infant some
other human environmental elements are necessary to explain

---

4. The question of social components in prenatal conditioning is here left out of the question. The reasons
for this are of two sorts: (1) there is the general lack
of knowledge of the extent and nature of prenatal conditioning, let alone the social components involved; and (2)
it is difficult for the author to imagine findings on this
score that would change the present argument materially.

survival, and without such survival a unit such as that which we have defined as society would be impossible.[5] Despite the use of the case of infancy because of its ease of establishment the same point can be made for the biological requirements of the adult members of society. The heredity of the organism is always such that it must have food, and in many areas at least it must have clothing and shelter. These do not come automatically to the adult any more than they do to the infant. The range of action open to an adult in terms of physical possibilities might in theory make it possible for each adult to cope with the situation without regard for other human elements. But this is also unlikely since there is a learning element of a nonhereditary nature involved in such activity on the one hand, and on the other, the "scarcity"[6] of resources

---

5. In addition, of course, there is no reason to believe that the care of human infants by adults is completely explicable in terms of the factors of human heredity and nonhuman environment. In the case of many other species of animals care of the young can apparently be explained in these terms. The provision for their young by the solitary hunting wasps, so charmingly described by Fabre, is apparently of this order. In these insects the range of variation possible permits of relatively narrow choices. The insects pick spots for their burrows, and there is variation in this respect, but all of a given species dig burrows of a given type. All of certain species supply the larva to be hatched with a food supply, and in some cases there is not even any range of variation of food supply, that being, in some cases, confined to the members of a particular sex of a particular species of insect or spider. Furthermore, in some of these species there is no evidence of any sort of conditioning of the adult by other adult members of the species. One is forced back in such cases on the factors of species' heredity and nonspecies' environmental factors for explanations of the care of the young. It is this possibility which seems closed in the case of the "human" species -- a species in which adequate provision for the young is by no means a certainty in terms of these factors, but rests, where achieved, on others.

6. This "scarcity" may be a product of man as well as of nature. If five objects of a given type exist when only two are wanted, it is not scarce in the sense intended

would involve a plurality of individuals of any sort in
contacts with one another. Because of the relative efficiency of the use of force and fraud for limited purposes,
the action of the members of a plurality of the sort
envisaged here, without regard for one another, i.e., with
a view solely to instrumental efficiency, would result in
the state of war of all against all. The absence of any
human social elements (i.e., elements not explicable in
terms of human heredity and nonhuman environment) would,
because of the purely physiological aspects of the membership, result either in biological extinction or the war of
all against all.

In this connection something must be said about the
term _adequate_. Here reference is made to a question
treated above.[7] The term _adequate_ does not cover measures
sufficient to ensure survival in the face of _variations_ in
the limits set by heredity and nonhuman environment. In
no known society are the members able to insure the survival of the society against a meteoric catastrophe or
shifts in the nonhuman environmental limits of this sort.
Adequate in this sense means a type of social system sufficient to insure survival when failure to survive could
not be explained solely in terms of human heredity and
nonhuman environment.

The second of the points mentioned above has specific
reference to the human aspects of the setting apart from
the factors of heredity. If the society is to persist,
the results of the operation of the structural features of
a society must be such that factors other than those

---

here. If six are wanted, it is scarce. Furthermore, a
good or service is scarce in this sense if more than one
person desires the particular one involved. There is an
absolute sense in which empirical resources on earth are
finite. This being the case, depending on the state of
demand, any good may become scarce.

7. See pp. 14-15, 135-136.

explicable in terms of human heredity and nonhuman environment, i.e., that social factors, do not prevent the biological persistence of the membership. It has been suggested immediately above that, the facts of human heredity
and nonhuman environment being what they are, some social
structures must be present if there is to be biological
survival of an adequate membership. Social factors may
also interfere, however. Some structures of land ownership
and control are such as to result in a "mining of the soil."
The continuation of such a system would in the long run
prevent biological survival in the area. There are, however, other problems of quite another sort on the social
level. The question of neighboring societies of a hostile
and aggressive orientation is an obvious case in point. In
the face of such neighbors the lack of structures of resistance would result in extinction, dispersion, or enslavement.

The third of the points mentioned above is virtually
self-explanatory. The definition of the unit concerned
involves recruitment at least in part by the sexual reproduction of the members. Such reproduction is not automatic,
and structures ensuring "motivation" and opportunities for
such reproduction are required. Certain ascetic structures,
if widely enough institutionalized, would certainly prevent
such reproduction. From another point of view structuring
in this respect is also necessary. Sex partners are from
one point of view "scarce goods," as are all other empirical objects which are at all desired. In the absence of
structures of access to and allocation of sex partners some
reproduction would no doubt take place, but, the capacity
of human beings for emotional reactions in this sphere
being what it seems to be, if this sphere of action were
socially undefined, the determination of action on the
basis of instrumental efficiency (i.e., the war of all
against all) would certainly develop rapidly with all its
disruptive possibilities.

In the absence of these provisions, the membership of

a society will suffer biological extinction through the death of the members or absorption into another social system. A society, however, need not provide equally for the physiological needs of all its members. Infanticide, geronticide, limitation of marriage, and birth control may be necessary to maintain certain societies. Which members, and in what proportions, are most important for the functioning of a society depends on its social organization. There are certain minimal limits, however. Every society needs enough adult members to ensure reproduction and to man essential "roles" if it is to persist.

The members of a society must adapt to, manipulate, and alter their situation. Among the features thus dealt with may be chronically threatening aspects of the situation. In a dry region a society may employ techniques of food storage, irrigation, or nomadic migration. If neighboring societies are hostile, an army may be essential -- further evidence that no society needs to keep all its members alive. The existence of Murngin society depends partly upon the destruction of a proportion of its adult males by chronic warfare. Resistance is only one possible response to hostile neighbors. Certain "men-o-bush" tribes of New Guinea make but little resistance to raids. These raids do not threaten to extinguish the society. Only if they do can such a passive adaptation be said to be inadequate to meet the functional requisite.

The inclusion of such apparently disparate features as maintenance of the organism, defense, and provision for sexual reproduction under one heading is by no means arbitrary. From the point of view of a social system, the nonhuman environment, the biological nature of man, and the existence of other societies[8] are all part of the setting

---

8. And from the point of view of any given individual his own society, at least in some respects, is part of the setting of action too.

of action. To none of these aspects of the setting is passive adaptation the only mode of adequate relationship. In fact, a purely passive mode of adaptation to them cannot be maintained if a society is to persist. Thus, the biological limits of society are themselves molded. Individuals have constitutional differences, but the latter are variously evaluated and dealt with in various societies. The biological birth-growth-death cycle is a process in its own right,[9] yet societies both are adapted to it and modify it in a number of ways. In noting the necessity for a society to meet certain biological requisites, one must also remark upon the great plasticity of individuals. It is scarcely necessary to remark that societies alter concretely the modes of relationship of their members to their situations, that technological changes occur, sometimes through loss, more often by invention and diffusion.

B. ROLE DIFFERENTIATION AND ROLE ASSIGNMENT

In order to avoid confusion it is advisable to preface the discussion of the necessity of role differentiation and role assignment with a definition of the term role as it is used here. Unfortunately, it is not possible simply to stop with this definition since the term role has been so intimately involved in past literature with such terms as status, position, stratification, etc. For reasons of consistency and clarity it is not possible to use here the exact formulations on this score used elsewhere in social science literature. At the same time, the formulation used here rests heavily upon the work of Kingsley Davis, Ralph Linton, and Talcott Parsons.[10] Some of the defini-

---

9. i.e., subject to analysis in strictly biological terms.

10. See: Kingsley Davis, "A Conceptual Scheme of Stratification," Am. Sociol. Rev., Vol. VII, No. 3 (July 1942), pp. 309-321; Ralph Linton, The Study of Man.

tions used here will be virtually identical with those
used by these writers. The major distinction between the
present and past treatment will come with reference to the
concept role.

On the subject of status and role difficulty in the
past has arisen from the general tendency to define role
as the actual way in which a given individual performs in
his status or position. Davis says, "Following Linton, we
define Role as the manner in which an individual actually
carries out the requirements of his position."[11] Parsons
in his use of the term also refers to Linton and uses
essentially the same definition.[12] There is no difficulty
about making the distinction in this manner, but once made
it has not been commonly observed. If one defines role in
the above manner, one can subsequently speak only of the
roles of particular individuals or groups of particular
individuals. Such terms as occupational roles (not the
roles of specific individuals in specific occupational
statuses or positions), role differentiation, etc., would
have to be abandoned -- at least in their ordinary application. Without any intention to disparage the real contributions of these three men to this field, the difficulty
of this usage can be illustrated from the work of the men
already quoted. Davis, in a recent book which uses the
same system of definitions as that of his article, speaks
of the "dual role of the social scientist."[13] Linton, in
his volume, speaks of the "warrior role."[14] Parsons, on
the same page on which he defines role, speaks of "the
role of surgeon."[15] In all these cases what is meant is

Appleton Century, New York, 1936, Ch. VIII; Talcott Parsons,
Essays, Ch. I, III, and VII.

11. op.cit., p. 311. The relevant portion of Linton
is Ch. VIII (op.cit., supra), especially p. 114.

12. Parsons, op.cit., pp. 34, 43.

13. Human Society, Macmillan, New York, 1949, p. 11.

14. op.cit., p.480.

15. op.cit., p. 43.

what these writers have defined as either <u>status</u> or <u>position</u>. Given <u>role</u> as defined, there is no "social scientist role" or "warrior role" or "role of surgeon"; there are only roles of particular individuals who occupy the status (or position) of social scientists, warriors, or surgeons. If the term <u>role</u> is used consistently with its definition, then there can be no talk of people acting in terms of roles. Their actions <u>are</u> their roles. There can be no talk of systems of roles that are abstracted from specific individuals. The difficulty may be extended to multifarious different uses of the role concept.

Now, the distinction at which the above concept of role is aimed is a very important one. The system of definitions which follows attempts to retain a place for that concept while avoiding the type of difficulty mentioned above.

The term <u>role</u> will be used to mean any position differentiated in terms of a given social structure whether the position be institutionalized or not. A given role is the classification of the social position given to the individual who performs an activity differentiated in terms of the social structure. These roles involve obligations, rights, and expected performances of the individuals who hold them.[16] The positions of thief, doctor, outcast, injured man, etc. are all roles in this sense. A distinction may be drawn between <u>ideal</u> and <u>actual</u> roles. An <u>ideal</u> role is an <u>institutionalized role</u>. Such a role involves normative standards, conformity with which is generally to be expected, and failure to conform with which is met by moral indignation.[17] An <u>actual role</u> is the position in fact occupied by an individual. It is what he in fact does with regard to any socially differentiated

16. These three factors are advanced by Parsons as basic aspects of status as he defines the term. See <u>op.cit.</u>, p. 43.

17. See definition of institution above, p. 102.

position whether institutionalized or not. The concept of
actual role conforms very closely to that of role as defined by Davis, Linton, and Parsons. The concept ideal
role conforms rather closely to status as that term is used
by them. By status in this treatment we shall mean the
sum total of an individual's (or group's) institutionalized
positions in a social structure -- the sum total of his
ideal or institutionalized roles. Specific ideal roles
may be called aspects of status. Thus, a given man's ideal
roles as a father, a doctor, a taxpayer, a citizen of the
United States, etc. are all aspects of his status. A
person's total social standing is the sum total of all his
roles both ideal and actual.[18] Thus, a given man may have
as components of his total social standing not only the
fact that he is a father but that he is a "good" father,
not only that he is a doctor but that he is a "mediocre"
doctor, not only that he is a taxpayer but that he is a
somewhat "delinquent" one, and so forth. The definition
of office used by Davis[19] will be used here, but it will
be distinguished from an institutionalized or ideal role
rather than from status. An additional remark may be made
about office. It is true that, as Davis would hold, an
institutionalized role need not involve an office, but, on
the other hand, an office almost always, if not inevitably,
involves some institutionalized role. In the concept of
station Davis' usage is followed roughly, and the concept
means a cluster of roles "which may be combined in one individual and recognized as so combined in a great many
cases."[20] The term stratum, used by Davis to mean "a mass

---

18. The sum total of an individual's actual roles
will be termed his actual social standing. The sum total
of an individual's ideal roles may be termed his ideal
social standing, or alternatively, his status. The term
ideal social standing may be substituted for status by
those who find the present use of the term status confusing.

19. op.cit., pp. 309-310.

20. ibid., p. 310.

of persons in a given society enjoying roughly the same station,"[21] will be used in the same way here.

With so much by way of introduction attention may now be turned to the functional requisite of role differentiation and role assignment. <u>Role differentiation</u> as a function may be defined as that state of affairs in which the roles[22] involved are heterogeneous. <u>Role assignment</u> as a function may be defined as the state of affairs that exists when the obligations, rights, and expected performances involved in roles are taught and allocated to an individual or individuals.

In any society there are activities that must be regularly performed if the society is to persist. If their performance is to be dependably insured, these extensive and varied activities must be broken down and allocated to capable individuals trained and "motivated" to carry them out. Otherwise, everyone would be doing everything or nothing -- a state of indeterminacy that is the antithesis of a society and that precludes getting essential activities carried out. The universal problems of scarcity and order are insoluble without an institutionalized allocation of property rights and authority, and these in turn are unattainable without reasonably integrated role differentiation.

There is another line of reasoning bearing on the classifications of this condition as a functional requisite. Not all individuals are capable of performing the same activities, and some are even unable to perform activities on which their own survival depends. Furthermore, even were every member of a society capable of performing every conceivable activity necessary for his survival, it would not be possible for each individual to carry on simultaneously all the activities that often have to be carried on

---

21. <u>ibid</u>., p. 310.

22. See definition above, p. 159.

in that manner. Again, in this respect one may point to
such obvious cases as that of infants who are everywhere
in human society unable to shift for themselves at birth.
Sex differentiation is another such factor. For all the
remarkable plasticity of the human individual and for all
the similarities between the males and females of the
species, the males are everywhere unable to bear children,
and some differentiation of roles on the basis of sex must
reckon with this factor if a society is to persist.

While a given individual is always the locus of several roles, he can never combine all the roles of his society
in himself. He can never combine all the requisite roles
of his society either, and, in fact, he cannot even combine
all the requisite roles for his own survival. The real or
fancied cases of Crusoe existence do not shake the validity
of this point. Virtually all the Crusoe examples feature
an individual already at the adult stage, and none involve
an individual at birth. The survival of a Crusoe would
not, of course, be the same as the survival of a society,
but even the survival of a Crusoe of the human species
presupposes some societal background for the individual
concerned.[23] Age and sex differences, given the heredity

---

23. The interesting facet of the Crusoe case is not
how free these heroes are from all societal taints, but
rather the uncommon degree to which in one person they are
held to combine both knowledge and skill of the wide variety of roles of the societies from whence they came. In
this connection it is of interest to examine a particular
variant of the Crusoe example, i.e., that furnished by the
Swiss Family Robinson, Johann David von Wyss, E. P. Dutton
and Co., N. Y., 1910. This involves a group isolated (by
shipwreck, of course) on an island. The fortuitous addition of outside individuals permits this group to avoid
incest taboos, and by the end of the volume a small society seems to be in full swing. The reader will find many
gaps in this story as far as structural requisites are
concerned, but a close examination of the lengths to which
the author goes to develop his little group throws an amus-
ing light on some of the problems treated here.
    At this point it might be well to raise one fur-
ther point about the distinction between human societies
and cultures and those of other animals. It has already

and nonhuman environment, everywhere impose a degree of
role differentiation on human societies as mentioned above,
but the exact ways in which this role differentiation takes
place are not apparently determined by human heredity and
nonhuman environment. An extremely wide range of variation
is possible, and it is for this reason that one speaks of
the existence of role differentiation and role assignment
as a requisite of the society. If such differentiation
can be shown to be fully explicable in terms of human heredity and nonhuman environment, i.e., <u>if there is no range
of variation in this respect</u>,[24] then it becomes part of
the limiting factors in the setting of the society concerned rather than of the society itself. It is because

---

been pointed out that the range of variation possible within the limits set by the species' heredity and the nonspecies' environment seems to be at least greatly different in
degree for the human and any other animal species. A further factor may be added to this. Survival of the members
of some of the other species, at least, is possible without role differentiation on the basis of different members
(e.g., species whose members can shift for themselves at
birth and reproduce by parthenogenesis) and for others the
role differentiation on the basis of different members may
be confined to that necessary for sexual reproduction (e.g.,
the case of many insects). And this activity in turn may
be explicable on a heredity-environment basis. In such
cases the range of variation possible is certainly relatively small as compared with that possible in other species, and it may conceivably be nonexistent. It may well
be that there are many different species the activities of
whose members are completely explicable in terms of the
species' heredity and the nonspecies' environment, but this
is an hypothesis that requires proof. If it can be proved,
there remains the further intriguing problem of where, if
anywhere, in the scale of evolutionary development a line
can be drawn between those creatures which fit the category, <u>social</u>, and those which do not.

    24. If these factors are explicable in terms of human
heredity and nonhuman environment, they may still have a
range of variation insofar as the factors of human heredity
and nonhuman environment have a range of variation such as
that mentioned above (see Chapter I). In this case they
do not, however, have a range of variation <u>in the respect
relevant here</u>, i.e., specifically a range of variation not
explicable in terms of the limits themselves.

the limits of human heredity and nonhuman environment require some role differentiation if a society is to exist,
but do not determine exactly what it must be, that role
differentiation is a functional requisite of a society.

In some societies "class" and "occupations" may be
taken as examples of the many additional possible bases of
role differentiation. Arguments for the necessity of
specialization (and hence role differentiation) based on
differential ability in a broader sense than that mentioned
above in relation to sex and age differences, while of
great force in relation to complex societies, have less
bearing on societies so simple that any technique can be
learned by any individual who is not feeble-minded or
crippled.[25] Whatever the society, however, activities
necessary to its survival must be worked out in predictable
determinate ways, or apathy or the war of all against all
must prevail. Without reliable provision for child rearing
activities and without their assignment to specific persons
or groups, the society invites extinction for reasons discussed above. A system of role differentiation alone would
be ineffective without a system of selection for assigning
individuals to those roles. The absence of role differentiation and role assignment thus makes for three of the
conditions negating a society.

Mention should be made of one particular type of role
differentiation that is a requirement for any society,
i.e., stratification. Stratification is the particular
type of role differentiation that differentiates higher
and lower standings in terms of one or more criteria.[26]

---

25. A serious question may be raised, however, as to
whether any society is in fact so simple as this. Even if
the simplicity did exist in fact, differences in skill and
limitations of time and the number of things that can be
done at once would still be formidable arguments for the
inescapability of some specialization.

26. In stratification systems the political factor
(i.e., power and responsibility considerations) are fre-

Given the universality of scarcity, some system of differential allocation of the scarce values of a society is
essential.[27] These values may consist of such desiderata
as wealth, power, magic, women, and ceremonial precedence.
That conflict over scarce values may destroy a society will
be shown in another connection below. The present point
is that the rank order must be legitimized and accepted by
most of the members -- at least the important ones for the
maintenance of order -- of a society if stability is to be
attained. Allocation of ranks may be on the basis of
ascribed or achieved qualities or both.

Role differentiation implies organization. Precedence
in specialized activities must be correlated to some extent
with rank order. Coercive sanctions and initiative must
be vested in specified role holders. Some individuals will
thus receive more than others. These privileges are usually made acceptable to the rank and file by joining to the
greater rights of the "elite" a larger share of the responsibilities. The Brahmins stand closer to other-worldly
nonexistence than do the members of any other Hindu caste,
but they also have to observe the most elaborate ritual
obligations. The Trobriand chief enjoys a multiple share
of wealth and wives. He must also finance community enter-

---

quently of the essence of the matter. This is true to
such an extent that stratification systems are sometimes
defined in such a way that the political criterion is written into the definition. It is not felt necessary to do
that here. This whole question of stratification, however,
is discussed at greater length below in Chapter VII on the
analytic structure of role differentiation.

27. As may be seen from this and other portions of
this study, scarcity is not a factor whose relevance is
limited to the economic sphere in its usual sense. There
is a sense in which power, for example, may be considered
a good or at least a service just as there is a sense in
which goods and services contain elements of power. The
implications of this are explained to some degree in subsequent portions of this study. Suffice it to say at this
point that the present use of scarcity suggests, for peripheral uses at least, the relevance of economic analysis
in the ordinary sense for other fields and vice versa.

prise and exhibit at all times more generosity than anyone else.

Even the "simplest" societies have hierarchical sex and age gradings. Modern societies are much more elaborately stratified. Symbolic activities or ritual must be carefully organized to effect successfully such eufunctions as allaying anxiety and recreating allegorically the basic meanings and affirmations of the society. In group enterprises some roles tend to rank others, though the individuals filling the roles may rotate relatively freely as in the case of the citizens of the Greek city-state. Regardless of the type of stratification and authority system, an institutionalized scale of priorities for allocating scarce values (precedence, property rights, power, etc.) is always a vital portion of the differentiation of roles in any society.

C. COMMUNICATION

Communication for present purposes is defined as the activity or process whereby one or more individuals of a given species infers from the behavior (whether language of both oral and written types, gesture, or posture) of another individual (or group of individuals) of the same or different species an idea or feeling or state of affairs that the other individual(s) is trying to convey.[28] Evidence from deaf-mutes, "isolated" children,[29] and bilinguals

28. This definition, with slight emendations to increase its generality, is taken from Kingsley Davis, Human Society, Macmillan, New York, 1949, p. 149.

29. The category of "isolated" children for present purposes refers to those children who have been the victims of extreme separation from other humans in their early years though not completely abandoned by other humans. See in this connection Kingsley Davis's articles, "Extreme Social Isolation of a Child," Am. Jour. of Sociol., Vol. 45, No. 4, (Jan. 1940), pp. 554-564 and "A Final Note on a Case of Extreme Isolation," ibid., Vol.50, No. 3, (Nov. 1947), pp. 432-437.

shows that speech, which is perhaps the most obvious form of communication among human beings, is learned and that only rudimentary communication is possible in the absence of shared, learned, linguistic symbols. Without learned symbolic communication it would seem that only a few highly general emotional states -- anger, sexual passion, and the like -- in one individual can evoke an appropriate response in another, and only a few skills and techniques can be conveyed solely by imitation. Even this is perhaps doubtful.

No human society, however simple, can exist without shared, learned, symbolic modes of communication because without them it cannot maintain the common value structure or the protective sanctions that hold back the war of all against all. In a sense, this argument may be referred to the extreme plasticity of the human species in certain respects, i.e., to the fact that the range of variation within the limits of variation is so great. This fact, in conjunction with the scarcity aspects of the nonhuman environment, would seem to rule out an automatic adjustment, explicable solely in hereditary terms, of the individual to his nonhuman environment (let alone the human elements). With this sort of adjustment ruled out, the requisite character of social factors is apparent, and for these factors to be effective, they must be communicated. Communication is essential if socialization and role differentiation are to operate successfully. That the achievement of a given functional requisite thus depends in part on other functional requisites does not vitiate the present argument so long as the functional requisites are clearly differentiated from one another. They must be analytically separable, but they need not be empirically distinct conditions, since any action system may, and commonly does, involve several functional requisites.

In a simple society in which relationships are largely "face-to-face," shared speech-forms, shared gesture-forms, and shared posture-forms may suffice. In complex ·societies other communications than these are necessary for the system as a whole though not necessarily for the subsystems. Thus, in China writing facilitates the survival of the society despite local dialect differences too great to permit oral communication without bilingual intermediaries. Apparently, no modern industrial society could survive without writing.[30]   Thus, communication requires language, a medium of communication, and channels of communication.

D. SHARED COGNITIVE ORIENTATIONS

By the term _cognition_ is meant knowledge or understanding of a situation or phenomenon. This knowledge or understanding may be of an empirical or of a nonempirical sort. If it is of an empirical character, it is subject to the categories of ignorance and error as well as to those of validity[31] in the scientific sense. If it is of a nonempirical sort, any given observer may consider it real or fancied knowledge or understanding, or some combination of the two. Regardless of what category cognition may fall into in these or in other respects, for the purposes of social analysis the important consideration is not primarily the "reality" or even the "tenability" of the cognition, but rather the empirically observable effects of a given type of cognition on the actions of those who hold it and/or on that of those with whom interaction takes place. Questions of the "reality," "tenability," "empirical or nonempirical nature," etc., of the cognition are relevant for the purposes of social analysis only insofar as they throw light on the effects of such cognition

---

30.   This involves modern industrial societies in a whole series of problems centering about literacy.

31.   The question of empirical and nonempirical factors in cognition is taken up in some of its aspects in discussing certain ranges of variation in the institutionalized patterns of cognition involved in different relationships. See below, pp. 240-248.

on the actions of those who hold it and/or on that of those with whom interaction takes place.

In any society the members must share a body of cognitive orientations[32] that (a) make possible adaptation to and/or manipulation of the situation of action; (b) make stable, meaningful, and to some extent predictable the social situations in which they are engaged; and (c) account for those significant aspects of the situation over which they do not have adequate prediction and control in such a way as to sustain and not destroy "motivation."

If the first criterion were not met, biological existence of the members of the unit would be impossible. If the second were not, interpersonal and intergroup relations could not exist. Private definitions of social situations or the absence of such definitions could lead only to mutually incompatible actions and the war of all against all. In no society are all conditions predictable and controllable. The frustration of expectations is, therefore, a chronic feature of social life. Without a reasonably determinate explanation of such areas of existence, the individual would exist in an unstructured world and could not avoid psychological disorganization. In the absence of shared cognitive orientations, serious clashes would ensue.

---

32. This argument is an example of the dependence of present system of analysis on an underlying, i.e., more general, theory of action. A theory of action that includes a cognitive aspect of the actor's orientation can and must include this functional requisite in the analysis of any society. On the other hand, this analysis presupposes a theory of action involving a cognitive aspect of the actor's orientation. Parsons is currently at work on a systematic generalized formulation of such a system. Elements of it have emerged previously in his work from The Structure of Social Action on. Both in his published materials and in his lectures this cognitive orientation has always played its analytic role.

Other examples of this sort of dependence are taken up below. See the sections on goal orientations and affective orientations, pp. 175-177, 183-186.

Cognitive orientations must be shared, but only insofar as the actors are involved in the same situation of
action. A housewife may not distinguish a colonel from a
corporal; a soldier may not appreciate that he is using
his hostess' "wedding silver." They must agree, however,
that a foot is "so long" and that that gentleman is a
"policeman." But though a farmer may pray for rain and an
aviator rub a rabbit's foot for good weather with no resultant difficulties between them, both must define the
American political system in a roughly similar fashion if
they are to vote. Here again levels of generalization are
important. Specific members of a given society, on some
levels of generalization, may have relatively little in
common with one another. On levels of generalization at
which this is true shared cognitive orientations may be at
a minimum,[33] but, if they are to be members of the same
society, some elements of cognition must be shared. Without such elements, communication, for example, would be
impossible. Communication is not cognition, but there are
of necessity elements of cognition involved in communication. A couple must "know" a common language of some sort
to communicate linguistically, or "know" a common set of
gestures if communication is to take that form. The
element of cognition in communication is only one example

---

33. Several years ago a famous American cartoonist
ran a series of cartoons based on this theme. These cartoons were usually built around three persons, two of whom
share common occupational roles. The conversation of these
two, whether about their jobs or other considerations, is
conducted in the jargon peculiar to their shared roles.
The third person, an outsider in this respect, is thoroughly baffled, and the punch line is of the order, "They don't
speak our language." The jest involved has two essential
elements. One is the specialized unintelligibility of the
"experts" for the "nonexpert," but the other and no less
important aspect is the note of grievance of the outsider,
arising in essence from the fact that, after all, they are
members of the same social setting in some respects and
therefore should share cognitive orientations sufficiently
for intelligible communication to be possible.

of the relevance of this functional requisite for others. Elements of cognition are involved in all the others as well, and this is of course true of each functional requisite relative to every other. Each functional requisite is, after all, a functional requisite of the same unit in the same setting. For the unit to exist in its setting all must exist. The situation in this respect is a sort of analytical all for one and one for all. This does not, of course, mean that all are the same.

Those elements of cognition that are on the more general "shared level" may be called the basic cognitive orientations of a society. This concept may be phrased more precisely: the basic cognitive orientations are those elements of cognition in a society that must be institutionalized[34] for every member of the society at some stage of his or her development if the society is to persist as defined. It will be noted that this definition allows for elements of cognition that pertain to one stage of development and perhaps not to another, e.g., there are elements of cognition which one expects every child to have but not every adult and, of course, vice versa. It focuses attention on an expectation of knowledge with regard to every member of the society. At the same time it must be noted that the inclusion of the term "institutionalized" takes cognizance of the overwhelming probability that not every member will in fact know the basic cognitive orientations. All cognitive orientations other than the basic ones in a society will be termed the intermediate cognitive orientations. These may be of two sorts, institutionalized and

---

34. By "institutionalized" it is, of course, meant that conformity (i.e., in this case knowledge of the element concerned) is generally to be expected, and failure to conform (i.e., in this case, lack of the relevant knowledge) is a reason for moral indignation on the part of other members of the society. This phenomenon is a tediously familiar one as is witnessed by the familiar expression of indignation expressed in some such form as the following: "Any adult should know better...."

noninstitutionalized. The institutionalized intermediate cognitive orientations are those intermediate cognitive orientations (1) possession of which is generally to be expected of some of the members of a society some of the time in some of the substructures of action of the society, and (2) failure to possess which is met with moral indignation by the members of the substructure concerned or by other members of the society in general. The noninstitutionalized intermediate cognitive orientations are residually defined relative to the institutionalized ones. It must be borne in mind that the noninstitutionalized category is by no means socially insignificant. Many, if not most or all, of the theoretical discoveries of science, for example, would fall into this latter category.

The number of members of a society holding the various intermediate cognitive orientations will, of course, in any given case be smaller than those holding the basic cognitive orientations. Furthermore, there will be great variation in the numbers of persons concerned or the level of generality of the specific intermediate cognitive orientations. Those pertaining to steel workers, for example, will cover a larger group than those pertaining to diamond cutters in modern United States society. The variation possible in these respects is at least as great as the variation possible in the concrete substructures of a society.

One further factor should be noted in this connection. There is a sense in which some of the cognitive orientations in a society are more important than others for the survival of the society. Those which are necessary for the maintenance of structural requisites are more important in this sense than are others. In this connection adaptation can be made of some of the qualifying terms used above in connection with institutions.[35] These terms are crucial

---

and strategic and the qualifying aspects of strategic,
i.e., substantive and critical. Cognitive orientations
may be crucial, or more or less strategic, and if more or
less strategic, they may be so with regard to their substantive or critical aspects.[36]

E. A SHARED ARTICULATED SET OF GOALS

To phrase this requisite in terms of ultimate or immutable ends of action produces a vague and extremely
general formulation like Thomas' four wishes. It is equally difficult to operate in terms of "motivations," since
these are exceedingly diverse and are intricately articulated with social structure. The statement in terms of
goals seeks a middle ground and is couched in terms suita-
ble for considering a system of action. By the term goal
is meant a state of affairs deemed desirable by the actors
concerned.[37]

The same factors that make role differentiation
necessary for a society also require that considerations
be given to a set of goals rather than to a single common
goal. The facts of scarcity and of differential individual
endowment, features of all societies, make it necessary to
speak of a set of goals. The range of goals, however
narrow, provides alternatives for individuals and thus
reduces one serious source of conflict in societies.

---

36. It is no doubt unnecessary to define separately
the application of these qualifying concepts here. Re-
course to their original appearance above in Chapter II
will make the matter obvious enough. It will also be obvious that these same qualifications may be made with regard to goal (or value) orientations and affective orientations as a minimum. There are basic goal and affective
orientations, intermediate ones, institutionalized and
noninstitutionalized ones, crucial and more or less strategic ones, and they may be more or less strategic in a substantive and/or a critical sense(s).

37. This definition follows that of Parsons, op.cit.,
p.32.

The possibility of some universally sought goals is
not, of course, ruled out. In fact in the absence of some
goals that, if not universally sought, are at least held
in common by an effective majority of the population of a
society, a society could not persist. Man as an animal is
capable of conscious teleological action.[38]   That is to
say, men consciously seek to bring about a state of affairs
which at least in theory from the actor's point of view
would be different in some degree if they did not orient
their actions to a particular goal (or set of goals). The
source of this capability in the species homo sapiens[39]
may perhaps be explained in terms of human heredity, but
whatever the scientific findings on this score, they do
not at least for the present establish anything more than
a range of variation in this respect. Although conscious
striving for goals may be biologically determined, the
exact goals striven for cannot with present biological
knowledge be determined. In addition, current research in
the field of biology does not offer any glowing prospects
for such determination. The existence of such a range of
variation in a setting involving such factors as the
nonhuman environment with its aspects of scarcity, etc.,
requires some commonly held goals for the members of a
society, if the society is to persist in its setting.
Without them a war of all against all would be inevitable,
and indeed even apart from such a state of affairs as that,

---

38. Men may be, and no doubt are, capable of "unconscious teleological" actions if that phrase does not involve a contradiction in terms. It is not necessary for
present purposes, however, to explore this aspect of the
question. The existence of any such teleological action
whether conscious or unconscious will establish the present
point.

39. The capability is by no means confined to this
particular species. At least one may say with due view
for scientific caution that science has not demonstrated
any such restriction of the trait.

the absence of such a set of commonly held goals would
make biological survival of the members impossible on other
grounds. In addition to being commonly held these goals
are further restricted if a society is to exist. For
example, some "motivation" or goal orientation to the care
of children must exist if the children are to survive to
play their role in the continuity of a society. Those
goals that are such that the members of a given society
must hold them sufficiently in common to "motivate" the
performance of the functional requisites of that society,
and that are such that the holding of them is institutionalized for each member of the society at some stage of his
development, will be called here the basic value or goal
orientations of that society. There are some basic value
orientations that must be common to all societies, but
these are, of course, to be formulated only in the most
general terms. For example, in all societies the members
must hold some acts of murder to be bad. The range of
definition of this basic value orientation for different
societies ranges from a radical outlawing of all forms of
taking life (including pacifism in the face of any aggres-
sion) to societies in which vendettas of the bloodiest
sort are part of the social structure. However liberal
may be the definition of those eligible for slaughter,
there is always some limitation placed upon it, and if
those limitations break down completely, the society will
dissolve into a war of all against all.

All of the less general forms of the basic value
orientations need not have the quality of being held in
common that is necessary for the basic value orientations,
nor the quality of institutionalization, though some will
have the latter quality albeit in a more limited form.
The less general forms of the basic value orientations
will be called the intermediate goals or the intermediate
value orientations. Here exists a state of affairs
analogous to that discussed above relative to basic cogni-

tive orientations and intermediate cognitive orientations.
A housewife need not know a corporal from a colonel, and a
corporal need not be able to tell a head butcher from his
subordinate, but both of them need to know something about
the position of the president of the United States. Similarly, the value considerations involved in the employment
of baseball players and automobile workers may be quite
different in specific respects, but in both cases universalistic criteria[40] must be emphasized if the system is to
operate effectively. There is, in the matter of intermediate goals, a whole hierarchy for any given society.
The hierarchy contains classes like those discussed above
under the heading of cognitive orientations. Thus, there
will be institutionalized and noninstitutionalized intermediate goals, crucial and/or more or less strategic ones,
etc. They may also be more or less strategic in their
substantive or their critical aspects.[41] The hierarchy is
susceptible to almost endless variations of both types and
levels. About this variation one generalization may be
made: the more differentiated the structural features, the
more elaborately differentiated will be the system of
intermediate goals.[42] A kinship system that institutionalizes the recognition of three hundred different kinship
positions will involve a much more elaborate set of intermediate goals, at least in this respect but almost certainly in others as well, than one that institutionalizes the
recognition of only twenty-four. This is, no doubt, a
statement of the obvious and banal. Insofar as action is
purposive, the more differentiated the action the more
differentiated the goals when considered on the lowest

---

40. The concept of universalism is taken up for definition and discussion below. See pp. 248-255.

41. See above, pp. 172-173.

42. The same generalization in this respect has been
made above about intermediate cognitive orientations.

level of generalization. If one shifts, however, to consider institutionalized patterns, a less obvious consideration emerges. The more elaborately differentiated one
institutionalized pattern is from another the more elaborately differentiated the institutionalized goal system
will have to be. This is not necessarily so of the total
goal system, however, though one might reasonably expect
it to be. There are always to some extent goal orientations that are not institutionalized,[43] and in some cases
the noninstitutionalized goal orientations might conceivably offset a difference in complexity of institutionalized
ones. Ordinarily one would not expect this to be the case,
however, since the elements of unpredictability and lack
of control to which such a situation, if general, would
give rise would almost certainly negate the functional
requisites at some point or other.

The goals, whether of the intermediate or basic value
orientations variety, must be sufficiently articulated to
insure the performance of socially necessary activities if
the society is to persist. This they must do positively,
and on the negative side they must not insure action that
threatens the existence of a society. A cult of sexual
abstinence, if sufficiently widespread, would terminate a
society. All the above must not, however, be construed to
mean that the systems of goals in societies cannot contribute to the disorganization and instability of a society.
To do so would be to fall into the fallacy of functional
teleology. The goal systems of a society commonly and, no
doubt, inevitably have dysfunctional as well as eufunction-

---

43. The inevitability of noninstitutionalized aspects
of action in societies is not to be overlooked. Just as
the factors of human heredity and nonhuman environment set
limits within which variation may take place, so do the
functional and structural requisites and the institutionalized structures. If all action were completely institutionalized, action would be completely determinate. This
point is discussed at somewhat greater length in another
connection. See below, pp. 180-181.

al aspects. If the society is to persist, their dysfunctional aspects cannot, of course, outweigh their eufunctional aspects. The dysfunctional aspects, however, may
be strong indeed, even though the society persists. For
example, if an industrial society is to operate, great
emphasis must be placed on competition and on achieved
roles. For reasons too complex to go into here, a significant proportion of the members of such a society must have
as one of their goals a rise in the stratification system
through objective achievements in competition on a highly
universalistic basis. This goal orientation is eufunctional in that it affords a large field from which to pick
persons for increased efficiency and achievement rather
than a more restricted one, and this in turn is eufunctional because the industrial society is one in which comparatively small differences in ability may have dispropor-
tionately large effects on performance because of the
complex multiplication of effort added by the use of
modern machines and because of the relatively delicately
balanced interstitial adjustments of machine processes.
This is patent in the sphere of occupational roles, but it
is true in other respects as well. On the other hand, in
the face of widespread "motivation" for upward social mobility based on competitive achievement, many of the striv-
ers are bound to be frustrated in seeking their goals.
This frustration has dysfunctional aspects that may take
many forms of socially disruptive behavior. Such behavior
is to some degree offset by still other goals such as the
observance of the rules of fair play, the conduct of a
good loser (or winner), etc. This is one form of the
articulation of goals, but the fact remains that one given
goal may, as in the example chosen, have both eufunctional
and dysfunctional aspects.

There are other sources of dysfunctional aspects than
that mentioned above. One of the commonest met in societies is the presence of goals that are to some extent

mutually incompatible. "Individualism" and "maximization of the general welfare," for example, may result in quite sharp conflicts under some circumstances. Some of both may be functionally requisite in a given system, in which case the dysfunctional aspects of the contradiction must be kept below a point negating the eufunctional aspects if the society is to persist as defined.[44] If this is not done, change will take place. Some goals may be mutually incompatible without being destructive to the society, though this cannot be the case if both are functional requisites for the society and affect the same members at the same time.

It has already been said above that the goals must be shared to some degree, though this will vary with the differentiation of the society. The goals of one individual must also be meaningful to another insofar as they share a common structure of action. Finally, the goals concerned will be both empirical and nonempirical. If no one sought empirical goals, the minimum of subsistence necessary for biological survival could not be maintained. A state of apathy would exist. The material goals sought in societies are never confined solely to the biological minimum, but these must obviously be present if there is to be persistence. But the nonempirical goals are of no less importance. It is in terms of ultimate ends (or goals) (i.e., ends that are not considered means to further ends) that men order their intermediate ones. These nonempirical goals may take conventional religious forms such

---

44. It must be kept in mind continuously that the terms eufunctional and dysfunctional do not mean good and bad. They are defined relative to a particular unit the adjustment or adaptation of which to its setting furnishes the criteria for a given function's classification as a eufunction or dysfunction. Nothing need be said in the course of analysis about the goodness or badness of the unit or the goodness or badness of its adaptation and adjustment or its lack in these respects.

as admission to heaven, attainment of _nirvana_, unity with
the _tao_, or the like. They may also take the form of
seeking to attain ethical values that are never completely
identified with empirical states of affairs in the minds
of the individuals concerned (e.g., the role played by
"democracy" in the value systems of many "idealists").
Men who scorn the conventional religious systems may still
seek "the good life," and when asked what this consists
in, they are rarely able to give definitions of the end
sought in solely empirical terms.

It is thus understandable that the goal systems in
all societies be to some degree indeterminate. The concept, _indeterminate goal systems_, is defined as goal
systems that do not identify all possible goals in the
actions of the members of the society. To some degree
elements of indeterminacy exist because some of the goals
are of a nonempirical character and have not been tied to
particular empirical referents. Another element of indeterminacy exists in that even those goals that are empirically defined do not eliminate all possible ranges of
variation in the intermediate means-ends schema leading to
their own accomplishment. Whatever may have been the
"cause" of this universal lack of determinacy, it is easy
enough to discern the apparently insuperable obstacles to
complete determinacy. In the first place, a completely
determinate goal system would have to encompass the entire
range of _possible_ variation of action within the society
concerned. If this range of variation does not permit of
an infinite number of different goals, then at least the
number is such a large finite one as to make the establishment of the goal system an unending task from the point of
view of any particular group of humans. In the second
place, such a system of goals, if possible, would be so
enormously complex and extensive as to preclude any individual's learning of all of it even insofar as it applied
to him. And finally, if these first two difficulties could

be overcome, there would result a fixity of action such
that the members of such a society could not adjust to any
new circumstances that might arise from even slight changes
in the limits of possible variation. The whole argument
about such a completely determinate goal system is, of
course, in essence beside the point, if only because of the
cognitive problems involved. For such a goal system to
exist, there would have to be complete knowledge of the
limits of possible variation of social action, and for the
present at least three sources of indeterminacy have been
listed in these factors themselves.[45]

It may be added that this indeterminacy is one well
understood in a sense by the members of all societies; at
least all societies seem to make allowances for this condition because in all known societies there are understood
arbiters of these matters when indeterminacies arise.
These arbiters may be more or less well defined, but in
some degree they are always present. Some groups rest
responsibility in these respects on the individual members.
The Anabaptists carried this principle to an extreme. Some
groups allocate these decisions to priests, chiefs, courts,
parents, dictators, legislative bodies, synods, and an
unending list of other socially defined positions or organizations. In the absence of such resorts or in defiance
of the established ones, social conflicts ranging from the
hysteria of a child to social revolution of the bloodiest
sort may result without checks.

Nevertheless, despite the mixture of empirical and
nonempirical goals, the indeterminacy of goal systems, the
presence of mutually incompatible goals, and the lack on
the part of each member of the society of complete knowledge about the total goal system of the society, without
a relatively well-articulated and clearly defined set of
goals a society would invite extinction, apathy, or the

---

45. See above, pp. 12-18.

war of all against all.

F. THE REGULATION OF THE CHOICE OF MEANS

This functional requisite is the prescription of means
for attaining the socially formulated goals of a society
and its substructures. It complements but is not identical
with the functional requisite of "the effective control of
disruptive forms of behavior," including as this latter
does the control of the use of force. The regulation of
the choice of means defines positively the means (mostly
noncoercive) to the society's goals. There is another
obviously complementary relationship involved, that with
the systems of goals, since many of the goals in a goal
system are goals from one point of view and means to other
goals from another.

That some of the means for the attainment of social
goals must be clearly stated for the sake of order and the
effective functioning of the society follows from the
problems posed by the unit society in its setting. Given
factors such as scarcity, the interdependence of individuals (e.g., infants cannot survive without adults, societies cannot persist without infants), and the like, social
anomie would result from the lack of recognized legitimized
means. First, patterns of role differentiation tell who
is to act, while the common articulated set of goals
defines what is to be done. There must be regulation of
the choice of means to tell how these goals may be won.
Secondly, the absence of regulation of means invites apathy
or the war of all against all. Without socially prescribed
means, a goal must either be devalued or the road to its
attainment must be left open to considerations based solely
on instrumental efficiency. As the loss of a bolt may
permit a great machine to beat itself to pieces, so the
absence of regulated choice of means operates cumulatively
to destroy the social structure.

Especially in ritual and initiatory activities must

procedures be specified. The contents of prescriptions
may vary greatly among societies. What is indispensable
is simply that there exist socially accepted directives
for ceremonial and symbolic action. This point emphasizes
the necessity for the category of regulation of the choice
of means, in addition to the effective control of disruptive behavior. Moreover, there are often alternative
noncoercive ways of realizing goals, and they must be differentially evaluated for the sake of order, or some must
be ruled out.

G. THE REGULATION OF AFFECTIVE EXPRESSION

The term _affect_ as used here follows Parsons' usage[46]
in that it includes "components of pleasurable or painful
significance to the actor, and of approval or disapproval
of the object or state which occasions the reaction," but
it includes also those reactions to stimuli that are
commonly catalogued under the term "emotions," covering as
that does such inadequately defined and understood terms
as "anger," "hate," "fear," "love," "pity," etc.[47] Four
aspects of the regulation of affective expression will be
touched on here. In the first place, in any society the
affective states[48] of the members must be mutually communi-

---

46. _op.cit._, p. 32.

47. The present highly unsatisfactory definition of
the term _affect_ is one of those cases in which, for the
present at least, it seems wise to "sin bravely" and go
ahead with the work.

48. The affective orientations of individuals in a
society are capable of the same classificatory distinctions
made above in relation to cognitive and goal orientations.
It is thus useful to distinguish in the same way among
basic affective orientations, intermediate affective orientations of both the institutionalized and noninstitutionalized sorts: there will be crucial or more or less strategic ones, and they will be more or less strategic substantively and/or critically speaking. See above pp. 171-173.

cable and comprehensible. Secondly, not every affect can
be expressed in every situation. Some must be suppressed
or repressed. Thirdly, there are affects that must be
produced in the members if the social structure is to survive. Finally, there must be regulation of the lengths to
which affective expression is carried even when it is
comprehensible, appropriate, and socially eufunctional.
All of these aspects are included in the regulation of
affective expression.

In the absence of the first of these conditions stability of expectations between individuals is destroyed, and
apathetic or destructuve reactions will occur. This is
true both of states of anger and of affection, love, lust,
and the like.[49] Without comprehensibility and communica-
bility, mutually inappropriate responses in affectively
charged situations can only result in the destruction of
the relationship. In a love affair, if one member's
expression of affection has the meaning to her of a flir-
tation, while to her partner it signifies willingness to
consummate the affair, and he is affectively involved, the
relationship is headed for a crisis. The same state of
affairs with regard to the expression of affect in an
entire society is clearly incompatible with the continuation of that society. This is not a matter of a lack of a
shared cognitive frame of reference; the conflicts are
potentially explosive because of the emotional involvement,
or the situations are potentially apathetic because of a
lack of such involvement. The cues that make affective
expression comprehensible range from obvious and subtle
linguistic behavior to posture, facial expression, gesture,
and tone of voice.[50] Many of these are not consciously

---

49. It may be that gross affective states are mutually communicable in the absence of regulation, but such
communication is not sufficient to obviate all the problems raised here.

50. e.g., consider that recurrent opening phrase for

recognized by the actors themselves. There is, of course,
a cognitive element involved in all this. One must learn
to know the signs of the affective states, and these, like
other cognitive matters, must to a degree be shared in
common. But the communication and comprehensibility of
affective states cannot be confined to the cognitive level.
It is not enough in many social situations to know that
another is angry. It is necessary to respond affectively
in some appropriate way whether this be sympathetic anger,
pity, antagonistic anger, or one of a large number of other
affective possibilities. The person who does not respond
affectively in affectively charged situations is sometimes
invaluable, but he is also often the most upsetting sort
of person possible.

In the face of regulated competitive, cooperative, and
authority relationships, some of which are entailed in any
conceivable system of role allocation, taken together with
disturbances of expectation and scarcity situations, no
society can survive a complete latitude of affective expression. The ungoverned expression of lust and rage leads
to the disruption of relationships and ultimately to the
war of all against all. At the other extreme, apathy may
result. Expression of fear and grief, for example, must
be kept within certain bounds -- granted different ones in
different situations and in different societies, but always
within some bounds. Love is another obvious case in these
respects, especially when considered in its sexual aspects.
In all societies some bounds are placed on this expression
to avoid conflicts (e.g., incest taboos, adultery taboos,
premarital taboos, etc.) and some to prevent preoccupation
with this emotion and no other action (e.g., limits on
appropriate times, ages, and places for this activity).

---

conflicts between all sorts of persons (e.g., small boys,
husbands, and wives, etc.) in our society; "It ain't what
you said: it's the way you said it."

A society must not only structure the way in which affects are expressed and restrict certain forms of affective expression, but it must also actively foster some affects. Unless one adopts the view that all relationships in all societies can be rational and contractual in character, one must take the position that some relationships depend on regulated affects for their perpetuation.[51]   In the absence of the production of appropriate affects, the "family," for example, would not survive. The question of what affects must regularly be produced in any society is closely related to the way other functional requisites are fulfilled. In American society the "urban middleclass conjugal family" depends heavily upon the establishment of strong affective ties based on romantic love between spouses. Japanese society deemphasizes structures of romantic love, emphasizes respect between son and father, and uses an individual's strong reaction to ridicule and shame to control such behavior.

Finally, there must be further regulation of affect even when the three above forms of regulation are in effect. The primary bond of solidarity in the American family is that between husband and wife, and it is based upon romantic love. It is, however, a sign of immaturity, even of prolonged adolescence, if the individuals let their affective preoccupations with one another make them irresponsible in other respects. It is good in that situation to love fiercely, sincerely, monogamously, and even to the death, but, after the courtship and perhaps the honeymoon period, devotion to one's wife becomes ridiculous if it prevents responsible performance of an acceptable occupational role. In Tokugawa Japan, respect for one's father took a secondary place if its dictates conflicted with one's loyalty to one's overlord. So it goes. The situation

---

51. The material discussed above in Note 32, p. 169, may be applied here in connection with affective orientation.

is perhaps not one of the Aristotelian mean, but it is one
of limits. However praiseworthy the affect, it can be
overdone from the point of view of the patterns of the society. Uncontrolled, a just anger becomes a blind rage,
a touching love becomes maudlin, prudent fear becomes
neurotic anxiety, and so it goes.

One further word may be said of these four aspects of
the regulation of affective expression. They not only appear in the actual affective patterns of society, but they
also appear powerfully reflected in its systems of humor.
A moment's reflection will call to mind jokes based on
failures to respond correctly in one or another respect.
There is, for example, in the system of American humor a
well worn stock of these jokes. There is the husband who
cannot understand his wife's chagrin or the wife who cannot understand her husband's humor; there is the person
who laughs and cries at the "wrong" time; there is the
person who fails to laugh at the "right" time; and finally
there is the person who laughs "immoderately," though at
the right time. All of these serve their roles as figures
of fun just as in other connections they may become vil-
lains in novels or hapless strugglers in motion pictures,
and in so doing they illustrate the extreme breadth of the
understanding of these matters.

H. ADEQUATE SOCIALIZATION

By the term socialization is meant the inculcation of
the structure of action of a society on an individual (or
group). Socialization in this sense is a matter of degree.
An individual may be more or less socialized. An individual is adequately socialized if he has been inculcated with
a sufficient portion of the structures of action of his society to permit the effective performance of his roles in
the society. There is adequate socialization in a society
if there is a sufficient number of adequately socialized
individuals for the structural requisites of a society to
operate.

The requisite nature of adequate socialization arises
from the hypothesis that it is not the nature of human
beings to acquire on a hereditary basis or through the
interaction of heredity and nonhuman environment the structures of action necessary for effective functioning in
their minimally required roles. Although it has not in any
strict sense been proved that specific structures are not
acquired in such a fashion, the general plasticity of human
beings in these respects, the wide range of structures of
action extant throughout the world, and the lack of knowledge of any genetic structures directly determining specific social structures[52] would seem to make the foregoing

---

52. The concept of <u>social structures</u> used here relative to human beings refers, of course, to those structures
of action that occur within limits set by human heredity
and nonhuman environment. If it can be demonstrated that
no such range of variation exists, that in fact the specific structures of action are capable of analysis and explanation in terms of heredity and nonhuman environment, then,
of course, it follows that all social studies become a
branch of biology and that all work of a nonbiological nature is beside the point. Whether this is true <u>sub specie
aeternitatis</u> may never be known to modern scientists, but
at least it has not been proved by them as yet.
    The above may seem to be simply a matter of defini-
tion, but this is not the case. It is true that by definition <u>social</u> structures refer to structures not uniquely determined by the factor of species' heredity and nonspecies'
environment, i.e., structures within a range of variation
having these factors as limits. The question raised, however, is not whether the analysis is consistent with the
definition but rather whether the concept as defined has
in fact any empirical referent. It is the assumption for
the present that it does for the reasons given. Further,
the contrary hypothesis has not been proved, and work based
on the assumption used here, and used implicitly or explicitly by virtually all social analysts, does seem to throw
some light on human action. If the contrary hypothesis can
be demonstrated, i.e., if the concept used here can be
shown to have no empirical referent or if the use of the
present assumption adds nothing to the fruitfulness of
analysis as compared with analysis based on the contrary
hypothesis, then much, if not most, of the works of the
"social sciences" will have proved a waste of effort, and
that which remains will be more "biological" than "social."

hypothesis a reasonable one until facts to the contrary are produced. Even those social structures most directly and obviously related to hereditarily determined structures show few signs of specific genetic determination. Structures of walking, defecation, sexual contacts, breathing, and the like, all exhibit a range of possible variation within limits set by heredity and nonhuman environment rather than an exact determination. If one uses the contrary hypothesis to that used here, all further analysis of the acquisition of the structures of action must be in terms of advance in the knowledge of human genetics and the nonhuman environment.

Societies can, of course, persist with some inadequately socialized members, and the number or proportion of these relative to the total membership of a society will vary from society to society. Nevertheless, for the society to persist there must be transmitted specifically to each individual so much of the minimum necessary quota of adequately socialized personnel, so much of the modes of dealing with the total situation, of the modes of communication, of the shared cognitive orientations, goal systems, attitudes involved in the regulation of means, modes of affective expression, and the like, as will render him capable of adequate performance in his several roles throughout life, both as respects skills and attitudes. Socialization is thus a different concept from the maintenance of the individual in a state of biological well-being.

Socialization is not, of course, confined to the necessity of inculcating the social structures on the infant of a society (those individuals comprising what has sometimes been called the "periodic barbarian invasion of a society"). Socialization includes both the development of new adult members from infants and the induction of an individual of any age into any role of the society or its subsystems in which new learning is required. By definition the infants will be there as members of the unit here called society, but other new members may come from other sources than the sexual reproduction of the members of a society. Furthermore, in some societies new roles are continuously being opened up. This is most striking perhaps in so-called "modern industrial" societies, but it has to some degree been a prominent feature of many societies, and it is probably not entirely lacking in any society.

A society cannot persist unless it perpetuates a self-sufficient system of action, whether in changed or traditional form, through the socialization of new members drawn in part from the maturing generation. Whatever the defects of any particular mode of socialization, a universal failure of socialization means the extinction of the society through a combination of at least three of the terminating conditions mentioned previously for reasons which are certainly sufficiently obvious.

The complexities of individual development arising from the interaction of individuals of varying constitutional endowment with the modes of child care and socialization and various other aspects of the social interaction, as well as with less predictable situations, cannot be dealt with here. It is sufficient to say that no socialization system is ideally efficient, that in no society are all individuals socialized equally well, nor is any one individual perfectly socialized. One individual cannot become equally familiar with all aspects of his society; indeed he may remain completely ignorant of some. But he must acquire a working knowledge of the behavior and attitudes relevant to his various roles, and identify to some degree with such values as are shared by the whole society or segments thereof, whenever his behavior articulates with that of other members of the society. A Brahmin and an Untouchable learn some skills and attitudes unknown to one another. Both, however, must learn that the Hindu world is made up of castes and that this is the way things "should" be. Socialization is to a large extent a "learn-

ing-teaching" process, if indeed it is not that exclusively. As such it involves elements of cognition as well as
others. It is not, however, identical with cognition any
more than role differentiation is synonymous with provision
for adequate physiological relationship to the setting of
action, though the two certainly are mutually involved.

I. EFFECTIVE CONTROL OF DISRUPTIVE FORMS OF BEHAVIOR

Prominent among these disruptive forms of behavior are
force and fraud. The extent to which such behavior will
occur is dependent on the way that various other functional
requisites are met: role allocation, goal systems, regulation of means and of expression, and socialization being
the more obvious cases in point. All of these functional
requisites, it should be clear from the preceding discussion, are conditions that tend to prevent the occurrence
of disruptive behavior but that may also bring it on.[53] In
addition to, and separate from, these is the effective
control of such behavior when it does occur. To understand
why this function is a requisite, one must ask, "Why would
not a perfectly integrated society exist in its absence?"
The answer lies in three conditions inherent in the
relation of any society to its setting: (1) scarcity of
means, (2) frustrations of expectations, and (3) imperfections of socialization. That many of the desiderata of
life are ultimately scarce needs no further emphasis. It
is not simply a question of quantity. For even if more
food than could be consumed were readily available, there
would still remain the possibility of two or more persons
wanting exactly the same pig. Since sexual objects are
differentially evaluated by the members of society, those
few at the top of the scale tend to be sought by a large

---

53. i.e., they may have dysfunctional aspects as well
as eufunctional ones.

number of the opposite sex. Wealth, however defined, is
basically scarce for the mass of individuals everywhere.
Force and fraud are in many situations the most efficient
ways of acquiring scarce values. Indeed only scarce values
can be objects of rationally directed coercive effort.
Even if in fact "crime does not pay," disruptive behavior
can result if individuals are convinced that it will. To
argue that a society without coercion and deceit can exist,
one must first demonstrate the absence of scarcity.

Frustration of expectations is inevitable for some
individuals in any society as long as there are such universal realities as unexpected consequences of purposive
behavior, scarcity, and uncertainty. Uncertainty alone
would account for the presence of some such frustration.
To banish all possible uncertainty would require complete
and accurate knowledge of all empirical phenomena, past
and future, by every member of the society, and this would
only eliminate the cognitive problem involved. With complete knowledge the problem of control would still remain.
Lack of control would carry with it some inevitable frustrations as the result of sickness, storms, and the like,
not to mention the lack of social controls.

Imperfections in socialization result, among other
things, in evasions of the institutionalized structures of
action. Together with frustrations of expectations it
results in explosive outbursts of anger and violence.[54]
Thus, both rationally directed exercise of force and
fraud[55] and nonrational outbursts of emotion continually

---

54. Other disruptive modes of behavior, including
apathy, also may occur. But a refined analysis of the
problem of deviant behavior is beyond the scope of the present work.

55. There is always some rational component intended
in the case of fraud at least. Fraud consists for most
purposes of definition in the conscious attempt to gain
empirical ends by means, short of the use of force, that
are institutionally defined as illegitimate.

press to disrupt stable social relationships. If resort to these disruptive behaviors is restricted only by opportunity, the war of all against all will ultimately result either from rational, irrational, or arational calculations.[56] Some disruptive action may also tend in the direction of an apathetic breakdown, though it is perhaps unnecessary to elaborate on this aspect of the argument.

The system of goals tells _what_ must be done; the regulation of means prescribes _how_. It also includes prescriptions and proscriptions regarding the use of force and fraud. In addition, however, the society must have techniques for handling those who, for reasons outlined above or for others, use these disruptive means or are subject to disruptive outbreaks. The structures of control and the degree of their efficiency may vary greatly. What type of action is directly destructive of a given society will vary with the nature of that society: parricide in a society based on patriarchal clans, violation of property rights in a society emphasizing property, and so on. Conversely, some societies can tolerate forms of these behaviors that others cannot. Chukchee social structure, for example, withstands a high homicide rate if one is to believe the anthropological materials available. But no society can withstand any and all of them without exception or control.

J. ADEQUATE INSTITUTIONALIZATION

The term _institution_ has been defined above.[57] The existence of institutions in a society is a functional requisite for the existence of any society. Discussion of the standing of institutionalization as a functional requisite may be broken down into the categories of normative

---

56. For definition of the terms rational, nonrational, irrational, and arational see below, pp. 242-244.

57. See p. 102.

patterns, the conformity aspects of institutions, and the sanctions aspects. It will be readily seen, when this is done, that this functional requisite, like its fellows, involves aspects of other functional requisites. To a greater extent than is true of the others, it may seem to be analytically mixed up with its fellows, to lack distinctness. This may be a valid objection to its separate standing in the list of functional requisites, and yet the combination it represents of normative patterns, conformity aspects, and sanctions aspects does seem to have an analytical distinctness.[58] At any rate, whether this factor deserves a separate listing in such a treatment as this, the condition referred to deserves a special emphasis that would be lost in the absence of separate treatment.

One of the major concepts of the general theory of social action which underlies a treatment of this sort is the concept of the normative orientation of action. And one of the major tenets of that theory is that action is normatively oriented. This argument has been most systematically explored in the work, both published and unpublished, of Parsons. One sees elements of it in his early essays on Marshall,[59] the English economist, and it continues throughout his books, essays, and lectures. Given the fact that human heredity and nonhuman environment determine, in general, a range of possible variation of action rather than specific forms of action, it is hard to see an alternative to the assumption that man's actions are consciously oriented to normative considerations of objects and standards held to be "good" and "bad," more or

---

58. Testing of the separate status of this functional requisite by the use of symbolic logic is, unfortunately, beyond the capabilities of the author.

59. T. Parsons, "Wants and Activities in Marshall," Quart. Jour. of Eco., Vol. 46, No. 1 (Nov. 1931), pp. 101-140, and "Economics and Sociology: Marshall in Relation to the Thought of His Time," Quart. Jour. of Eco., Vol. 46, No. 2 (Feb. 1932), pp. 316-347.

less "valuable," and so on. If this is not the case, the
analyst is faced with two problems in the place of one:
(1) what alternative exists to play the role of normative
orientation in a theory of "motivation" of action, and (2)
what explains the extremely persistent illusion on the part
of men that they do act in terms of such orientations?

At any rate, in all of the functional requisites
treated above normative structures enter. There are normative structures involved, for example, even in such categories as cognitive orientations and communications (e.g.,
that these systems should be intelligible and eufunctional
for the operation of the system). The normative aspects
of other of the categories is more obvious. Goals are
norms or contain normative elements by definition, and an
attempt has been made above to demonstrate the necessity
of the existence of a system of them if a society is to
persist. In the regulation of means and affective expression the normative aspects are equally obvious. In essence,
social regulation, whatever its form, be it persuasion or
force, involves evaluation and discrimination. A vital
element in socialization is the learning of the normative
structures that are maintained in a given society and so
forth.

If one studies the normative structures of a society,
one finds that, with regard to some of them as a minimum,
conformity must be generally expected. In the absence of
normative structures, given the assumption of the normative
orientation of action, apathy would certainly exist. In
the absence of a generally expected conformity with certain
of these structures it would be impossible to predict one's
own actions and those of others sufficiently to carry out
action. The way would be open for either a bewilderment-
produced apathy or a war of all against all undertaken
because of the efficiency of the use of force in a chaotic
situation.

The sanction aspects of institutions seem to enter as

a necessity as a means of bringing about conformity and
handling failures to conform. The structures of sanctions
may vary, but what is involved here is more than the control of deviant behavior. Something has been stated about
those structures. The sanction elements must contain elements of affective expression on the part of the populace
at large. In the absence of such elements it is perhaps
impossible to maintain the sanctions in sufficient force
to maintain conformity. There is no known case in which
affective neutrality to the normative structures of a society is maintained throughout the society, and indeed this
is not to be expected, since actors orient themselves affectively as well as normatively and cognitively.

Discussion may now turn to the qualifying term
adequate which precedes institutionalization. Institutionalization is "adequate" if its conformity and sanction
aspects are carried sufficiently far to permit the persistence of the minimal normative structures involved in other
functional requisites. In structural terms this means the
existence of a full set of crucial institutions, that is
to say, the structural requisites of a society must be
institutionalized if a society is to persist. The absence
of such institutionalization would leave a situation of
indeterminacy incompatible with the existence of a society.
It must be noted that the institutionalization of a structural requisite does not guarantee its existence or its
maintenance. These matters will depend upon the degree to
which its conformity and sanction aspects are in fact
carried out. Nevertheless, the contrary situation, the
noninstitutionalization of the structural requisite, would
guarantee chaos through nonconformity alone. Empirically,
neither possibility is ruled out. In a given social system a structural requisite may be more or less institutionalized or it may be noninstitutionalized. If the
former is the case, then on this particular score the
system will be more or less stable (depending, in this

respect, on the degree of institutionalization). In the
latter case, or cases of extremely low degrees of institutionalization, the nonpersistence of the system may be
predicted. If, in fact, there is <u>no</u> conformity, the structure does not exist as a structure of a society, and its
only possible "existence" is as an aspect of culture as
that concept is used here.

The reader will note throughout the above treatment,
and nowhere more markedly than in the last topic treated
above, a continual reference to structures (or patterns),
though, in fact, the chapter has been concerned primarily
with functions. The close relation is not to be avoided,
for functions are the results of the operation of structure. Subsequent treatment, with the help of the above,
will now pass directly to structural considerations.

C H A P T E R   V

SOME METHODOLOGICAL PROBLEMS

This chapter is intended to serve as an introduction
to the second part of this volume, which concerns itself
with the structural features that are present in any society. This treatment in turn will be divided into two parts.
The primary consideration will be a series of chapters
dealing with the analytic structural requisites of any society. A chapter will be devoted to each one of these requisites and will treat it and its substructures insofar as
it is possible for present purposes to derive these categories without departing at any great length from the most
general level of the present type of analysis, i.e., structures present in any society. Preceding this there will be
a chapter on certain structural aspects of any relationship.
The reasons for this procedure will be discussed in the
present chapter. The general topics to be covered in the
present chapter will be the following: (A) the distinction
between concrete and analytic structures, and the difficulties attendant to the use of the concept, concrete structural requisites, on the present level of analysis; (B) the
relationship structures and their general relevance to the
discussion of analytic structural requisites; (C) some of
the uses and difficulties involved in the application of
this type of conceptual development to comparative social
analysis; and (D) the relationship between conceptual development and its corresponding theoretical development.[1]

---

1. The reader may well view the treatment of the

A. THE DISTINCTION BETWEEN CONCRETE
AND ANALYTIC STRUCTURES

This distinction has been defined above in the second chapter of this volume. Concrete structures have been defined as "patterns of action that define the character of membership units involved in social action." Concrete structures include such structures as societies. Concrete substructures of societies may be defined as "the patterns of action that define the character of membership units involved in social action within a given society or those relating two or more societies." Analytic structures have been defined as "patterned aspects of action that are not even theoretically capable of concrete separation from other patterned aspects of action."[2] Society, as defined here, is the most general type of concrete structure. It is that concrete structure of which all other concrete structures are substructures (or they are substructures of two or more interacting societies). In any given case of a society there are concrete substructures. This condition is a corollary of the functional requisite of role differentiation.[3] Furthermore, given the definition of a particular society to be studied, it can be shown to have certain specific concrete structural requirements. For example, if one defines "United States society" in sufficient detail to isolate its present form, then a particular form of family structure, several specific forms of predominantly economic structures, and several specific

---

third and even the fourth of these topics as premature in this chapter -- as more properly following the discussion of structure rather than preceding it. The discussion is intended to give the reader further material on the specific orientation of the work so that he will have in mind, whether he agrees with it or not, the intention of the work.

2. See above, pp. 88-89.

3. See below, pp. 206-207.

forms of predominantly political structures can be shown to be structural requisites of the society.[4] If it is defined simply as a "modern industrial" society, some of these concrete substructures cease to be structural requisites while others will remain at least in a more general form. For example, in the first case, predominantly economic structures involving "factory" structures of production and "business" structures of management wil be requisite structures. In the latter case, there will also have to be predominantly economic structures involving "factory" structures of production although "business" structures of management need not be present.[5] "Traditional" Chinese society, on the other hand, required a specific type of family structure and virtually eliminated predominantly economic structures since the economic aspects of action were, at least in theory, almost inevitably organized on a family oriented basis rather than on the basis of "production-consumption" considerations isolated from family considerations.[6]

---

4. This, of course, says nothing of their being "good" or "bad," simply that they have some eufunctional implications for the persistence of the unit as defined. It may well be that within the society "liberal," "conservative," "radical," or "reactionary" opinions might be dedicated to their overthrow.

5. The entire argument necessary to support these examples is not produced here for obvious reasons. Quotation marks are placed around those terms whose definitions have not been given here but would be required for the supporting argument. It is hoped that a sufficient ground of common understanding exists in these cases to make the examples useful for heuristic purposes.

6. This, of course, does not mean that economic aspects were ignored or were only slightly valued. It does mean that in the case of a conflict of family interests and production-consumption interests, the former, ideally speaking, took precedence. The society was so structured that in fact such conflicts were reduced to a minimum. In "transitional" China many of the current problems stem in a sense from the fact that this situation no longer obtains. For analysis of this example ad nauseam see M. J. Levy, Jr., Family Revolution.

If one asks, however, what concrete structures are
structural requisites of <u>any</u> society, the matter is immensely more difficult. Here one is faced by the tremendous versatility of concrete structures. It is perfectly
true, and quite easy to show, that there must be concrete
structures in terms of which the allocation of goods and
services (i.e., the economic aspects of action) is carried
out. It is not, however, easy to show that they must be
carried out in terms of any particular concrete structure.
Such functions may be achieved largely by predominantly
economic structures, and one sees examples of this in the
United States where business managed membership units
carry out many of the major aspects of economic production
in the society and many of those of consumption as well.
In "traditional" China these functions were almost inevitably carried out by family units which, if predominantly
oriented to one or two analytic structures above all
others, may be said to have been oriented to the structures
of role differentiation and solidarity of that society.
In Soviet Russia one may hazard the guess that these functions are in fact carried out in terms of membership units
that are more predominantly politically oriented (i.e.,
oriented to power-responsibility allocations) than to
economic considerations. This is not to say that the
economic considerations are not of extreme importance in
the latter two cases, but merely that, if noneconomic considerations conflict with economic ones, the former and
not the latter take precedence, or are conceived to take
precedence by the actors involved.[7]

_____

7. For example, in "traditional" China aged fathers
were sometimes denied <u>de facto</u> power by their sons, and
often because of the fear of the sons that their fathers'
exercise of <u>de facto</u> power would be economically ruinous.
But such action was, ideally at least and probably actually, inevitably undertaken because of what such economic
action would mean to the future of the family. If the future of the family was not threatened, such restraint of
the aged fathers was not in order. See M. J. Levy, Jr.,
<u>op.cit</u>., pp. 64-65 and 128-133

One is forced to recognize the fact that various types
of functions can result from the operation of concrete
structures not primarily oriented to any one of the particular functions or even to a specific group of those
under study at any one time. The analytic structures are
another matter. It is relatively easy to demonstrate that
certain specific analytic structures must be present in any
society. For example, in the absence of some structures
having to do with the allocation of goods and services,
i.e., some economic structures, it can be shown that certain aspects of the list of functional requisites cannot
be met.[8] On the other hand, the very flexibility of concrete structures, the fact that one primarily oriented to
role differentiation, for example, may also determine the
allocation of goods and services, militates against pinning
down a specific list of concrete structural requisites.
The present writer suspects that in each society there are
in fact some concrete structures primarily oriented to
each of the analytic structural requisites, that some are
predominantly role differentiation structures, some predominantly solidarity structures, some predominantly
economic structures, and so forth. If, however, any sound
argument of an empirical rather than an a priori nature
exists to prove this point, it has for present purposes
proved elusive. The possibility must not be ignored,
however, for if a group of concrete structural requisites
for any society can be demonstrated, it will add immensely
to the power of the present tools for comparative analysis.
It would provide a whole range of an alternative type of
structures which could, with a high degree of certainty, be
relied upon as sine qua non structures for any society.
The use of this range of structures in conjunction with the
analytic ones would greatly increase the known factors,
specific exemplifications of which would have to be sought

---

8. This matter is taken up below in Chapter IX.

in any particular society.

In order to elucidate this whole problem further, it is useful to consider a particular possibility in this connection. Some forms of "family" structure appear apparently in all known societies. By family structure is meant the smallest kinship unit on a membership basis that is treated as a unit for generalized purposes by other parts of the society and by other parts of the kinship structure. By kinship structure is meant that portion of the total institutionalized structure of the society that, in addition to other orientations, sometimes equally, if not even more important, determines the membership of its units and the nature of the solidarity among its members by orientation to the facts of biological relatedness and cohabitation.[9]

It is at least a possibility that a given society have only two types of concrete substructures on the level of generality immediately below that of the society itself. It is possible that all other structures, both analytic and concrete, in the society are either concrete subdivisions of, or analytically differentiated, aspects of the family type structure and one other. The one other structure would be some structure specifically interrelating different families. The necessity of a second type of concrete structure arises from the apparently universal factor of the incest taboo and its parallel explanation as a functional requisite of family structures. It would take the argument too far afield to discuss these aspects of the incest taboo in this place. It has been discussed with varying emphases in many sources well known to students of social phenomena and specifically, though briefly, in this connection in at least one place.[10]   Suffice it to

---

9. These definitions of family and kinship structure follow with only slight modification those advanced by M. J. Levy, Jr., op.cit., pp. 3 and 5.

10. M. J. Levy, Jr., op.cit., pp. 19-22.

say that for present purposes the empirical generality of
the incest taboo rests on the same sort of evidence as the
empirical generality of the family. As far as is known to
the author no unit conforming to the definition used here
of a society is totally lacking in either family structure
or incest taboos. This factor alone would require some
differentiation of the families of orientation and procrea-
tion of some of the individuals in the society. Hence,
not all the individuals can be in one family unit, and so
there must be more than one family unit. This in turn
argues for the necessity of some concrete structure to
regulate, arbitrate, and otherwise mix in interfamilial
relationships. Such a structure might be a family council
or a "government" or any one of a number of types of concrete structure, but it could not very well be in turn a
family. As a minimum it would have functions and structures different for general purposes than those of other
family structures.

The line of reasoning above is undertaken briefly to
illustrate the fact that, given any particular type of concrete structure in a society, one can say something of
other concrete structural requisites, but this does not
establish any particular concrete structure as a requisite.
The generally accepted prevalence of the family structure
seems to argue strongly that it is a structural requisite
of any society, but it does not prove it, and to assume
that it does is to fall into the error of structural teleology.

One may even go a step further without reaching con-
clusive results in this case. On the basis of evidence
such as cited above in Chapter IV,[11] it may be assumed that
the infant of the human species needs a great deal of
attention from adults if it is to become a reasonably
stable and mature individual. Much of this attention must

---

11. e.g., pp. 166-167.

apparently be of a sort such that the infant is given a
sense of "security" and "belonging," a sense that he is
"loved," etc. Apparently, in all societies this has been
done at least to some extent in terms of family units.
Only in utopias and other imaginary societies are all the
infants in general turned over in toto to total "strangers,"
i.e., to persons who have no particularistic connection
with the infant. But this is not the same as proving that
in fact these functions of socialization and others associated with them cannot be performed by any other concrete
structure. The presence of a family system in every known
society may be the result of a lack of social invention.
One may, and the present author belongs to this school,
suspect that this latter is not the case, that on the contrary a family system is a concrete structural requisite
of any society, but it has not yet been proven.

On the other hand, the flexibility of concrete structure is quite well known and is relatively well understood.
It is, for example, well understood that functions (on the
most general level) performed in one society by operations
in terms of predominantly economic structures may be performed in another by operations in terms of the family or
in terms of predominantly political structures. In the
modern United States a great deal of economic production
is handled in terms of nonfamily structures. In "traditional" China relatively little was. There is hardly any
general type of function performed by operation in terms
of one type of concrete structure in one society that cannot be performed in terms of the operation of another in
some other society. It is the flexibility of concrete
structures in these respects, coupled with the lack of any
concrete evidence that even so empirically ubiquitous a
concrete structure as the family is a concrete structural
requisite, that leads this study to sidestep for the present any direct attack on the concrete structural requisites
of any society.

At the same time, one must not jump to the conclusion

that the same difficulty faces one in the consideration of
any specific society. In any specific society there will
be, of course, some concrete structures which are requisites of the society. The degree to which one may specify
them will vary with the level of generality of the definition of the unit, but as long as the unit is a particular
society, or even a particular type of society and not any
society, something more definite can be said on this score
since some specific concrete factors will have to be present in the definition of the unit.

With what has been said above as a basis of understanding, something may now be said to modify the position
taken in these respects. For the reasons given above the
approach here will proceed in terms of the analytic structural requisites of any society. But in the course of
their development and subsidiary to it, something may be
said of certain concrete structures. For example, in the
discussion of the structure of role differentiation it will
be shown that some differentiation of roles on the basis
of age must be made, and in the structure of economic
allocation it will be shown that some differentiation between production and consumption must exist if the society
is to persist. Thus, it may also be said that there will
be concrete structures of some sort in which age differentiations play a defining part and some in which production considerations play a defining part. Thus, it is
possible to isolate certain considerations that will prove
to be defining elements in some respects for concrete
structures in any society. What cannot be said is how
these defining elements will enter specific concrete structures. For example, the units of production may be made
up solely of members of particular age groups, or both the
units of production and the age groups may be parts of the
family structure. There may exist in a society a differentiation between infants and children but no organization
of infants and children as such except in family terms.

The same may be true of production workers. On the other
hand, this may not be the case. Male children may be
organized in membership units outside the family. These
units may even take precedence over family considerations.
The possibilities seem endless if viewed from the level of
any society. On the level of analysis of any society it
seems for the present advisable to stop with certain defining elements of the concrete structures of any society
rather than to attempt to derive the concrete structural
requisites themselves, if indeed the concept of concrete
structural requisite has any empirical referent on this
level of analysis.[12]

B. THE RELATIONSHIP STRUCTURES AND THEIR GENERAL RELE-
VANCE TO THE DISCUSSION OF ANALYTIC STRUCTURAL REQUISITES

    In discussion of societies or of any sorts of social
systems one is forced to consider these systems in terms
of some combination of their concrete structures and analytic structures. When one is not dealing with isolated

---

    12. Before leaving this point on so pessimistic a
note, a word of encouragement is possible. The analytic
structure of solidarity treated below in Chapter VIII may
be used in the case of any particular society to isolate
the concrete structural requisites. The material on the
analytic structure of solidarity attempts to isolate certain bases on which there must be solidarity among the
various members of any society and hence of relationships
that must be handled in terms of concrete structures. Examination of material gathered in these terms will highlight such concrete structures and hence lead to their isolation for any specific type of society. Such isolation
may also be arrived at by intuition or insight or previous
knowledge. Any advantage that lies in the technique referred to here lies in its systematic character and its
usefulness for these purposes relative to any society. The
discussion of the analytic structure of solidarity below
should make the use of that material for the purposes suggested here sufficiently obvious so that lengthy examples
are not required at this point.

individuals,[13] one is in addition always dealing to some
degree with the problem of relationships between individual
actors. In the case of concrete structure one deals with
membership units which from one point of view are aggregates of relationships in a particular type of socially
defined unit. In the case of analytic structure one deals
with different aspects of relationships or other concrete
structures. This suggests, then, a general approach to
social analysis via an investigation of the relationship
structure of the particular social unit under discussion.

There are, unfortunately, certain difficulties involved in such an approach. The approach has not, however,
been ignored by social scientists. The stronghold of what
may be called the relationship approach has, of course,
been the analysis of kinship structure. The fundamental
technique of this approach is to single out some individual
member of the unit to be studied and to ascertain his relations to all other members of the unit and to such other
outside units as interest dictates. The difficulty of the
technique is twofold. In the first place, to elaborate a
particular unit under study requires going through all its
aspects from the point of view of every conceivable member
of the unit since in relationship terms the unit is never
exactly the same from two different points of view (given
two different egos). In the second place, the kinship
structure of many, if not most, societies operates largely

---

13. The value for some purposes of dealing with isolated individuals may be considerable, and such researches
may well throw invaluable light on factors of general
structural relevance. This is especially likely to be so
relative to the general limits of possible variation. In
using and doing such research two precautions must be observed, however. First, one must be extremely careful to
state explicitly in just what sense the isolated individuals are isolated. Second, in using the knowledge acquired
from such researches one must take great care that the
sphere of application of such knowledge does not violate
the assumptions and specific state of affairs on which its
validity may hang.

in terms of membership units rather than in terms of individual relations. The preoccupation of past social science literature with the relational type of analysis of kinship is interesting from the point of view of wissensoziologie. It is possible that analysis tended in this direction partly because it developed in a society which not only placed great emphasis on "individualism" but also had a kinship structure that was unusually individualistic.[14] It is interesting to note that outside of kinship analysis this relationship approach has not been widely utilized. This is, on the whole, not difficult to understand. Complex though it may be, kinship structure isolates a segment of a society, and specific units isolate the analysis still further. A strict relational approach to a society numbering no more than a thousand members would no doubt furnish insupperable obstacles in terms of time and facilities for recording data. The permutations and combinations of relationships qua relationships even in a society of such small numbers would reach staggering proportions.

The difficulties of a strict relationship approach to the analysis of structures other than kinship structures, and especially of societies, are simply more or less magnified versions of the difficulties involved in confining kinship analysis almost entirely to the relationship approach. In the first place, the problem of going through an entire analysis from the point of view of each possible ego (or even type of ego)[15] is surely impractical from the

---

14. There is in this no intent to stigmatize the notable researches carried out in these terms. Work by social scientists along these lines has contributed markedly to the general store of knowledge. It may, however, be suggested that the contribution might be even greater if the relationship approach were at least combined with a systematic organizational or membership unit approach.

15. To the extent that the problem is broken down into types of egos, as it commonly is, elements which depart from a strict relationship approach are present. This is all to the good from the point of view of getting on with

point of view of a society.[16] In the second place, many,
if not most, societies and other social systems are not
"individualistically" oriented, and to the degree that this
is so, use of the relationship approach may lend a none too
subtle bias to the analysis.

On the other hand, relationships are not to be ignored
either, for they are certainly a ubiquitous phenomenon in
all societies and all other social systems as well. For
that reason two of the succeeding chapters focus attention
on relationship structures. Chapter VI, which follows,
concerns itself with certain general characterizations and
ranges of variation of any type of relationship, and Chapter VIII is concerned with the structure of solidarity of
a society in which considerable attention must be focused
on individual relationship patterns.

For the present, however, concern is with the considerations to be taken up in Chapter VI. At least six different aspects of relationships may be distinguished
analytically. These are as follows: (1) the cognitive
aspect, (2) the membership criteria aspect, (3) the substantive definition aspect, (4) the affective aspect, (5)
the goal orientation aspect, and (6) the stratification
aspect. The first five of these aspects are perhaps best
known for their appearance in an essay by Parsons.[17] The
sixth has long cropped up in one form or another in the

---

the job, but a systematic approach to such departures --
an approach such as that furnished by the membership unit
approach -- makes perhaps for more explicit analysis and
for wider coverage.

16. Some societies differentiate as many as some tens
of thousands of occupational roles alone. These represent
only different types of some different possible roles of
different egos.

17. "The Professions and Social Structure," Social
Forces, Vol. XVII, No. 4 (May 1939). Reprinted in Essays,
pp. 185-199. The reader who is familiar with this essay
will note the obvious indebtedness of Chapter VI to this
source despite some fairly considerable departures in definition from the original.

general tradition of social science. There is little question that in the course of development of the field other
ranges of variation relative to relationships will be added
to the list treated here, and furthermore, development of
those treated here will no doubt make considerable progress.
The matter is explored in this volume only within a quite
restricted range. Just enough of it is developed here to
provide some useful tools for characterizing the relationship structures relevant to the other concrete structures
and the analytic structures treated here. Relationships
insofar as they are not unique and unpatterned are, of
course, concrete structures that vary enormously in complexity depending upon the number of persons involved and
so forth. Even the limited analysis of these ranges of
variation available in Chapter VI should facilitate the
analysis of the other structural categories treated insofar
as relationships are relevant in these respects. Furthermore, some of these ranges of variation have implications
for one another and hence the presence of one of these
aspects means that the range of variation of the other aspects is in turn limited.

C. SOME OF THE USES AND DIFFICULTIES INVOLVED IN THE APPLICATION OF THIS TYPE OF CONCEPTUAL AND THEORETICAL DEVELOPMENT TO COMPARATIVE SOCIAL ANALYSIS

The first and most obvious case of the uses and difficulties of the matter treated here is that of comparison
of two different societies. One may assume for the present
that there are five analytic structural requisites of any
society and that each of the analytic structural requisites
has six subcategories. One may identify the structures by
the letters A,B,C,D, and E, and each of the subcategories
by one of the numbers, 1,2,3,4,5, or 6. The number of
structures and subcategories is here chosen merely for illustrative purposes. If there are in fact five analytic
structural requisites for any society, and each one of them

has six subcategories, then for each society one may set up in effect a box like that illustrated in Table 1. That

Table 1. General structural requisites
(and their subcategories) for any society

	A	B	C	D	E
1					
2					
3					
4					
5					
6					

is to say, there will be thirty different types of structures about which one must know something if that society is to be covered. Take for example the structure of role differentiation. In each society, as will be brought out below, there must be some structure of role differentiation, and as a minimum roles must be differentiated on the basis of age, sex, generation, economic allocation, political allocation, and religion.[18] If this is the case, then one must know as a minimum about six different types of role differentiation in any society, and so forth, with regard to the other structural requisites. Assuming the model used here for illustrative purposes is correct, the initial step in comparing two societies is to determine under thirty different headings in each case how these societies handle the structural requisites of any society. The dif-

----

18. At this point no attempt is made to define these terms or justify these statements. They are here used solely for illustrative purposes. The structure of role differentiation and the other structures and their subcategories mentioned here are taken up in the following Chapters. In the following treatment there are in fact five structural requisites, but it is not true that each has six subcategories.

ferences and similarities that emerge will give one the differences and similarities between the two societies on the most general level.

And now the cautions must begin. First, the fact that these two societies come up with similarities in all thirty categories on this level does not mean that they are identical or almost identical. It would merely mean that they are identical or almost identical on this particular level of generalization. At lower levels of generalization further differences may and commonly will emerge. Thus, on this level the United States and Great Britain would be very similar indeed, whereas at lower levels of generalization quite striking differences would emerge. There is a sense in which, in one respect, all societies are identical if this type of analysis is valid, and that is, of course, in the sense that all have these thirty different categories of structure. On the other hand, if at this level of analysis differences emerge, then differences of the societies at lower levels of generalization is a foregone conclusion (see Table 2). Thus, if the societies are similar in respects $A_1, A_3, A_5, B_1 \cdots$ and different in respects $A_2, A_4, B_2 \cdots$, two conclusions may be drawn: (1) further differences at lower levels of generalizations are to be looked for as a minimum in the development at lower levels of generalization of the categories $A_2, A_4, B_2 \cdots$, and (2) differences with respect to still other categories, which on this level are similar, are to be expected on lower levels of generalization insofar as it can be shown that at such levels the factors treated in $A_2, A_4, B_2 \cdots$ are interdependent with other structures.[19] Thus, even if effort were confined to this most general level at the

_____

19. This whole discussion involves the relation between the conceptual scheme used and the theoretical structure which accompanies it. This matter is taken up specifically in the final section of this chapter. See pp. 226-237.

Table 2. Comparison of two societies in terms of structural requisites (and their subcategories)

	A		B		C		D		E		F		G		H	
	SocI	SocII	SocI	SocII	SocI	SocII	SocI	SocII	SocI	SocII	SocI	SocII	SocI	SocII	SocI	SocII
1	√	√	√	√							√	▨	√	√	▨	√
2	√	X	√	X							√	▨	√	√	▨	√
3	√	√									√	▨	√	√	▨	√
4	√	X									√	▨	√	√	▨	√
5	√	√									√	▨	√	√	▨	√
6	√	√									√	▨	√	√	▨	√
7																
8																
9																

[dashed box]	-- Structural requisites that emerge on levels lower than that of any society
√ | √	-- Data similar for societies A and B
√ | X	-- Data different for societies A and B
▨	-- Structure lacking

outset a quite systematic location of possible similarities and certain differences would result, and in addition it would suggest systematic ways of following up, on lower levels of generalization, the differences located at this level.[20]

Another caution has already been mentioned in the general discussion of structural-functional requisite analysis. Suppose under heading C_5 one finds no structure. In that case one (or some combination) of three conclusions may be correct. Firstly, the observer may have simply failed to observe the structure though it in fact exists. Secondly, the structure may not in fact exist although the unit studied is a society. This raises the question of the requisite status of type of structure C_5. This is, in turn, studied by reexamining, firstly, the derivation of the structural requisites from the functional requisites and, secondly, the derivation of the functional requisites themselves. If no error is found at this juncture, one may even raise the question of the advisability of changing the general definition of the unit. Thirdly, the structure may not in fact exist and the second type of difficulty mentioned above may not exist either, but the unit which has been called a society may in fact on closer examination be shown not to conform to the definition of society.

These three possible explanations of the absence of structure C_5 highlight types of difficulty that may arise in the use of such a system of analysis as this one, but they highlight a certain source of strength as well. They indicate with some precision the three general lines that

---

20. Another possibility of differences lies, of course, in the fact that on lower levels of generalizations categories such as F and G may be added in one case and G and H in the other. Additional subcategories, e.g., A_7, C_9, etc., may also emerge at these lower levels of generalization. The possibilities in these respects are limited by what is found to be the case relative to A,B,C,D, and E, but they are not necessarily ruled out by what is known of these five categories. See Table 2.

inquiry must take when difficulties of this sort arise. They give systematic ways of locating error by tying down the error to one or some combination of: (1) failures of observation, (2) errors in the development of the theoretical structure and useless or difficult elements in the conceptual scheme, and (3) failure to establish the fact that the supposed empirical referents of the concepts are in fact empirical referents of those concepts. The examples which have been taken for present purposes are, of course, societies, but exactly the same things may be said of comparison by means of structural-functional requisite analysis of different examples of other types of units. Furthermore, the remarks here made about societies have been confined to the most general comparative level, whereas, with the additional necessity of ascertaining the levels of generalization under examination, the same methods may be followed at any levels of generalization.

Perhaps the greatest difficulty of this approach to the comparative analysis of two different societies is a sort of sin of omission rather than one of commission. Properly used and with, of course, much greater development than is now present, this approach can with genuine certainty isolate and identify the minimum ranges of difference and similarity between two societies (and among more than two if that is desired). It can not, however, isolate and identify the maximum possibilities in these respects except insofar as the maximum possible range is limited by the minimum necessary range.[21] This is not an unexpected difficulty. It confronts all comparative analysis of empirical phenomena. Complete identification of the maximum range in these respects would involve complete empirical description of each of the units concerned. In respect to this difficulty, too, the method of analysis has at least

---

21. The terms *maximum possible* and *minimum necessary* apply, of course, only insofar as one accepts as given the units as defined.

a partial solution. If for any reason it is suspected that the minimum comparative range established is not sufficiently detailed for the purposes of the researcher, he may seek further help by proceeding with the same methods to the next lower level of generalization. He will never achieve complete knowledge by this or any other technique, but he will achieve closer and closer approximations to it, and that by steps which can be checked and rechecked with some accuracy and precision.

There is another application of the combined conceptual scheme and theoretical system advanced here. If it is a valid observation that <u>society</u>, as that unit is here defined, is the most general social unit,[22] then it will follow that the structural requisites of any particular unit other than a society will have fewer than the total number of requisite structures of the society of which it is a part (or of the societies which it interrelates) on any particular level of analysis. This, too, can be adapted to varying levels of generalizations. For example, if one assumes for a moment that all societies have family structures of some sort but that no society can consist solely of family patterns, then it will follow that one can delineate family structural requisites as the list of thirty types of patterns minus certain of the types (or subcategories of the thirty types). On lower levels of generalization one may do the same thing with the relation of the U. S. family system to the United States society. This gives the analyst a rather precise way of relating in terms of general structural requisites any given unit to the society of which it is a part. It is useful in another respect as well. For example, in any society there must be role differentiation, and there must also be role

---

22. i.e., in the sense that all other social units are either subcategories of societies or the result of the interrelationships between two or more societies. See above, pp. 22-26, for a brief discussion of this point.

differentiation in the case of kinship structures. The
role differentiation in the kinship structure is obviously
relevant for that of the society. But the role differentiation of the parts of the society, other than the kinship
structure, is also relevant for the role differentiation
of the kinship structure. They must be mutually compatible
to some degree if the society (or the kinship structure)
is to persist. And so from a careful examination of this
sort, a systematic approach to the interrelationships of
any given substructure of a society and the total society
may be gained. By extension of the process the interrelationships of two or more such substructures with one
another may also be systematically explored. This can be
done by direct comparison or by first relating each of the
substructures concerned to the total society in terms of a
structural requisite comparison. There is something to be
said for the latter alternative since it provides a systematic way of ascertaining on any given level of generalization whether "all" of the relevant interrelationships have
been covered.[23]

Another example may be relevant at this point. In
terms of the United States family structure, institutionally speaking, the person holding the role of father or
husband (depending on whether ego is a child or a wife) is
expected to produce the major economic income of the family
unit. The wife or mother produces household services and
to some extent goods, but the husband or father is the

----

23. This statement is obviously made in terms of any
specific stage of development of the conceptual scheme and
its accompanying theoretical system. "All" of the interrelationships relevant on a given level of generalization of
two substructures in terms of the present stage of development may be only a fraction of what they may be five years
from now. In any sort of analysis one works within limits
of this sort, but further development is both easier and
more likely if the limits in these respects are clearly
and explicitly recognized rather than merely appreciated
intuitively.

major producer of goods and services. He is the "bread-
winner." When one looks at the economic aspects of the
family, however, it is also clear that his economic production is not carried out in terms of the family unit
which is a unit of production only for extremely limited
purposes.[24] This means quite clearly that there must be a
major interrelationship between the family unit and some
system of occupational roles outside of family units in the
society. If one turns and examines the system of occupational roles in the society, one finds that in theory at
least family considerations are not expected to enter.
This in turn suggests all sorts of leads on distinctions between ideal and actual structures, sources of tension, and
other interrelating structures vital to both the system of
occupational roles and the family system. But it is only
in terms of relating both these structures to the society
of which they are parts that these factors come to light
systematically.

Corollary to the uses of this approach for the analysis of a given substructure of a society or in relating
two or more such substructures are its uses for comparing
two or more such substructures. By relating the substructures to the total society one may pinpoint their similarities and differences. For example, using Table 3 substruc-
ture I may lack structures of the types A_4, C_6, D_5, E_1, E_2, and
E_3. Substructure II may lack these same structures and in
addition those of the types C_1, C_2, and C_3. Of the types of
structures they possess in common they may have virtually
identical forms of structures A_1, A_2, A_3, A_5, A_6, B_1, B_3, B_4, and
C_5 and different forms of the rest of those types of struc-
tures which they have in common. Thus, even on a high level
of generalization one may discover what type of structures

----

24. This is, of course, particularly and most spectacularly true of the "urban middle class" family and perhaps least true of the relatively poor rural families.

Table 3. Comparison of two substructures (Substr.) of a society in terms of
the structural requisite (and their subcategories) of any society

	A Substr. I	A Substr. II	B Substr. I	B Substr. II	C Substr. I	C Substr. II	D Substr. I	D Substr. II	E Substr. I	E Substr. II
1	√	√	√	√	√	▨	√	X	▨	▨
2	√	√	√	X	√	▨	√	X	▨	▨
3	√	√	√	√	√	▨	√	X	▨	▨
4	√	▨	√	√	√	X	√	X	√	X
5	√	√	√	X	√	√	▨	▨	√	X
6	√	√	√	X	▨	▨	√	X	√	X

▨	-- Data lacking
√ √	-- Data similar for substructures I and II
√ X	-- Data different for substructures I and II

these substructures share, which ones are peculiar to each, and where and how the shared ones differ. By going to lower levels of generalization, the amount of detail obtainable in all these respects can be greatly increased.[25] Finally, in the process one develops knowledge of the degree to which each such substructure approximates or fails to approximate a society.

In the course of such analysis differences of levels of generalization as between one substructure and another would of necessity come to light. In relating each substructure to a society the level of generalization of initial definition of each substructure has to be made explicit, and as a result the confusions which sometimes plague social analysis because of lack of clarity in these respects is at least easier to avoid.

What has been said above about substructures has been applied to substructures within a given society, but the method can equally well be applied to the comparative analysis of similar (or different) substructures within two or more societies which may in turn be more or less similar or different. For the most thorough work of this kind one would follow the lines of comparative analysis of both the societies and the specific substructures concerned. One may, of course, confine one's attention to specific substructures and proceed systematically in terms of structural-functional requisite analysis, setting for the purpose the functional and structural requisites specific to the substructures concerned, but the systematic relation of the substructures to the societies concerned would certainly serve as a convenient checking device and should serve to limit some of the many possible errors of omission.

---

25. Further differences or similarities may exist between them in terms such as those of additional subcategories of the structural requisites of any society (see Table 2, A_7 and C_9) and/or additional requisite categories and their subcategories (see Table 2, F_{1-6}, G_{1-6}, H_{1-6}).

Finally, one other purpose may be served by an analysis of the structural requisites of any society. These
structural requisites may be studied with a view to ascertaining whether or not any particular combinations of
particular ways of handling the structural requisites seem
to characterize groups of different societies. That is to
say, one may be able to erect a taxonomy (or taxonomies)
of societies on a structural basis. For example, one might
find that all societies would fall into, say, five or six
different types, members of each of which has on the level
of generalization concerned the same manner of handling
the structural requisites of any society. The structural
requisites of each of these types might then be derived.
These types could in turn be further broken down and so
forth. The results of particular studies of particular
societies or particular substructures of particular societies could thereby be arranged in a framework such that
the general relevance of particular studies would be systematically available for other students.[26]

---

26. Very little work of this sort has been attempted
systematically. The most obvious taxonomy which has been
used is the division between literate and nonliterate societies. Much interesting material has been assembled by
use of this division, but even so it has been an obvious
and none too critically examined distinction. A major
criterion of a useful taxonomy would certainly be its a-
bility to group together those societies with the maximum
structural similarity and separately those with sharp differences. The determination of which taxonomy will prove
most useful will take years of research, and it may well
be years before some genius in the field develops a taxonomy of societies that has even a shadow of the usefulness
of that which characterizes biology, for all its many problems. Certainly signigicant possibilities have been overlooked. Structurally speaking at least it would seem, for
example, that the industrial society -- nonindustrial society dichotomy might be more useful in these respects
than the literate-nonliterate distinction. It can be shown
that industrial societies must have high literacy rates
while nonindustrial societies may or may not have them.
Nevertheless, the two dichotomies do not even approximate-
ly correspond to one another in any save this one respect.
At the same time it can almost certainly be shown that any

By working to lower levels in this fashion and by making empirical studies at the various levels delineated, there should develop in this field a substantial backlog of knowledge for use by various and subsequent scholars. For present purposes it may sound outlandish to say, as has been suggested above, that if one is to compare the economic substructure of the U.S.S.R. with that of the U.S. one may do so best by relating each to the societies concerned as a whole and so forth. But it cannot remain ever so if the field of social analysis is to make progress in scientific development. One of the real shortcomings of social analysis at its present stage of development is that so few of its many admirable researches have been so framed as to make possible a cumulative effect, or at least that so few have been so used. One of the reasons for this may well be the lack of any reasonably acceptable, explicitly worked out, systematic approach to the general problems. One may turn to the field of biology as an obvious source of insight in these respects. Where would the biologists

---

two nonindustrial societies, whether they be similar with regard to their literacy rates (or the presence or absence of literacy) or whether one be literate and the other not, have more in common with one another, structurally speaking, than either has with an industrial society. Structurally speaking a strong case can be made out for the proposition that thirteenth century English society has more in common with Trobriand society than either has with modern English society despite the fact that the later form of English society evolved from the earlier one. That is to say, structurally speaking, a literate society may have more in common with a nonliterate society than with another literate society if one of the two literate societies is industrialized and the other is not. If this proposition can be successfully defended, the distinction based on the industrial factor would be a better basis for a taxonomy, given the criterion for taxonomies suggested here, than the one traditionally used. The further question may be raised as to whether or not failure to make systematic analysis of the structure of society on the most general level may have played a major role in the almost traditional acceptance of the literate-nonliterate distinction and the relative lack of attempt to seek or test other taxonomies of a similar level of generality.

be today if each researcher had, in the sense true of social analysis today, to relate all over again the particular organism(s) in which he was interested to living matter
in general and other specific types in particular, and
perhaps more importantly, to work out anew the relations
of portions of an organism in which he was interested to
the whole? A researcher in botany can test the effects of
auxin on plant growth using coleus blumei Bentham for his
experimental work only if someone else has worked out a
great deal of knowledge about plant structures in general.
If much work on the general circulatory systems of plants
were not available, he would have to do it himself. Furthermore, if something were not known of the general relations between coleus blumei Bentham and other plants, the
research scientist could say nothing of the relevance of
his results beyond their application to coleus blumei
Bentham.

Social science must seek comparable frameworks in
terms of which knowledge may come to have a powerfully
cumulative effect if the usual goals of scientific development are to be sought. There is a sense in which all
knowledge has some cumulative effect, but one of the major
sources of advance in scientific knowledge has been the
erection of frameworks of analysis that greatly facilitated
the systematic relation of bits of knowledge to one another
and hence increased the cumulative effects of these bits.
It is with acute awareness of the size of the job to be
done that this work suggests that the systematic structural
requisite analysis of societies may be a step in that
direction.

In the use of this approach for comparative analysis
one general overriding word of caution must be issued. For
any specific case of analysis it presents a framework, but
it does not make the analysis automatic. It does furnish
a systematic answer to what sorts of data must be sought,
and depending on the level of generalization to which the

approach is carried, this systematic answer may be more or less detailed. As has been pointed out above, the approach as here presented will not be carried beyond the most general level, i.e., that applicable to any society, but from the work done at this level it should be possible to set up tentatively a taxonomy of societies,[27] then to work out the structural requisites of each type, then to set up subtaxonomies, and so forth. The tremendous job of empirical research remains to be done, of course, and at any particular level the bulk of the theoretical analysis remains to be done as well. Even at the most general level this treatment gives only a tentative formulation, and in the future, when work at this level is much advanced, it will still be tentative. No empirical scientific systems have a priori validity. It is important that a student not underestimate the usefulness of general analysis, but it is equally important that he not overestimate it too.[28] This line of development will give conceptual tools for analysis, a theoretical framework useful for either isolated or comparative analyses, some empirical generalizations, a systematic set of indications of important lines for further development, and explicit indication of the lines to be checked (and to some extent how to check them) as to sources of error in such analyses. It does not, however, solve the problems of data gathering. It merely highlights important areas in which data gathering must take place. The use of the approach for particular analyses, the further

---

27. Of course, more than one taxonomy could be set up. Like taxonomies in other fields, those in this field will go through a long period of erection, reexamination, refinement, substitution, etc.

28. The frequent and persistent underselling of social science in the past and present should not blind either the social scientist or the lay public to the possibilities of overselling that may be present in some respects today.

development of the approach, and its detailed validation
(or invalidation) at its present stage of development --
all rest in important respects on the gathering of data.
Such an approach as this one is explicitly and emphatically
not advanced as an alternative to statistical work, to cite
only one highly developed form of data analysis. The detailed usefulness of such an approach as this one will rest
on its direction of data gathering and the development of
ability to gather and analyze data in terms of it. The
concepts of such an approach as this will remain at best
significant for purposes of theoretical exercise if they
are not capable of operational definitions, given the use
of that term in its broadest sense.

Development of this sort must go hand in hand with the
development and application of data gathering and analysis
if it is to be effective. Both lines of development must
be stressed. Statistical techniques and studies, for example, may suggest or prove, on the one hand, inadequacies
of the present conceptual scheme and theoretical system
and, on the other, lines of improvement. Development of
this type of conceptual scheme and theoretical system may
in turn suggest the need for statistical techniques or
other techniques of data gathering and analysis of a sort
which do not now exist, or their application in areas in
which they have not heretofore been applied. Failure to
understand at all times the mutual relevance of such an
approach as this and data gathering and analysis may be a
source of the gravest types of empirical errors or sterility from the point of view of the development of social
science.

D. THE RELATIONSHIP BETWEEN CONCEPTUAL DEVELOPMENT AND ITS CORRESPONDING THEORETICAL DEVELOPMENT

One of the more dangerous pitfalls attendant upon the
use of the kind of analysis attempted here is the confusion
of concepts and theories and consequently of conceptual

schemes and theoretical systems. This distinction is sufficiently obvious to any of the scientists who have followed an explicit interest in general methodological problems and to many who have not. Nevertheless, discussion
of the point is undertaken here on the theory that it is
better to bore the initiated than to risk unnecessary confusion of those who have not given the matter their attention.

A concept, as that term is used here, is a means of
intersubjective communication. For these purposes concepts
are represented by signs, mostly words. These words, in
order to fulfill such purposes, must have intersubjective
meanings. At the risk of being somewhat less precise the
matter may be put in another way which is less satisfactory
from the point of view of the epistemologist but may,
nonetheless, be clearer for the average reader and do no
harm to the use intended here.[29] A concept may be defined
as simply a name for the members of a given class; the
class may be of any sort. The definition or referent of a
concept involves the logical analysis of the class to which
the concept in question is applied. Concepts may have
empirical referents, e.g., the concept "dog," nonempirical
referents, e.g., the concept "God" as conventionally used,
or some mixture of the two, e.g., the Pope of the Catholic
Church as conceived by a member of that faith. A group of
concepts used in conjunction with one another for any
particular purpose is a conceptual scheme. For example,
the set of concepts used for the scientific analysis of
"living" phenomena forms the conceptual scheme of biology.
That conceptual scheme is one among many scientific

---

29. The difficulty of this second formulation from
the point of view of the epistemologist is that it defines
concept extensionally and not intensionally and thereby
overlooks the combination of the two. Since the present
emphasis is on scientific concepts which involve primarily
the extensional aspect, little harm is done here by the
second formulation.

conceptual schemes. It is "scientific" in the sense that
it is erected for the purposes of scientific analysis. The
set of concepts used by Kant in his <u>Critique of Pure Reason</u>
forms a philosophic conceptual scheme because those concepts are derived as parts of a philosophic system and so
forth. On the most general level the possible different
conceptual schemes and the possible different concepts are
infinite, given the definition of concept used here.

A great deal can be said about the concept of concepts
in general, and much has no doubt been said about them by
the epistemologists in particular. It would be beside the
present point of interest to go deeply into this matter on
the most general level. For present purposes interest
focuses on concepts for use in scientific conceptual
schemes and on others only insofar as their development is
relevant for scientific purposes.

For scientific purposes certain criteria for concepts
may be set up. <u>First</u>, a scientific concept must be clearly
and precisely defined. That is to say, it must be possible
to ascertain exactly what the referent of a scientific
concept is, and it must be possible to distinguish that
referent precisely, either analytically or concretely, from
the referents of other concepts that are in the conceptual
scheme and that are conceived to be different from the one
in question. <u>Second</u>, if it is a concept in an empirical
as opposed to a formal science, the concept must have an
empirical referent. These empirical referents may be
concretely distinguishable or only analytically distinguishable from one another; that is to say, the referents
may be concrete empirical objects or analytically distinguished aspects of concrete objects (e.g., molecules or
the mass and volume of molecules). The concept "God" as
ordinarily used is a nonempirical concept and hence has no
status in an empirical scientific conceptual scheme. On
the other hand, the concept of "human belief in a God" is

an empirical concept and may have such a status.[30]   The
concept of "God" in this sense has only the status of a
nonempirical concept in terms of which human beings orient
their action in particular ways.

Third, unlike theories, concepts in scientific systems
are neither more nor less valid. They may be more or less
well defined, and they may be more or less well identified
with empirical as opposed to nonempirical referents, but
one cannot prove or disprove concepts in a scientific
system. Here, of course, the arbitrary nature of definitions in scientific systems is relevant.[31]   If a physicist
chooses to use the term "boojum" for the referent which
every other physicist calls an "atom," his concept is
neither more nor less valid than theirs. His divergence
in this particular will be regarded by his colleagues as a
more or less perverse personal eccentricity, but it need
not interfere with the validity of his research in any
particular. The great test for concepts in scientific
systems is quite different from that of validity. Concepts
in scientific systems prove themselves to be more or less
useful as tools for the derivation of knowledge. If, for
example, the concept society as defined here proves less
useful for the systematic general analysis of social
phenomena than the same term given a different referent,
then the social scientists will presumably abandon the one
and use the other. It is possible to examine the society
of the United States with only one concept of occupational

---

30. It may be more or less difficult to measure and
ascertain "human belief in a God," but the concept can at
least in theory be given an empirical referent operationally defined in terms of specific types of observations of
the actions of members of a particular biological species.

31. See M. J. Levy, Jr., "Methodological Difficulties
in Social Science," Jour. of the Phil. of Sci., Vol. 17,
No. 4 (Oct. 1950), pp. 287-301.

roles, for example the "farmer concept," but one will get
far more information about the society in general and even
about the farmers if one adds other occupational role concepts to the scheme.

One may recapitulate the basic observations about
concepts. For empirical scientific purposes they must
first be precisely defined and precisely differentiated
from other concepts. Second, they must be given empirical
referents. Third, they are not more nor less valid, but
only more or less useful for a given purpose of analysis.
It is important that these points about concepts as used
in empirical scientific systems be understood if concepts
are to be used successfully and not abused for scientific
purposes. Conceptual work in empirical science cannot be
carried out in a vacuum. One must always know to some
degree for what purpose concepts are to be used. With this
point of view and the nature of concepts clearly in mind,
work on a conceptual scheme may prove brilliantly fruitful
for a given scientific problem. Confusion about the nature
and role of concepts in empirical scientific systems is
likely to lessen the chances of such fruitfulness.

The term theory as used here refers to generalized
statements containing one or more variables. These statements are made in terms of a conceptual scheme, and they
relate in some fashion the referents of two or more of the
concepts involved. Here, however, interest lies in one
particular type of theory, i.e., empirical scientific
theory, and the short term theory will be used hereafter
to refer to that particular type of theory unless otherwise
specified. Theory in this special sense consists of
generalized statements containing variables that (1) are
made in terms of concepts having empirical referents, and
(2) draw an empirical relationship between the referents
of two or more such concepts. Theory in this sense may be
opposed to singular statements. These singular statements
may also state empirical relationships of concepts with

empirical referents, but they are not generalized and do
not contain variables (e.g., "The ninth chair in this room
is broken now"). Theories may be of three types: (1) universal theories, (2) existential theories, and (3) mixed
theories.[32] Universal theories apply to all possible cases
concerned. They take a form such as the following: "All
swans are white" (i.e., no swanlike thing is not white).
They may be disproved or disconfirmed by finding a single
empirical exception to the statement, e.g., in this case
by finding a single swanlike thing which is not white.
Thus, these theories can be disconfirmed by finding a
single exception to them, but they cannot be completely
confirmed, if they are empirical theories, since it is not
possible to examine all possible data. Existential theories assert the empirical existence of some case of the
sort concerned. They take a form such as the following:
"There exist white swans (i.e., the class of things
swanlike and white exists)." These statements can be disproved only by examining all possible phenomena and not
finding the class asserted (i.e., in this case no swanlike
things which are white). Thus, although they can be confirmed by finding a single case, they can never be completely disconfirmed though their state of confirmation
becomes less and less adequate (or reliable) as more and
more research fails to locate one of the cases asserted by
the theory. Mixed theories contain elements of both sorts
and consist of statements such as the following: "All swans
have a swan ancestor." They can be more or less well confirmed or disconfirmed by a combination of the two above
procedures.

Two other types of theory may be distinguished. These

----

32. It is not proposed here to define the three types
of theory in an epistemologically sophisticated form. An
attempt is made merely to clarify these concepts sufficiently for the less precise needs of the present analysis.

two types cut across the triple classification mentioned
above. These two types may be called isolated theories
and integrated theories. The distinction between these
two types of theories is not based on the content of the
theory itself as was the preceding distinction but rather
upon the derivation of the theories concerned or their relationship to other theories. An isolated theory may be
defined as one which in its derivation is not dependent in
any way on other theories. An integrated theory may be
defined as one which in its derivation is at least in part
deduced from other theories. Any particular theory may be
either a completely isolated one or a more or less integrated one. In either case the tests of the validity of
the theory are the usual empirical ones. The important
difference between the two types lies in the different
sources of error one examines when a particular theory is
more or less disconfirmed. In the first case, i.e., the
isolated theory, the error is simply straight empirical
error, in this case either wrong observations or a generalization broader than justified by the data or one's
estimate of the data. In the second case, i.e., the integrated theory, the source of error may be incorrect
observation as in the first case, although here the
incorrect observation may have been made either in the
special observations involved in deriving the particular
theory under consideration or in those observations involved
in the theory (or theories) from which it is partially deduced. The source of error may be of another sort, however,
i.e., of a logical sort. Insofar as the theory is partially, at least, deduced from other theories, error may have
resulted simply from improper procedures of deduction.
Deductive procedures are not entirely absent in the case of
isolated theories either, of course, insofar as some deductive element is involved in proceeding from any specific
data to a generalized formulation about it, but this element of deduction holds for all empirical scientific
theories of whatever type.

One may take as an example of the distinction between isolated and more or less integrated theories the following theory: "The family system of any nonindustrialized society, if that family system is not of the multilineal conjugal variety, will change in the direction of a multilineal conjugal family system if the society of which it is a substructure changes in the direction of an industrial society." If this theory is presented as an isolated theory, a single empirical exception to the theory disproves it. One may have fallen into the error involved by wrongly observing (or positing observations of) societies in which one thought the change in question took place but in which it did not in fact take place. One may also have observed correctly in all cases studied but then have wrongly jumped to the conclusion that what was true in the cases observed held for all societies.[33] On the other hand, the theory may be presented as a more or less well integrated theory in which case it may be in part deduced from another theory such as the following: "Multilineal conjugal family units are structural requisites of an industrial society." Now given an empirical exception to the first theory under discussion one may either show this second one also is invalid or that, insofar as the first is thought to involve logically the second (or vice versa), one's deduction is faulty.

This distinction carries the argument on to the question of systems of theory or theoretical systems. Systems of theory may be defined as groups of theories that are all to some degree more or less well integrated theories relative to one another. It is toward the development of

---

33. This in essence amounts to changing the isolated theory to a more or less integrated one because implicitly, at least, it involves the addition of another theory such as the following: "Other societies than those I have observed cannot in fact differ from those I have observed in a fashion such that this generalization under consideration will be invalid."

empirically tenable systems of theory that empirical scientific work is oriented. This is not to say that poorly integrated or isolated theories have no place in science. It is rather to say that aggregates of poorly integrated or isolated theories are relatively far less fruitful for empirical understanding than are highly developed systems of theory. The advantage of highly developed theoretical systems is obvious to the point of banality. With such systems the relevance of new observations about phenomena and the implications of new theories hitherto poorly integrated or even of the isolated sort are spread widely and quickly, and a systematic basis for the development of their implications is furnished. Furthermore, systematic attempts to develop theoretical systems by forcing the careful examination of the general implications of existing theories may bring to light new theories[34] which can then be subjected to processes of empirical testing and may even indicate possible sources of data which otherwise might go undetected. In some cases highly developed theoretical systems make it possible, temporarily at least, to bridge gaps which exist in the data.

There is a grave danger involved in the development of theoretical systems. This is not, however, a difficulty inherent in such systems but rather in the attitudes and characters of the men who use them. If a given scientist becomes so attached to or so bemused by a given theoretical system that he ignores empirical exceptions to the theories, or overlooks them entirely, the theoretical system may become a device for the perpetuation of error and an obstacle to scientific advance. For this reason, if for

---

34. One may prefer to call those theories that have not yet been subjected to empirical testing <u>hypotheses</u>. This is certainly conventional application of terminology and will be followed in this volume whenever that distinction is of the essence of the argument. In such cases empirically tested theories will be referred to as more or less <u>well confirmed</u> or more or less <u>disconfirmed theories</u>.

no other, social systems for which scientific advance is
important must place great emphasis on a highly developed
orientation to critical rationality in such fields if the
aims sought by the members of such a system are to be
achieved.

The grave danger involved in the use of theoretical
systems is, however, more than offset by the advantages of
such systems. In this respect one of the basic difficulties of social science is not, as has been so often alleged,
that it has as a discipline been too theoretical but rather
that it has had, relative to the other sciences, such
poorly developed and poorly tested theoretical systems.
If one looks at the sciences in terms of a hierarchy based
on scientific achievement, i.e., contributions to empirical understanding, one finds that those at the top have
the most highly developed systems of theory and those at
the bottom the least developed systems of theory. In
biology there are more isolated or poorly integrated theories than in physics, and there are more in social science
than in biology. In fact, in some areas of social science
there are almost no empirical scientific theories of any
other sort; such theoretical systems as exist in some of
these fields are either of a more metaphysical or of a
more formal (i.e., mathematical) scientific nature[35] rather
than of an empirical scientific nature. Interest in the
development of theoretical systems cannot be the sole
interest or even the main interest of a science if this is
taken to imply a relative lack of interest in the development of techniques of empirical confirmation and disconfirmation of hypotheses.[36] On the other hand, it must be

---

35. Those of a mathematical or formal scientific sort
have been relatively few and far between, the most notable
examples having cropped up in the field of economics.

36. There is, of course, no reason why it should imply such a disastrous lack of interest, in fact quite the
contrary.

<u>one</u> of the main interests of any scientific field.

Now it is necessary to turn to the distinction between concepts (and consequently conceptual schemes) and theories (and consequently theoretical systems). Concepts are some of the tools in terms of which theories are constructed. Unlike theories, concepts are not confirmed or disconfirmed. They are simply shown to be more or less well (i.e., precisely) defined, to have (or not have) empirical referents, and to be more or less fruitful. Their fruitfulness lies in the degree to which they facilitate the development of confirmable theories in the areas to which they are applied. The selection of concepts for empirical scientific purposes is arbitrary provided the concepts are (1) precisely defined and differentiated from other concepts, and (2) have empirical referents. Theories are not arbitrary. They are more or less well confirmed or disconfirmed. Furthermore, the fruitfulness of a theory is not necessarily related to its degree of confirmation. Well confirmed theories may be relatively fruitless (i.e., trivial) for the further development of theory, and it is even conceivable that poorly confirmed or even disconfirmed theories might be fruitful in these respects. Although one would on the whole expect well confirmed rather than disconfirmed theories to be fruitful for further development, there is a genuine and inescapable sense in which disconfirmed theories are important building blocks of science.[37] Without "good" (in the sense indicated above) concepts it is impossible to develop confirmable theories,[38]

---

37. In a sense one of the naive aspects of social science is the extent to which "negative" results in this field are held by some to be worthless.

38. Sometimes one hears statements like the following from social scientists: "Precisely the value of the concepts, <u>ego</u>, <u>superego</u>, and <u>id</u> lies in the fact(?) that they are undefined and hence can be used on more than one level at the same time." If there is any methodological validity in what has been said here of the relation between concepts and theories, statements like the one quoted are a counsel of despair.

and without the development of confirmable theories the
fruitfulness of concepts cannot be determined. This is in
essence the relation between concepts and theories in empirical science.

This particular work attempts a combination of conceptual and theoretical development. Such combinations are
to be expected. If the concepts one uses are precisely defined and have generalized and variable empirical referents,
then generalized and variable statements relating two or
more concepts will be theories. In this volume terms such
as <u>society</u>, <u>functional requisites</u>, <u>structure</u>, <u>structural
requisites</u>, <u>role differentiation</u>, <u>setting</u>, and so forth,
are concepts. Statements that "<u>societies</u> have <u>settings</u>,"
that "<u>societies</u> in their <u>settings</u> have <u>functional</u> and
<u>structural requisites</u>," that the "existence of <u>role differ-
entiation</u> is a <u>functional requisite</u> of any <u>society</u>," and
that "a <u>structure</u> of <u>role differentiation</u> is a <u>structural
requisite</u> of any <u>society</u>" are all theories; they can presumably be subjected to empirical testing. The validity
of the theories will rest on such tests or on the production of empirical exceptions to the theories as framed.
The fruitfulness of the concepts, given the orientation of
this volume, rests on whether or not their combinations
and permutations can be put to use and made to result in
confirmable theories about social structure in general and
about comparative aspects or parts of the same or different
societies in particular.

C H A P T E R   VI

THE ANALYTIC ASPECTS OF RELATIONSHIP STRUCTURES

It has been suggested above that it is difficult, if not impossible, at this stage of theoretical development to discover and analyze the concrete structural requisites of any society.[1] In the same chapter, however, something has been said of the ubiquity of relationship structures in general and of certain analytically distinct aspects of those relationship structures. A relationship structure, as that concept will be used here, is defined as any social structure (or set of structures) that defines the actions, ideally and/or actually, that interrelate two or more individual actors. In a sense relationship structures of this sort conform to the definition used here of concrete structures. The doctor-patient relationship is a membership unit in any specific case. Relationship structures in this sense are the building blocks, if one will, of membership unit structures such as the "family," a "business firm," the "U.S. Congress," etc. The difference is largely one of approach. Analysis in terms of relationship structures focuses attention on the individual actor components of any particular action. Analysis in terms of membership units such as the family focuses attention on the unit in terms of which action takes place rather than on the individual actors participating. Wherever one is unclear about the nature of these more general membership unit structures, he is forced to seek clarification by examina-

---

1. Supra, pp. 198-207.

tion of relationship structures. From such examination indications of social orientations and other structures may
be gleaned, and explicit indication of the more general
concrete structures may follow therefrom. Thus, if a social scientist were placed in a group of people about whom
he in fact knew nothing beyond their being human and
numerous, he could only bring order out of chaos by first
observing relationship structures. Fortunately for social
scientists this situation almost never arises. Something
of more general concrete structures is almost always known
or fairly obvious from the start. Only in the most excep-
tional cases of ignorance on the part of observers or
casuistry on the part of the observed does one face a
situation in which only the fact that there is a human ag-
gregation is known.[2]

The ubiquity of relationship structures and the necessary resort to them whenever one is at a loss or whenever
question arises as to the more general membership unit
structures of a society (or a part of a society) suggests
that any generally applicable knowledge of any relationship

---

2. The impatience sometimes shown by laymen toward
"social science" "discoveries" and proofs of the "obvious"
is not unrelated to such considerations as this. The a-
mount of sophistication in these respects built into the
average individual by the time he has reached adulthood is
quite remarkable. This is evidenced in many ways. The
average adult in United States society, even in the absence
of identification by clothing, etc., can quickly estimate
whether he is in an aggregate picked more or less at random, or forming a "family," a "businessman's club," a "university faculty," and so forth. Not only can he estimate
such distinctions, but in terms of those distinctions he
can and usually will alter his own actions with a thoroughness and plausibility which only the most skilled actors
can achieve for dramatic purposes. It may also be posited
that activities in quite strange and foreign societies, if
at all similar to such well-known structures, are likely to
be caught by an observer. Serious mistakes may perhaps be
made by observers by accepting such impressions uncritical-
ly, but, if such sensitivity to such similarities were totally absent, it is questionable whether any work on foreign groups could be done at all.

may prove extremely useful. It is extremely useful both
from the point of view of possible taxonomic development
and from the point of view of comparative analysis. One
may get at such knowledge by distinguishing analytically
six aspects of relationships: (1) the cognitive aspect,
(2) the membership criteria aspect, (3) the substantive
definition aspect, (4) the affective aspect, (5) the goal
orientation aspect, and (6) the stratification aspect.[3]
The remainder of this chapter will be broken into two
parts: (A) discussion of the aspects of relationship structures, and (B) discussion of the usefulness of such distinctions for the purposes of comparative analysis.

A.   THE ASPECTS OF RELATIONSHIP STRUCTURES

1.   The cognitive aspect

However elementary it may be, every socially defined
human interrelationship involves some elements of cognition. There is, for example, the cognition involved in the
recognition of those eligible for the relationship, and
there is always some cognition involved in the action
carried out in terms of the relationship. It is impossible,
perhaps, to say anything very definite of the substantive
content of the cognition involved since virtually any substantive content may be covered. Something may be said,
however, of the general character of the cognition involved.
Here as in the other aspects of relationship structures a
sort of polar scale along which variation may take place

---

3.   These have been mentioned above, p. 210. At that
time the explicit indebtedness of this work to that of Parsons on this subject was mentioned. It must be reiterated
here. Credit for the usefulness of at least the first five
of these concepts belongs to him though he cannot, of
course, be held responsible for any of the problems raised
by the numerous departures taken here from his original
usage of the terms.

is necessary. In this case the basis for distinction is
the consequence for cognition of the distinction between
the concepts _empirical_ and _nonempirical_ insofar as this
distinction is relevant to the cognitive aspects of social
action. _Empirical_ phenomena may be defined as those phenomena about which data may be apprehended directly through
sensory perception (i.e., by one or more of the five
following: taste, touch, sight, smell, or hearing) or indirectly inferred by the use of instruments in which a
sensory chain of connection is clear or presumed to be
clear.[4] The concept of nonempirical "phenomena" is a residual category relative to the concept of empirical phenomena. Thus sticks, stones, societies, atoms, microbes,
etc., are empirical phenomena. God, heaven, beauty (in
the abstract), ultimate values of all sorts, etc., are
nonempirical. As has been pointed out above, although
social science does not analyze nonempirical phenomena
directly, it may and must concern itself with the variety
of empirical fashions in which empirical beliefs in nonempirical phenomena can and do affect the empirical actions
of empirical individuals in empirical social systems.[5]

Before going further it is necessary to insert some
definitions of types of social action in which the differentiation of types is based first on the cognitive aspect
of action and secondly on the empirical-nonempirical distinction insofar as that is relevant to such a classification. This classification takes as its starting point a
distinction previously made by Pareto. The classification
has been previously presented elsewhere by the author,[6]

---

4. If the chain is shown unclear or nonexistent, the
instrument is, of course, revised or discarded.

5. _Supra_, pp. 228-229.

6. M. J. Levy, Jr.: "A note on Pareto's Logical-
Nonlogical Categories," _Am. Sociol. Rev._, Vol. XIII, No. 6
(Dec. 1948), pp. 756-757.

but it is presented here for the sake of convenience. The set of definitions is the following:

(A) <u>Logical (or rational) action</u> is that action in which the objective and subjective ends of action are identical. That is to say, it is action in which the end that the actor seeks to achieve by the means he has chosen is identical with the end that a qualified scientific observer (with, theoretically, perfect scientific knowledge) knows that the actor will achieve. In such action as this both the means and the ends of the action must be empirical. This is obvious since, if the end(s) is nonempirical, the scientific observer cannot determine whether it can or will be reached and since, if the means are nonempirical, the scientific observer cannot judge whether their use (or the "believed" use of them) will in fact attain the end(s) sought, or if they are attained, the scientific observer cannot judge whether or not the means used were conducive to the end(s) sought.

(B) <u>Nonlogical (or nonrational) action</u> is all conscious action other than logical action. Nonlogical action may be subdivided into two parts:

(1) <u>Illogical (or irrational) action</u> is that action in which the objective and subjective ends of action are not identical although both ends and means are empirical. This covers the ordinary categories of ignorance and error, i.e., the case in which the actor's choice of means can be shown empirically to be inadequate to attain his ends. The attempt to boil an egg in the same minimum time at an elevation of ten thousand feet as that required at sea level would, other things being equal, fall into the category of illogical action. As in the case of logical action, the ends and means in the case of illogical action must be empirical. If either the ends or means contain a nonempirical element, the action cannot be classified as illogical for the same sort of reasons given above for

logical action. A scientist cannot know scientifically that one won't attain a nonempirical end anymore than he can know that one will, regardless of the means involved, nor can he know scientifically that nonempirical means "properly applied" (from the point of view of the actor) won't attain a given empirical end anymore than he can know that they will, though of course he can tell whether or not such an end is achieved.[7]

(2) <u>Alogical (or arational) action</u> is all nonlogical action that is not illogical. It may also be subdivided into two parts:

(a) <u>Methodologically alogical (or arational) action</u> is that action in which the ends of the actor are empirical but the means are nonempirical, at least in part. This type of action is a common component of the phenomena generally termed <u>magic</u>. In fact <u>magic</u>, as that term will

---

7. If, for example, an actor believes that he can bring rain by invoking the aid of "gods" by means of prayer, two outcomes are possible. It rains to some extent, or it does not. If it rains, the scientist may offer alternative explanations that run in purely empirical terms. These explanations may satisfy the believers in science better than do the actor's explanations in terms of magic, but they are not disproof of these latter explanations. On this score the scientist can only take an agnostic position or assert that these magical explanations are not scientifically meaningful. The scientist can no more prove scientifically that nonempirical entities like "gods" lack powers than he can prove that they have them. If, on the other hand, it does not rain, the scientist can at most observe that the prayers <u>as performed</u> were inadequate to the end sought. If the actor, as is frequently the case in these circumstances, insists that the magic always works when "properly" performed but that some "improper" element must have entered this case, the scientist is again thrown back on the agnostic position. It is child's play epistemologically speaking, to show that nonempirical causal arguments generally are scientifically meaningless since they involve elements outside scientific methodology, but by the same token scientific proof of their falsity is also barred. By what scientific means, for example, can one prove that the "rain god" of the "X" tribe does not "exist," however meaningless such an entity (or its existence) may be from the scientific point of view?

be used in this work, will be so defined insofar as it is defined in terms of its cognitive aspects.[8]

(b) Ultimately alogical (or arational) action is that action in which both the ends and the means of the actor are at least in part nonempirical. The case of action in which the ends are nonempirical and the means completely empirical is not considered because it is self-contradictory. If the end is nonempirical, there must be some nonempirical content in the means, even if it is no more than the faith that the means are conducive to nonempirical ends. From the point of view of its cognitive aspects religious action may be defined as ultimately alogical action. In religious ritual, as that term is commonly understood, there are endless examples of the nonempirical elements involved in means viewed by the actors concerned as conducive to nonempirical ends.[9]

In terms of its cognitive aspects relationship structures may be classified in terms of whether or not the cognition involved is logical (or rational) or nonlogical (or nonrational). If it is nonlogical, the category and degree of nonlogicality are both subject to variation. If it is logical, there are not degrees of logicality involved, but the specific sphere of cognition about which the logicality is relevant is subject to wide variation. For example, the actions involved in both doctor-patient and businessman-customer relationships in modern United States society are institutionally defined as logical although the sphere of cognition involved, on the one hand, has to

---

8. Magic may of course be defined in terms other than its cognitive aspects.

9. This set of definitions, with some slight changes and additions, is quoted from the source cited above (see Note 6, p. 241, of this chapter). The indebtedness of this set of definitions and its relationship to Pareto's work may be seen more fully in that source.

do with biology (and to some extent psychology) whereas, on the other hand, it has primarily to do with the allocation of goods and services. With regard to relationships which in whole or in part are institutionally defined as nonlogical, the possibilities are methodological alogicality or ultimate alogicality with the great possibility of all sorts of differences in degree and kind under each heading or some combination of the two.[10] For example, magic as opposed to religion, and more or less of the one or the other, may be involved. One type of magic or religion as opposed to other types may also be involved, and so forth.

Ordinarily when a given relationship is discussed in this work as logical in its cognitive aspect, reference will be made to the institutionalized form of the relationship. It must, however, be borne in mind that many significant relationships are noninstitutionalized and many specific instances of relationships of an institutionalized sort do not conform to the institutionalized structure con-

---

10. The reader will note the lack of reference here to institutionalized illogicality. It is omitted because of the difficulty which the author has of envisaging this form of action as the institutionalized cognitive aspect of a relationship. This is not to say that some degree of ignorance is not often institutionalized for one or both parties to a relationship (e.g., two poker players), but rather that whenever the ends and means are both institutionalized as empirical, logical action is institutionalized insofar as possible. One might perhaps say that in such cases illogical action is institutionalized in a very restricted sense, i.e., that, if the action of one party to the relationship is nonlogical at all, it is expected that it be illogical rather than alogical. This, however, amounts to little more than the reassertion of the statement that the relationship is institutionalized without nonempirical elements in the means-ends structure. These remarks should not cause one to overlook the many important functions of ignorance in social systems. For some extremely interesting remarks on this general question see W. E. Moore and M. M. Tumin's article, "Some Social Functions of Ignorance," Am. Sociol. Rev., Vol. 14, No. 6 (Dec. 1949), pp. 787-795.

cerned. Whenever reference is made to forms of relationships other than the institutionalized sort, specific
notice to that effect will be given.

The importance of the cognitive aspects of a relationship are not to be overlooked. If one wishes, for example,
to compare the relationship of therapist to patient in the
society of the modern United States and that of "traditional" China, important distinctions arise in these respects.
Logical elements appear in both, but nonlogical elements
are, institutionally speaking, entirely ruled out of the
doctor-patient relationship in the United States. This is
not to say that they never enter, but ideally they are
either radically excluded from the picture, as in the case
of magical cures, or in the therapeutic aspect of the relationship are held neutral, as in the case of friendship.
In the doctor-patient relationship in the United States no
doctor is expected to use magical cures, and whether or
not a patient is also a personal friend of his doctor is
in theory irrelevant to either the course of therapy prescribed or the quality of the treatment given. In the
"traditional" Chinese case, however, magical practices are
an important part of such relationships as are considerations of personal relationships.

The contrasts between different types of relationships
in a single society differ in these respects just as
significantly, structurally speaking, as do similar relationships in different societies. The mother-son relationship in U.S. society is not like the doctor-patient relationship in these respects. Certainly, many rational
elements are involved in the mother-son relationship. In
modern industrial societies the rational elements in such
a case are probably carried further than in any other type
of society. Feeding, exercise, and the like are expected
to be carried out on the basis of rational action, and the
current popularity of books on character building and the
like maximizes the rational emphasis in these respects as

well, perhaps. At the same time either a mother or son
swayed only by rational calculations in her or his treatment of the other would be acting quite out of the institutionalized structures even for U.S. society. In other
relationships the contrast is even more clear-cut. The
rejoinder "You can't prove it scientifically" is no acceptable remonstrance on the part of a parishioner to his
priest when questions of ethics and faith in general are
concerned.

It must be borne in mind when discussing the cognitive
aspect of a given relationship that not even the institutionalized form of the relationship is by any means always
clear-cut in these respects. Even those relationships in
which logicality is most heavily emphasized often contain
some nonlogical elements of action, and the exact form and
degree of nonlogicality of a given nonlogically institutionalized relationship may be quite hard to determine.
The same is true of virtually every one of the six paired
terms here applied to six different aspects of relationship
structures. One cannot oversimplify concepts at the expense of having no empirical referents for them if one is
to do scientific work. Despite this sort of difficulty
these concepts can be shown to be useful both for comparative analysis and noncomparative structural analysis.[11]

The distinction used here between logical (rational)
and nonlogical (nonrational) is a departure from the usual
pair of rational and traditional.[12] The difference is
more apparent than real. The institutionalization of
traditional action as differentiated from logical action
in this sphere involves one or another of the forms of
nonlogical action. If both ends and means are empirical,

---

11. Some uses of these terms will be suggested by
examples of their application at the end of this chapter.

12. See Parsons, op.cit., p. 188, for the use of the
term traditional in this connection. See above, p. 108,
for the definition of the term as used here.

traditional action, if different from logical action, falls
into the category of illogical action. In the medical
sphere, for example, this would amount to justifying a
therapy because it had been considered proper in the past
rather than because it cured. If the means are nonempirical but the ends are empirical, it is methodologically
alogical. Traditional action such as magic falls into
this category. If the perpetuation of a way of doing
things is observed simply as a good in and of itself, it
would fall into the category of ultimately alogical action.
Because the categories used here make possible these distinctions, and perhaps others as well, among the different
cognitive aspects of different sorts of tradition this
departure in terminology has been employed.

2. The membership criteria aspect

In all relationships the question of choice of membership in the relationship is posed. On what basis may a
person become a member of any given relationship, say that
of doctor and patient? Do the bases differ from one society to another? Do they differ for different relationships in the same society? The specific bases or criteria
for eligibility are susceptible to the widest sorts of
variation. In theory, if such criteria are not infinite,
the number of possibilities is at least of so large a
magnitude as to make any attempt at listing foolhardy.
This would hold true from the point of view of any particular society and hence would present an even more insuperable problem from the point of view of any society. In an
attempt to bring order out of this sort of chaos, one
seeks categories of criteria for selection that will at
one and the same time be clearly and easily applicable
(i.e., on the basis of which clear-cut distinctions can be
made) and form a distinction of general relevance in the
development of empirical theory. The paired terms which

serve these purposes are <u>universalistic</u> and <u>particular-istic</u>.[13]

The membership criteria for a relationship will be called <u>universalistic</u> if persons are chosen for it or admitted to it on the basis of criteria that satisfy two conditions: (1) that they be criteria such that no individual is barred by social structures from possessing or acquiring them, and (2) that they be criteria such that they are germane to the purpose for which selection is made. The membership criteria for a relationship will be called more or less <u>particularistic</u> to the degree and in the respect that any departure whatever is made from the two conditions set up in the definition of <u>universalistic</u>.[14] Of the distinction between universalistic and particularistic a remark of Parsons' may be quoted: "Like all such analytical distinctions it does not preclude that both elements may be involved in the same concrete situation. But nevertheless their relative predominance is a

---

13. These terms are taken over from the work of Talcott Parsons. They are differently defined, however. Parsons' definitions are to be found in his article, "The Professions and Social Structure," <u>Essays</u>, p. 192. Although the definitions are different, the terms have been retained since the author believes that the empirical referent aimed at is identical. As formulated, the Parsons definitions would admit as <u>universalistic</u> criteria certain criteria that are almost certainly not intended as <u>universalistic</u>. The change in definitions is simply the result of an effort to tie down the concepts a bit more precisely to the referents for which they are ordinarily used.

14. The definition of <u>particularistic</u> need not be left residual if there is a preference for a more "positive" formulation of it. More positively the matter may be put as follows: the membership criteria for a relationship will be called <u>particularistic</u> if persons are chosen for it or admitted to it on the basis of criteria that satisfy one of the two following conditions or both of them: (1) that they be criteria such that some individual(s) is (are) barred by social structures from possessing or acquiring them, and (2) that the criteria are in some respect not germane to the purpose for which selection is made.

matter of the greatest importance."[15] Selection criteria
that tend to minimize but do not entirely eliminate particularistic elements will be called predominantly universalistic. Those that tend to minimize but do not entirely
eliminate universalistic elements will be called predominantly particularistic.

These definitions need some explanation by example if
there is to be clarity about their referents and their
application. Examples of purely particularistic criteria
are not difficult to find. Succession to the throne of
Great Britain is a case in point. At any one time, ideally
speaking, all individuals save one are socially barred from
the criteria for succession, and those criteria are not
necessarily germane to the purpose of selection if that
purpose includes such factors as governing ability, fitness
as a representative of the nation, etc. The criteria are
kinship criteria, and they are confined to a particular
kinship unit. The fact that an individual is the eldest
son (or eldest daughter, if there are no sons) of the
current king and queen (the criterion for being first in
the line of succession) is certainly socially barred to
all persons save one, and it is no guarantee of germane
ability or achievement of any sort. It must be added that
in modern times at least some universalistic elements are
injected into this selection by virtue of the operation of
the modern English political structure. Succession by
relatives felt to be more able than the person in the
direct line of succession may be obtained via the forced
abdication of the person deemed unfit, and on occasion the
British have shown themselves capable of changing royal
families altogether.

Examples of purely universalistic criteria are perhaps
harder to find. Ideally speaking, the distinctions by the
court and jury systems of the United States between the

---

15. Parsons, op.cit., p. 192.

guilty and the innocent are made on purely universalistic
bases. In theory all men are equal before the law. Ideally speaking, the only germane question, and the only
question in theory taken into consideration, is whether or
not they committed the act as charged. In fact, such
distinctions often are affected by particularistic elements.
The personality and appearance of the defendant may sway
the jurors. In some courts there are detectable differences in the treatment of Whites and Negroes, and in some
there are differences in treatment of wealthy and in-
fluential defendants as opposed to those who are not, and
so forth. Ideally speaking, however, these particularistic
elements do not enter. In theory, at least, many other
selections are carried out on completely universalistic
bases. The choice of members of Phi Beta Kappa in schools
for which only academic ability and achievement, ideally
speaking, determine admission and the choice of scholars
for the Nobel peace prize fall into this category.

The mixed case is, however, the more ordinary form.
Examples of this will be confined to the occupational
sphere because it is in relation to this sphere that these
concepts have had their greatest application and usefulness
so far. In the occupational sphere the distinction can be
phrased in more popular and easily understood terms.
Criteria for selection are more nearly universalistic the
more they are concerned with what a person can do that is
relevant to the job, and they are more particularistic the
more they are concerned with who he is regardless of the
relevance of his identification to the job. The general
conditions must, however, be kept in mind because the same
quality may in some cases give a particularistic emphasis
and in others a universalistic one. If an employer
announces he will hire only redheaded machinists to run
his lathes, and if he seeks the usual ends of running his
business efficiently, he is including a definite particularistic element in his criteria for selecting individuals

for the employer-employee relationship, unless it can be shown that red hair is an index of greater efficiency in lathe operation. The fact that he chooses the most efficient lathe operators from among the redheads who apply indicates that the inclusion of universalistic elements is present, but if it takes a secondary position relative to the color of the hair of the candidates involved, the criteria may be described as predominantly particularistic. The criteria in this case may also be described as more particularistic than those of an employer who chooses lathe operators on the same basis as that used in the former case, save for the fact that hair color is held by him to be irrelevant. The criteria in the first case are also less particularistic than they would be if the employer made his first selection on the basis of red hair, his second on the basis of whether or not the applicants wore blue shirts, and the third on the basis of ability as lathe operators.

Redheadedness is not, however, intrinsically particularistic. If one wishes to make colored motion pictures, and the color process is such that only "natural" redheads can be photographed distinctly, then the choice of redheaded actors and actresses is quite germane to the purpose, and assuming the society has no rules such that only redheads from particular families may be permitted to remain in the society, the characteristic is not one people are socially barred from acquiring or possessing. In such a situation placing redheadedness ahead of acting ability is not a movement in the direction of particularistic criteria but rather involves a choice between different universalistic criteria.

The example of "redheadedness" is an extreme case and focuses its attention on the question of the germaneness of the criteria. It is hoped that it is extreme enough to be easily understood, while at the same time it is not too extreme to be relevant. Less extreme examples are not difficult to find. Industrial societies in general place heavy emphasis on universalistic elements in the criteria for occupational roles,[16] but industrial societies by no means completely eliminate particularistic elements even when universalistic ones are heavily emphasized. For example, workers are often chosen on the basis of sex when the physiological distinction and even accompanying social distinctions are not germane. Only men are eligible for some jobs although the choice among the men may be almost entirely on universalistic grounds. In some areas of the United States the Negro-White or the Japanese ancestry-non-Japanese ancestry distinction is a criterion of employment, and so forth.

Another point mentioned above cannot be overemphasized. The question of the universalistic or particularistic nature of a criterion does not necessarily inhere in the criterion itself although it does inhere in some criteria. Again, another example may be given lest the case be biased by the hypothetical nature of the "redheaded" example. Given the aims of American movie producers and the tastes of the American public as they are, the choice of women for movie heroine roles on the basis of "physical beauty" rather than "acting ability" is not necessarily particularistic. On the other hand, the selection of women for admission to the Phi Beta Kappa Society on the basis of "physical beauty" most certainly would be.

The examples given above focus on the condition of germaneness, but the other condition given in the defini-

16. In three studies the present author has tried to show the relevance of the universalistic-particularistic distinction for problems of industrialization in general and that of China in particular. Though in some of these sources the definition of the concepts has differed slightly, their use and application has been identical with that sought here. See M. J. Levy, Jr., Family Revolution, Some Problems of Modernization in China, and (with Shih, Kuo-Heng) The Rise of the Modern Chinese Business Class, Institute of Pacific Relations, New York, 1949. These concepts have been very widely employed by other students in this and other connections as well.

tion is in many cases equally important. If, for example, only the lineal descendants of participants in the American Revolutionary War were admitted to colleges in the United States, both conditions would be involved, and selection would be on a predominantly particularistic basis. This type of factor certainly enters in the exclusion of Negroes from the polls in some states, from certain residential areas, etc. Relationships of various sorts in which determining criteria are kinship considerations take this form. This is no less true of industrial societies than of nonindustrial ones. There is, however, a major difference between industrial and nonindustrial societies in this respect. Industrial societies minimize the legitimate role of kinship criteria, and nepotism, for example, is inevitably regarded as a sin in many contexts in such societies. Nonindustrial societies often make such criteria the major legitimate basis of selection, and in such societies the failure to practice nepotism in many, if not most, situations may be a sin.

The universalistic-particularistic distinction as applied to criteria for selection is a distinction on quite a high level of generalization. For many problems in social analysis even so abstract a distinction is useful. This must not, however, lead one to presume that two relationships that admit persons on predominantly universalistic criteria are identical in any other specific sense.[17] The criteria may be widely different in all other respects than this one. Doctor-patient, businessman-customer, and employer-employee relationships in the United States are

---

17. It is, however, possible to say that some of these relationship aspects combine more readily with one another than do others. Predominantly universalistic relationships are likely to emphasize both rationality and functional specificity. Relationships are rarely both predominantly universalistic and predominantly functionally diffuse. This question is explored briefly later in the present chapter.

all predominantly universalistic ones, institutionally
speaking, and a rather high level of institutionalization,
especially with regard to the conformity aspects of the
institutions involved, is maintained. Nevertheless, the
concrete criteria involved differ very widely indeed. In
the first case, the criteria are professional achievement
on the one hand and state of health on the other; in the
second, property ownership (or control) on the one hand
and inclination and ability to purchase on the other; and
in the third case, control of jobs and of wages to pay for
performance on the one hand and ability to perform the
jobs on the other. The variation possible with regard to
particularistic criteria is no less great. In comparing
two relationships the classification of each with regard
to membership criteria gives one insight into the possible
range of differentiation on one particular level and in
one particular respect. Whether this distinction is a
useful one can only be determined by its application, and
the ability consequent to that application, to judge
whether or not the distinction proves to be useful in the
construction of more or less well confirmed theories.[18]

3. The substantive definition aspect

In every relationship there are activities or considerations or rights and obligations or performances that
are covered by the relationship. These factors comprise

---

18. In this connection the author is of the opinion
that the usefulness of this pair of concepts with reference
to certain problems of analysis is beyond doubt. These
problems fall into the category of studies of changes from
states of nonindustrialization to industrialization (more
specifically, obstacles to industrialization). Certainly
in the case of China many "influences" of the "traditional"
structures on the structures of industrialization and vice
versa can be explored in these terms, and these "influences" are "important" in the sense that they are "influences" that must be understood if the problem of current
social change in China is to be understood.

the substantive definition of the relationship. For example, in the employer-employee relationship in an industrial society the employer usually provides the worker
with tools, materials, working premises, and a payment of
some sort for the work done. The employee on his part
provides a more or less well specified form of services.
Obviously, the substantive definitions of relationships
are also subject to the widest kind of variations, and
here again a distinction among such definitions is sought
on a level of generalization relevant to any relationship
and at the same time useful for empirical analysis. For
those purposes the distinction is drawn between functionally specific and functionally diffuse relationships. A
functionally specific relationship is one in which the
activities or considerations or rights and obligations or
performances that are covered by the relationship are
precisely defined and precisely delimited. The modern
business contract relationship is a typical example of a
functionally specific relationship. In a modern contract,
ideally speaking, an attempt is made to state explicitly
everything involved in the particular relationship concerned.[19] If the contract is between two parties, A and B,
the contract defines what the relationship is to cover,
say the sale of a piece of land, what A must deliver to B,
and vice versa. As Parsons points out in such relationships, the burden of proof of obligation falls upon the
person claiming it.[20] Thus, if, after B has delivered the
title of the land to A and taken A's check for five

---

19. This is within the social context of such relationships. As Durkheim has pointed out (see De la division
du travail social, Felix Alcan, Paris, 1932, 6th ed.,
pp. 184-197), the phenomena of contract relationships are
not comprehensible save in the context of quite specific
noncontractual social structures. Nevertheless, within
such a context contracts are, ideally speaking, functionally specific.

20. Parsons, op.cit., p. 190.

thousand dollars, assuming that the title and the land are as described in the contract, B claims that A owes him an additional twenty-five hundred dollars, B must show that promise to pay this additional amount was called for by the contract. Now it is obvious, of course, that all contracts are not completely clear-cut documents leaving no room for alternative interpretations, but in theory they are drawn to serve this purpose.[21] The plaintiff and defendant in such relationships, should disagreement arise between them, both refer the case to the substantive definition of the relationship which is conceived as affording a precise answer to any question that may arise on this score.

Parsons uses the doctor-patient relationship (in modern industrial society) to illustrate the functionally specific type of relationship.[22] The doctor-patient relationship is not ordinarily carried out on an explicit contract basis. Nevertheless, the range of the doctor's "authority" over the patient, his access to the patient's body, etc., are all justified only in terms of a quite specific end, the patient's physical (and mental) well-being. Furthermore, it is expected that the doctor's contributions to this end will be made in quite specific ways and only in these ways, ideally speaking. These ways

---

21. One source of ambiguity in contract relationships may arise from the following situation. It is often to A's advantage to have the contract precisely drawn with regard to his maximum obligations to B and B's minimum obligations to A. It may also be to A's advantage to have the contract imprecisely drawn with regard to his minimum obligations to B and B's maximum obligations to him. The same possibility is present from B's point of view. A contract is badly drawn from B's point of view if A succeeds in such a plan and vice versa. It is badly drawn from both points of view if it emerges so vaguely defined that it is either unenforceable or only enforceable through litigation more costly than the net advantages sought by the parties to the contract.

22. Parsons, op.cit., p. 190.

are the techniques of a supposedly scientifically based therapy.[23] Use of other types of therapy (most particularly magically based therapy) are most strongly indicted and constitute a violation of the institutionalized terms of the doctor-patient relationship.

The concept of <u>functional diffuseness</u> explores the opposite type of substantive definition. A <u>functionally diffuse</u> relationship is one in which the substantive definition of the relationship is more or less vaguely defined and delimited. The relationship between husband and wife is more or less functionally diffuse in most (and probably in all) societies. Modern United States society probably limits the husband-wife relationship about as much as any society ever has, and even so the relationship is conspicuously different in this respect from the contract relationship. The relationship is institutionally defined by some set of more or less vague terms as mutual love and respect, companionship, financial support of the wife by the husband, etc. Some unusually explicit limits are placed on the relationship. The husband is ordinarily not expected to let his marital relationship inject particularistic elements into his operations in his occupa-

---

23. The doctor-patient relationship is institutionalized as predominantly rational in its cognitive aspect. In fact, save for the areas in which lack of scientific knowledge prevents the determination of rational action, the action in terms of this relationship strictly defined is institutionalized as wholly rational. Irrational action is considered inevitable to some degree, but the number and sort of irrational decisions a doctor makes classify him as a good or a bad doctor. Some irrational decisions may even result in his loss of the right to practice medicine. Since the end of the doctor-patient relationship is empirically defined, the only type of alogical action open to doctors is methodologically alogical or magical action. Such action, while present to some degree or in some attenuated forms, is in theory never tolerated by either the members of the profession themselves or the general lay community of industrial societies. Actually, of course, there may be a considerable amount of such action.

tional sphere, etc. Nevertheless, when a wife asks for a
new dress, a husband reluctant to grant the request (or
demand) does not decide the question in terms of explicit
agreements verbal, written, or mutually understood at the
time of marriage or reformulated explicitly periodically
after marriage. Only in quite extreme cases of nonsupport
could a wife, for example, take her case to a court.
Again, Parsons has pointed out[24] in such relationships the
burden of proof is placed on the person desiring to evade
the obligation alleged under the relationship. In the
functionally specific case defense for evasion centers on
the specific substantive definition of the relationship
itself. In the functionally diffuse case the implications
of the request for other relationships or other standards
becomes the basis of defense. When a wife, five years and
six months after marriage, requests a new red wool dress
costing a hundred dollars, a husband may expect to evade
the obligation by stating that he lacks the money, the
request is extravagant, or that, if granted, it will mean
that clothes necessary for the children can not be pur-
chased. He can not ordinarily expect to get by as would
an employer, suddenly faced with a request for an extra

---

24. Parsons, op.cit., p. 190. Parsons states: "The
burden of proof [in the functionally specific relationship]
is on him who would exact an obligation, that it is really
owed, while in many other relationships [i.e., functionally diffuse ones] the opposite is true, the burden of proof
is on the one who would evade an obligation, that it is
not due. Thus in the ordinary case of commercial indebtedness, a request for money on the part of one party will be
met by the question, do I owe it? Whether the requester
'needs' the money is irrelevant as is whether the other
can well afford to pay it. If, on the other hand the two
are brothers, any contractual agreements are at least of
secondary importance, the important questions are on the
one hand, whether and how urgently the one needs the money,
on the other, whether the second can afford it. In the
latter connection it comes down to a question of the possible conflict of this with what are recognized as higher
obligations."

hundred dollars in wages by an employee for past work, by
maintaining that he did not <u>owe</u> it to the claimant and
that the claimant could not prove the indebtedness in any
court in the land.

Modern industrial societies institutionalize functionally specific relationships on a scale probably equaled
in no other type of society. At the same time it may well
be that in no society are institutionalized functionally
specific relationships totally lacking. Nevertheless, in
all societies more or less functionally diffuse relationships are always institutionalized for some relationships
that are crucial or more or less strategic for the society.
The differences in a society between the relationships
strictly institutionalized on a functionally specific
basis and those institutionalized as more or less functionally diffuse are important, but the differences among the
relationships of differing degrees of functional diffuseness are also important.[25] In "traditional" Chinese
society both the father-son and husband-wife relationships
are to a high degree functionally diffuse, but those
between father and son are more diffuse than those between
husband and wife and also take precedence over the latter.
In modern American society both these relationships are
functionally diffuse too, but, if a difference in degree
can be discerned, the reverse of the Chinese situation
holds. In both societies the father-son relationship is
ordinarily more diffuse than the relationship of friends.
Considerations of this sort are of great significance in

----

25. In the mixed case containing both elements of
functional specificity and functional diffuseness a distinction like that drawn relative to membership criteria
aspects may be used. Mixed cases emphasizing functional
specificity more highly than functional diffuseness will be
called <u>predominantly functionally</u> specific; the reverse
will be called <u>predominantly functionally diffuse</u>. Here
too, both ideally and actually speaking, the mixed case is,
usually, the one more often met.

the analysis of the structure of solidarity[26] of a ·society or of many types of concrete social structures.

There are also extremely important distinctions in these respects relative to relationships that are institutionalized as either functionally specific or only slightly functionally diffuse. The degree to which these factors are well institutionalized both with regard to their conformity and sanctions aspects may be strategic for certain types of analysis. The great emphasis on functional specificity in many different relationships in an industrial society is almost certainly one element in the type of dissatisfaction summed up in the objections of individuals to being treated as "cogs in a wheel." In attempts to offset this, some personnel managers try to impress their workers with the feeling of belonging to a "family." Because of the dysfunctional aspects of functionally diffuse relationships for modern industrial concerns,[27] such techniques have to be most carefully limited. These and other moves in a functionally diffuse direction will no doubt lessen certain tensions, but they may create new problems of equal magnitude. They may, for example, increase the complexity of dealing with employees beyond any practicable limits. A large scale mass production firm cannot operate on the basis of vaguely defined obligations to thousands of employees.[28] On the other hand, there may also be difficulties from the workers' point of view. Paternalistic policies on the part of employers may be

---

26. See below, Chapter VIII.

27. This point is discussed below in Chapter IX, e.g., pp. 431-437.

28. The essence of the distinction lies in exactness as opposed to vagueness. Extremely complex relationships may be highly functionally specific. It would be interesting to investigate in these terms the great emphasis that has been placed by businessmen on the need for legislation legally binding unions to their contracts. A contract that is not binding on one of the parties to it and subject to abandonment at will injects a functionally diffuse element into a type of relationship (i.e., the contract relationship) which is habitually thought to exclude such elements.

bitterly resented as "undue interference" with the private
lives of the employees. From the employee's point of view
the employer-employee relationship is institutionalized as
a functionally specific one too, and the violation of this
institution may well be one of the elements of resentment
sometimes encountered in "company-run" housing and community developments for employees. Such attitudes often
exist even though the material standard of living of the
employees is improved by them.

Finally, with regard to elements of variation in the
substantive definition aspects of a relationship, the
question of the actual content of the relationship must
always be kept in mind. Two relationships may be functionally specific (e.g., the doctor-patient and the
employer-employee relationships in modern industrial society) and yet differ widely in what they are functionally
specific about. The same may be true of relationships of
comparable or differing degrees of functional diffuseness.
One must not, therefore, assume that similarity in these
respects means a general similarity in the relationships
(e.g., the relationship between witch doctor and patient
may well be functionally specific in some societies just
as that between doctor and patient is in modern industrial
society). The use of these concepts gives one insight
into only one type of extremely general distinction between different types of substantive definition aspects of
relationships. It cannot be applied beyond those lengths
except insofar as the presence of functional specificity
or various degrees of functional diffuseness in a given
relationship can be shown to have structural implications
for other aspects of the same relationship or for different
relationships connected in some fashion with the one
immediately concerned.

4. The affective aspect

The difficult state of the concept of _affect_ and the

definition of it used here have been stated above in another connection.[29] The definition, such as it is, may be repeated here: the term _affect_ as used here includes components of pleasurable or painful significance to the actor, and of approval or disapproval of the object or state which occasions the reaction. It includes also those reactions to stimuli that are commonly catalogued under the term "emotions" covering as that does such inadequately defined and understood terms as "anger," "hate," "fear," "love," "pity," etc.[30] There is certainly no question but that many relationships involve rather high degrees of affectivity of rather generally appreciated sorts. In U.S. society, for example, mothers are expected to "love" their children, and husband and wife are expected to "love" one another at least in the early stages of their marriage. The sense of the word "love" is quite different in some respects although there is generally assumed to be some common element involved. The average member of the society expects to see examples of this sort of reaction about him in everyday life, and he is usually of the opinion that he can identify these reactions and distinguish them from others of different types.

It may also be true that there are relationships

---

29. See p. 183ff.

30. One may certainly wonder whether such a definition is really any better than a less imposing one which is perhaps more stimulating, intuitively speaking, though no more or less precise than the definition given here. Such an alternative definition might run as follows: the term _affect_ has as its referent the phenomena which people describe or exemplify when they respond to questions such as "How did you 'feel' about that situation or that person?" In a sense this definition is, perhaps, easier to frame in operational terms than the one given above. The distinction drawn, for example, between "feeling" and "knowing" is generally understood as a distinction, and although the concept of "feeling" may include many different reactions for many different people, it always seems to cover the body of referents generally termed "emotions," "affects," etc.

involving no affectivity whatever. Exact determination of
this point, and it cannot be determined in any manner
except exactly since it is an all or none proposition, will
have to wait upon a much more precisely and operationally
defined concept than the one in use here. However, even
if such cases exist, it is perhaps not unreasonable to
maintain, until the contrary is demonstrated, that the
quantity of such cases actually would be relatively small
and (and this is a more extreme hypothesis) that the relevance of such cases for the operation of societies is not
on the whole great. The reverse might, of course, be true,
ideally speaking. The second of these hypotheses about
completely nonaffective relationships is based on a line
of speculation such as the following: actions in terms of
structures of no affective significance to an actor are not
likely to have appreciable effects on structures which do
have affective significance for an actor; if they did, by
reason of their implications for the other classes of
structures, the actions of the first type would acquire
affective significance, etc.[31]

The distinction between relationships on the basis of

---

31. The rather cavalier fashion in which this problem is discussed must not lead the reader to treat the
matter as of little significance or to assume that the
writer holds such views about it. The treatment given the
matter here is given in despair of something better and
with the feeling that something, however badly formulated,
must be said on this score. The precept involved here is
that any bad theory which is explicit is easier to correct
and alter than a bad or even somewhat better theory left
implicit. Quite important problems are involved in this
matter. For example, the relation between affects and the
general problem of "motivation" is of the essence of the
matter so briefly mentioned here. It is also a central
problem for the whole question of the analysis of social
action. Parsons, in his current work on the general conceptual scheme and theoretical system of action phenomena,
seeks to make headway with just this type of problem. To
the degree that he and others are successful in this effort
the whole question under treatment here would have to be
reexamined and restated, if not totally changed.

affectivity as opposed to nonaffectivity will not be made
here because of the considerations just mentioned. There
is, however, a basis of distinction that has something in
common with this one. There are relationships that tend
to minimize direct contact, to carry out such contact as
does exist on a relatively "formal" basis, and to maximize
restraint of overt affective displays. There are other
relationships that tend to emphasize direct contact, "informality," and overt display of affects.[32] In the first
case, the term avoidance, and in the second, the term
intimacy will be applied. Here one is faced with polar
types. Perhaps no relationships are at either pole, but
the gamut that can be run is wide. It varies from relationships which, though quite important for the parties
concerned, require the members to avoid any direct contact
with one another, including seeing or being seen by one
another, to relationships in which direct, "informal,"
almost constant contacts with overt displays of affect are
both expected and demanded by the participants and/or by
other members of the society. The relationship between
mother and infant in many, if not most, societies is to a
high degree intimate in this sense. The relationship
between husband and wife is an intimate one in both the
modern United States and "traditional" China in many respects, but in the latter case it is far less intimate
than the former, involving as it does, in the stricter
Confucian families, genuine avoidance in many contexts.
The doctor-patient relationship contains major elements of
avoidance. The contacts involved are direct, but emotional restraint, especially on the doctor's part, is
expected and the contacts are to a high degree "formal" in
their precision of definition and their confinement to a

---

32. The terms formal and informal are defined below,
pp. 267-268.

highly specialized context.[33] The businessman-customer relationship also has major avoidance aspects in this respect.

Since the "all or none" cases of avoidance and intimacy are rare, if not totally absent, the classification of relationships in these respects is always clearer on a

---

33. The usual connotations of the word "avoidance" interfere with its application to the doctor-patient relationship, and yet in the sense in which it is used here it is applicable. Institutionally speaking, it is frequently expected that one's doctor in western society also be one's friend so that the doctor-patient relationship is quite frequently seen in combination with that of friend-friend. This is particularly striking in the case of the general practitioner role in the United States. Nevertheless, this is not essential to the doctor-patient relationship. Displays of affect by the doctor toward the patient are justified only insofar as they have therapeutic value. Displays of affects such as pity, sympathy, and even anger are legitimate only if they can be viewed as in some way therapeutic. The "bedside manner," for example, is considered "good" if it has such an effect and is considered "bad" if it does not, smacking as it does in the latter case of meretricious action. Displays of affect that lack a genuine or at least fancied therapeutic value are supposedly ruled out of the relationship. The institutional structure in these respects is carried so far that in cases of serious illness doctors are expected not to treat those with whom in other roles they are deeply involved affectively. Furthermore, insofar as the doctor does react affectively toward the patient, and that is certainly inevitable in some kind to some degree, he is expected to observe affective restraint at least to the degree that it not influence either the character or the quality of his treatment.

On the other hand, the patient often comes to the doctor in a state of extreme affective display. Such lack of restraint on the part of the patient whether directed at the doctor or not is something to be treated or kept out of the relationship. Ideally speaking, one goes to a doctor to be "cured" or "kept cured." No affective display save that of "confidence in one's doctor" is encouraged in the patient unless there is therapeutic value in such a display. For example, patients who "fall in love" with their doctors and openly display their love in the therapeutic situation place no less a strain on the doctor-patient relationship then doctors who do the same with their patients. The psychoanalytic situation offers certain exceptions to this, of course, but here in theory a definite therapeutic consideration is involved.

comparative rather than an absolute basis. The doctor-patient relationship is clearly more of an avoidance one
than the mother-child relationship, for example. This
makes for difficulty in discussing examples of a particular
type of relationship on a noncomparative basis. To avoid
that difficulty the concepts of <u>predominantly avoidant</u> and
<u>predominantly intimate</u> relationships will be used to
classify relationships from the point of view of their
affective aspects. A relationship will be termed <u>predomi-
nantly avoidant</u> if it is one that emphasizes restraint or
formality[34] in the overt display of affect and/or subordi-

---

34. A given type of action will be termed <u>formalized</u>
or <u>formal</u> to the degree that its structures (but not necessarily the specific obligations covered) are precisely and
minutely defined and/or institutionalized for the context
of action in which it appears <u>regardless of the specific
individuals involved</u>. It will be termed <u>informalized</u> or
<u>informal</u> to the extent that variations in its structures
actually develop and/or are institutionalized on the basis
of the specific individuals involved. Again the mixed
case is frequent, and depending on emphasis, the terms
<u>predominantly formal</u> and <u>predominantly informal</u> may be
used. Thus, the display of "respect" by a "traditional"
Chinese son for his father has been predominantly and highly formalized by the developments of that society. The
relationship between a peasant son and father is usually
less formal than that of a gentry son and father in that
society, for the latter are expected to observe the rules
of etiquette in all their minutiae. By comparison at
least the display of "love" or "respect" by an "American"
son for his father is predominantly informal, placing
heavy emphasis as it does on the specific personalities
involved and the uniqueness of the relationship. In the
"American" son-father case certain minimal formal elements
are, of course, institutionalized. The "American" son is
institutionally expected to "love" and "respect" his father
within certain limits regardless of the specific individuals involved.
    Because the formal-informal distinction is rela-
tively, at least, more precise than the avoidant-intimate
distinction, and because of the large role played by the
former in the latter, it might be better for the present
stage of development at least to replace the latter by the
former. This has not been done in the present tentative
version of this work because it is felt that to do so
would excessively minimize the "affective" elements in the
usual sense, however poorly developed that concept may be

nates the overt display of affect to other aspects of the
relationship. A relationship will be termed <u>predominantly</u>
<u>intimate</u> if it is one that emphasizes lack of restraint
and informality in the overt display of affect and/or
subordinates other aspects of the relationship to the overt
display of affect. In terms of these concepts the relationship between husband and wife in a "traditional"
Chinese gentry family is a predominantly avoidant relationship whereas that between husband and wife in modern
American society is a predominantly intimate one.

The use of the concepts of avoidance and intimacy
merely provides a highly generalized distinction between
relationships in terms of their affective respects. It is
only one of, perhaps, several possible distinctions of
this sort. It is a distinction between relationships on
the basis of their affective aspects on the highest level
of generalization possible in these respects because all
relationships may be classified affectively in these terms.

---

for the present. The substitution might also do less violence to ordinary usage than the terms avoidant and intimate as applied here. Here as in all cases throughout
this volume the reader should feel free to revise, refine,
change, and improve the concepts as presented here wherever
any useful theoretical purpose would be served.

One further caution should be mentioned. The
terms formal and informal are not coterminous with functionally specific and functionally diffuse. In the latter
case, the emphasis is on the elements covered or not covered by the relationship. In the former, the emphasis is
on the manner in which the members of the relationship
deal with one another. The analytic distinctness of the
two does not, however, mean that they have no implications
for one another. Some elements of informality are incompatible with some elements of functional specificity, and
some are not. Some elements of formality are incompatible
with some elements of functional diffuseness, and some are
not. "Traditional" Chinese society, for example, emphasizes both formality and functional diffuseness in the
father-son relationship. United States society emphasizes
informality and functional diffuseness in that relationship. Many examples of possible and impossible combinations of this sort come readily to mind and testify to the
analytic distinctness of these concepts.

The possibility of alternative taxonomic development or
further development of this particular taxonomic suggestion cannot in the long or short run be neglected by
social scientists because of the central importance and
the general prominence of the affective aspects of action
in general. The present basis of distinction has been
chosen with a view to its general relevance to the analysis of social structure. The line of empirical theoretical
speculation involved in this particular choice may be
briefly stated with regard to a general line of justification of this choice and one specific instance of that
general line.

In all societies situations arise in which the unre-
strained display of affective responses would or could be
peculiarly disruptive, and there are also situations in
which affective expression is to a high degree eufunctional.[35] Current work in the field of "personality" development would even seem to indicate that rather lavish informal displays of affect toward children are highly
eufunctional for the development of stable adult personalities. The distinction used here is based largely on a
distinction between types of regulation of affective
expression and hence is germane for those reasons.

More specifically, in all societies the question of
the allocation of power and responsibility is one of
central importance. Furthermore, in all societies there
are some socially defined structures in which a premium is
placed upon the efficient and even rapid exercise of
responsibility. Even slightly uninhibited displays of
affect can be extremely disruptive in such situations.
Hence it may be argued that in all such situations the
institutionalization of predominantly avoidant rather than
predominantly intimate relationships is eufunctional. One

---

35. This matter is discussed in Chapter IV in the
section on the regulation of affective expression.

of the most obvious cases of such a relationship is that
between superiors and subordinates in a military organization, but this is by no means the only case. One sees
similar factors involved in the relationship between a
"traditional" Chinese father and his son. Because of the
manner in which the family structure fits into the total
structure of Chinese society, that relationship is far more
important in these respects than the same relationship in
modern American society.

In general, wherever the intimate type of affective
expression is not a central element of the substantive
definition of the relationship, or at least whenever it is
subordinated to other aspects of the substantive definition
of the relationship, a premium is placed upon the institutionalization of avoidant elements in the relationship.
It is not enough apparently to repress intimacy in such
situations. Apparently formal modes of affective expression are also needed. Because of the ubiquitous relevance
of such considerations, the particular dichotomy suggested
here will be used until one of greater relevance is suggested.

5. The goal orientation aspect

The discussion above of the substantive definition
aspects of relationships centered attention on the kinds
of activities covered by the relationship. The goal orientation aspect of a relationship focuses attention on what
might be called "motivational" aspects of the relationship. Insofar as the ends of a relationship are manifest
to one or all of the parties concerned, what can be said
about them further that is of general usefulness in analysis? Here the distinction has tended to focus on such
polar terms as "egoistic" and "altruistic," "self-inter-
ested" and "disinterested," etc. Parsons in his original

discussion of this matter was quick to point out[36] in his
distinction between doctors in their relations with
patients and businessmen in their relations with customers
that the one group was by no means necessarily more "selfish" or "greedy" than the other, and so forth. He states
that one must look at the ways in which the two different
situations are institutionally defined to see that the
same individual cast in one role would very probably act
quite differently in these respects than he would if cast
in the other, and so forth. For example, doctors would
appear to be very much more lenient in their reaction to
patients who do not pay their bills than are businessmen.
Moreover, patients feel in time of genuine need that it is
legitimate to request that a "sliding scale" of medical
fees be applied to them, and doctors feel that it is
legitimate too. In fact, it is assumed that the doctor
determines all fees partially on such grounds. Customers
do not expect such treatment from businessmen or vice
versa, and the only legitimate way to force it is the
economic last resort of bankruptcy proceedings. While
these marked differences exist, it is not hard to indicate
that the relation of the distinctions involved is to
differently institutionalized situations rather than to
basic differences in the character structure of doctors
and businessmen.[37] One need only ask whether as a whole
doctors who also own property of various sorts conduct
themselves in their management of these assets in the same

---

36. Parsons, op.cit., pp. 196-197.

37. It is not meant to say that there are no basic
differences in character structure between doctors and
businessmen. It is only intended to say that, if such a
difference exists, it is related to these structures and
that such a difference need not and cannot be invoked
apart from these structures to explain the differences between the activities of doctors and businessmen in these
specific respects.

way that they do with their patients. Or perhaps one
should ask more accurately, is it institutionalized that
they will do so? The answer is surely a negative one. A
doctor who is terribly exacting with his patients over
fees is a subject for adverse comment. If he carries his
conduct to the point of refusing to treat the patient when
the patient is in need and gives as an excuse the fact
that the patient has not paid his last bill, he is certainly violating the institutional elements of the medical
profession. On the other hand, a doctor who, having
failed to receive payment for one bit of land, refuses to
sell another to the farmer concerned, comes in for no
community censure regardless of how dire the farmer's need
for land may be. One may suggest that the term doctor
defines a role and not a man and that qua doctor one does
not buy and sell land. Qua doctor one treats patients.
This is, of course, correct and is the essence of the
matter. It brings out the fact that it is by no means the
total character of the individual actor that is of concern
but only his actions in a particular socially defined role.

This rather lengthy introduction to the main argument
here is intended to obviate any ethical overtones or
general character judgments from the use of the concepts
to be suggested here. The concepts that will be used here
are individualistic and responsible. A given relationship
is more or less individualistic to the degree that each of
the parties to the relationship may be expected to calcu-
late how best to secure maximum advantage from the relationship for himself without regard to the goals sought by
the other parties to the relationship. A given relationship is more or less responsible to the degree that each
of the parties to the relationship may be expected, in
seeking to realize his own goals, to safeguard, even at
the expense of some of his own goals, such goals of the
other parties as are relevant to the relationship. Again
the terms are polar, and cases at the poles are perhaps

difficult to find. Again the use of the prefix <u>predomi-
nantly</u> can be of service. A relationship will be called
<u>predominantly individualistic</u> if the emphasis is placed on
each party to the relationship "looking out for himself,"
i.e., on each member acting in his own behalf to safeguard
the realization of his goals with relatively lesser emphasis on those of the other member(s). A relationship will
be called <u>predominantly responsible</u> if the emphasis is
placed on one (or more) of the members safeguarding the
relevant goals of the others if he is (or they are) to
achieve his (or their) own goals at all.

The distinction may be illustrated by examples already
mentioned above. A business relationship between two men
in the United States today is a predominantly individualistic one. Each party to the relationship is expected
(institutionally expected in this case) to seek to maximize
his own interests. The situation is not devoid of responsible elements. Presumably negotiations are carried out
in terms of a general framework of honesty on which neither
side is expected to infringe. Straight misrepresentation
of the property involved is fraud as is payment for it
with a bad check. On the other hand, if the customer is
willing to pay twice as much for the property as would be
necessary if he knew the situation better, the seller is
not expected to enlighten him or to price the property at
the going rate despite his customer's ignorance. Students
of social change could no doubt trace a very interesting
development of the businessman-customer relationship in
the United States. At no time was the maxim of <u>caveat
emptor</u> completely without limit because the courts stood
ready to act on certain practices classified as illegitimate. Nevertheless, the change has certainly been marked,
and "deals" which were commonplace in the heyday of the
"captains of industry" would be considered definitely un-
ethical today. Despite these changes, the "good businessman" is expected to be able to take care of himself and is

not expected to look out for the interests of others. If
he does look out for the interests of others in business
relationships with him over and above the minimum degree
required by the general framework of expected probity, and
if he does so to the detriment of his own business interests, whatever may be the evaluation of him in other respects, he has shown himself to be a "poor businessman."

On the other hand, the doctor-patient relationship
may be described as a predominantly responsible one. The
doctor is responsible for protecting the patient's interests. He is not only expected to avoid direct misrepresentation, but he is also expected to ensure the protection
of the patient from any ignorance the patient may have in
this connection. If the patient wants an operation unnecessary for his health, the doctor, whether to his own
financial hurt or no, is expected not to perform it. If
the accepted scale of fees for patients of a given income
group is five dollars a visit, it is not ethical for a
doctor to charge such a patient ten simply because the
patient is ignorant of the situation. Again it must be
insisted that this tells one nothing of the personal character of the doctor.. A doctor who scrupulously observes
these standards may be "selfish" in the extreme, and a
businessman who follows the others may be the "soul of
generosity." The practice of medicine is, however, very
differently institutionalized than is the conduct of business. The achievement of success in the one is in part
dependent upon the observance of this type of responsibility, and in the other it is in part dependent upon the
observance of the type of individualism pointed out. Two
men almost identical in their personal ambitions for money,
power, and prestige may neverthless be forced to engage in
strikingly different types of concrete acts if one is in
the medical and the other is in the business sphere. There
is in all this a striking instance of the relevance of an
understanding of general social structure for the under-

standing of differences in the actions of individuals.

6. The stratification aspect

This aspect of relationships is fortunately considerably simpler than those that have been discussed above. Stratification has been defined for present purposes as "the particular type of role differentiation that differentiates between higher and lower standings in terms of one or more criteria.[38] In some relationships one party to the relationship is expected to have a higher ranking than the other. The relationship between a "traditional" Chinese father and his son is of this type. On the other hand, there are relationships which are such that, regardless of the ranking of the parties concerned in their other roles, in their roles as members of this particular relationship and relative to one another their ranking is either considered equal or any question of differences in rank is considered irrelevant.

A relationship of the former type will be called a hierarchical one. A hierarchical relationship is defined as one in which the relative rankings of the members are expected to be different and the actions involved in the relationship are differentiated with regard to this difference. The latter type of relationship mentioned above will be called a nonhierarchical one, and special cases of this will be called egalitarian. A nonhierarchical relationship is one in which no differential rankings of the members in any respect are considered relevant to the relationship. When a relationship is one such that it is specifically required that the members treat one another without reference to differential rankings, it will be termed egalitarian. The term egalitarian is used to distinguish this type of relationship from those in which

---

38. See above, p. 164.

differences in rank are irrelevant but are so simply by lack of institutional definition of the relationship in this respect, i.e., in which the members are neither equals nor unequals ideally speaking.

More or less hierarchical relationships are familiar enough to require little or no comment. The example of a "traditional" Chinese father and his son has been given, but other examples are even more obvious. The relationship between officers and enlisted men in military organizations is definitely of this sort, and given the usual objectives of military organizations, the presence of hierarchical aspects can be shown to be definitely eufunctional to such a system in its usual setting.

Nonhierarchical and purely egalitarian relationships are somewhat harder to find. It is probably only in relationships of very short duration and in relationships such that any one specific case of the relationship is socially defined as unimportant that one finds nonhierarchical relationships of a nonegalitarian sort. So pervasive are rank order systems and so strategic, if not crucial, are they structurally speaking that some definite institutionalization is usually required to keep hierarchical considerations out of the picture. Furthermore, only in rather fleeting relationships, specific cases of which mattered little, would it be possible to have no definite structuring of the hierarchical elements which do exist because of the great relevance of such elements to the sort of things which can be done in terms of the relationship. Relationships of the casual meeting or crowd contact sort would fall into this category. This is not to argue that such relationships in the aggregate are unimportant for the society in which they occur. It can probably be demonstrated, for example, that it would not be possible for an industrial society to operate unless it could be expected that a tremendous number of acts would be carried out in terms of the "casual meeting" type of relationship.

On the other hand, in some nonindustrial societies relationships of this sort are reduced to a very small number,
and any great expansion of such relationships would be
dysfunctional for the society concerned.

The egalitarian relationship, while perhaps, on the
whole considerably less frequent than the hierarchical
type, is also quite familiar to most scholars in this
field. The relationship of friend to friend is of this
order in modern western societies. Friends are expected
to treat one another as equals and to consider one another
as such regardless of other factors. During the last war
the egalitarian character of friendship as opposed to the
hierarchical character of the officer-enlisted-man relationship was a frequent theme of conflict in comic strips,
in the movies, on the radio, etc. Bosom friends who met
but could not eat together because of the military distinction appeared in all sorts of stories. Whether or not
old friends in uniform, meeting in a nonmilitary context,
could treat one another as equals became as it were a test
of the strength of the friendship, and so forth.

Strong egalitarian elements often enter relationships
that are in other respects hierarchical. In many respects
the members of a university faculty are equals despite the
fact that for some purposes the hierarchy of professors,
associate professors, assistant professors, and instructors
is of great significance. The faculty situation becomes
tense at once if it is felt that the hierarchical aspects
are being pushed beyond their institutionalized sphere.
The emphasis on egalitarianism in the face of hierarchical
distinctions is perhaps symbolized by the official university use of the term of address "professor" for all three
ranks of the professor category and by the fact that
faculty members among themselves frequently avoid such
terms altogether and use the more general term, "mister."

For comparative purposes the distinctions concerned
with the stratification aspects of relationships are often

quite revealing. Military systems seem everywhere to have been hierarchically ordered if successful. But other relationships show greater contrasts. Take, for example, the husband-wife relationship. In modern American, urban, middle class society the relationship, if not regarded, ideally speaking, as egalitarian, is institutionalized as very close to egalitarian. In "traditional" China it was definitely a hierarchical relationship with the husband very much more highly ranked than the wife. There may very well be societies in which the relationship is hierarchical but with the wife ranked well above her husband in most respects. With factual knowledge of only these three differences with regard to one aspect of one type of relationship, one may make a considerable number of predictions about other types of differences that must exist in these societies. Predictions based on these three facts taken alone might be extremely risky, but they would tell something, and the more such facts one has the less risky prediction would become.

In conclusion of Part A of this chapter it should be reiterated that the list presented here of six different aspects of any relationship is not presented as a definitive list. How much longer the list can be made usefully remains to be seen. That is a question for which in essence there is no final definitive answer. One simply adds to or changes the list whenever it can be shown to be useful to do so for the further development of empirical knowledge. The same caution must be reaffirmed about the specific distinctions made in terms of the six different aspects discussed above. The particular distinctions made are believed by many to be quite useful and are believed by some to be tremendously valuable tools for analysis. No one would seriously maintain, however, that those concepts are either definitive in number or so well and precisely worked out as to make further effort in this direction unproductive.

B. COMPARATIVE ANALYSIS IN TERMS OF THE CONCEPTS
OF RELATIONSHIP ASPECTS

The concepts discussed above are tools for the comparative analysis of social structure in several senses
that may be illustrated here. In the first place, they
are concepts such that in terms of them some empirical
statements can conceivably be made about any relationship.
This means that, for comparative purposes, questions asked
in terms of these concepts are always capable of yielding
some answers. Furthermore, an attempt, however unsystem-
atic or elementary, has been made to employ concepts whose
referents are especially significant for the understanding
of the part played by specific relationships in the total
social structure. Thus, these concepts are expected to
have empirical referents in the case of any and all relationships, and the particular form that that referent takes
is expected to be of considerable significance for understanding the larger social systems into which these relationships fit. For example, in any recurrent type of
relationship, and certainly in any institutionalized type
of relationship, something can be said about the criteria
for membership in the relationship. What is said about
those criteria can be stated in some respects in terms of
the distinction between universalism and particularism.
Finally, it can frequently be shown that the fact that the
criteria for membership are predominantly particularistic,
for example, is of considerable significance in understanding not only the operation of the relationship itself,
but also in understanding the operation of other social
systems into which it enters. To put the matter another
way, in any relationship of a recurrent sort, such material
will frequently, if not always, have important implications
for the relationship itself and for the other social sys-
terms into which it enters. That is to say, if the criteria for membership are shifted from predominantly particularistic to predominantly universalistic ones or vice

versa, the structural implications of that will extend
considerably beyond the shift itself.

One need only to think of the businessman-customer
relationship in a modern industrial society to see how
important such shifts can be. If businessmen were to
choose customers and customers businessmen on predominantly particularistic grounds, the whole economic structure
of industrial society would have to be altered, and, in
fact, it is doubtful whether any industrial system conducted on a business footing could survive such a switch.
This brings up another general consideration. As knowledge
accumulates in the field of social analysis, tools of this
sort should become increasingly valuable. Already one may
make out a reasonably strong case for the theory that, at
least in the economic structure of a society, heavy emphasis on rationality, functional specificity, universalistic
criteria, to mention only three aspects of relationships,
is a functional requisite for an undustrial society.[39]
One can contrariwise make out a very strong case for the
necessity of heavy emphasis on nonrationality, functional
diffuseness, and particularism if the economic structure
of the society is to be based on highly self-sufficient
agrarian units. As a larger and larger number of more or
less well-confirmed theories of this sort accumulate, that
is to say, as the amount one knows about the general implications of relationship aspects for social structure increases, one will be able to make increasingly fruitful
predictions about the possible range of variation in
structural patterns of the society concerned by asking a
minimum number of questions about more or less strategically selected relationships.

Like most scientific concepts these are intended to

---

39. The author has tried to sketch the case for such
a theory briefly in Family Revolution and in Some Problems
of Modernization in China, cited above.

make possible the greatest accumulation of scientifically
defensible knowledge about a given type of phenomena with
the least amount of effort, and to have that knowledge of
maximum general relevance to the development of the general theoretical system of the field concerned. It is to be
hoped that these concepts will in some measure prove themselves useful in the obviously utopian effort to reach
such a goal. More specifically, however, this set of
concepts is useful because it provides a framework in
terms of which one may compare the following different
sets of relationships: (1) different types of relationships in a single society, (2) similar types of relationships in different societies, and (3) different types of
relationships in different societies. For the purposes of
rapid sketching of examples, Table 4 is set up.

Table 4. Polar terms for relationship aspects

	x	y
1. Cognitive aspect	rational	nonrational
2. Membership criteria aspect	universalistic	particularistic
3. Substantive defini- tion aspect	functionally specific	functionally diffuse
4. Affective aspect	avoidant	intimate
5. Goal orientation aspect	individualistic	responsible
6. Stratification aspect	hierarchical	nonhierarchical

Using the table, a relationship that is described as
of the type $x_1, x_2, x_3, x_4, x_5, x_6$ is a relationship which emphasizes rationality in the cognitive sphere, universalistic selection of members, functionally specific substantive definitions, avoidant affects, individualistic
goal orientations, and hierarchical ranking of the members
of a relationship.

In terms of this framework, for the purposes of example one may compare: (1) the doctor-patient relationship and the businessman-customer relationship in modern United States society, (2) the businessman-customer relationship in modern United States society and in that of "traditional" China, and (3) the businessman-customer relationship in modern United States society with that of gentry father and son in "traditional" China.[40]

1. The doctor-patient and the businessman-customer relationships in modern United States society

The doctor-patient relationship may be described in the terms used here as $x_1, x_2, x_3, x_4, y_5, y_6$. The doctor is

---

40. An attempt is made here to use statements about these relationships which are as tenable empirically as possible. The statements made about these relationships are, however, made primarily for the purposes of illustrating the technique involved and not for the sake of comparative analysis of the relationships themselves. For the latter purpose the statements given will, as a minimum, be seen to be oversimplified. For the former purpose this is not the case since the illustration can be made in terms of statements which are in fact empirically tenable or are only assumed to be so. It will also be noted that the relationships presented here are relationships which have, at least in the opinion of the writer, rather well-institutionalized relationship structures.

It must be stated that the material presented here on the doctor-patient relationship was first brought to the attention of the writer by the work of Parsons. Some of this material has been published by Parsons in his article on the "Professions and Social Structure" already cited. A tremendous amount of Parsons' material on the medical profession has unfortunately been presented only in lectures. Most, if not all, of the material presented here has been presented in one of the two forms mentioned by Parsons, though he cannot, of course, be held responsible for any misuses or mistakes in the present use of this material for purposes of example. Use has been made here only of factors thought by the writer now to be well known to both professional social scientists and laymen, though perhaps in the case of the latter not generally conceived as presented here.

expected to employ rational techniques in his treatment of
the patient. It is well understood that occasionally,
because of the limitations of knowledge in the field and
the fallibility of man, the doctor will act irrationally,
but the range of irrational actions is limited. Many
medical errors are considered inescapable and nonculpable,
but others, e.g., repeated failures to diagnose correctly
common ailments appearing in common uncomplicated forms,
are likely to result in pressures of some sort being
brought to bear on the doctor concerned. Some irrational
actions are considered sufficiently egregious to be grounds
for civil suit against the doctor, and some are even
grounds for his loss of license to practice. The latter
form of discipline is relatively rare, probably because of
the reluctance of qualified personnel to testify against
such doctors. This reluctance is by no means wholly understandable in terms of a "guild" or "there but for the
grace of God go I" spirit. It is at least in part understandable in terms of the reluctance to shake by such
exposure the element of public confidence in medical men.
This element of confidence is certainly of vital importance
to the current forms of medical practice, and whether it
would be broken down or bolstered by more frequent ex-
posures of this sort is as yet an undetermined point. The
fact that overt sanctions are not so evident as might seem
justified on the basis of expressed licensing standards,
medical society membership criteria, etc., does not mean
that sanctions in this respect are totally lacking by any
means.

The doctors may often act arationally in their treatment of patients. If they do, the action is methodologically arational since the relationship is to a high degree
functionally specific and the specific goal involved is a
quite empirical one, i.e., the health of the patient. The
use of arational techniques by doctors is either definitely condemned or is not specific to the relationship. The

complete substitution by a doctor of nonempirical means
for empirical ones in the treatment of a patient is, perhaps, never sanctioned. Nonempirical means of some sorts,
e.g., prayers in terms of one of the established religious
systems of the society, are acceptable as means supplemen-
tary to the application of scientific knowledge, but such
activities are definitely not an institutionalized part of
the relationship. They are tolerated but not required.
Nonempirical means of other sorts are strongly condemned
and are considered applications of "superstitions" or
"magic," both of which are felt to have no place in this
field and are felt to be "very, very, bad things."[41]

The patient on his side is also expected to act rationally in the following respect. He is expected to
choose his physician on the basis of predominantly universalistic criteria. This, of course, involves an element
of rationality since there is involved the process of
understanding what criteria are germane to the ends sought
and the process of judgment as to whether the doctor chosen
in fact measures up to such criteria. Another rational
element enters from the patient's point of view in that he
is expected to know within limits when it is and is not
necessary to consult his doctor (i.e., put the relationship into operation), and he is expected to follow his
doctor's "orders" rationally. Both with regard to conformity and sanction aspects, however, the rational action
by the patient is less well institutionalized than that by
the doctor.

---

41. Medical faddism is a somewhat different matter
than methodologically arational action. It is a specific
form of irrational action. Medical faddism may be defined
for these purposes as the process of, at some times, using
some medical techniques more than is objectively justified
on known medical grounds and at others using some medical
techniques less than is objectively justified on medical
grounds. Parsons, in the lectures mentioned in the preceding footnote, has discussed the basis for medical faddism and the analogy of this phenomenon to that of magic
in some societies and in some respects.

The doctor-patient relationship is at least in theory a predominantly, if not completely universalistic, one. The patient is expected to choose his doctor on grounds of competence and availability. The doctor is expected, within quite broad limits, to accept patients on the basis of need for treatment. This structure breaks down in many respects. Patients often choose or reject doctors on bases that are medically irrelevant. Such considerations may range from "liking a doctor's looks" to not liking his political or religious affiliations. Doctors, on the other hand, sometimes choose or reject their patients on the basis of the patient's ability to pay. Again, the structure seems to be better institutionalized for the doctors than for the patients in both conformity and sanctions aspects. While the structures are often violated in these respects, the remarkable feature of the situation is perhaps that they are not violated more given, among many other relevant factors, on the one hand the medical ignorance of the patient and on the other hand the tremendous emphasis in the society in general on monetary income as a symbol of success.

The relationship is, of course, in theory functionally specific. It is the doctor's obligation to do what he can medically for the patient, and all of his "orders" and access to the patient must, in theory, be justified on the grounds of their relevance to the patient's health. The patient on his part is expected to follow the doctor's "orders" (and to pay his fees unless he is being treated on a charity basis). The doctor with respect to fixing fees is expected to take into consideration the patient's ability to pay. Often functionally diffuse elements creep into the relationship, particularly in the case of the general practitioner or "family doctor," who is frequently a close friend and advisor of the patient in matters medical and otherwise. The appearance of functionally diffuse elements in the relationship almost inevitably goes hand in hand with predominantly intimate rather than

predominantly avoidant affectivity in the relationship.
Again, as a matter of hypothesis at least it may be suggested that the lead in breakdowns in these respects is
more likely to be taken by the patient than the doctor.

The relationship is expected to be a predominantly
avoidant one, the more so the more it is confined to
strictly medical matters. Departures on the doctor's part
are only in theory justified if they contribute to the
patient's health. Departures on the patient's part may
range from the often unobjectionable combining of a friend
to friend relationship with that of doctor and patient to
excursions into intimacy of a sort most strongly condemned
in such circumstances. Both the doctor and the patient
may be strongly condemned for some of these departures in
the direction of intimacy, and the profession as a whole,
as well as the public, is well aware of this. The profession is so thoroughly aware of it that in certain respects elaborate precautions and procedures have been set
up to eliminate as far as possible any such breakdowns in
the strictly medical sphere.

The relationship is responsible rather than individualistic. The doctor rather than the patient is primarily
affected here since he plays the more active role in the
relationship. The whole structure of prestige in the
medical profession is so set up as to require even the
most "selfish" of doctors to place the interests of his
patients both actual and potential before any goals of his
own that do not involve their medical welfare. The most
"selfish" of doctors dares not acquire a widespread repu-
tation for demanding assurance of payment before treating
an emergency case or for "ordering" on a wide scale
profitable but medically unnecessary operations and the
like. Again, the experts in the field are reluctant to
testify openly in such cases, but the sanctions brought to
bear are none the less strong. The patient on his part is
expected to take into consideration the doctor's various

problems in certain respects, but the question of individualism or responsibility is not quite so relevant from the
patient's point of view since the doctor's role is so much
the more active of the two. In the ordinary case the
question in terms of which the individualistic-responsible
distinction is phrased does not characteristically arise
for the patient. Both he and the doctor in theory share
the end of restoring the patient's health. Other goals
such as minimizing the doctor's fee, etc., are not supposed
to enter since the doctor's "responsibility" covers making
such fees "reasonable."

Finally, the relationship is of a relatively nonhierarchical sort. Of course, the roles are sharply differentiated, but as far as general social standing the doctor
may be of either higher or lower rank than the patient.
In theory at least none of the action takes place because
one member of the relationship is a superior of the other
in any power sense. A doctor's "orders" are not "orders"
in the ordinary sense that implies an enforcement agency
outside the person "ordered" and the possibility of "orders" not to the subordinate's best interests. In theory,
the doctor's "orders" are given the patient only in order
that the patient may achieve his own goal, e.g., restoration or maintenance of health. The only hierarchical
aspect involved, ideally speaking, is that of medical
knowledge, but even this is by no means a hard and fast
requirement since doctors are usually patients of doctors
other than themselves and sometimes of less able ones.
However the members of the society as a whole may rank
doctors relative to patients, and in this there is certainly an hierarchical element, the treatment by the doctor
of the patient is in theory determined by medical criteria
and not by criteria of any relative social standing. For
most purposes of the relationship such differences in
ranking as exist are, institutionally speaking, irrelevant
to the determination of action in terms of the relationship.

The relationship between a businessman and his customer in the modern United States may be described as
$x_1, x_2, x_3, x_4, x_5, y_6$. Both the businessman and his customer
are expected to deal rationally with one another. Not to
do so is "bad business," and in this relationship both
parties are expected to behave in a "businesslike" fashion.
Irrational action on the part of either member is the mark
of a fool. Nonrational action in general simply isn't
"good business," and in some cases comes in for the harsh-
est sort of criticism.

The criteria for membership in the relation are predominantly universalistic. Both parties are expected to
pick fellow members on the basis best calculated to serve
the empirical ends sought. The businessman seeks to make
a "profit"; the customer seeks to get the best possible
value for his money. To refuse to sell at a profit to
second generation Scandinavian citizens because one does
not like them is "bad business," as is refusal to buy from
them on this ground. There are many departures from these
standards by both types of parties, but such departures
become increasingly less common as business becomes large
scale. Large scale firms such as some of the automobile
manufacturers would find insuperable obstacles in trying
to enforce such particularistic criteria, and individual
customers find their effect in such matters negligible and
such activities likely to fall into the category of "cutting off one's nose to spite one's face." The heavily
institutionalized criteria for businessmen in selecting
customers is "ability to pay," and that of customers in
selecting businessmen is the "ability to deliver the 'best'
goods at the lowest price."

The relationship is kept as functionally specific as
possible. Ideally speaking, it is perfectly functionally
specific from both points of view. The contract relationship is the archetype of this quality. If a contract is
vague, it is a bad contract, at least from the point of

view of the person who may find added unanticipated obligations as a result of such vagueness. In only a fraction
of such relationships are actual contracts drawn, but the
usual structures of a "one-price" system make such things
quite clear. A customer buys a soft drink. His obligation
is confined to the payment of its price; the dealer's
obligation is to deliver the product as defined by quite
specific standards. If there is an insect in the drink,
the dealer is liable; if the payment is less than the
stated price, the customer is liable. One could go at
some length into the nature of this functional specificity
as a functional requisite if a modern industrial society
is to operate, but that would be beside the point here.
To leave the obligations of such a relationship vague is
always potentially "bad business" from someone's point of
view.

The relationship is institutionalized as a predominantly avoidant one. Often there are departures in the
direction of intimacy, but these departures are more likely
to characterize small firms with a restricted, relatively
unchanging set of customers. On the whole, the attitude
in this respect is that "business is business" and that
affective involvement with one's customers, insofar as it
is permissible, becomes inadmissible if it interferes with
the profit goals of enterprise. Roughly the same situation
exists from the customer's point of view.

The relationship is a predominantly individualistic
one. It is not, however, completely individualistic with
a completely unhindered caveat emptor outlook. In general,
there are restrictions on both parties. Certain standards
of honesty, for example, are not only expected but are
enforceable at law on both parties. At the same time,
neither the customer nor the businessman is held responsible for protecting the other against his own ignorance
as is the case with the doctor. Within a certain framework
of mutual regard for each other's interest the businessman

and his customer operate on an "every man for himself"
basis, while in theory this is never true of the doctor's
relation with his patient.

Finally, this relation is, institutionally speaking,
nonhierarchical and in some respects even egalitarian.
The customer has neither higher nor lower rank than the
businessman in general, and of course one individual may
at any time be playing both roles in different operations.
Theoretically, the parties to a transaction of this sort
deal with one another as equals, and proof of deliberate
tinkering with this equality may be the basis for setting
aside such transactions legally. Much of the antimonopoly
legislation rests on the legal philosophy that the parties
to a valid contract should be equals for the purposes of
that transaction. Of course, there are many departures
from the ideal structures in this respect.

One may now compare briefly these two relationships.
In doing so there are three levels of procedure. In the
first place, one may compare the two relationships on the
most general level discussed here. In that comparison the
basic difference between the doctor-patient and the businessman-customer relationships lies in the fact that the
former is predominantly responsible (y_5) and the latter
predominantly individualistic (x_5). On this level these
two relationships are identical in all other five aspects.
Now there is considerable feeling that the doctor-patient
relationship, institutionally speaking, is very different
indeed from that of the businessman and his customer. For
purposes of comparative analysis of the two, one would
first attempt to see how much of the differences between
the two can be explained in terms of the difference between
x_5 and y_5.

Insofar as explanation in those terms is not sufficient for the purposes sought, one must proceed to the
second level of analysis. Both relationships institutionalize rational action (x_1) and predominantly universalistic

criteria (x_2). The specific content of the rational action
and of the universalistic criteria are, however, quite
different. If one looks at the specific content of rational action, for example, in these two cases, one sees that
in the one case rational action is focused on the restoration and maintenance of health, and on the allocation of
goods and services in the other case. In theory at least
those differences between the two relationships which are
not explicable in terms of the differences between x's and
y's (i.e., differences on the most general level) may be
explicable in terms of the differing contents of a given
x or y. If these second differences are insufficient to
explain the differences noted between two relationships
being compared, then one of four possibilities remains:
(1) differences on the first level of generalization have
been overlooked, (2) differences on the second level of
generalization have been overlooked, (3) the list of aspects of relationships needs reformulation and/or additions
at least on lower levels of generalization, or (4) some
combination of the three foregoing difficulties is present.

In the third of the foregoing possibilities lies the
third of the levels of procedure. If two relationships
are in fact different in their structure but also in fact
identical on the two levels of procedure cited above, the
difference must be in aspects of one or the other or both
of the relationships not given in the original list of six
aspects. Even if the relationships are not identical on
the two levels previously cited, differences on this third
level may still be present. Any failure to explain differences between relationships on the previous two levels
must explore this third level. The exploration of this
third level is quite important for further development in
this sphere. Exploration of this level may discover
aspects that apply only to one or both of the specific
relationships under discussion, but it may also discover
an aspect or aspects that are empirically observable in

any relationship and hence should be added to the original list of six aspects.

2. The businessman-customer relationship in modern
    U.S. society and in that of "traditional" China

The material on the businessman-customer relationship in modern U.S. society need not be repeated. It takes the form $x_1, x_2, x_3, x_4, x_5, y_6$. In "traditional" China the relationship takes one of two forms. If the relationship is the usual particularistic one, it takes the form $y_1, y_2, y_3, y_4, y_5, y_6$ (or x_6). Ideally, it is expected to be based on particularistic criteria such as friendship, family connections, and neighborhood consideration that are already present or are established by a "go-between." If particularistic connections of this sort do not exist, the relationship is likely to take the form $x_1, x_2, x_3, x_4, x_5, x_6$ (or y_6).

This difference between the businessman-customer relationship in China, when it is based on certain particularistic, rather than universalistic, criteria of choice, accounts for many differences in accounts as to the "reliability" or "honesty" of Chinese businessmen.

In "traditional" China, if one is dealing with a friend or a relative or a family which has dealt with his family for years, or a person from his own village or a person introduced by a "go-between" who possesses some one or some combination of these connections with both businessman and customer, then the businessman emphasizes the preservation of the relationship. He operates in a nonrational (traditional) fashion.[42] The relationship is

---

42. This is not to say that his action is irrational, and it is not intended to indicate that no rational action takes place. It is rather intended to indicate that, unlike the western structure, when rational and nonrational considerations conflict with one another, the nonrational ones on the whole take precedence.

by definition highly particularistic, but it is also predominantly functionally diffuse. "Extra" requests by the
customer may well be granted. It is predominantly intimate
in the sense that something like friendship dominates the
relationship. Either party is more or less accessible to
the other, and displays of affect are by no means out of
the question although it must be borne in mind that that
society generally sets a broad framework of highly formalized, predominantly avoidant relationships. Most importantly, it is a highly responsible relationship. The
merchant is expected to protect his customer at all costs
even to the extent of his own financial ruin in some
extreme cases. The relationship may or may not be hierarchical. If a merchant is dealing with a member of the
gentry class, the relationship is almost certainly hierarchical, in other cases it might not be.

On the other hand, if the expected particularistic
connections do not exist, the picture is almost exactly
opposite to that given above. A ruthlessly caveat emptor
situation exists and is carried as an ordinary matter to
an extreme that western business has not tolerated for some
decades. Under these circumstances, both businessman and
customer act as rationally as possible in an attempt to
maximize their material gain from the relationship. The
relationship becomes as specific as possible, and it is an
avoidant one. It is ruthlessly individualistic, and that
within a framework in which force and fraud are only
limited by what the parties concerned think they can get
by with. It may be hierarchical or not, but, if possible,
one party will utilize hierarchical factors to secure an
advantage. It must be noted that it is not institutionally
expected that businessman-customer relationships will be of
this second type, and this type of relationship is institutionalized little if at all. This does not mean that the
structure is not frequently observable. In this particular
case conformity with the structure is much greater than

its sanction aspects, but both aspects are minor relative to the institutionalization of the other Chinese structure sketched above.

In comparing the businessman-customer relationship in modern U.S. society and "traditional" China, one is first forced to consider the differences in the relationship as it occurs in China. Here the distinctions are almost, if not completely, understandable in terms of differences on the most general level of relationship aspects. In comparing either of the Chinese patterns with the U.S. pattern, differences on both the most general level and the second level of generalization mentioned above are significant. One may set up the comparison as in Table 5.

Table 5. Comparison of businessman-customer relationships in U.S. and China

	U.S.	China	
		Type A	Type B
1. Cognitive aspect	x	y	x
2. Membership criteria aspect	x	y	x
3. Substantive definition aspect	x	y	x
4. Affective aspect	x	y	x
5. Goal orientation aspect	x	y	x
6. Stratification aspect	y	(or ^{y}x)	(or ^{x} y)

Seen in this form, it is immediately obvious that the differences between type A and type B in China apparently lie on the first level of procedure since the structures are exact opposites except with regard to the possibilities of variation with regard to the stratification aspects. The differences between type A and the U.S. type again lie apparently almost wholly on the first level of procedure, but the differences between type B and the U.S. type will obviously have to be sought on the second level of procedure or in additions to the lists of relevant aspects.

Actually, in comparison of the U.S. type and type B the differences lie largely in differences in the cognitive aspects and the goal orientation aspects both of which on the first level of procedure fall into the same category.

3. The businessman-customer relationship in modern
U.S. society and the father-son relationship
in "traditional" China

The businessman-customer relationship used here has already been described above. It takes the form $x_1, x_2, x_3,$ x_4, x_5, y_6. The father-son relationship in "traditional" China takes the form $y_1, y_2, y_3, x_4, y_5, x_6$. On the most general level of analysis these two different types of relationships in different societies have only one element, x_4 (predominantly avoidant affective aspects), in common. On the most general level these two relationships emerge as almost wholly different from one another. But there are differences on a lower level of generalization as well. For example, the matters about which the one relationship emphasizes rationality and the other nonrationality are quite different. Even when there is a similarity on the most general level, as in the case of the institutionalization of avoidance aspects, the differences do not end, since the types and degrees of avoidance are quite different (i.e., there are differences on the second level of procedure). Whether such a comparison as this one is likely to be of great interest may be doubtful, but some comparison of different types of relationships in different types of societies may be of considerable importance, and such comparisons can be handled in these terms.

The above examples have been given in order to illustrate the analysis of different types of relationships and their comparison in terms of the concepts suggested here. In the course of these examples four systematic approaches to sources of differences have been suggested. They are

differences which arise from: (1) differences on the most
general level (i.e., the x or y classification); (2) differences on the second level of generalization (i.e., the
relationships whether similar or different with regard to
x or y classification are different in the kind or degree
of "x-ness" or "y-ness"); (3) differences in aspects on
the most general level of relationships or on lower levels
for which no concepts have been provided (i.e., aspects of
any relationship or of specific ones that are not included
in the present list of six); or (4) some combination of
the three foregoing differences. A brief attempt has been
made to show that different or similar types of relationships in the same or different societies may be compared
usefully in these terms.

Two further observations must be made about these
relationship aspects. They are observations of some importance for any estimate of the general utility of these
concepts for the purposes of analysis. In the first place,
there is some basis for believing that some of these more
or less polar types of relationship aspects are more likely to go together than others. There is not space to go
into the matter in great detail here, and in fact the
attention necessary to go into the matter in such detail
has not yet been given it, but some suggestions in these
respects are in order. Rationality, functional specificity, universalism, and avoidance are quite likely to go
together. When rationality is involved both ends and
means must be empirical and, to a high degree, explicit.
Functionally diffuse elements are likely to interfere with
rational action and force inclusion of nonrational elements
if only by adding vagueness to an otherwise explicit
situation. Again, rational factors are likely to be inter-
fered with by particularistic selection since such selection will not guarantee the ability of the members of the
relationship to carry out rational action. Intimacy as
opposed to avoidance, affectively speaking, is more likely

to involve departures in the direction of nonrationality, functional diffuseness, and particularism. These four by no means always go together. For example, in some societies rather high levels of universalism are maintained in picking wives for one's son, whereas the relationship may be, and commonly is, nonrational, functionally diffuse, and more or less intimate. Nevertheless, there is some promise of finding out which of these aspects are more likely to cluster together and which ones seem to vary most nearly independently for any society or for particular societies or for general types of concrete structures or for specific examples of concrete structures. There is also the possibility of discovering the conditions under which certain clusters can be avoided. To the degree that theories of this sort can be formulated and confirmed, these concepts will become increasingly useful. If the probability is very high that any relationship which institutionalizes rationality will also institutionalize functional specificity, then the amount one can learn about a given relationship relative to the effort needed to learn it is greatly increased. The discovery of whether it is either rational or functionally specific will at the same time tell one what the probability is that the other factor is also present. The more one can learn in these respects, the wider become the implications of what is known, and the more economical it becomes to gather knowledge.

In the second place, in addition to the possibility of establishing a whole set of theories about the tendency of some of these factors to go with one another, it is certainly possible to say that some types of social structure cannot operate in the presence or absence of certain types of relationship patterns. For example, in order to operate a modern automobile industry within the commonly accepted standards of efficiency, management-employee relationships must emphasize rationality, universalism, functional specificity, avoidance, and hierarchy to a high degree and responsibility to some degree, although in this last factor the possible range of variation is somewhat greater. The same is generally true for such relationships throughout an industrial society. To the degree that such theories as this can be confirmed, again one is able to learn more, more economically. If the above theory is true, one can say a lot about the management-employee relationship simply from measuring the efficiency and type of operation carried out in a given automobile industry. If the rulers of a society without such an industry decide to establish one, a social engineer applying scientific knowledge can make some immediate suggestions as to auxiliary conditions that will have to be present. By studying the society he (or others) can formulate theories about possible obstacles and aids to the proposed change and so forth.

The set of concepts discussed here in one form or another has been put to some use already by social scientists, but it has not on the whole been carefully or precisely used, and what is perhaps more important, it does not seem to have been generally employed with any very clear picture of what could be done with it. Its use has appeared on the whole in lists or fragments of application. It is hoped that more systematic application of it, preferably in statistically tenable forms, will either prove it worthless so that social science can be done with one more useless apparatus or greatly improve its precision and general relevance.

C H A P T E R   VII

THE STRUCTURE OF ROLE DIFFERENTIATION

The concept of the analytic structure of role differentiation in any social system may be defined as the structures of distribution of the members of the system among the various positions and activities distinguished in the system and hence the differential arrangement of the members of the system. In Chapter IV above an attempt has been made to show minimal reasons why the existence of a society, as that concrete structure has been defined here, requires a differentiation and assignment[1] of the roles of its members. The present chapter is not concerned with the functional aspects of role differentiation except insofar as they are relevant to the structural requisites under examination. The concern here is with role differentiation as a structural requisite of any society. It is not difficult to establish with some reasonable degree of certainty the hypothesis that some structures of role differentiation are necessary if any society is to exist. The present argument attempts to go one step further. It attempts to develop the hypothesis that for any society to exist there must as a minimum be role differentiation on

---

1. The present concern is with the structure of role differentiation. The structures of role assignment are treated only incidentally at this stage. The structural requirements of role assignment are treated explicitly in Chapter XI.

several different specific bases.[2]

In this respect two cautions must be observed. In the first place, the argument as ever throughout this book proceeds on a minimal rather than on a maximal basis. That is to say, no attempt is made to give all of the reasons or even, perhaps, the "basic" reasons why a given type of structure of role differentiation is a structural requisite. The attempt is only to give _some_ reason why the structure concerned is a structural requisite for any society. As development of this type of analysis goes on, more and more attention will have to be given to fuller treatment of the basis of the "requisite" character of the various structural requisites of any society. Here the attempt is merely to discover the structural requisites,

---

2. In the first of the conferences called in connection with the general research program for empirical work in terms of the present volume (see above, Preface, pp. xii-xiii) serious question has been thrown on the level of generalization of the structure of role differentiation relative to the other analytic structural requisites discussed in this volume. The attack was not on the substantive content of the present chapter. It rather raised the question as to whether or not both theoretical development and actual empirical work in terms of the conceptual scheme and theoretical system presented here would not benefit from the inclusion of this material under the various other structural headings. This criticism met with unanimous acceptance in general. Specifically it was decided to offer and discuss detailed suggestions for such reformulation in the meeting of the conference to be held in the fall of 1951. That meeting was to be devoted to general substantive revisions of the present manuscript. It was decided to go ahead with the publication of the manuscript in its present tentative form without delay for that substantive revision in order that the work proposed in these terms have at the earliest date the advantage of the widest possible criticism and suggestions from other students concerned with these problems. The most useful place for the concepts of role differentiation in such a scheme of analysis raises genuine problems. They cannot be ignored, and yet they must be so integrated with the other concepts involved as to give rise to theoretical implications and developments rather than merely a more or less systematic catalogue for description of a unit. The latter tends to be their present status.

however crudely that may be done. In the second place, it
must never be forgotten that a basis (or the various bases)
for the standing of a type of structure as a structural requisite is by no means necessarily the factor exclusively or
even most prominently reflected in the specific structures
themselves. For example, one might say that some distinctions between "adult" and "child" roles are structural
requirements if a society is to survive because of the
inability of very young children to satisfy their minimal
requirements for food and shelter. There is no reason to
believe that this is the only reason why some such differentiation must exist if a society is to survive. Moreover,
there is no reason to believe that in any particular society the specific differentiation of "adult" and "child"
roles will focus predominantly or exclusively on the
particular functional requisite used to establish the
structure as a structural requisite. The functional requisite concerned may be a latent rather than a manifest
function of the structure (or structures) from the operation of which the function results.[3] On the level of

---

3. In the example given here the function is not
likely to be a latent one. The feeding and care of the
young by the more mature is apparently a manifest function
of some structure (or structures) in every society. This
does not weaken the need for caution in these respects,
however. There is an additional problem which may also be
suggested in this connection. One or more of the functional requisites involved may be a latent function of the
system concerned, but the structure performing it may be
latent too. This might not be expected because, as is
brought out below, the structural requisites must in general be institutionalized and hence manifest structures.
There is, however, some possibility that some latent structures may be structural requisites of a system. For such
a system to persist the latent structure concerned would
have to be an inevitable by-product of other structures
that were well institutionalized. This would amount to a
sort of institutionalization at second hand for the latent
structure. Latent structures that are also structural requisites of a system may not in fact exist on the levels
of generalization concerned here, but they are nevertheless

generalization under consideration here the functional
requisites of the system are not likely to be latent functions. Still, if one is to believe the observers who
report on these matters, there are societies whose members
are unaware of the physiology of conception.[4] These societies have structures concerned with heterosexual intercourse, but the members of the group are presumably unaware
of the relation of such intercourse to conception. The
functional requirements related to sexual recruitment in
such a society are latent functions of a manifest structure. The structure concerned is a structural requisite
of the system because of the latent functions it performs
quite apart from any manifest functions connected with it,

-----

a clear theoretical possibility. On very low levels of
generalization they certainly exist. In specific analyses
a careful eye should be kept on this possibility. Latent
structures that are also structural requisites obviously
might be either a source of instability or a major obstacle
to gradual orderly change in the systems in which they occur. Because of these two possibilities such structures
cannot be ignored.

4. See B. Malinowski: The Sexual Life of Savages,
Halcyon House, New York, 1929, pp. 179-186. Some caution
must be stated about this example. In the first place,
the facts involved may be questioned by some scholars
though believed by others. Should this example prove a
bad one, others might be substituted. Perhaps a more important caution, however, is that one must be careful to
keep in mind the differences in types and levels of generality of structures when discussions of latency are at
issue. Thus, in this case, assuming the physiological ignorance, the conception of children is a latent function
of the structures of intercourse. The conception of children is not, however, necessarily a latent function of
marriage structures. It may be an intended and recognized
consequence of marriage that the couple involved have children, and the structures may and usually, if not always,
permit of this even though the persons concerned are unaware of the physiological processes involved. Discussion
of this point with Professor Melvin Tumin has proved illuminating and has led to the suggestion made that in the
general development of the concept of latency in social
phenomena the question of differences in levels of latency
cannot be ignored and is susceptible of considerable fruitful development.

although the latter may also make the structure a requisite one.

The position of the structure of role differentiation as an analytic structural requisite of any society follows as a minimum directly from the discussion of role differentiation as a functional requisite. If it is sound to maintain that the condition of differentiated roles must exist if any society is to exist in a given setting, then there must be patterns or structures the operation of which results in such a condition if such a unit in fact exists. Briefly, the establishment of role differentiation as a functional requisite rests on the following considerations: (1) there are differentiated activities which must be performed if the society is to persist; (2) these activities must be assigned to capable persons trained and "motivated" to carry them out; (3) not all individuals are capable at all times of performing all requisite activities, and some are even incapable of performing activities on which their own survival depends; and (4) even were all individuals equally capable at all times, it would not be possible for all individuals to carry on simultaneously all the activities that must be carried on simultaneously if the society is to persist.[5]

While it is not true that all of the structures of role differentiation of a society must be institutionalized, it is necessary, if the society is to persist, that the structural requisites of role differentiation be institutionalized in such a way that the functional requisites of the system be provided for in a manifest, latent IUR, UIR form or some combination of these forms. The argument about the institutionalization of these structures rests on the standing of adequate institutionalization as a functional requisite of any society. It has been pointed out

----

5. Fuller development of these points may be found above, pp. 161-166.

above[6] that adequate institutionalization may not justi-
fiably be listed separately as a functional requisite on
any grounds save those of emphasis. In any case, however,
the condition involved, whether separately listed or included in the other functional requisites, must be present
for the reasons suggested as a minimum if the society is to
persist. Briefly, if institutionalization of these structures were lacking in the conformity aspects of institutionalization, the necessary functions performed by the
structures would not be performed, and if institutionalization in its sanctions aspects[7] were lacking, there would
be no reason to believe that the required level of conformity could or would be maintained.

The structure of role differentiation is an analytic
structure as that term has been defined here. The structure of role differentiation does not define a membership
unit even theoretically capable of isolation from the
structure of political allocation or any of the other
analytic structures, nor does it define a unit separable
from any concrete unit. It does not define a unit at all
in this sense. It merely defines an aspect of social
action that is observable in all social action. Role differentiation can be distinguished as an aspect of any
concrete structure, but one can never exhaust the possibilities of concrete structure or concrete social actions
solely in terms of the role differentiation involved.

While the structure of role differentiation is not a
concrete structure, different types of role differentiation may be, and to some degree always[8] are, bases for

_____

6.   See pp. 193-197.

7.   It must be kept in mind that the use of force as
a sanction is by no means the only or the most important
or the most prevalent form of sanctions in these respects.

8.   There is one obviously tautological sense in which
role differentiation always is a basis for defining con-

defining concrete structures. For example, distinction of
the role of women is an essential part of the definition
of a concrete structure such as the Women's Club of Duluth,
but of course it does not define that concrete structure
completely. It merely tells in part what sorts of people
are eligible for membership. Often two or more types of
role differentiation are combined as partial bases for
definition of a concrete structure. In many societies,
for example, the boys of a particular age group are organized into membership units for specific or general purposes. Not all of the different types of role differentiation structurally required in any society form partial
bases for the definition of membership units. Role
differentiation on the basis of "relative age" is obviously a difficult, if not impossible, criterion for these
purposes since it is difficult, if not impossible, to get
a group of persons of the identical "relative age," and
the introduction of other criteria in these respects tend
to change the basis to one of "absolute age,"[9] or at least
to a combination of "absolute and relative age" considerations. On the other hand, the other requisite forms of
role differentiation seem capable of the widest variations
of application in these respects.

Nine different types (some of which have differentiated subcategories) of role differentiation necessary
for any society will be discussed here. The list is not
advanced as definitive either in its exhaustiveness or in
its form. It is advanced merely as a first step in that

_____

crete structure. Concrete structures are specifically differentiated from one another, and hence one has or has not
a role as a member or nonmember of any specific concrete
structure. This is not the sense of role differentiation
as a basis for definition of concrete structure intended
here.

9. The distinction between "relative and absolute
age" considerations will be brought out below.

direction. The basis of all of these distinctions is, of
course, the implications of the list of functional requisites of any society, and those follow from the implications of a unit such as that defined here (i.e., a society)
in its setting (i.e., the limits of variation set by the
factors of human heredity and nonhuman environment). The
remainder of the present chapter will be divided into two
parts. The first will be devoted to a discussion of these
bases of role differentiation as structural requisites of
any society. The second part will be devoted to a brief
discussion of one implication of role differentiation in
any society, i.e., stratification.

A. BASES OF ROLE DIFFERENTIATION IN ANY SOCIETY

Prior to discussion of the different bases of role
differentiation in any society, a brief outline of the
types may be presented so that the reader may have some
advance notice of the matter covered in this part of the
chapter. Under each basis of role differentiation the
basis will be defined and the reasons for its characteri-
zation as a structural requisite will be discussed. The
bases may be outlined as follows:

    1. Role differentiation on the basis of age.
        a. Absolute age.
            (1) Infancy.
            (2) Childhood.
            (3) Adulthood.
            (4) Old age.
        b. Relative age.
    2. Role differentiation on the basis of generation.
    3. Role differentiation on the basis of sex.
    4. Role differentiation on the basis of economic
        allocation.
    5. Role differentiation on the basis of political
        allocation.

6. Role differentiation on the basis of religion.
7. Role differentiation on the basis of cognition.
8. Role differentiation on the basis of nonhuman environment.
9. Role differentiation on the basis of solidarity.

1. Role differentiation on the basis of age

The unit as defined here involves a membership of human beings. To a very great extent, if not to an unusual extent, differences in age are relevant to differences in capabilities for biological individuals of this type. The concept of age employed here is the usual one. The age of an individual refers to the passage of time during which the biological individual lives. For present purposes the period of life will be reckoned from the beginning of the operation of the individual as a biologically separate entity from other individuals of his species. This is done despite the fact that different societies reckon age from different starting points; some from conception, some from birth, and so forth. Here the duration will be reckoned from birth.

The general necessity for structures of role differentiation on the basis of age rests as a minimum on the functional requisite of role differentiation and that of provision for an adequate physiological relationship to the setting. As a minimum the "infants" of the species are unable to shift for themselves and can not survive if other individuals of different capabilities do not make such provisions for them. This is merely a minimal justification of some differentiation on the basis of age. There are many others beyond such a minimum. Other capabilities than the meeting of physiological needs are in a high degree correlated with age differences in the human animal. The necessity of observing and manipulating the rather complex social structures necessary for the existence of a society apparently cannot be taught biological

"infants" immediately. A rather prolonged period must
elapse, apparently, before the average individual can
attain sufficient maturity, emotionally, cognitively, and
in other respects, to carry on without roles differentiated with respect to age. The sexual recruitment of
members of the society is another case in point. The
exact age at which sexual capabilities develop and the
period over which they endure are open to considerable
variation, but the passage of time is certainly not an
irrelevant factor. It is hard to conceive of any human
society in which age does not at some point enter the
qualifications for full performance of the marriage roles.

The necessity of some role differentiation on the
basis of age is, perhaps, obvious and banal enough. If it
is obvious and banal, it is well then to require of an
ostensibly thorough study of a society that it tell systematically and thoroughly how the factor of age enters
role differentiation, that it answer, on whatever level of
generalization the study may be posed, the question, "Who
does what insofar as his (or her) right or obligation to
do it is determined by or related to the elapse of time
since birth?" As a minimum such questioning will elicit
a life cycle picture of the development of the different
types of individuals distinguished in the society on the
level under consideration.

a. Absolute age. The term absolute age as a basis
of role differentiation refers to the use of age as a
criterion of role differentiation in such a way that the
persons given a particular type of role on this basis are
eligible for it because they are conceived as being in a
particular age span and that age span is conceived as
being such that an individual can be a member of one and
only one such span at any one time. If one considers the
matter in terms of groups based on absolute age, the
matter becomes, perhaps, a little clearer. In modern U.S.
society a distinction is usually drawn among infants (or

babies), children, adolescents, and adults (subdivided into
young adults, middle-aged adults, and old-aged adults).
The reader may prefer a somewhat different set of distinctions for the case in point, but however the lines may be
drawn, a given individual is conceived as fitting into one
and only one such category at any one time. He may be
classified as a "child who acts like a baby" or a "young
adult who acts like an old man," but he is classified
primarily in one group on the basis of age however much he
may take over characteristics usually associated with
another group. This concept of absolute age is not absolute in the sense that a sharp, clear-cut, temporal line
is necessarily drawn between one absolute age classification and another. It is not that one ceases to be an
infant and becomes a child when exactly two years have
elapsed since birth. In some cases the basis of role
differentiation may be so sharp as that, but it is probably more usual for temporal demarcation to be more elastic.
Some individuals cease to be classed as babies at the age
of eighteen months, for example, some at the age of twenty
months, and some at the age of two years perhaps. The
important point is that, once so classified and once roles
are assigned on this basis, one and only one set of roles
on this basis is considered fully appropriate to a given
individual.

The basis for the standing of such distinctions as a
structural requisite for any society appears to lie in the
general functional requisite of role differentiation and
the fact that on the whole there is an age scale of development of the capabilities of individuals to perform the
roles differentiated in a society. It may be true in fact
that in any particular society the evolution of the individual may be continuous and gradual in these respects and
perhaps different to some degree for each individual. But,
for the society to persist, the roles must be differentiated with some view to the capabilities of the individ-

uals concerned (in this case with a view to differentiations based on age), and those role differentiations must
be institutionalized at least within certain limits. For
these reasons societies must have structures which apparently assume a definite more or less discontinuous or
jerky sort of development of the capabilities of different
individuals on the basis of age since it would not be
possible to institutionalize slightly different structures
for each individual in the society. The cognitive problems
involved alone would make such a solution impossible.
Apparently, within some limits there are such discontinuities in individual developmental curves. At least, if
there are not, the discontinuities imposed by the social
structures on the individual in a given society do not seem
to be sufficiently incompatible with the development of
the individuals of that society to prevent the persistence
of the society, though of course it is conceivable that
they could be. To some degree adjustment to individual
differences in development in these respects is made by
having the beginning and ending points of these age classifications more or less flexible rather than clear-cut and
by provisions, via structures for handling deviants, for
individuals whose development for one reason or another
does not conform even to the rather flexible limits usually set. Thus, for example, an individual who is slower
than usual in learning to walk and talk may be classified
as an infant, rather than in the next age classification,
longer than is ordinary in his society, but there is some
point beyond which, if he is still undeveloped in these
respects, he is placed in a category such that the usual
age classifications become irrelevant, e.g., crippled,
mentally retarded, etc. The number or percentage of such
deviants that can be produced without affecting the survival of the society is subject to some variation, but in
any specific society the range of tolerance is in theory
discoverable. In general, it cannot go beyond the point

at which the minimum functionally required roles cannot be
performed.

It is perhaps dangerous to proceed beyond this point
in the development of the concept of absolute age from the
point of view of any society. Certainly, different societies vary widely in the distinctions drawn on the basis of
absolute age. Nevertheless, some extremely general remarks
can be made with a possibility, if not a probability, that
they will apply to any society. The periods that suggest
themselves are: (1) infancy, (2) childhood, (3) adulthood,
and (4) old age. After discussing the bases for suggesting
these particular distinctions, a few remarks will be made
about the limits of their application to any society.

(1) Infancy. Infancy may be defined for present
purposes as that period in the life cycle during which the
"average" (or "normal") individual is ordinarily completely dependent upon the intervention of more fully developed
individuals for survival. For some individuals due to
physical or other defects this period covers their entire
life cycle. The term infancy applies merely to that portion of the life cycle during which this is the statistically "normal" expectation concerning every individual.
As a minimum this period covers that stage of the individual's development during which he is either completely
incapable of recognizing the implications of his environment for his survival and/or completely incapable of
coping with such factors as he does recognize. In a rather
pragmatic sense these restrictions on the capabilities of
an individual correspond roughly to the period during
which he can neither communicate nor move about in the
generally accepted fashions in the society. Generally,
for any society this involves as a minimum the ability to
speak the language of the society (or the portion of it in
which the individual lives) and to walk.

Because of the more or less complete helplessness of
the individual during this stage of development, special

provisions must be made to cope with it if the membership
of the society is to perpetuate itself via sexual recruitment. It is by no means true that in all societies this
period is institutionalized as being of the same duration,
or that it is covered by a single category, but it must
cover some period of development in all societies since to
some degree members of the species everywhere have a stage
in their life cycle during which these conditions hold
true. Differences in the nonhuman environment and differences in the human environment may necessitate or make
possible the prolongation or shortening of this period or
its division into several categories, but no known case of
the environment or the heredity of the members of any society makes possible its complete elimination.

It is also not intended to suggest that the absolute
age classification suggested here occurs in just this one
period in every society. It is quite conceivable that a
society recognize this period of development by breaking
it up into several stages. One stage might end when the
individual is able to turn over, another at the start of
the crawling period, another when the individual can first
stand unsupported, and so forth. The important point is
that, however the stage may be split up or prolonged or
shortened, some recognition of this stage of complete dependency must be given and specific structures of role
differentiation institutionalized to cover the period. As
a minimum these structures must differentiate those cared
for and those responsible for their care in addition to
certain behavior considered appropriate to the infants and
those responsible for their maintenance and care. It is
suggested as an hypothesis that there is no known society
without such structures and that no society which failed
to maintain such structures could survive in that form.
Insofar as this hypothesis is confirmed, no treatment of a
society that fails to yield some data on this score can be
complete. In fact one may go further. No treatment of a

society that fails to yield sufficient data to account for
the survival of a sufficient number of infants to enter
the next absolute age classification is complete. By "sufficient" in this case is meant, of course, sufficient to
permit (as far as numbers are concerned) the continuous
manning of those roles necessary to the persistence of the
society in the form in which it is being studied. Lack of
such data on a society can mean only one (or some combination) of three things: (a) the hypothesis advanced here is
invalid, (b) the data gathering has been incomplete, or
(c) the society studied is either not in fact a society or
is in the process of changing the structures in terms of
which it is defined or possibly tending to complete dissolution.

Finally, as a further hypothesis, it may be suggested
that the behavior institutionalized for the individuals
expected to act in terms of the roles differentiated in
these respects must not only permit the survival of "sufficient numbers" for the purposes mentioned above, but
must also provide the social instruction necessary at this
stage to equip the individuals for their future roles.
Again, in the absence of data on this score the same statements may be made as have been made above.

(2) Childhood. Childhood may be defined for present
purposes as that stage of development during which the
individual, while no longer dependent on others for all
factors necessary to his survival, is nevertheless dependent upon them for instruction and guidance in the institutionally permissible and necessary behavior of individuals
in his society. It is the period during which an individual is expected to learn the types of behavior that are
institutionally expected of him for the remainder of his
life or at least how to find out by his own initiative
what is institutionally expected of him in his activities
present and future. To put the matter a third way, it is
the period during which the individual learns what he must

know in order effectively to be held responsible for his
actions in the society.

The limits of what can be learned by an individual
during the infancy period is marked by contrast with what
can be learned during the years between, say, two and
fifteen in the life cycle of an individual. One need not
minimize the plasticity of the members of the human species
at any stage, but it is, perhaps, tenable to hold that it
is greatest during this period. During infancy the difficulties and limits of communication, comprehension, and
performance are more marked than during childhood. After
this period, or even toward the end of it, sufficient
training has been undergone that marked departures from
the past structures face not only the obstacles of inculcating the new, but also that of overcoming the old insofar
as the old conflict with the new.

This period is conceived here as lasting as a minimum
through the period at which sexual maturity develops since
sexual capabilities and the patterns appropriate to them
are crucial for the persistence of the society. Ordinarily, these capabilities do not develop fully until the
"teen-age" period. They carry with them apparently not
only notable physiological changes but also as a minimum
new orientations and interests if not more or less subtle
changes in intellectual and emotional capabilities about
which little is known in a definitive scientific sense
that applies to individuals in any society. It is maintained, of course, by some that quite a bit is known about
this question with regards to specific societies, and
there are some whose claims cover mankind everywhere.
Theories of the latter type, however, are especially questionable either because of the basis on which they are
derived or because of lack of evidence to confirm them
and/or because of contradictions to them. Whatever may be
the state of the prevailing theories on this score, it is,
perhaps, safest until and unless the contrary is demon-

strated to take into account at least the possibility, if
not the probability, that such changes are involved. Whatever may be the definitive findings, they will affect the
minimum length of necessary duration of this period rather
than its existence. Even if no general changes of this
particular sort can be shown, the existence of some period
of childhood will not have been substantially shaken because of the other reasons given for its necessity.

Again, notice of the variability of different societies in their recognition of this period must be given. It
is not intended to suggest that the period must be handled
as a whole. It is merely suggested that a period or periods must be recognized during which the individual must
learn the basic structures institutionalized for one of
his type in his society if he is afterward effectively to
be held responsible for their performance. Obviously, if
no individuals can be held responsible in some manner for
their activities, the society cannot persist. Not only
must there be responsibility for some, but also the proportion and types of individuals who may be exempted from
responsibility is strictly limited.

The variability of societies is exceedingly great in
these respects. In the United States the period is split
into at least two and perhaps more. For example, small
children, who are emphatically not "babies," are distinguished from "big children" ("big boys" and "big girls"
are not classifications primarily oriented to size), and
both are distinguished from adolescents. "Traditional"
Chinese society, as far as the peasants were concerned,
institutionalized one basic classification, yu-nien, to
cover this period. Depending on the environment, both
human and nonhuman, the possibilities of variation are
enormous, however, and no attempt will be made here to
delimit them further. For the general understanding of
social phenomena some development of the minimal distinctions necessary in these respects for different types of

societies would be extremely illuminating.

The general implications for specific studies of societies of what has been said here of the childhood period
are almost, if not exactly, identical with those suggested
above relative to infancy with, of course, the obvious
changes necessary to fit the distinction between infancy
and childhood. The cautions, limitations, and suggestions
made relative to infancy as to the meaning of lack of data
on this score will also apply here.

(3) Adulthood. Adulthood may be defined as that
period of life in which the average member of a society is
held to be capable of full responsibility for his activity
in the society. In the period of infancy such responsibility is wholly out of the question, and in the period of
childhood only partial responsibility can be expected, if
for no other reason because of the sheer element of time
required to inculcate the minimal patterns necessary for
the effective expectation of such responsibility.

In quite a large number of societies adulthood is
institutionalized as beginning not later than actual effectuation of marital ties. Childhood betrothals and even
marriages are not uncommon, but in such cases there are
usually, if not always, definite expectations as to when
the complete practice of the marital bond will begin. The
frequent institutionalization of the beginning of adulthood not later than the effectuation of marital ties,
including as that does heterosexual intercourse, is one of
the main reasons for suggesting that childhood must extend
at least to the development of mature sexual capabilities
on the part of the individual.

Insofar as there is for any given society a definite
period in the life cycle of an individual during which he
is fully capable of being held responsible for his behavior, roles must be differentiated with respect to this
period. There are many roles that must be performed by
persons of such capabilities, and not all of those

individuals can be doing the same things at the same time. The production and rearing of children is an obvious case at point.

In respect to this age classification the possibilities of variation are also great. One of the more obvious distinctions within the classification is that between "young" adults and "middle-aged" adults. This one happens to be particularly evident in modern industrial societies like the United States, but it is also to be found in both Chinese and Japanese societies. However great the variations may be and whether or not the age classification starts with marriage performances or on a quite different basis, the classification is of importance to any society. This is the age group that alone can produce and rear the new members of the society, or at least that portion of them stemming from sexual reproduction of the members themselves. This is the group that must inculcate on the younger members the structures of behavior, the elements of cognition, and the like necessary for the operation of the society. If they are not the exclusive teachers of these factors, and they need not be, they are at least indispensable for the inculcation of many of these factors.

Again, the general implications for specific studies of societies of what has been said here of the adult period are almost, if not exactly, identical with those suggested above relative to infancy with, of course, the obvious changes necessary to fit the distinctions between infancy and childhood on the one hand and adulthood on the other. The cautions, limitations, and suggestions made relative to infancy as to the meaning of lack of data on this score will also apply here.

(4) Old age. Old age may be defined as that period in the life cycle of an individual during which, either by the institutionalization of special privileges or by other means, the full responsibilities of adulthood are no longer expected of the individual who has passed through the

period of adulthood. The minimum necessary basis for the
distinction of this period is, of course, the physiological factors of senility and the general infirmities of old
age.[10] Many individuals no doubt live out their life span
with no diminution of capabilities important for the performance of their adult roles, but this is not true on the
whole for a society if the life span of its members is
sufficiently prolonged. Just as infants and children are
in different ways and varying degrees incapable of the
performance of certain roles crucial for the existence of
any society, so do such incapabilities develop in the
average individual if his life span is sufficiently prolonged. The usual physical infirmities and the loss of
sexual powers are clear enough cases of this, but the frequent decline in "mental" capabilities is no less important.
The implications of these as yet unalterable aspects of
the animal are many and diffuse. The implications with
respect to power and responsibility roles and the possibility of a "true gerontocracy" have been touched on elsewhere,[11] but these implications go into virtually all other
crucial and more or less strategic roles in a society with
the possible exception of those played by the aged as an
object of veneration.

The aged cannot be treated completely as infants or
children either, for they have not the same problems of
learning and development. Their need for special treatment
lies in their inability to continue the use of what they
have learned and in their inability to develop alternatives. Even though in some cases they, like infants, are
completely helpless and dependent, they cannot be treated
exactly as are infants for the reasons given. Increase of

---

10. An additional factor is, of course, the relatively shorter life expectancy of the aged.

11. See M. J. Levy, Jr., Family Revolution, pp. 128-
129.

the life span of individuals may have prolonged the possible span of adulthood, but it has not yet eliminated the problem of senility. There is, of course, one possibility open to a society with respect to all of the aged that is not open with respect to all of the infants or children. They can be killed or left to die without terminating a society. However much such a structure as this with regard to the aged may shorten the period or lessen its problems or minimize the complexity of role differentiation relative to it, it does not eliminate such role differentiation for as a minimum it enters consideration of who is eligible for such treatment.

Once more the remarks made above about the possibilities of variation and the implication of the factors mentioned here for studies of society must be borne in mind. In any specific society, however, the classifications are made, the facts of senility and the infirmities of old age, actual, possible, and probable, must be dealt with, and in this dealing there must be aspects of role differentiation.

In regard to all four of the above absolute age classifications certain reservations have been made. Most notably it has been pointed out that these four classifications set the minimum range of variation but by no means set the maximum. A given society might distinguish many or few absolute age classifications, but no society can ignore the four suggested here, however much they may subdivide or overlap them. The position taken here is not that all societies must distinguish the four classifications given here. It is rather that all societies must distinguish absolute age classifications and that, however variously these are distinguished, the distinctions must permit and institutionalize the kinds of role differentiation which here have been shown to fall into four categories. To the degree that one can confirm (or in the absence of disconfirmation of) the basis on which these four categories are

distinguishable, such a position as that taken here is
difficult to contradict.

The fact that a given society distinguishes eight
rather than four absolute age classifications does not mean
that the four classifications suggested here are useless
concepts for structural analysis. Although one may start
out seeking data in terms of these four categories, one
need not maintain them in the face of contradictory facts.
Since the facts one derives will presumably be explicit
and since, under such a procedure, one's concepts and theories will be explicit rather than implicit, it should be
far easier to correct for the actual situation than would
be the case if one's initial concepts and theories were
implicit as they are presumably in the case of the "tabula
rasa" school of investigators of societies. Furthermore,
the questions asked in terms of these four age classifications seek not to find exactly those classifications but
rather to find how a specific society handles the inescapable factors of human development in age terms of which
these four categories are advanced as the minimum necessary
distinctions.

There is another type of problem involved here. It
has already been suggested in the general discussion above
that these categories are not absolute in that every individual must enter them after exactly the same lapse of time
since birth or any other starting point. Variation in
these respects may, however, take other forms as well.
The distinction of roles on other bases may be combined
with distinctions on this basis. For example, sex role
distinctions may be so combined. Females may be conceived
as having the same age classifications as males, but may
enter or leave such categories after markedly different
lapses in time. Females may even be conceived as having
an almost entirely different set of age classifications
than males, both in the number of categories and their
starting and ending dates and so forth. Differences in

social positions of various sorts may be a basis for such
distinctions. The category of ch'ing-nien, for example,
was found at one time primarily among the gentry of China,
and was rarely applied to the peasants of the period.

Yet another type of variation is possible and of considerable importance in these respects. Depending on the
type of roles institutionalized for different individuals,
or the manner in which the individual is expected to gain
his various social positions (whether by achievement or
ascription or some combination of the two), the emphasis
placed on role differentiation on the basis of absolute
age may differ considerably. This difference is in addition to whatever differences in beginning and ending ages
or actual differences in classifications may exist. In
"traditional" China, for example, role differentiation on
the basis of absolute age was both more flexible and more
casual, especially among the peasants, in the case of
females as opposed to males.

Again, it may be reiterated that, however much the
different possibilities of variation may complicate the
absolute age classification, the factors symbolized by the
four categories set up here must be dealt with in terms of
institutionalized structures of action. Failure to find
such structures in a society will, as has been suggested
above, indicate one or some combination of the following
three sources of difficulty: (a) the hypotheses advanced
here are disconfirmed, (b) the data gathering has been
incomplete for some reason, or (c) the unit being studied
does not in fact conform to the definition of a society or
is in process of changing the structures in terms of which
it is defined or is possibly tending to complete dissolution.

b. Relative age. Role differentiation on the basis
of relative age has reference to a distinction of roles
among individuals on the basis of their comparative ages.
Role differentiation on this basis is constant only as

between specific individuals. Thus, two specific individuals have either been born at exactly the same time or one
is older than the other. The designation of older and
younger never changes as applied to this pair, but the
individual with roles appropriate to older classification
in this relation may also have roles appropriate to younger
classifications relative to some third individual. This
age basis of role distinction is fundamentally different
from that of absolute age, the essence of which is that
one individual, institutionally speaking, fits into one and
only one age role classification of that type on any one
level of generalization at any one time. The essence of
role differentiation on the basis of relative age is that
the number of different role classifications conceivable
for one individual on any one level of generalization at
any one time is limited only by the number of persons to
whom he is so related and the extent to which they and he
do or do not have identical ages.

The basis for distinction in terms of relative age is
that some differences in capabilities and requirements for
survival (to put the matter in minimal terms) do in fact
vary in a relatively smooth and continuous fashion. The
discontinuities or breaks in the developmental cycle may
require absolute age distinctions, but however those categories may be set up, there are relative differences within them. A three-day-old infant and one of six months are
both to all practical intents and purposes helpless and
completely dependent upon others, but they cannot actually
be treated in an identical fashion, however much this may
be possible on a more general level. The birth order of
children frequently, if not always, makes some differences
for the relative development of the individuals concerned.
Furthermore, some of these differences are differences
that cannot be completely ignored by the other members of
the society or by the individuals concerned, provided individuals with this sort of difference operate in contact

with one another, and, of course, to some extent they
always do.

Role differentiation on the basis of relative age is
always present to some degree, but the degree to which
such differences are institutionalized is subject to the
widest sorts of variation. In "traditional" China relative age was a major criterion of status in family, neighborhood, friendship, and other units. In the modern
industrial societies emphasis on relative age is perhaps
reduced to a minimum. The difference between such emphasis
in "traditional" China and the modern United States family
systems is most instructive in these respects. Briefly,
in the Chinese case it is quite sufficient to explain many
differentiations in the treatment of siblings in relative
age terms (e.g., "Ma-Yüan can do so and so because he is
your eldest brother.") without reference to differences in
capabilities. In the urban middle-class U.S. family such
differentiations are also made, but the need is felt to
justify such distinctions on the basis of capabilities
correlated with the age differences (e.g., "Your older
brother may cross the street alone, and you may not because
he can look out for the cars."). The implications of such
differences between societies goes far beyond the differences in emphases on relative age criteria. In the case
of the examples given the individuals of one society grow
up to operate in a society that allocates roles on a predominantly particularistic basis and those of the other in
a society that places, perhaps, the maximum known emphasis
on predominantly universalistic criteria. The experience
of the child in the latter case of having role differentiation on the basis of relative age tied directly to germane
criteria no doubt plays its role in preparing the child
for an outside emphasis on universalistic criteria in later
life for which the general family emphasis on particularistic criteria does not prepare him.

Finally, it must be noted that in a sense role differ-

entiations on the basis of absolute and relative age cut
across one another. Within absolute age classifications
there are relative age differentiations, and as between
absolute age classifications there are also relative age
differences. Most children are relatively older than infants, presumably, and most adults are relatively older
than children. There may be cases that do not conform to
the majority rule in these respects, of course. If marriage is the criterion of adulthood in a given society,
some married individuals may actually be younger than some
unmarried ones. This would not be true for large segments
of the population, however, unless one type of role differentiation on the basis of age were sharply subordinated
to the other, or unless they were defined so as not to
conflict in any crucial or highly strategic structures in
the role differentiation of the society concerned. To the
degree that the two bases of role differentiation do define
such important social structures, they must on the whole
reinforce rather than contradict one another if serious
sources of instability and change are to be avoided.

2. Role differentiation on the basis of generation

For the present purposes the concept of generation is
that which is apparently generally accepted in social
science usage. The generation of an individual refers to
his position relative to other individuals in terms of the
number of births of individuals involved in his direct
biological line of descent from some (arbitrarily chosen)
ancestor in that line. Thus, an individual is one generation "younger" than his biological father or mother, one
generation "older" than his biological offspring, and of
the same generation as his biological siblings. If one
wishes to compare the generational status of two individuals in the strict sense of the term used here, it can be
done only if some common direct biological ancestor can be

found for the individuals concerned. In a colloquial or
loose sense, two individuals are considered in the same
generation if they fall into roughly the same absolute age
classification, but the term will be used here only in its
strict sense.

The minimal functional explanation of role differentiation on the basis of generation as a structural requisite of any society lies in the requisite of sexual
recruitment and its implications. The minimal basis for
the structural requisite is an obvious one. Neither the
biological mother nor father can possibly be given identical roles with the child. Furthermore, even though the
biological paternity of the child may be unknown in a
given society, the same cannot be true generally for all
aspects of its biological maternity. At least at the time
of birth there must be distinctions of role in this latter
case even if in later periods of development children are,
institutionally speaking, so mixed as to make unknown
either their biological maternity or paternity. As far as
is known to the author no such situation exists in any
known society. If one adds to this picture the fact that
in all known societies some family structure is apparently
present despite the fact that one may not be able to
demonstrate conclusively that family structures are concrete structural requisites of any society,[12] then the
necessity of some role differentiation on the basis of
generation becomes an even more obvious requisite for any
society. Under such conditions a family unit without
older siblings or relatives other than husband and wife,
or even of only wife and child, is at least conceivable,
and in this case, despite the fact that the role differentiation on the basis of absolute age and generation
might coincide, both factors would be operative. In any

---

12.   See above, pp. 199-207.

case they conceivably need not coincide, and if they conceivably need not coincide, a minimal basis for role
differentiation on the basis of generation may be considered established as an hypothesis, however much it may
lack detailed confirmation.

As in the other bases of role differentiation there
is, of course, no case known in which the role differentiation on the basis of generation is confined to the
minimum necessary for any society. Generational differences in the strict sense used here rest to some degree on
the recognition of kinship structure. Often the differences are generalized to cover persons not related directly
to an individual but of age groups corresponding to the
generational standing of the individual's relatives. If,
however, all kinship considerations, including the connection between biological mother and child, could be eliminated, role differentiation on the basis of generation
could be handled on the basis of absolute age or other
considerations. Insofar as real or presumed biological
parents are recognized, however, role differentiation in
generational terms is inescapable. In most cases generational and absolute age classifications coincide to a
rather marked extent. The fathers of children of roughly
the same age tend to fall into roughly similar absolute
age groups, for example. But this is not necessarily the
case, and many, if not all, societies recognize clear-cut
cases where these factors contradict one another. In
"traditional" Chinese society children of the same age may
be of different generations, and their roles in their
family are sharply differentiated because of this factor
despite the fact that one would expect similarity on the
basis of their absolute age classification. This, of
course, is a rather clear case of role differentiation on
the basis of generation taking precedence over that on the
basis of age, but it indicates the possibility of these
factors contradicting one another to some extent.

Ordinarily one would expect to find certain types of
roles differentiated on a generational basis. Those concerned with the rearing, socialization, etc., of children
are obvious cases in point. Frequently, allocations of
power and responsibility have important determinants in
these terms, and in societies that institutionalize family
units including members of several generations at once,
this sort of allocation of power is to some degree necessary. In societies whose economic structure features
highly self-sufficient units of production and consumption
organized on a family basis, one might expect generational
factors to play an important role in training and allocating economic roles and the like.

It would be out of place to prolong these speculations
further here. Apart from the minimum inescapable differentiation of mother and child at birth, if it were possible
to have a society without any concrete kinship units, it
would be possible for a society to do without structures
of role differentiation on a generational basis. It would
seem to follow, particularly in view of the strict definition of generation used here, that it is primarily in
kinship units of a particular society that the social analyst must expect to find the basic structures of role differentiation on the basis of generation. Insofar as these
distinctions are extended outside the kinship units, they
are in present terms at least extended on a simulated
rather than on an actual generational basis, much as one
in western society refers to the children of one's non-kin
contemporaries as "members of the younger generation"
relative to oneself. In the strictest sense of the term
these differentiations cannot be carried outside a sphere
in which at least one common ancestor can be traced. In
this respect, unlike some of the other sorts of role differentiation, the initial sorts of data to seek and sift
are rather clearly and conveniently indicated.

3. Role differentiation on the basis of sex

The distinction of sexes used here is that between
male and female in the accepted sense of those terms. In
physiological terms, the sexes are differentiated in terms
of the roles members of each of these two types are capable
of performing on the average in the production of new members of the species. Unlike some other species this particular one can be understood in terms of two sexes, male
and female, for present purposes since it is at least
within the realm of theoretical possibility that deviants,
if any, from these two types might be eliminated without
preventing the existence of some sort of society. The
females of the species may be designated as those individuals who on the average are capable of the physiological
processes of conceiving and bearing children. The males
of the species are those individuals who on the average
are capable of the physiological processes necessary if
the potentialities of the female for conception are to be
realized.[13]

At the present stage of biological engineering it is
quite necessary to have members of both these sexes if a
society as defined here is to exist. Without them the
provision for recruitment of the society by sexual means
is out of the question. Since it is the case that, banal
and obvious though it may be, women cannot father children and men cannot conceive and bear them, and since
the fathering and conception and bearing of children

---

13. One should at this point emphatically refer to
the present state of technology. Should biological discoveries relative to the mammalian orders permit of the
continued production of fertile female individuals by
stimulations of the eggs other than by male produced sperm,
the possibility of single sex societies sans males would
be opened. Experiments in mammalian parthenogenesis are
currently being carried out with some tentative suggestions
that may lead in that direction.

necessitates some minimal special forms of activity by the individuals concerned directly in these processes and by others related to these individuals in such a way that these activities have implications for their actions, roles must to some degree be differentiated on the basis of sex.

The obvious starting point for investigations of role differentiation on the basis of sex is the data concerned with the sexual reproduction of the members of the society. Closely associated with this is likely to be the allocation of roles with regard to the care and rearing of children. This, too, is associated with an obvious physiological distinction on the basis of sex since the women of most societies are both capable of and actually do nurse their offspring or delegate this duty to other mothers in the society. This factor, however, is not at the present stage of technology a necessary basis for role distinction on the basis of sex since it is by no means out of the question for a society to survive in which no woman nurses either her own offspring or those of other women.[14]

Other role differentiations on the basis of sex than these are subject to the widest sorts of variation, and the specific forms even of these may vary widely. Commonly, power and responsibility roles, production and consumption roles, religious roles, and many others are differentiated on the basis of sex, but, except insofar as these differentiations can be shown to be directly dependent on

---

14. This is an excellent example of variability of the limits of variation of social action. This is a variation in the limits set by human heredity and nonhuman environment that has resulted from the actions that previously took place within these limits prior to their variation. Were it not for social action within such previous limits, the techniques and facilities for nurturing infants without the use of human milk would not exist. Even in the present stage of technology the possibilities involved have never been completely institutionalized for any society, of course, but the fact remains that they now exist.

the physiological processes mentioned above, and few if
any of them are, it cannot be proved that they are role
differentiations on the basis of sex that must appear in
any society. It may or may not be true that women are
inherently weaker than men on the average, but there are
societies in which women and not men do the heavy work
just as there are societies in which they do not. Similar
remarks can be made about most, if not all, of the other
supposedly inherent physiological capabilities of men and
women. The hypotheses that are inescapable, however, are:
(1) that there is always some role differentiation on the
basis of sex, (2) that it is always related to the physiological factors of reproduction, and (3) that it is never
confined solely to considerations inescapably involved in
the physiological factors of reproduction.

4. Role differentiation on the basis of economic allocation

Economic allocation in concrete social structures may
be defined as the distribution of the goods and services
making up the income of the concrete structure concerned
and of the goods and efforts making up the output of that
structure among the various members of the structure and
among the members of that structural unit and other structural units with which it is in contact in these respects.[15] The structure of economic allocation may be
subdivided into two parts; the structures of production
and consumption. The structure of production includes all
of the structures from whose operation goods and services
accrue to the concrete structure concerned. The structure
of consumption includes all the structures from whose opera-

---

15. The goods and services referred to may, at least
from the point of view of the actor(s) concerned, be
nonempirical as well as empirical ones (e.g., some magical
and religious goods and services).

tion goods and services are allocated to the various members of the concrete structure concerned and for the purposes recognized by that structure.

In any society roles must be differentiated on the basis of economic allocation, i.e., who does what and when with respect to the allocation of goods and services, and these roles may be differentiated as production and consumption roles. The functional requisite basis of these differentiations lies as a minimum in the functional necessity of providing for the physiological adjustment of the members of the unit to the setting of the unit. Without institutionalized provision for the structure of production roles some, if not all, of the members of the society would starve let alone their possible death from lack of shelter or the like. Certainly, the infants of the society would die, and the society would not be able to persist.

Without institutionalized structures of consumption roles the same and other sorts of difficulties would arise. Even with food produced for them, infants without help could not consume it. Furthermore, given the facts of scarcity and the like, the absence of institutional structures as to who might consume what and when would leave the way open at any point for the war of all against all. Here, the functional requisite of regulation of the choice of means as well as other functional requisites is involved.

The production and consumption of food, clothing, shelter, and the like are obvious minima in these respects. Who produces and consumes particular goods and services can be distinguished, but sometimes the distinctions are subtle and complex. Often overlooked are those goods and especially services which are at one and the same time produced and consumed, as, for example, the care of children.

For quite simple and obvious reasons no society can have a structure of economic role differentiation such

that each individual is completely self-sufficient in both
production and consumption aspects of activities. The
ubiquity of helpless members of the society (infants and to
a lesser degree small children) forbids this quite apart
from other considerations. The famous Marxist formula,
"from each according to his ability, to each according to
his need," is perhaps a more possible solution, but one
might speculate that, for no other reasons than the political implications of economic roles, such a solution is unlikely. More realistic questions in these respects center
around the kinds of concrete structures in terms of which
production and consumption roles are carried out. Are they
combined in a single unit? Are the units of one or the
other or both highly self-sufficient, highly interdependent, or whatever? Are such units organized primarily with
reference to the allocation of goods and services as is
predominantly the case in industrial societies, or are
they organized on bases in which quite other considerations
(e.g., kinship) play a sufficiently prominent role to
determine or take consistent precedence over other criteria
in the allocation of goods and services? To what extent
are economic roles allocated on predominantly particularistic as opposed to predominantly universalistic criteria?
The range of variation is, of course, extremely wide.
These roles, however, are never completely separate from
other bases of role differentiation. To some extent considerations of absolute age classification and sex as a
minimum play a role in the definition of who does what and
when with regard to the allocation of goods and services.

5. Role differentiation on the basis of
political allocation

Political allocation for the purposes of this study
may be defined as the distribution of power over and responsibility for the actions of the various members of the

concrete structure concerned, involving on the one hand
the use of coercive sanctions, of which force is the extreme form in one direction, and on the other accountability to the members and in terms of the structure concerned,
or to the members of other concrete structures. The term
power is defined for these purposes as the ability to
exercise authority and control over the actions of others.
Responsibility may be defined as the accountability of an
individual(s) to another individual(s) or group(s) for his
own acts and/or the acts of others. The general functional requisite basis for the structure of political allocation will be taken up in detail when that analytic structure is discussed below.[16] For present purposes it need
only be said that the functional requisite of effective
control of disruptive behavior would in and of itself require the existence of some structures of political allocation.

The matter of concern here is the hypothesis that
there must be a differentiation of roles in terms of who
has what powers and responsibilities at what times. Obviously, there must be differentiation with respect to
power and responsibility holders. It is possible for a
given relationship to involve mutually equal powers and
responsibilities as in some forms of "friendship," but one
cannot be held effectively responsible to the same person
and in the same respect and at the same time relative to
whom, which, and when one wields power. Furthermore, it
is always possible that the individual in a given power
role will not have a balancing role of responsibility.[17]
At the same time the intimate relationship of power and
responsibility roles should not be ignored. In one sense

---

16. See Chapter X.

17. The implications of this possibility for the
stability of the concrete social structures in which it
occurs will be taken up in Chapter X below.

these elements form the obverse of one another. To some
degree one is responsible in some respect(s) to whomever
wields actual power over one, and conversely one has power
to some degree over whomever is actually responsible to
one. There is no effective power that does not involve an
effective responsibility, however the effectiveness of
these factors may be obtained.

Apart from the minimum necessity of role differentiation implicit in the empirically observable distinction
between power and responsibility, there are role differentiations that must exist in these respects on quite different grounds. Again, the convenient and familiar case
of the implications of infancy may be cited. Infants
cannot in their own persons either wield power or bear
responsibility in any effective sense of those terms. To
a lesser degree the same may be said of children. At the
same time individuals in both categories must be subjected
to controls to prevent harm to themselves as well as to
prevent deviant activities that might become a menace to
others.

The obvious distinctions that must be made in any
society in these respects are those between power holders
on the one hand and responsibility bearers on the other,
and of course distinctions between the different categories
or types of power and responsibility. A given individual
during the course of an ordinary life cycle will, of
course, hold numerous and different roles with regard to
both power and responsibility. And certainly after the
infancy period there will be no time in which, institutionally speaking, he will be completely free of either or
both types of roles.

It is not the task in this present consideration of
the allocation of power and responsibility to go into the
rather far-reaching implications of such structures for
the stability of any society. That matter will be discussed in Chapter X below on the structure of political

allocation, but one or two indications may be made at this
point of the manner in which role differentiation in these
terms must be related to role differentiation on other
bases. There is first the question of the importance for
stability of a relatively close balance between power and
responsibility. Briefly, instability may result from power
not balanced by responsibility because of the possibility
of capricious (that is capricious in terms of the social
structure concerned) exercise of power with all the disruptive effects possible under those conditions. Responsibility without corresponding power is equally a source
of instability since, in the absence of some power to enforce responsibility on the individuals concerned, the
responsibility bearer can not be held responsible effectively. Insofar as these hypotheses hold true, it follows
that role differentiations on other bases that contradict
these criteria will interfere with the stability of the
society.

The second question in these terms is that some bases
of role differentiation may determine the allocation of
factors of primary significance in the allocation of power
and responsibility and hence these role differentiations
cannot contradict those on a political basis without a
resultant instability. The best understood case is perhaps
that of role differentiation with regard to economic allocation. The production and consumption of goods and
services is always to some extent germane to the exercise
of power and responsibility since some minimal command of
both is necessary to political role holders, if only in
order that they may have at their disposal the minimum of
goods and services necessary to make any action at all
possible. The implications of these mutual involvements
cut both ways, of course. Without some powers and responsibilities goods and services cannot be allocated.[18]

_____

18. See above, Note 68, p. 98.

In a sense all of the different bases of role differentiation are mutually involved with one another and interdependent since they look at the same empirical phenomena
from different points of view. Nevertheless, some of these
omnipresent bases of role differentiation are more immediately and directly useful in the analysis of specific
problems than are others. With regard to the general
question of stability in social systems the political roles
are an obvious case in point involving as they do a focus
of concern on problems of control and an investigation of
other factors only insofar as they are relevant to these.
By studying carefully enough all of the role differentiations in a society on the basis of absolute age one will
uncover all the relevant data necessary for the analysis
of the problem of stability, but there will be an enormous
task of sifting it out of other factors. The data assembled in terms of role differentiation on the basis of
political allocation will already be in terms immediately
useful for such a study.

6. Role differentiation on the basis of religion

The term religion as used here refers to aspects of
action directly oriented to ultimate ends (or goals), i.e.,
to ends that are not conceived as means to other ends but
rather as desirable in and of themselves, as their own
basis of justification.[19] Concrete structures or specific
actions will be termed predominantly religiously oriented

---

19. This definition of religion is perhaps not the
conventional one. It would cover major aspects of the
conventional religious systems, but it would also cover
major aspects of many systems not ordinarily classified
under that category, e.g., communism and nazism as practiced in some respects by their believers. The general
question of this kind of structure and the usefulness of
this particular definition with some subcategories of it
is explored below in Chapter XI.

if the religious aspects of the structures of action take
precedence over all other aspects. The usual possible
discrepancies between the ideal and actual state of affairs
both from the points of view of the actor and the observer
are, as might be expected, present in these respects.
Role differentiation on this basis has reference to the
distinction of who does what and when with regard to the
portions of the system of action that are directly oriented
to ultimate ends. The general functional requisite basis
of some religious structural requisites of one sort or
another rests on the discussion of a shared and articulated
set of goals. In Chapter IV above the necessity of such a
set of goals has been explored briefly with some attention
paid to the fact that some nonempirical ultimate goals are
inevitably involved in societies.[20]

Although religious aspects of action are here defined
as aspects of action directly oriented to ultimate ends,
and although aspects of this sort are empirically observable, there are, of course, many other aspects of action
involved in concrete structures predominantly oriented to
religious aspects of action. In conventional predominantly religiously oriented structures like the various western
and oriental churches, such activities, intermediate in a
sense to the religious concern, are well known and understood. They involve administration, fund raising, and
hundreds of other considerations. Insofar as an individual is involved in such roles in a predominantly religiously oriented structure his roles are at least in some
respects differentiated from similar roles in the society
on a religious basis.

It is doubtful whether religious structures of the
sort necessary for any society can be organized on a basis
other than this sort involving as it does considerable

---

20. See pp. 173-181.

differentiation of the individuals so involved from others
in the society. The solitary ascetic sects of the world
do not provide the general framework for ethical principles
that can serve in the persistence of society as that unit
has been defined here since they tend specifically to ignore or deny common articulated sets of goals. The minimal
necessity for religious role differentiation may, however,
rest on quite different grounds. There must in the last
analysis be some differentiation between the initiated and
the uninitiated, the teachers and the student, in these
respects. Man's capacity for orienting his action to such
considerations is undeniable. It may even be true that in
the absence of any training some such orientation would
develop, but it is also true that the wide range of variation possible in these respects requires some systematic
development and training if any particular society is to
remain stable. As a minimum for stability in a society
the ultimate goals must permit of the intermediate goals
necessary for the persistence of the members of a society.
In substructures of societies there are examples of sects
whose adherence to the ascetic interdiction of sexual
intercourse, for example, has resulted in the extinction
of their systems of action. Some of the nihilist theolo-
gies would also end a society if they were sufficiently
widespread and faithfully enough adhered to. If such
possibilities are to be avoided, alternatives consistent
with other requisite structures must be inculcated, and
this in turn involves some minimal differentiation of
roles.

7. Role differentiation on the basis of cognition

Cognition has been defined above as "knowledge or
understanding of a situation or phenomenon," and different
types of cognition and cognitive orientations have been

discussed there.[21] The necessity of cognitive orientations
is discussed there also, and on this general functional
requisite rests the requisite basis of cognitive structures
in general. Role differentiation on the basis of cognition
has several necessary bases, all of them reasonably obvious.

Most obvious, of course, is the fact that the new
recruits for a society must be taught the various types of
cognition necessary if they are to operate in the society.
This, of course, implies the minimal distinction between
teacher and student. Hardly less obvious are the implications for role differentiation of the different types of
cognitive orientations. In the first place, there is the
distinction between the basic cognitive orientations and
the intermediate ones. The former must by definition be
shared by all to a large degree; the latter are not, and
role differentiation follows automatically.

There is another basis for differentiation in these
respects however. One may distinguish at least two empirically observable types of systems of cognition which
are of great importance in societies. In the first place,
there are the technologies, the systems of cognition that
serve as the basis for rational action of whatever sort.
In the second place, there are systems of cognition about
value standards, the normative structures of the society,
including both the values involved in ultimate and intermediate ends. These are different bases for cognitive
role differentiation, and the different subcategories possible within each serve as further bases for cognitive
role differentiation. The enormous range of possible
variation in these latter respects permits of extremely
complex systems. In a modern industrial society, for example, the technological roles are carried to extremely

---

21. See pp. 168-173.

sophisticated and specialized lengths of differentiation.

Finally, differences in cognitive ability, whether physiologically innate, socially determined, or both, always open the possibility for the distinction of the "expert" in these respects. Because of the importance of cognition in any society, the cognitive expert is always important, but as societies become increasingly complex in their technologies or general social structure, the role of the expert, and consequently the distinction between the expert and nonexpert, becomes of greater and greater importance for the stability of the system.

8. Role differentiation on the basis of nonhuman environment

Features of the nonhuman environment of a society such as seasonal, topographical, and other factors are subject to extremely wide variations. It is perhaps conceivable that a society exist in an area with nonhuman environmental conditions so invariant through time and space as to require no specific variant adjustments of social structures to such factors. If that is the case, role differentiation on this basis does not properly belong in the present list. Suffice it to say that, whatever may be conceivable, actual cases of such invariance are very rare indeed if not altogether nonexistent. For that reason brief consideration of the matter is given here.

Perhaps the most obvious case in point in these respects is seasonal variation.[22] In some sections of the earth the seasonal differences of temperature, humidity, and the like are less variable than in others, but they

---

22. A student at Princeton, Mr. D. S. Bingham, in the course of research in terms of this system of analysis suggested to the author that role differentiation on a seasonal basis would seem to be one of the minimally necessary bases of role differentiation.

are never absent. Furthermore, seasonal variations with
respect to food supplies both agrarian and others are never
completely lacking. Insofar as this is the case, some
seasonal (or to put it more generally, some nonhuman environmental) bases for role differentiation must exist.
In some societies the difference may be small indeed, but
for most of the world's population they are neither small
nor negligible. Failure to note them is, therefore, in
most cases almost certain to be a serious source of inadequacy in understanding society. The functional requisite
basis involved here is, of course, the provision for adequate physiological relationship to the setting. One need
not fall into the difficulties of geographical determinism
in these respects, but one cannot ignore the nonhuman environmental factors either.

9. Role differentiation on the basis of solidarity

     The structure of _solidarity_ in a society may be de-
fined as the structure in terms of which relationships
among the members of a society are allocated according to
the content, strength, and intensity of the relationships.[23] Given the definition of society used here such
that a plurality of members is always involved, the presence of relationships among the members is an inevitable
factor. In all of the functional requisites discussed the
presence of relationships among the members is involved.
It is not intended to discuss here the classification of
the structure of solidarity as a structural requisite.
That will be done in the following chapter. The concern
here is only with role differentiation on the basis of
solidarity.[24]

---

     23. The general discussion of the structure of soli-
darity is deferred until Chapter VIII. In that discussion
the subsidiary terms of the definition as well as other
aspects of the concept will be discussed in detail.

     24. A student at Princeton, Mr. H. Kaufman, in the

Many, if not most or all, of the functional requisites
of any society are conditions that can be fulfilled only
by the actions of individuals in relationships with one
another rather than by individuals operating in splendid
isolation. Solidarity structures have reference to an
aspect of relationship structures in general and consequently to an aspect of the larger membership unit structures
of a society as well. Insofar as such units, however they
may be defined, are present in all societies, role differentiation in terms of such units is an inescapable feature
of any society. While it is true that specific concrete
structural requisites cannot with any certainty be derived
for any society,[25] there is no reason to doubt that some
concrete structures must exist for any society. When one
asks the question who does what and when in terms of the
membership units to which he is attached, one discovers
material not only on role differentiation but also on the
kind of membership unit distinguished in the society.
Given the theoretical difficulty for the present at least
of deriving the concrete structural requisites of any society, examination of role differentiation on the basis of
solidarity promises to be a useful tool if only in that it
suggests a systematic fashion of locating the concrete
structures of a specific society.

It should be noted that any type of role differentiation may serve as a basis for a concrete structure. There
could conceivably be concrete structures involving all
children, or all women, or all food gatherers, or all milk
drinkers, or all people with power over children, etc. Of
the extremely large number of possibilities, relatively
few alone or in combination become the bases of the insti-

---

course of research in terms of this system of analysis
suggested to the author that role differentiation on the
basis of solidarity would seem to be one of the minimally
necessary bases of role differentiation.

25. See above, pp. 199-207.

tutionalized concrete substructures of a society. These
concrete substructures are of the utmost importance involving as they do the differing degrees of loyalty of
their members with the consequent possibilities for conflict or cooperation or what have you between the members
of one concrete unit and another. Unless it can be demonstrated that societies without such substructures can
exist, role differentiation in terms of solidarity can not
be avoided, nor can the roles so differentiated be ignored
by either the individual who has them or by his fellow
members of the society. If there are family units, Mr. X,
in addition to all his other roles, has a role as member
of the X family, and in the respects that such units are
crucial or more or less strategic for the society, Mr. X's
behavior in terms of his role as member of the X family
must be more or less well institutionalized if there is to
be a stable situation.

B. STRATIFICATION

Stratification has been defined above as the particular type of role differentiation that differentiates between higher and lower standings in terms of one or more
criteria.[26] The standing of stratification as a subcategory of the functional requisite of role differentiation
has been discussed above and need not be repeated here.
What must be pointed out here is the fact that, if the
condition involved is to exist, there must be structures
such that operation in terms of them will result in such a
condition. It is not intended to discuss the matter of
stratification in any detail or with any thoroughness.
The general question of stratification is currently receiving both wide and specialized attention of a sort which
cannot be given it here.

---

26. See p. 164.

The criteria in terms of which a particular stratification structure may be defined are, if not infinite, then
at least extremely numerous. Any of the bases of role
differentiation mentioned above and any specific case of
any of them may be made a criterion of stratification. It
has been the custom in the past to use economic and/or
political criteria as the bases of defining stratification
structures. This is not difficult to understand for two
reasons: in the first place, there is the obvious ease of
ranking individuals in these two respects; and in the
second place, there is their obvious mutual relevance for
one another that has been mentioned before in this chapter.
Political and economic criteria are by no means the only
possibilities, and in fact it may be advanced as an hypothesis here that they can never be the sole criteria of
stratification in a society. There can never be one or
two bases of stratification in a society; there are always
many. In some societies one or more may override in importance the others as in the case of societies institutionalizing caste systems, whatever the basis of the castes
may be. The others are never completely eliminated, however.

Wherever there is a question of learning or of ability
or of any quality crucial or more or less strategic for
the existence of the society, if that quality can be held
in varying degrees, it is a basis for stratification of
some sort in the society. To the degree that the development of that quality in individuals is crucial or more or
less strategic for the society some stratification in terms
of it must exist. The absence of such a discrimination
would involve difficulties of "motivation" as well as performance. Societies with more elaborate distinctions of
qualities, skills, etc. than others must have more elaborate systems of stratification. The caste system of India
seems to the western observer to be an incredibly and
almost unimaginably complex system of stratification.

Actually, this impression is the result of the fact that
the observer is not usually familiar with elaborate stratification on that type of basis. He is familiar, to the
extent often of being unaware of it, with a system of
stratification that is vastly more complex. The stratification of a modern industrial society is almost certainly
the most complex system of stratification in social history,
at least in terms of distinctions observed and stratified.
The different stratifications in the field of production
alone stagger the imagination. Some tens of thousands of
occupational roles, let alone differences of skill inside
them, are distinguished as a minimum. They are ranked
relative to one another in highly complex ways, perhaps
not any one relative to all the others, but at least each
with regard to some of the others. It is not a matter of
accident that, despite the ethical principle that "money
isn't everything" and "doesn't measure the true worth of a
man," the criterion of monetary income becomes so important
as a general basis of stratification in such societies.
It is a relatively objective and highly general and easily
understood criterion, and the other bases of distinction
that underlie monetary differences are so complex that
they cannot be grasped by the general membership of the
society.

While it cannot be said that only one or two stratification criteria operate in a specific society, there is,
of course, a limitation on elaboration in these respects.
It is quite out of the question that from the point of
view of each member of the society each other member be
differentially ranked in all respects. It is, perhaps,
even out of the question that from the point of view of
each member of the society each other member be differently ranked in any particular respect. The cognitive problem of recognition alone would prevent such a situation.
To some extent there must be stratified groups whose members from some point of view are conceived to have roughly

equivalent rankings. The permutations and combinations
possible vary widely. In an individual's immediate circle
of acquaintance everyone may conceivably be ranked differentially, but for the society as a whole there must be
some clustering of individuals in these respects.

While it is a mistake to ignore all other bases of
stratification than that of power, it would be equally
mistaken to ignore the importance of this basis. Involving
as it does the control of individuals, this basis is always
a crucial consideration for any society. The problems of
regulating means and affective expression controlling
deviant behavior, and the like, indicate sufficiently the
necessary role played by a system of stratification in
political terms. Furthermore, these problems alone suffice
to indicate the impossibility for the society as a whole
to institutionalize a completely egalitarian system of
political allocation. Whatever else may be said of the
structures of stratification, they are always in some respects crucial institutions as far as the problem of order
is concerned in any society.

In conclusion to these remarks on role differentiation
some further distinctions must be drawn. Much has been
made of the bases of role differentiation. These are the
criteria in terms of which society distinguishes who does
what when. An attempt has been made in the case of each
of the bases of role differentiation discussed to indicate
why such a basis must to some extent be recognized in any
society. Furthermore, an exploratory and tentative attempt
has been made to isolate the minimum number of different
bases of role differentiation that must be present in any
society. This effort must not be confused with the exploration of the causes of role differentiation. No attempt
is made in this volume to treat the evolutionary development of societies. Neither the necessary nor the sufficient conditions for the development of the structures of

role differentiation discussed here have been explored
here tentatively or otherwise. Nor can one suggest that
the functional requisites involved furnish a causal explanation of these structures. To do so is to fall into the
fallacy of functional (or structural) teleology warned
about above.[27] These structures cannot be said to exist
because in their absence the functional requisites would
not be fulfilled, for to do so is to assume a priori the
necessary persistence of the society in which they are
found. That such structures exist, and must exist in any
society that is to persist in its setting, is advanced as
an hypothesis here. No hypotheses about their causal
factors are advanced. It is not suggested that such considerations are unimportant, but merely that they represent
an attack on another set of problems. This distinction is
a familiar one in other fields of study that depend upon
structural-functional requisite analysis. One may say
that some given organ or process is a structural requisite
of arachnids, and this theory and the results for analysis
of many problems which will in part follow from the theory
may be well confirmed. This alone tells one nothing, however, as to how arachnids came to have such structures or
processes. Such is the distinction intended here.

In the consideration of social change these causal
questions are of the essence of the matter. In such problems one must, however, deal in terms of functional and
structural prerequisites as well as in terms of functional
and structural requisites. In problems of social change
the types of theories evolved by the use of functional and
structural requisite analysis will tell one a great deal
about the range of possibilities for change, just as in
biology it will tell the researchers what will be lethal
mutations, but the complete answer to these problems can
never come in terms of such concepts alone.

----

27. See pp. 52-55.

It must also be stressed in closing that the structural requisites of role differentiation for any society
are not the sole structural requisites for any specific
society. In any specific society there may well be requisite structures of role differentiation on bases other than
those given here though the ones given here will always be
present too. United States society as presently constituted must, for example, differentiate roles on the basis
of state membership, whereas Trobriand society as presently constituted need not. Furthermore, the subdivisions of
the bases of role differentiation given here will in the
case of any specific society be vastly elaborated in ways
that cannot be common for all societies. The specific
absolute age classifications found in "traditional" China,
for example, do not fit any and all societies.

Finally, it must be reiterated that what has been
said here merely sets the minimal bases for role differentiation in any society. It does not tell the researcher
the lengths of elaboration to which such differentiation
may be carried. It indicates, for example, that there
must be differentiation between males and females in certain respects, but it does not indicate that their clothing
or adornments need be differentiated, though they are to
some degree in all known societies. It tells one that
some distinctions on these bases must be sought and, to
some degree, what sort must be sought, but it does not
tell how far they may be carried save in one sense, i.e.,
that they cannot be carried so far in one or more senses
as to prevent totally the recognition of other bases.
These hypotheses about role differentiation are, therefore,
presented on an extremely general level. On that level
they have many and varied uses for the purposes of social
analysis. They must not, however, be used as would be
justified if the present form of analysis had already been
carried to much more specific levels.

C H A P T E R   VIII

THE STRUCTURE OF SOLIDARITY

The structure of solidarity has been defined above[1]
as the structure in terms of which relationships among the
members of a society are allocated according to the content, strength, and intensity of the relationships.[2]
Solidarity as used here will cover an aspect of phenomena
of infinite gradation between two poles. The negative
pole will be taken to mean complete antagonism -- war at
sight as it were. The positive pole will be taken to mean
complete agreement and complete and mutual affective
accord. The only element of discontinuity of the variation between these poles is at the point of perfect neutrality. This point may be ruled out with reference to
the relations of members of any concrete structures that
are concrete structural requisites of a particular society
being studied, since some affective orientation of members
of such units toward one another must be institutionalized
if that unit is to be sufficiently stable to permit of its

---

1. See p. 341.

2. The definition and discussion of the structure of
solidarity represents a modification and expansion of an
extremely brief treatment of this structure in the author's
previous volume, Family Revolution. In that volume (pp. 15-
22) this structure was briefly developed as a structural
requisite for any concrete kinship structure. Here it is
briefly developed as a structural requisite for any society. With additions and changes made necessary by this
different and more general application of the concept much
of that previous material is used, and some portions of it
have been used without change.

operation and the resultant performance thereby of the
functional requisites (or portions thereof) on which its
classification as a structural requisite rests. In the
definition of the structure of solidarity used here, the
subsidiary terms, content, strength, and intensity, have
appeared. By the term content is meant the definition of
the type of relationship that is to exist and the members
between (or among) whom it is to exist. Thus, all societies must have relationships of some sort between the
adults and the children and infants who are members of the
society. The factors that necessitate role differentiation in these terms also require relationships of some
sorts in these respects. As a minimum, for example, factors of maintenance and training for the young are involved.
The content of such a solidarity structure, for example
that of parent and child to cite a common form of such a
relationship, would include the parent and child as the
persons concerned. The type of relationship would be
subject to wide variation, but it would involve production
of certain necessities of life in the form of goods and
services either directly or indirectly by the parent.
Obedience of the child to the parent, or at least power on
the part of the parent to curb and direct the child, would
be involved as a minimum if any major part of the training
of the child were institutionally defined as taking place
in terms of such a relationship. Finally, some mutual
"emotional" attachment between (or among) the parties
would be necessary and would presumably have to be of such
a nature as to permit and ensure the general effectiveness
of the maintenance and training involved. Current research
on child development would lead one to expect that, at
least in the early stages of the infant's development,
intimate rather than avoidant affects would have to be
involved.

By the term strength is meant the relative precedence,
or lack of precedence, taken by this relationship over

other relationships of its general sort, and over other
obligations and commitments in the larger social sphere.
This aspect of the structure of solidarity is well recognized in both scientific writing and common sense knowledge. In the family system of a modern industrial society
the husband-wife solidarity is institutionalized as
"stronger" than that of husband-husband's father or wife-
wife's father, unless the husband or wife acts in such a
way as to violate rather markedly the institutionalized
form of his or her respective role. It is "stronger" in
the sense that it is institutionalized that the mutual
obligations of the husband-wife relationship be given priority over the obligations of either of the other two relationships. It is weaker in some specific respects than the
husband's relationship with some of the concrete politically oriented structures of his society. His wife's objections to his paying taxes or serving in the armed forces,
for example, is not a legitimate excuse for his failure in
either respect, although it is a legitimate excuse for his
failing to take a government job offered through ordinary
channels.

In consideration of the strength of solidarity structures one element of variation of tremendous significance
must be noted. The strength of the relationship need not
be identical from the point of view of all the parties to
the relationship. A two-person relationship may be used
as an example. Individual A's obligations to individual B
may be much greater than the reverse. For example, in
"traditional" China the strength of the father-son relationship was overwhelming from the son's point of view,
but this was by no means always the case from the father's
point of view. From the son's point of view this solidarity took precedence, institutionally speaking, over his
relationship with his mother, but from the father's point
of view his relationship with the son's mother, his wife
or concubine, took precedence over that with his son in

many respects though, ideally speaking, conflicts of this
sort were certainly not expected. The father's obligations
to his own father, of course, also took precedence over
his obligations to his son. On the other hand, relationships may be institutionalized as involving equal strength
from both A's and B's points of view. The relationships
between friends in "traditional" China were of this sort.
The solidarity was not the strongest or the weakest possible for either, but for each the same sorts of solidarities
were stronger or weaker.

　　　The significance of the concept of strength of solidarities is not difficult to see. It has an obvious
relevance for the ranking and ordering of relationships in
the society. The various strengths of various solidarities
is, of course, a part of the general structure of political
allocation, or rather is that structure viewed from a
somewhat different standpoint. No single concept will
give the researcher more insight into the interrelationships of various concrete structures in a society nor will
any more readily locate the concrete structural units of
major significance for the operation of the society. This
consideration is quite useful in approaches to the analysis
of different societies. If, for example, there is good
reason to conjecture that the strength of the solidarity
institutionalized for one particular type of concrete
structure is in general far greater than any other, it is
reasonable to conjecture that virtually the whole of the
social structure can be derived by the analysis of the
particular type of concrete structure involved. This hypothesis is suggested on the following basis: if one unit
takes such precedence, the structures that are structural
requisites and fall outside the concrete structure concerned must be so devised and so oriented that operation
in terms of the concrete structure of overwhelming strength
of solidarity will involve the maintenance of the other
structures or at least that the latter be so arranged as

not to conflict with the former. This would seem to hold
simply because under such conditions in cases of conflict
the probability is that the structural requisites lying
outside the concrete structure would not be observed, and
either change or dissolution of the society would result.
If no structures outside the structure concerned are
structural requisites, then on the level involved the analysis need go no further than that concrete structure in
any case. "Traditional" Chinese society institutionalized
a concrete structure of such overwhelming strength of
solidarity, and to a considerable degree analysis in terms
of family structure will get at the major structural requirements of that society. On the other hand, no such
single concrete structure can be easily distinguished in a
modern industrial society, and approaches to such a society
through a single concrete substructure are considerably
less promising.

By the term intensity is meant the state of affect
involved in the relationship. The intensity of solidarity
is subject to two major types of variation. There is first
the question of the type or types of affect involved; respect, love, fear, and so forth. Though there are many
different affects that may be listed according to whichever
psychological taxonomy may be preferred, the important
distinction for present purposes is the dichotomy set up
above[3] of avoidance and intimacy. Briefly, the essence of
avoidant affects is their tendency to deemphasize direct
contacts and to conduct such as exist on a relatively
formal basis. The essence of intimate affects is their
tendency to emphasize direct contact, informality, and the
overt display of affect. Certain affects are more easily
combined with avoidance (e.g., fear, respect, etc.), and
others are more easily combined with intimacy (e.g., love,

---

3. See pp. 262-270.

joy, etc.), but this is a highly relative matter. The relationship between a Navaho man and his mother-in-law, according to many anthropological accounts, is of considerable importance, but his avoidance of her in the fullest sense of the term is carried to considerable lengths, all direct contact with her being taboo for him. At the other extreme, perhaps, is the institutionalized form of the husband-wife relationship in a society in which the choice of marital partners is on the basis of "romantic love."

The second consideration relative to intensity is the degree of affective involvement expected from the parties to the relationship. This factor is also open to the widest sorts of variation. In modern western society one is expected to "love" one's mother a great deal. One is also expected to love one's aunts, but not to nearly the same degree, and legitimate grounds for withholding love in the latter case are both more numerous and less serious in terms of the general values of the society.

It must be noted in the case of intensity as in the case of strength that a range of variation exists in terms of the different parties involved. A's affects toward B may differ in both type and intensity from those of B toward A, institutionally speaking or otherwise. In the teacher-student relationship the point of view of teacher and student is quite different in these respects, certainly in degree and often in kind as well. The relation of friendship, on the other hand, generally institutionalizes identical intensities just as it institutionalizes identical strengths.

In consideration of the structure of solidarity another range of variation is of considerable significance. It is in a sense compounded of those which have gone before. It is possible to have solidarities in which the degrees of strength and intensity tend to vary in opposite directions. It is possible for there to be relatively little strength but relatively great intensity in a rela-

tionship, for example. There are presumably limits on
this type of variation, however. Insofar as the type and
degree of affect is relevant to the strength of it, the
institutionalized form of the one cannot contradict that
of the other if the relationship structures are to remain
stable.

In considering the different units of solidarity in a
society a consideration of quite another sort arises. One
must ascertain the various factors concerning the solidarity of the members of the unit vis-à-vis one another.
There is also the question of the various aspects of the
solidarity patterns of the members of the unit concerned
vis-à-vis other such units. Thus, in the United States
one must study not only the internal solidarity patterns
of the family structure but also those relating the family
to the government, to business firms, and so forth. This
again brings one to the general consideration of the relevance of solidarity considerations for the relative positions of different concrete structures in a society.

Before discussing the requisite nature of the solidarity structure of any society a word or two may be said
about the relation between the structure of solidarity as
discussed here and the general analysis of relationship
structures discussed above in Chapter VI. The two are
obviously interrelated. The content aspect of solidarity
involves the membership criteria aspect and the substantive definition aspects of any relationship as a minimum.
The strength consideration involves the hierarchical aspect, and the consideration of intensity certainly involves
the affective aspects of any relationship. There is, however, a difference of point of view involved. In Chapter
VI the interest focused on the different aspects that can
be distinguished relative to any relationship. In the
present chapter the interest is focused on certain analytically distinguishable aspects of the structure of any
society. The basis of these particular aspects rests on

the inevitability and omnipresence of relationships in any
society, despite the difficulty of proving some particular
concrete structures to be requisites for any society.
Thus, Chapter VI concerns itself with analytically distinguishable aspects of any relationship, i.e., with aspects
of those concrete structural building blocks out of which
concrete social structural units of all types are built.
The present chapter is concerned with the analytically
distinguishable aspects of any society (i.e., one particular type of concrete social structure) that are implicit
in the fact that concrete relationships must be present in
any society.

　　As has been suggested above, the requisite basis of
the analytic structure of solidarity rests in the most
general sense on the fact that the various functional requisites of any society cannot be produced unless the members of that society enter into relationships with one
another. Obviously, for example, if there is to be adequate physiological adjustment to the environment by the
members of the society, the infants present must be cared
for in such a way as to permit some portion of them to
survive and reach maturity, if only in order to permit of
the production of still further infants. Since the infants
are "helpless" in the senses previously mentioned, there
must be relationships between them and other individuals
in the society if their survival is to be realized.

　　The above is, of course, only the statement of a
minimal basis for the existence of relationships in the
society. There are many others equally compelling and not
a great deal less obvious. This fact gives the student of
social structure an extremely helpful hand with a rather
perplexing problem. In Chapter V above the difficulty of
deriving the concrete structural requisites for any society
has been discussed.[4] Basically, this difficulty inheres

4.　See pp. 199-207.

in the fact that concrete structures are extremely flexible
in the functions that they may perform. Furthermore, they
are extremely flexible in the predominant orientation or
combination of orientations that may characterize them.
Thus, in a modern "capitalistic" industrial society concrete structures of the type "business firm" are, institutionally speaking, predominantly economically oriented.
They are ostensibly concerned first, last, and always with
the allocation of goods and services. In their operation,
however, hundreds of noneconomic functions are performed
simultaneously with the allocation of goods and services.
Roles are differentiated, power and responsibility are
allocated, and so forth. On the other hand, in the case
of a concrete structure such as the "traditional" Chinese
family it is not so easy to distinguish any particular
predominant orientation. Institutionally speaking, it is
not in any obvious sense more oriented to economic or
political allocation than to role differentiation, etc.
Although it lacks an obvious predominant orientation such
as that which characterizes the business firm, it shares
the complicating features of the latter in that it does
create by its operation a myriad of differentiable functions.

        Consideration of the analytic structural requisite of
solidarity gives the one general lead in the direction of
concrete structural requisites that is available to the
present writer. It is possible to indicate that certain
general types of relationship must exist if the society
is to exist. From this one may conclude that concrete
structures in terms of which those relationships may operate must exist. This does not tell one what predominant
orientation(s) these structures must have in any society
because of the flexibility mentioned above. It does indicate, however, certain relationships that must be investigated in any society, and the discovery of these relationships will at one and the same time give leads, if not full
information, on the larger concrete structures themselves.

In the remainder of this chapter an attempt at an
initial minimal list of these necessary relationships will
be made. Much of the material indicating the necessity of
these relationships has already been produced in the preceding chapter on role differentiation. Insofar as that
is the case the material will be indicated rather than
reproduced in full in this chapter.

A. CONCRETE UNITS INVOLVING AGE ROLE DIFFERENTIATION

1. Absolute age

a. Infant-adult. Relations of this sort must exist
if the infants are to survive physically. The training
and general care of the infants during this absolute age
period also requires this relationship. The relationship
between infants and children or old people could not alone
be counted upon to secure these ends. Obviously, mature
individuals are involved in the begetting of offspring,
but they cannot be eliminated from the relationships after
this point either. Children and the aged may take over
many responsibilities relative to infants in many societies, but they cannot be counted upon to do the full job.
The basis of their inability in these respects lies in
their incapability of bearing full responsibility. The
children cannot bear full responsibility because they
themselves are not fully trained in the ways of their society, and certainly in the earlier stages of childhood
their lack of knowledge and stability in crises of various
sorts would militate against their action without some
supervision and direction. Adults must not only supervise
the children in these roles to some extent, they must also
be available to take over in those situations in which
factors arise that go beyond the capabilities of the children. By the latter part of childhood such needs may be
reduced to a minimum, but over the general span they cannot be eliminated. In no society known to the writer is

the care and supervision of infants completely in the hands
of children.

The question of responsibility arises also in relation
to the possible role of the aged. Here it is not the question of knowledge that presents the primary problem. The
primary problem arises in two respects. In the first
place, the aged can not be counted on to survive for the
necessary period to nearly the same extent that is possible in the case of children or adults. In the second
place, the facts of senility being what they are, even if
the aged survive, they cannot be relied upon to be able to
perform the minimum functions necessary in relation to
infants.

Some relations between adults and infants must, therefore, be present. The fact that a one-to-one correspondence of infants and adults is unlikely, the obvious connections between mother and infant, the problem of "motivating" adults in these respects, and many other considerations militate against the possibility of each infant
having a relationship with one and only one adult or each
adult having a relationship with one and only one infant.
This would in turn suggest the inevitability of the infant-adult relationship taking place in terms of some
concrete structure of a more general nature than a two-
person relationship. This becomes the more obvious when
one considers certain necessary relationships between
adults and children, adults and other adults, and adults
and the aged. Some of these relationships must go on
simultaneously with those in connection with infants and
would, therefore, argue for the overwhelming probability
of this relationship being combined into some more general
concrete structure such as a family structure. Certainly,
there is no known society in which this is not the case.

b. Adults-children. The problem of training the
young for the minimum number of roles that must be perpetuated in the society is involved here. Obviously, the

infants cannot perform this function, and the aged cannot
do it for much the same reasons that they cannot bear full
responsibility for the infants. The attention required by
children in these respects is considerable, of course. No
society could remain stable or even persist at all if in
fact its children were permitted to run wild. The possible deviant behavior that would result would not only
threaten the lives of the young and possibly their elders'
as well, but also it would put an end to the production of
responsible adults in the society. Involved here are not
only the teaching of the normative structures of the society but also its necessary skills, knowledge, and procedures
in general. To a lesser degree, perhaps, than in the case
of infants the need for such attention by adults to children must be unremitting, but nevertheless it is a continuous matter to a very high degree.

The same argument given about infants would militate
against a simple one to one form of adult-child relationship. Other factors are also operative. The activity of
children can and must be vastly more varied than is that
of infants. The range of possible contact with adults is
increased tremendously. It is extremely doubtful, if not
completely out of the question, that the child-adult relationships institutionalized in any society can be confined
to as restricted a sphere as is that of infants. Certainly, it is not generally the case. The author knows of
no society in which institutionalized adult-child relationships are as restricted in number or type as those of
adult and infant, and one has only to look about modern
western societies to see how vast the discrepancy may be
in some cases in this respect. These considerations and
those suggested relative to infants would tend to indicate
that adult-child relationships are inevitably to be found
in several concrete structures of a more general nature
than two-party structures.

c. <u>Adult-aged</u>. The facts of senility argue for the

necessity of such a relationship as this in any society. Even if the aged are automatically killed off, some participation of the adults is involved. If they are to be preserved until death from "natural" causes takes place, the facts of senility require some care and provision for the aged. Obviously, infants cannot be counted on to provide this, and the limits to the possibilities of children, while less restricting than in the case of infants, are nonetheless obvious. The facts of senility argue against the possibility of complete self-reliance.

There is another factor that argues against the complete isolation of the aged from the adults. This is the fact that transition to the role of aged is a more or less continuous process. The transition between adult and aged roles, if the aged were to be isolated from the adults in a society, would involve a radical break at the point of transition between the aged-to-be and all of their past contacts with adults not yet aged. Such a radical readjustment short of compulsory execution of the aged (and the adults would be involved in that) is well-nigh inconceivable. To some degree such breaks occur, but complete severance of this sort is out of the question because of the difficulties presented by affective considerations if no others. The affective bonds necessary for the stable operation of many adult-adult relationships could hardly attain the necessary degree of flexibility in these respects in every case.[5]

d. <u>Adult-adult</u>. The importance of sexual relationships for the perpetuation of the society is sufficient to

---

5. An institutionalized execution of the aged is, of course, a possibility as has been stated. The point under discussion here is the impossibility of the complete isolation of the aged if they are permitted to live out their lives. Such complete isolation seems, at least on hypothetical grounds, much less of a possibility than their destruction.

argue for relationships of the adult-adult type. There
are many others as well. The necessity of curbing deviant
behavior by adults as well as children is a case in point.
So is the fact that single adults in general cannot be
completely self-sufficient in the matter of goods and services in a society. Minimal role differentiations of many
and various sorts would also be germane in this connection.
Unless it can be shown that each and every adult in isolation is capable of performing each and every necessary
adult role at the necessary time, the general necessity
for adult-adult relationships will remain.

The wide range of variation possible in adult activities is reflected in the wide range of possibilities for
concrete structures involving adult-adult relationships.
Because of the greater range of capabilities, both capabilities in terms of the factors of human heredity and
nonhuman environment and capabilities that involve clearly
social elements, present in adults, the range of variation
of adult-adult structures might reasonably be expected to
exceed the range of adult-child possibilities in these
respects.

e. Other absolute age classification structures. It
will be noted that nothing has been said about the concrete structures involving the following absolute age
classifications: (a) infant-infant, (b) infant-child, (c)
infant-old-age, (d) child-child, (e) child-old-age, and
(f) old-age-old-age. It is perhaps conceivable that there
be a society in which there be no concrete structures involving such relationships. On the surface at least the
minimal requirements of these absolute age classifications
can be met by relating their members to adults only.
Probability, however, would seem to be overwhelmingly
against such a situation. Infants could rather easily be
kept out of contact with other infants perhaps, and indeed,
because of the limited range of capabilities of infants,
the importance for social structure of infant-infant rela-

tionships would seem to be quite limited. For the other types of individuals the separation would seem to be more difficult. The common necessity of concrete structures relating all four classifications to adults would argue that, barring extremely rigid compartmentalization of adult lives, some relationships of these other types would inevitably appear. Certainly, in no known society are all of the six types of relationship listed completely absent, and with the possible exception of the first it is doubtful whether any of them can be entirely absent. Adult-adult relationships are likely to have some previous history in child-child relationships. The absence of old-age-old-age relationships would require a sharp break with previous adult-adult structures, and so forth.

Some of these six types of relationships are often of considerable significance in social structure. In fact, examples of the prominent importance of all save the first type can be found in almost any society. The family structure of societies quite commonly blends and combines all six of these plus the four previously given, and many other structures do so too. Some sorts of common play and educational groups of children are, empirically speaking, perhaps as ubiquitous as any other social phenomenon.

Before passing from this aspect of solidarity units one further point must be stressed. If the absolute age classifications in a particular society are more complex than the fourfold minimal classification given here, the implications for units of solidarity become correspondingly more complex. Here a minimum number of four relationships plus an almost certain additional five or six have been delineated as relationships that must be carried out in concrete structures of some sorts. If the initial list is six or eight, the various possible and probable permutations and combinations are likewise increased.

2. Relative age

Solidarity structures oriented at least in part to considerations of relative age are found empirically with great frequency. For example, the solidarity patterns between an elder and a younger brother in "traditional" China were of considerable importance not only among actual brothers but were sometimes relevant among individuals for whom a fraternal relationship was simulated. In Chapter VII above the structural necessity of relative age distinctions has been pointed out. This hypothesis, if correct, plus the empirical ubiquity of some such distinctions would argue that there must be solidarity patterns on the basis of relative age. Nevertheless, from the point of view of any society it remains at least theoretically conceivable that no distinctions on the basis of relative age exist within units such that solidarity structures oriented to those considerations exist. It may, for example, be true that a two-month-old infant and a one-year-old cannot be treated in the same way by their mother, but her relations with each may be structured in absolute age or generational terms, and no solidarity between the two infants on the basis of relative age would seem to be absolutely inescapable. Thus, at the present stage of development the position taken here on this question is that such structures would never seem to be empirically lacking in known societies, but they are not structural requisites. For this reason they are not taken up here. This should not lead any researcher to assume, however, that such structures are insignificant in any specific case. Rather than do this it would be better to assume them to be requisites without any well-developed line of argument to this effect. In such phenomena as leadership, responsibility, inheritance, etc., solidarity structures oriented to relative age may be crucial or highly strategic structures. In the case of "traditional" China, for example, the difference in solidarity structures between father and son on the one hand and eldest and younger brother on the other would

seem to have been one of the most significant avenues of
family flexibility.

B. CONCRETE UNITS INVOLVING GENERATIONAL
ROLE DIFFERENTIATION

This category is not on general theoretical grounds
at the stage of theoretical development reached here, a
minimal requirement as a unit of solidarity. While some
minimal distinction between generations is necessary as
indicated above, it is difficult, if not impossible, on
the level of generality attempted here to require the inclusion of relations between members of different generations in any single concrete structure smaller than the
society as a whole, just as in the case of relative age
mentioned above. If it were possible to demonstrate the
necessity of family structures at this level this would
perhaps no longer be the case. At any rate, given the development reached here, it is quite possible that infants
at birth be turned over to the care of adults who have no
clear generational relationship to them, and that such
relationships therefore do not form a basic element in any
particular concrete substructure of a society.[6]

Despite these theoretical cautions it would be unduly
squeamish to omit mention of such concrete units. Such
concrete units would, of course, be some type of family
unit since family units as defined here involve the criteria of biological relatedness and cohabitation with the
consequent implications of generational differences in
such units.[7] In no society known to the author are such
units totally absent. And indeed in many, if not most,

---

6. The importance of doing this in such a society
would not negate the necessity of role differentiation on
the basis of generation since this factor would at least
determine which adults could not rear which children.

7. See above, pp. 203-204 and 324-325.

societies not only these generational relationships but
also many of those involving absolute age classification
differences are found in terms of concrete structures of
the family or of a more general kinship type. Inevitably,
apparently, some of the adult-child and adult-infant relationships are institutionally allocated to concrete
units in which these age classifications coincide to some
degree with generational differences. Therefore, if not
on general theoretical grounds, then certainly on the
grounds of past experience some concrete substructures of
a society involving relationships between or among two or
more generations must be sought in the analysis of any society. At least this would seem to be the most prudent
procedure until and unless it becomes possible to demonstrate definitively that societies without family structures can persist.

C. CONCRETE UNITS INVOLVING SEX ROLE DIFFERENTIATION

The minimal implications for role differentiation of
the physical differences between the sexes and the defini-
tional element in the concept of societies of recruitment
by sexual reproduction of the members have already been
suggested in the previous chapter and need not be repeated
here. Suffice it to say that some such concrete heterosexual relationships must be formed if a society is to
persist. Although these relationships may be of a quite
fleeting and casual sort, some definite structuring of
them is required. Commonly, of course, although some of
these relationships may be fleeting and casual, some of
them are formed on a more permanent and enduring basis in
terms of the marital relationship.

Heterosexual relationships are by no means the only
possible ones in a society, however. Whenever roles are
differentiated on such a basis, relationships between
similar role holders as well as different ones may be

distinguished. Concrete structures involving only the
members of one sex are usual, if not inevitable, in all
societies. This is particularly important when one considers a factor that, if not demonstrable on the present
level of analysis, at least seems to be another of those
ubiquitous social features. This is the fact that some
forms of allocation of goods and services, whether productionwise or consumptionwise, always become identified with
the sex difference. The hypothesis that the distinction
between "men's work" and "women's work" crops up in some
respect in all societies does not appear ever to have been
successfully contradicted.

Insofar as factors of this sort crop up concrete
units involving relationships between members of the same
sex as well as those involving relationships between members of different sexes must be sought. In the latter
case some of the activities connected with the relationship must be reproductive in character. But it is by no
means necessary, or even possible perhaps, that they be
confined solely to such activities. Certainly the activities of groups consisting of members of a single sex need
not involve "sexual" activities in this special sense.

D. CONCRETE UNITS INVOLVING ECONOMIC ROLE DIFFERENTIATION

If there must be role differentiation in terms of
economic allocation, or even if there merely must be economic allocation, there must be concrete units in terms of
which activities with these aspects are carried out and
hence solidarity structures oriented at least in part to
these considerations. There must be both production and
consumption of goods and services if societies are to
exist, and these activities have to be carried out by concrete individuals. Furthermore, as a minimum some of the
individuals can consume but cannot produce what is necessary for their consumption, so the possibility of complete

individual economic self-sufficiency is out of the question for the members of a society. The concrete structures in terms of which these activities are carried out need not be structures that have predominantly economic orientations. The economic aspects must, however, be sufficiently well institutionalized so that the performance of these allocative functions is not a matter of chance if the society is to have a stable existence.

It is not inevitable that the concrete structures in terms of which production and consumption are carried out be identical; frequently they are different. In fact, it is probably inevitable that they be different in some respects. The degree to which these structures are separated is a matter of tremendous consequence for social structure because it determines in major respects the degree of self-sufficiency of concrete structures. The degree of separation has implications extending far beyond immediate economic considerations.

At the same time there are limits on the degree of separation. Some production and some consumption must take place within the same concrete structures. This is partly due to a factor involved in the definition of production and consumption and partly due to quite another factor. With regard to the former, the relevant consideration is that what is from one point of view production is simultaneously from another point of view consumption. A manufacturer, for example, is a producer from the point of view of his customers and a consumer from the point of view of his raw-material suppliers. With regard to the latter point, reference must be made once again to the fact that some services, if not some goods as well, are such that they must be simultaneously produced and consumed from the point of view of the same individual. This is true, for example, of all services produced by an individual for his own consumption provided the consumption of those services is not deferable.

E. CONCRETE UNITS INVOLVING POLITICAL
ROLE DIFFERENTIATION

If roles must be differentiated on the basis of political allocation, there must be concrete structures in
terms of which the factors of power and responsibility
operate. Quite obviously, relationships are involved here
and hence solidarity structures oriented at least in part
to these considerations. By definition, both the concepts
of power and responsibility involve other actors than the
individual wielding power and bearing responsibility.
Some of each may be relative to himself alone, but the
necessity of the institutionalization of some concrete
structures performing such functions as these remains.

There must be concrete units in societies in terms of
which power and responsibility are allocated. In any such
unit there will be elements of both power and responsibility. It is not possible for power alone to characterize
some units while responsibility characterizes others. The
importance of political allocation for social systems
carries with it an important complication for societies.
As previously suggested, societies can never be characterized by a single type of concrete structure. For example,
a society cannot be characterized by family units as the
sole type of concrete structure. The basic reasoning be-
hind this hypothesis rests on the possibilities of conflict
of various sorts among the memberships of any such single
type of concrete unit. There must be methods of settling
such conflicts if the society is to remain stable in any
given form. As a minimum this requires for a given society at least two types of concrete structure, one of which,
however casually organized, must allocate power and responsibility as among the other units if there is to be
stability. It would be theoretically possible, perhaps,
to have a society with only family units as concrete
substructures if one or more of those family units differed

in its power position substantially enough to perform this
function of maintaining order. If this were the case,
however, there would not be a single homogeneous type of
substructure, but a minimum of heterogeneity in the political structure.

Such experience in social analysis as exists does not,
of course, lead one to expect the minimum possible number
of concrete substructures. The simplest societies studied
have certainly given evidence of more concrete units than
this minimum of two. The minimum serves a limiting purpose, however, since it warns the scholar against oversights
in these respects. The principle may be extended with some
usefulness one step further. Not only must there be a
minimum of two types of concrete substructures in any given
society if it is to be stable, but for any given type of
concrete substructure there must also be at least one other
type of concrete substructure ensuring some minimum of
political regulation among the units of the original type.
This does not involve an infinite extension of concrete
substructures since the units regulating another type of
unit may in turn be regulated at least in part by the
units they control. It does mean, however, that no study
of a concrete substructure of a society is complete unless
there is some indication of where it fits into the total
political structure of the society. In this respect the
political aspects of concrete units differ from the economic aspects. It is at least conceivable that some given
types of concrete unit be economically self-sufficient,
though this is not the case for all the types of concrete
units of a society. It is not possible for a concrete
substructure to be politically self-sufficient. With respect to the latter there remains always the question of
responsibility of the unit.

In this connection it must be noted with particular
care that the reasoning here rests upon an assumption of
social stability on whatever level of analysis considera-

tion takes place. Manifestly such stability is by no
means ubiquitous in societies on any level. Failure to
note this assumption will automatically involve one in the
fallacy of functional teleology. On the other hand, observation of the assumption by no means paralyzes the
study of the various problems of social change. These
problems of change are, pragmatically speaking, the obvious questions of importance for social engineers. As in
all sciences, in the social sciences too one must in the
last analysis look to studies with some dynamic elements
for practical applications. The sort of analysis suggested
here should be an aid in these respects. One might in
studying modern Germany, for example, point to the fact
that the extreme difficulty (if not impossibility) of imposing responsibility from within a society upon a charismatic leader like Hitler was a specific source of instability in these respects, that any analysis of social
change in recent German history must, on a specific level,
seek out the implications of this lack of structured responsibility on the part of the charismatic leader concerned,[8] and that, on a more general level of greater
long-run interest, one must seek out what factors in German
social structure predispose, fail to inhibit, or contribute
to the fact that leaders with such unstructured responsibilities may arise in the society.[9] If sufficiently
developed, knowledge of the type of structural configura-
tion necessary to prevent changes cannot conceivably fail

---

8. Or, conversely, one must show that this was not
in fact the case and that sources of social change in
these respects must be sought elsewhere.

9. The implications of such studies would presumably
throw light on more than the past history of Germany. It
might have social engineering implications of the most
far-reaching sort for all of the modern industrialized
"democracies" whose members wish to avoid such structures
of authoritarianism.

to be of use in locating sources of change. The solidarity structures of units looked at in terms of their political aspects are of primary importance for the analysis of
such problems.

F.   CONCRETE UNITS INVOLVING RELIGIOUS
ROLE DIFFERENTIATION

     If there must be role differentiation on the basis of
religion, there must be concrete structures in terms of
which the holders of these minimal religious role differentiations come into contact with one another, and hence
there must be solidarity structures oriented at least in
part to such considerations. The range of variation possible is wide, but some concrete structures must appear.
Perhaps the most useful lead here is to raise the following
question, "In terms of what sort of concrete units can the
particular religious system be carried out, and in terms of
what minimal units must it be carried out?" Answers to
these questions involve an answer to the manner in which
the religious structures can and must as a minimum fit
into the general social structure.
     The possibilities are extremely complex and subtle.
There is no intention here to explore the matter deeply.
On the most obvious level relative to the implications for
solidarity two types of religious systems may be distinguished. In the first place, there are religious systems
that involve the presence of predominantly religiously
oriented concrete structures. Catholicism, Buddhism (as
often practiced), and many other religious systems are of
this sort. The distinct predominantly religiously oriented
concrete structure involved may be called a church. However many other functions or orientations a church may
take on, it remains a church in the sense intended here as
long as its religious orientation takes precedence over
all other considerations. The second type of religious

systems are those that do not necessarily involve a <u>church</u>.
These vary from systems involving the radical insistence
that religious practices are solely the responsibility of
each individual through systems involving the execution of
religious structures in terms of concrete structures that
are not predominantly religiously oriented. Protestantism
in some of its forms and Confucianism in "traditional"
China are examples of this sort of system. The former involves emphasis on complete individual responsibility, and
the latter requires the execution of religiously oriented
activities in terms of family units.

Both types of system are frequently found in mixed
forms. Religious systems of the <u>church</u> type frequently
involve the execution of religious activities in nonchurch
units, especially the family. Religious systems of the
<u>nonchurch</u> type (i.e., not by religious doctrine requiring
the presence of a church) frequently do have churches.
Some of the differences among the systems are simple, if
not obvious. In the mixed cases of the first type the
possibility of conflict between the church and other concrete structures is raised, and the religious practices
outside the church are always subject to church scrutiny.
Problems of the interrelation of the church and other concrete structures must be understood if the religious aspects of the society are to be understood. The church
type system, in theory at least, minimizes the possibilities of sectarianism, or more correctly minimizes the
possibilities of variation that involve the production of
new religious systems, whether of the church or nonchurch
type.

The nonchurch type, on the other hand, maximizes the
possibilities of religious deviance when it takes the
extreme form of emphasizing individual religious responsibility, and in any case greatly increases the possibilities
by comparison with the church systems. Insofar as such
deviance has implications for social change beyond the

religious sphere, this increase of the possibilities of
deviance is of major significance. Systems of the
nonchurch type also minimize the power of such churches as
do exist in these systems since such churches are not
necessarily the primary religious structures of the system.
In some sense this reduces the problem of integrating the
churches of such religions with other concrete structures
in the society.

There is one general factor concerning solidarity on
the basis of religion that may be stressed because of its
extreme importance in any society involving two or more
religious systems. This is, of course, the question of
the strength of this solidarity. This question has two
rather obvious general forms. The first is the question
of how strong the solidarity is in strictly religious matters. To what extent are other social considerations
subordinated to religious concerns? Elements of this sort
have cropped up in the works of many social scientists, an
obvious case being that of Auguste Comte, who suggested a
specific theological type of society in which such considerations override all others. The implications of differences in strength in this respect are much too broad and
specialized to be explored here, but their significance
for any typology of religious systems or for social structure in general cannot be overlooked.

The second question is the degree to which the practitioners of a given religious system are expected to act
in concert on nonreligious matters. In a sense this injects a religious element into these other matters, but
the difference from the question cited above lies in the
fact that here the question of specific religious priority
is not the question primarily involved. The question is
rather one of solidarity among religious practitioners.
Relative to these two questions the church-nonchurch distinction has many and varied implications.

G. CONCRETE UNITS INVOLVING COGNITIVE
ROLE DIFFERENTIATION

The most obvious units here are, of course, those units in terms of which teaching and research are carried out. To some degree such units must exist because of the minimal educational problem presented by infants and children. It is by no means necessary, however, that predominantly cognitively oriented concrete structures be distinguished in a society. The distinction between societies having such units and those lacking them is of some importance for understanding the social structure of the societies concerned.

One consideration here is, perhaps, especially revealing for modern purposes. It may be suggested that, for societies in which continued technological change is an important part of the social structure, some predominantly cognitively oriented concrete structures are concrete structural requisites. Modern industrial societies fall into this general category, and the importance for such societies of research organizations, universities, schools in general, and the like is certainly considerable. The matter may become quite complex. The necessity for such structures at an advanced cognitive level requires such structures at more elementary levels as well, if only because of the necessity of maintaining the minimum degree of cognitive uniformity that will enable large scale selection of individuals to continue more advanced work.

With regard to the cognitive components of concrete structures, and hence with regard to solidarity viewed in these terms, one distinction of major significance in all societies should be noted. This is the distinction between knowledge such that it may serve as the cognitive component of rational action and knowledge such that it may serve as the cognitive component of nonrational action, most espe-

cially in the arational forms of nonrational action. Only
a few decades ago in social science it was the fashion to
hold that "primitive" societies were to be differentiated
from others by virtue of the fact that the action of the
members of such societies was "prerational," i.e., that no
rational action existed. The work of Malinowski and many
others has long since disposed of this particular bit of
mythology. There is no known society in which no trace of
rational action is to be found. On general grounds it
seems quite easy to show that some rational action must
exist. There is, for example, no basis whatever for believing that nonrational techniques are sufficiently trust-
worthy and invariant in their yields to assure a food
supply for any population. Some rational action is necessary if food is to be gathered, stored, utilized, etc.
Along with the rational components of such action, nonrational ones may be mixed. The people making the mixtures
may make only rudimentary distinctions between the two
types, but the results of irrational action or the lack of
rational action are never completely explained in arational
terms in any society.

There is only one possibility of maintaining the "prerational" hypothesis in any form, but this possibility
throws out the whole problem of cognition, and what is
more to the point, perhaps, there is no definitive proof
of the possibility. If the minimum rational action necessary to cope with the problems of adequate physiological
adjustment of the members of the society to their nonhuman
environment can be shown to be fully explicable in terms
of an "instinct" theory or the like, then the discussion
of a cognitive basis for rational action is beside the
point, and the question of education would make even less
sense. There is every reason, perhaps, to maintain that
human heredity or, more properly, some combination of
human heredity and nonhuman environment, determine a range
of possible cognitive variation for the species as a whole

and even for specific members of it, but there is no
reason to believe that specific items of cognition are so
determined. The development of science with its excep-
tionally cumulative character is sufficient to refute any
such unqualified hypothesis, and definitive demonstration
of such a basis for even those bits of cognition universally found in societies has not been forthcoming.

The cognitive elements involved in arational action
are no less ubiquitous in societies than are the cognitive
elements involved in rational action. In all societies
there is some knowledge of a set of values, just as there
is some empirical knowledge as to how to effectuate some
of these values. For example, there is the value placed
on general survival and knowledge of it, just as there is
knowledge of how in some respects to secure survival.
Again, the possibility of complete explanation of such
cognition in terms of human heredity and nonhuman environment is, at least at the present stage of development of
biology, out of the question. Here again, however, there
is no doubt good reason for believing that the factors of
heredity and nonhuman environment determine a range of
possible variation. Reports, such as they are, on children raised in extreme isolation would seem to indicate
only the most rudimentary development of either type of
cognition, if indeed the development of cognition can be
demonstrated in such cases.[10] The value systems of most
societies have not permitted the type of experimentation
on human beings necessary to determine the minimal type of
development that would take place solely in terms of heredity and nonhuman environment, but the extreme range of
variation with regard to both types of cognition and the

---

10. See Kingsley Davis, "Extreme Social Isolation of
a Child," Am. Jour. of Sociol., Vol. 45, No. 4 (Jan. 1940)
pp. 554-565, and "A Final Note on a Case of Extreme Isolation," Ibid., Vol. 50, No. 3 (Nov. 1947) pp. 432-437.

great discrepancies in both kind and degree of development
of both types in different societies argue powerfully
against such explanations.

   If empirical cognition and nonempirical cognition must
and do exist in all societies, and if they do not come
automatically and without other human intervention to the
members of the species, they must be taught, and there must
be concrete structures in terms of which they are taught.
Not only must they be taught, but minimal distinctions between them also must be taught. Perhaps not all the members of a society, but at least some of them must know the
distinction between the results of "bad" workmanship and
"bad" magic, and between the results of empirically oriented
action and religious action. It goes without saying that,
wherever, no matter in how rudimentary a form, rational
action is recognized, irrational action is also recognized.

   To some extent the distinction between rational and
arational action must also be clear. To the degree to
which the structural implications for the society of one
or the other increases, the need for clarity in the distinction increases. The basis of this is twofold. In the
first place, the difficulty of development of empirical
knowledge is increased infinitely if it is not possible
clearly to distinguish nonempirical elements. In the second place, the intrusion of strictly empirical knowledge
into arational systems of cognition is either beside the
point of such systems or subversive of the faith that must
underlie them to some extent.

   The considerations in the preceding paragraph lead
one to a type of distinction that must appear in the concrete units in which cognition is taught even if the same
unit teaches both sorts of cognition. To some extent the
teaching of straight empirical cognition must emphasize
the use of critical faculties, and to some extent the
teaching of nonempirical cognition must deny the use of
such faculties. In the former case, the emphasis may not

go much beyond the necessary freedom to alter the use of a
digging stick in one type of soil as opposed to another.
In the latter case, it may not go beyond the general acceptance of the basic value orientations of the society.
In societies that emphasize the continuous development of
empirical technologies, emphasis on critical rationality
must be carried to a very high point indeed, and the converse is true of societies emphasizing highly developed
and rigid arational systems. Both of these hypotheses involve, of course, the assumption of continued stability of
the social structure, and neither will hold in the absence
of such an assumption.

Finally, these considerations suggest a need, if
stability is to exist, for the insulation of one type of
cognition from the other, particularly in the case of societies in which heavy emphasis is placed on either type.
In the one case, the subversion of the value system of the
society must be inhibited; in the other, the emphasis on
the traditional approach must be prevented from inhibiting
those changes in empirical cognition which may be necessary to survival. It must be pointed out that neither
inhibition is preordained in any sense. The spread of
critical rationality, for example, may be subversive of
the value structure of industrial society and result in
changes that negate critical rationality itself. Some
such factors certainly play a role in the development of
modern authoritarian systems. The emphasis on tradition-
alism may leave a society helpless to adapt to change or
even to avoid total destruction. In any case, whether the
inhibitions hold or fail to hold, whether the societies
remain stable, change, or be destroyed, some reflection of
these factors must be present in the solidarity structures
of the concrete units in which cognition is instilled.

H.   CONCRETE UNITS INVOLVING ROLE DIFFERENTIATION
     ON THE BASIS OF NONHUMAN ENVIRONMENT

Perhaps the most obvious of concrete units involving role differentiation on the basis of nonhuman environment are those distinguished on the basis of spatial location. However shifting such locations may be, as in the case of nomadic peoples, some grouping of individuals in these terms is inescapable. All individuals occupy space, and potential conflicts over who is to occupy what space, when, and how must to some extent be regulated if there is to be stability. This factor coupled with the necessary existence of some concrete structures involving more than a single member involves the presence of some units distinguishable in spatial terms however minor such an orientation may be. The importance of various spatial locations for the economic aspect of activities and the relative lack of homogeneity of spatial locations add to the importance of such factors.

One of the most obvious of such concrete units is that which has "legitimate" occupation, however fleeting, of a particular location. The solidarity features of such a group are directly germane to such considerations, as only a moment's consideration of such structures as primogeniture and equal inheritance will indicate.

Another of these nonhuman environmental considerations is the time element[11] involved in such locational structures. The distinctions among predominantly agrarian, predominantly industrial, and predominantly nomadic societies are in part understandable, for example, in terms of seasonal variations. The variations of concrete units in locational terms in such societies must be explored as a minimum in these respects.

Another consideration in terms of spatial location is that of neighborhood units. By neighborhood units is meant those concrete structures whose membership is

---

11. This is, of course, not in contradiction to the presence of quite important social elements in time considerations.

determined at least in part by criteria of spatial proximity and which include as a minimum concrete units or
parts of concrete units of other sorts. Neighborhood
units of some sort are minimally required because the factor of spatial proximity always involves some problems of
the regulation of the actions of individuals and concrete
units in such proximity. The variation possible is considerable. It may range from the simple elimination or
settling of conflicts to units of major solidarity strengths
in the society. In societies like "traditional" China such
concrete units are of major importance in the social structure. In the most highly urbanized portions of an industrial society they are often of minor significance.

   Perhaps the most fruitful general hypothesis relative
to variations in the strength of neighborhood solidarities
has to do with the degree of centralization of the general
political structure of the society. To the degree that
the political structure of a society as a whole is decentralized the strength of neighborhood solidarities must
be increased, all other factors remaining equal. The converse of this hypothesis may also be advanced. The cete-
ris paribus assumption is introduced here because other
concrete structures, such as the family, may to some degree
decrease or increase in strength with increases or decreases in over-all centralization and meet the minimal
requirements for stability, but to some degree neighborhood
considerations cannot be eliminated. The hypotheses advanced in this connection rest at least in part on the
hypothesis that certain minimal regulation must be maintained in any society to some degree on the basis of
spatial proximity. If these hypotheses are valid, many
specific hypotheses relative to social change as it affects
spatial units of solidarity would follow. For example,
industrialized societies of all sorts require high degrees
of political and economic centralization. In general one
would expect, therefore, to see any shift from a nonindustrial to an industrial form of society accompanied by a

weakening of neighborhood solidarities unless the society
concerned were of a nonindustrial type already highly centralized. The exception suggested in the hypothesis is,
perhaps, superfluous since it is at least doubtful whether
the kinds and degree of political and economic centralization required by industrial societies can be maintained by
nonindustrial ones.

Although there must be role differentiation to some
degree on the basis of seasonal variations and all of the
nonhuman environmental variations that accompany seasonal
changes, there need not be concrete structures specifically oriented to such factors. A working group, for example,
may remain the same in terms of its solidarity despite
seasonal changes. On the other hand, in societies in
which seasonal changes and the like are marked, concrete
units specifically oriented to these considerations may be
expected, if indeed they are not inevitable. In sedentary
agrarian societies, for example, harvesting groups are by
no means always identical with planting or cultivating
groups, and these activities are usually, if not always,
highly correlated with seasonal factors.

One would, therefore, expect to find some concrete
units that are seasonally oriented even though such groups
are not inevitable. Furthermore, one would in the ordinary
case expect that, whenever a seasonal orientation is present, some specific economic orientation be present as well.
It is, after all, to the allocation of goods and services
that seasonal variations are so immediately and directly
germane. Thus, even in the case of ceremonial activities
that are seasonally oriented and in connection with which
concrete social units are formed, some such economic aspect
is usually present or at least is involved in the origina-
tion of the ceremony. Such ceremonials frequently take
the form of religious or magical activities related to
food production or other such seasonally influenced factors
and are perpetuated long after their original manifest or

latent eufunctions or dysfunctions have disappeared.

There are unending considerations relative to nonhuman environment that in specific cases may permit or inhibit specific types of concrete units and hence specific types of solidarity structures. There are, for example, all sorts of topographical distinctions between hill and dale and the like. There are rivers, lakes, swamps, oceans, and seas to be taken into account, not to mention the climatic variations that so often accompany them. In relation to these factors, however, it is well-nigh impossible to derive hypotheses that will hold on the level of generalization under study here, i.e., that hold for any society. The reason for this is both simple and obvious. Societies may exist in areas where there are plains but no hills, rivers but no oceans, slight but no great temperature variation, and so forth. If for no other reason, this consideration would emphasize the importance of delineating the major factors of the nonhuman environment that hold for any particular level of generalization on which any specific society is being studied. Delineation of these factors will at least give leads in the case of any particular society on the maximum range of variation and the minimal requirements of variation in concrete units oriented to such factors. On the present level of generalization these factors cannot be further discussed beyond this indication of their significance for any specific case of analysis.

I. CONCRETE UNITS INVOLVING ROLE DIFFERENTIATION ON THE BASIS OF SOLIDARITY

There is a sense in which it is superfluous, or at least redundant, to include this category of unit in the present chapter on solidarity. All concrete structures involve questions of solidarity both internally among the members and externally in the relations of one such structure with another. On the other hand, there is a sense in

which it is not superfluous or redundant for there may be
concrete structures in a society that are predominantly,
or at least very strongly, oriented to solidarity considerations. In the last analysis some such structures must
probably be involved if there is to be stability, for in
the last analysis there must be some overridingly strong
solidarity or solidarities that can be used to control
deviance in the society. In the modern western world the
national unit is of this order in many respects. In "traditional" China the family and other concrete kinship
structures played such a role. In feudal societies like
those in Tokugawa Japan and medieval France the various
units in the feudal hierarchy played such roles. Examples
of this sort may be extended more or less indefinitely.

Perhaps one of the most obvious factors involved here
is the fact that concrete structures of this sort must be
very closely coordinated with the predominantly politically
oriented structures in a society if there is to be stability. The reasons for this are, of course, the obvious
implications of the strength aspect of solidarities for
the allocation of power and responsibility in the society.
"Traditional" China represents a classical problem in
these respects. In that society the basic unit of solidarity was the family unit, and the strength of family orientations took clear priority, institutionally speaking,
over other orientations. The imperial government was predominantly a politically oriented concrete structure.
Stability in "traditional" China could be maintained only
insofar as family and imperial interests did not conflict
or insofar as effective means were found by the imperial
bureaucracy to hold family heads accountable for family
actions. In the long run it had to be the former, for in
the absence of such a lack of conflict the problem of quis
custodiet ipsos custodes inevitably arose since the
"guards" always had roles as family members too. This
ambivalence was recognized in the Chinese doctrine of

sovereignty which held that the "Will of Heaven," the <u>sine</u>
<u>qua non</u> of imperial authority, was no longer possessed by
a particular emperor under whom conditions sufficient to
"motivate" his overthrow by his subjects existed.[12]   The
overwhelming loyalty owed by the individual to family interests and its priority even over imperial wishes played
no small role in the dynastic cycles so marked in Chinese
history.

Another type of concrete unit in which solidarity
seems to be the predominant orientation is that which is
described by the general connotations and denotations of
the term friendship. The term friendship, whatever else
it may imply, would seem always to imply a loyalty between
two or more individuals and a loyalty that is valued in
and of itself apart from any other specific functions it
may have. Friendships are often conducted in such a way
that specific functions of a predominantly economic or
political nature result, but if these functions come to be
valued primarily for their economic, political, or other
aspects, the usual connotation of the term is violated.
Although by definition the economic and political aspects
of functions performed by the operation of friendship
structures may not become the major "motivation" for such
relationships without violating their character, these
relationships are of considerable significance in social
systems because of their effects and their possibilities in
these respects. If a general picture of the solidarity
aspects of social structure is to be derived, some general
cognizance of the role of units predominantly or solely
oriented to solidarity considerations must be taken.

In conclusion of this treatment of the analytic

_____

12. For example, any suicide, the mark par excellence
of intolerable conditions in "traditional" China, had in
theory to be investigated and reported specifically to the
sovereign himself.

structure of solidarity a few final remarks may be made.
In the introductory material of this chapter the difficulties of deriving concrete structural requisites for any
society were once again cited, and their implications for
the treatment of the question of solidarity in any society
were briefly raised. If these problems can be solved, the
treatment of the solidarity aspects of any society will
become at one and the same time both more simple and more
specific than the treatment here has been. In any specific
society such a procedure could be followed, and for the
analysis of any specific society the usefulness of the
material presented here will rest on whether or not it is
an aid in the location and discovery of the specific concrete structures of that society. This will, perhaps,
remain the sole use of this material until or unless the
solution of the problem of concrete structural requisites
makes it obsolete.

Perhaps the most obvious feature of the treatment
attempted here is its extremely close dependence upon the
material developed in the chapter on role differentiation.
The factors that necessitate the differentiation of roles
in any society at the same time necessitate the organization of different roles in specific concrete structures.
The extreme flexibility possible in concrete structures
cited above prevents one's deriving the specific concrete
structures that must coordinate the differentiated roles.
It has been suggested that all of the roles could conceivably be coordinated by two types of concrete structures, one a family-type structure and the other a structure for interrelating and regulating the relations among
different families. No society as simple as this in its
concrete structure has, to the knowledge of the writer,
ever been described, however, and even had it been, the
possibility of variations not involving families cannot
a priori be ruled out even in the face of the ubiquity of
family structures in societies.

In this situation the writer has turned to the lead
provided by the material on role differentiation. If roles
must be differentiated and if differentiated roles must
somehow be coordinated in concrete structures, then a consideration of the requirements of coordination of roles
will tell the researcher that concrete structures containing certain types of role coordination must be present in
any society. It will not, and does not attempt to, tell
what types of concrete structures must exist in any society. It only seeks to ascertain the roles that the concrete
structures of any society must coordinate and hence between
or among which types of role holders solidarities must
exist.

In the application of this material to a specific society, failure to indicate some concrete structures relating to the differentiated roles discussed here will again
indicate one (or some combination) of three things: (1)
the theory presented here of the necessity of coordinating
such roles may be invalid, (2) the general unit under study
does not conform to the definition of society used here,
and does not conform in a respect relevant to this absence
of material, or (3) the data presented are incomplete.

One further paragraph of caution is necessary. In
this chapter the treatment has again been minimal, and the
general implications of this approach for any specific
social analysis apply. The hypothesis here is that the
concrete structures of any specific society must set up
the types of solidarity discussed here. It is specifically
not the hypothesis that only these types are necessary for
any specific society. Furthermore, aside from the possibility of a minimum of two types of concrete structure,
nothing is said about the limits on the number or types of
concrete structures in any specific society. Finally,
there is a double sense in which the treatment here is
minimal. It is not only minimal in the general sense indicated before; it is also minimal in the sense that no

sufficiently developed discussion of the minimal interrelationships between the different types of solidarity suggested is available for presentation here. These cautions are underlined because failure to notice them may obviate whatever usefulness these suggestions might otherwise have.

C H A P T E R   IX

THE STRUCTURE OF ECONOMIC ALLOCATION

Economic allocation in concrete social structures has
been defined above as the distribution of the goods and
services making up the income of the concrete structure
concerned and of the goods and efforts making up the output of that structure among the various members of that
structure, and among that structure and other structural
units with which it is in contact.[1] In this definition
the terms goods and services (or efforts) are conceived to
cover not only their unsophisticated material forms but
also rights and privileges in, legal claims to, goods and
services (or efforts), and the like.

Goods and services that contain nonempirical aspects
or are completely nonempirical by definition must also be
considered. It is perfectly true that from the point of
view of a scientific observer neither nonempirical goods
nor nonempirical services are facts to be reckoned with.
It is, however, a fact from the scientific observer's point
of view that many of the actors whom he observes orient
some of their actions to such considerations. That human
beings engage in both methodologically and ultimately
arational action is undeniable, and there is always some
allocation of empirical goods and services involved in
such action. From the point of view of the actor(s) involved, however, the allocation of nonempirical goods and
services that the actor(s) _believes_ takes place is no less

---

1. See p. 330.

important than the allocation of empirical goods and services involved that the scientific observer can check.
Thus, one may give a magician food in exchange for the
nonempirical service of coercing the spirits into hounding
a rival to his death. One may give to charity in an effort to secure the nonempirical goal of salvation, etc.
One may even exchange nonempirical goods and services for
nonempirical goods and services. However imaginary,
superstitious, illusory, or whatever, the scientific observer may, as an actor, feel nonempirical goods and
services to be, he cannot disregard the fact that many, if
not most, actors seem to believe in them some of the time
and some actors seem to believe in them virtually all of
the time. Furthermore, their beliefs have undeniable implications for their empirical actions and consequently
for the allocation of empirical goods and services. There
have been periods of religious revivals in societies all
over the world in which no sense whatever could be made of
the structure of allocation of empirical goods and services without consideration of such beliefs. In the most
modern industrial societies the economic allocation involved in magical action, let alone religious action, is
by no means negligible, and in societies in which critical
rationality has even a more limited standing such considerations may play an overwhelming part in the structure of
economic allocation.

The functional basis for the standing of a structure
of economic allocation as an analytic structural requisite
of any society is not difficult to establish. The members
of a society must have food and usually shelter and clothing as well if there is to be an adequate physiological
adjustment to the nonhuman environment. Without these
goods and the services connected with their collection and
preparation no members of the society could survive physically. As pointed out in Chapter IV above, the human
heredity and nonhuman environmental factors alone do not

suffice to explain the acquisition of the minimal requirements for human beings as they do in many other cases of
the animal and vegetable species. These requirements are
not even in the nature of "free goods," as that concept is
defined by the economists. Even if they were, the problem
of distribution would still arise in the social context to
offset the effects of jealousies that might well arise no
matter how homogeneous the articles concerned might be
intrinsically.

It is at least theoretically possible that the members of one or more types of concrete structures consume
such minimal goods and services without producing them or
others save in negligible quantities, but it is not conceivable that this be true for the members of all of the
concrete substructures of any given society. In a society
some groups may survive solely by virtue of economic
"exploitation" of others, but this cannot be true of any
save a relatively small proportion of the concrete structures of a society unless the society is on the road to
extinction or unless changes in technology make possible
as yet undreamed of changes in the range of variation set
by the factors of human heredity and nonhuman environment.

It is, of course, not conceivable that the members of
any group produce without consuming, though it is by no
means necessary that the members of any concrete unit consume exactly the same goods and services that they produce.
Limitations of this sort highlight the importance of economic structures for social structures generally and imply an
extremely limited range within which such structures may
change without changing the general social structure or even
resulting in the dissolution of the society as a whole.

The analytic structure of economic allocation may be
subdivided into two categories that can be distinguished
in any society. These are the structures of production
and consumption. The structure of production includes all
the structures from whose operation goods and services

accrue to the concrete structure concerned. The structure
of consumption includes all the structures from whose
operations goods and services are allocated to the various
members of the concrete structure concerned and for the
purposes recognized by that structure. In the treatment
of economic structure attempted here these two subdivisions
will be treated separately with attention being paid to
some of their various interrelations.

A. THE STRUCTURE OF PRODUCTION

1. The division of labor

Perhaps consideration of the division of labor is as
good a starting point for the analysis of the structure of
production as any. By the division of labor is meant role
differentiation on the basis of production. The basis for
minimal requirements in these respects have already been
cited above in both Chapters VII and VIII and need not be
repeated here in any detail. Suffice it to say that some
of the members of any society cannot produce at all save
for the gratifications implicit in their very existence
itself; some have extremely limited capacities for production; some have radically different capacities; and
finally, of those individuals with mature capacities, not
all can do at one and the same time all of the things
simultaneously necessary for a society or even for themselves.[2]

The first consideration about the division of labor
is, then, the discovery of who in a given society is institutionally expected to do what and when. Within the
limits set by the minimal necessities for role differentiation the range of variation possible is enormous. In
an attack on these problems one is led to the question of

---

2. See above, pp. 303, 307-310ff.

the source of income, i.e., what types of production are
minimally required. These may be divided into three categories. In the first place, there is the production (i.e.,
acquisition) of the raw materials of goods and services.
Raw materials for present purposes may be defined as those
empirical objects that exist in the nonhuman environment,
and are either directly dissipated upon their acquisition
or are dissipated in the creation of other goods or services. In the second place, there is the production of
manufactured goods. By manufactured goods are meant all
goods that are modified by human activity for human purposes from a raw material state. Finally, there is the
production involved in the allocation of goods and services itself. This third type of production may take the
form of management, delivery services in the ordinary
sense, salesmanship activities, gift bestowals, or whatever, but they are always germane either to production for
further production or to delivery for consumption.[3]

    a. Production of raw materials. The production of
raw materials may take many forms. Again, certain minima,
all of which are well known, may be stated. In the first
place, one may distinguish the minimal raw materials necessary for survival. These consist roughly of food, clothing, and shelter. These may be further subdivided into
the acquisition of animate products and inanimate products.
The former may be further subdivided into those animate
products of a botanical character and those of a zoological
character. Raw materials for products over and above the
minima necessary for survival may be similarly subdivided.

    Animate products. With regard to the production of
botanical raw materials for food, shelter, and clothing,

---

    3. Although limitations of knowledge and space have
not permitted detailed treatment of the question of nonempirical types of production, it must be kept in mind that
all three types distinguished here have implications for
the nonempirically oriented economic aspects of action.

the alternatives for production are confined to systems of
simple collection and to systems of collection based to
some degree on processes of cultivation. Collection in
the absence of cultivation may vary all the way from systems such as gathering nuts and berries found within easy
reach to systems involving the use of complex machinery in
a planned deforestation for the purposes of timber production. Societies resorting solely to collection activities
in order to secure a supply of organic materials will, of
course, have their range of variation more narrowly explicable in terms of human heredity and nonhuman environment
than would otherwise be the case. Depending on what proportion and how important the items concerned are in their
minimal necessary production, the activities of their members will be limited by the nonhuman production of these
raw materials. More or less nomadism and periods of prosperity and depression in such societies may be explained
to a large degree in such terms.

To the degree that mechanical aids for collection are
employed, flexibility in some of these respects will be
increased, but the requirements of production of such mechanical aids will introduce inflexibilities of another
sort, usually those involving an increased interdependency
of the concrete units in terms of which production takes
place.

The processes of simple collection of botanical raw
materials cannot be completely ignored because of their
possible role in the economic aspects of a society. It is,
however, fair to observe that, at least quantitatively
speaking, as one surveys however sketchily the descriptions
of known societies, one is impressed with the extreme importance of systems of cultivation whenever attention in
societies becomes focused on the use of botanical raw
materials. A few societies would seem to survive in the
absence of such a concentration, most notably certain Eski-
mo groups in which the concentration is perhaps, overwhelm-

ingly on animal rather than plant sources of raw materials. But on the whole some systems of cultivation of plants are, if not ubiquitous, at least present in a preponderant number of known societies. For want of a better word, the term agrarian will be applied to those aspects and structures of any society that are concerned with the cultivation of plant materials.

The presence of agrarian elements in a society always places limits on nomadism since it at least ties a portion of the members of a society to specific areas during planting and harvesting seasons. Ordinarily, its sedentary influence goes far beyond this minimum, however, because of the importance in most cases of constant care and attention between planting and harvesting activities if there is to be any considerable harvest at all.

The limits on nomadism are not the only implications for a society of agrarian elements of raw material production. Some concepts of rights and obligations as distributed among the members of the society to locational factors (i.e., property rights in land) are an inevitable concomitant. Not only must possible conflicts be held within certain limits, but also certain minimal responsibilities for the cultivation of certain areas must be allocated. Furthermore, there must be structures of distribution for the products of agrarian production as there must be for all forms of production. Here again the minimal structures not only reflect the necessity of inhibiting possible conflicts but also reflect the necessity of distribution of goods to nonproducers of various sorts or to producers of different sorts of products.

There are at least an extremely large number of aspects of agrarian production that involve considerable implications for general social structure. The different products themselves, the different characteristics of different lands, climates, and seasons, the different types of units in terms of which this work is done, all have

widespread implications that the student of societies can
not afford to ignore. For the present, however, one distinction of special significance will be explored briefly.
This is the distinction between industrialized and nonindustrialized agrarian production. Industrialized systems
of production in general may be defined as systems of production in which inanimate devices are used to multiply
the effects of human effort and in which inanimate sources
of power generation are employed in this multiplication.
Both of these criteria are necessary for the concept of
industrialization used here. The use of a shovel multiplies the effects of the digging efforts of a man, the use
of an electrical, gasoline, steam, or otherwise inanimate-
ly powered shovel makes possible indefinitely greater
multiplication of this effort. At least, at the present
stage of technological development no animate sources of
power make possible anything corresponding to the degree
of multiplication of effort possible with inanimate sources
despite the fact that many of the inanimate sources (e.g.,
coal, oil, etc.) have themselves a definite organic background or source. The use of inanimate sources of power
is perhaps inevitably more efficient in material terms and
hence capable of greater multiplication than the use of
animate sources because of the necessary expenditure of
effort in the maintenance and continuity of the animate
sources and because the point of marginal returns is so
much lower in the one case than in the other.

The use of this definition of the term industrial
permits of certain applications. In the first place, it
permits indefinite distinction of degrees of industrialization as well as kinds of industrialization. Degree will
vary with the amount of multiplication of effort from the
sources named in the society, and kind will vary with the
distinctions among the devices used to attain multiplication. When a waterfall is used to turn a paddle wheel
harnessed directly to a grindstone, some degree of indus-

trialization is present. A lot less is present than in
the case of harnessing waterfalls to dynamos and utilizing
the power obtained through electric motors. There is not
only a difference of degree involved but also a difference
of kind. The differences of degree and kind have implications that go considerably beyond the empirical multiplication of the effects of human effort. They extend to the
social structure itself. A society in which electric
power is derived from waterfalls cannot have the same
structures as a society in which waterfalls are harnessed
in other ways or not at all. Different roles, different
concrete units, different implications for the regulation,
training, etc. of such units are involved as a minimum.

There is another range of consideration involved.
The term _industrial_ as used in common parlance, and even
in technical social science literature, is rarely, if
ever, precisely defined in terms capable of measurement.
The definition given here is capable of measurement and
has a precise denotation. But by tying the term down in
this fashion or in some fashion similar to it[4] another
possibility is raised. The more or less precise statement
of the degree and kind of industrialization in a society
when viewed in the context of the structural requisites of
any society or of any specific society enable one to determine more narrowly the range of possible variation of
the structures of that society. For example, in highly
industrialized societies based on hydroelectric, coal, and

---

4. This attempt at definition is certainly not regarded as final or complete. For the purposes of social
analysis considerable modification or even complete change
may make the concept a great deal more useful. Nevertheless, any definition of the concept to be useful in social
analysis, if it is to capture any of the connotations generally associated with the term industrialized, must make
possible the precise distinction of degrees and kinds of
industrialization and of the development of the implications of those distinctions for social structure.

oil sources of power there cannot be institutionalization
of economically self-sufficient family units of anything
like the degree or kind possible in nonindustrial or only
slightly industrialized societies. The requirements of
occupational specialization and selection in the one case
are structurally incompatible with the requirements of the
other case. No attempt is made here to develop this and
similar points in any highly confirmed form, but it is
hoped that verification or disproof of such points will
result from the comparative analysis of different societies made in terms of the conceptual scheme and theoretical system developed here.

To return to the question of agrarian elements in raw
material production, one may differentiate societies with
respect to the degree and kind of industrialization or
lack of it involved in the system. The range of variation
possible under these different conditions will be widely
different. In many respects the range of variation possible in nonindustrialized or relatively little industrialized agrarian systems will be very much greater than in
the case of highly industrialized systems. The former,
for example, may organize such production in terms of an
almost indefinite number of different types of predominantly particularistically recruited units. The latter
must emphasize highly universalistic units to a much
greater degree and is less flexible in these structural
respects. The degree of self-sufficiency of the units
possible in the one case is radically different from that
possible in the other case. On the other hand, variations
in scale and variety of products, degree of specialization,
and so forth, practicable in the latter case, are very
much greater than in the former case. In the consideration of agrarian systems of raw material production some
recognition of these factors must be present. Because of
the relative ease of operational measurement of the degree
and type of industrialization, and because of the far-

reaching implications of such considerations for the range
of structural possibilities, recognition of these factors
are especially important for the comparative analysis of
societies, whether this be attempted relative to social
change in a given case or intersocietal comparisons in
widely separated cases.

Another type of animate raw material product that may
be differentiated here is that of animal as opposed to
plant products. Here again the distinction between simple
collection and cultivation (husbandry in this case) may be
drawn. In both cases, simple collection and husbandry,
the possibilities of combining production with nomadism
are considerable. In the former and the latter case the
details of the nonhuman environment plus the size of the
membership of the society place definite limits on the degree to which nomadism may be avoided and the degree to
which it may be practiced if the society is to persist.

Because of the greater mobility of animal as opposed
to plant stocks, the implications for sedentary structures
of husbandry are not nearly so great, at least on the
average, as is true in the case of cultivation of agrarian
products. The type of structures possible relative to
locational utilization are also considerably different.
The clear demarcation of hunting and fishing preserves as
well as of grazing possibilities is both more difficult
and less practicable in the case of animals than of plant
products. Again, the greater mobility of the product is
germane. Extremely small, highly parcellated land hold-
ings of the type characteristic in many agrarian based
societies are quite out of the question in husbandry based
societies. The implications of greater spatial mobility
of the membership of such societies for the organization
of different concrete units is considerable as are the
requirements of locomotion and the like.

When sedentary husbandry is the basic form of animal
production, the implications for general social structures

are again quite dissimilar from those of agrarian production. Given land capable of both cultivation and husbandry, other factors being equal and quite apart from the
differences in mobility of plants and animals, the amount
of land necessary to support human life via husbandry is
very much greater than via agriculture. For all the in-
efficiencies of agriculture, it is far more prolific per
acre in terms of food and other raw materials than is
husbandry, assuming land adaptable to either purpose.
Given land equally adaptable for either purpose, husbandry
can be more profitable than agriculture in terms of food
production. This is true, however, only under certain
conditions. First there must be a comparative advantage
with respect to husbandry between the area concerned and
other areas with which it is in contact. And second, it
must be possible for exchange to take place between these
areas such that the persons involved in husbandry can more
than equal their possibilities of agrarian food production
through the exchange of the products of husbandry for
agrarian products.

     Even apart from the differences in productivity be-
tween husbandry and cultivation, husbandry would still
require different social structures than agrarian production. The types of cognition necessary in the one case
differ markedly from those in the other. The care of the
animals differs from the problems of cultivation. Different labor structures are both feasible and necessary. The
differences involved in many of these respects is well
illustrated in societies in which agrarian and husbandry
and/or different types of husbandry production have come
into contact with one another. Frequently, situations of
considerable conflict have resulted. In the development of
the United States the conflicts between cattlemen and
farmers, cattlemen and sheepmen, etc., were not only no-
torious for the violence and bitterness involved, but also
clearly represented different ways of life. In England

the enclosure movement and in Chinese history the contacts
between the Chinese and the Mongols contain important
elements of this sort. Throughout history, the cases in
which changes from cultivation to husbandry or from one
type of cultivation or husbandry to another that have had
far-reaching social implications are too numerous to be
ignored. One need not fall into the intellectual traps of
a theory of economic determinism to agree that the structures of production are never without implications for
other types of structures in a society.

The distinction drawn above between industrial and
nonindustrial structures in relation to agrarian production may also be drawn relative to husbandry. Husbandry
may be carried out on the one basis or the other, and here
also the implications of the difference are far-reaching.
As in the case of agrarian production, industrialization
in husbandry increases the practicable scale of production
units and in fact in some respects places minimal requirements on the scale. It may increase the productivity of
labor tremendously although it need not increase the
absolute productivity of all the factors involved. Usually, it has the latter effect too, however, though not to
the same degree that the productivity of labor is increased. These considerations always involve questions of
alternative occupations for labor thus released or, if not
alternative occupations, at least structures to cover the
increased leisure time thus created.

Industrialization in this field, as in the agrarian
field, requires the integration of the raw material production sphere with some manufacturing sphere. The further
industrialization is carried, the greater the interdependence in these respects and the lower the degree of self-
sufficiency possible in the husbandry production units.
In a modern industrial society, for example, an obscure
grievance precipitating a strike of power workers could
create a major crisis within a matter of hours in the

dairy production of the area concerned. Prior to the invention and spread of milking machines such interdependency was unknown. Again, the presence of industrialization
both increases and decreases flexibility. In matters
having to do with self-sufficiency the decrease is, perhaps, the more noticeable. In matters having to do with
product differentiation, elaboration, etc., the flexibility is increased. The possibilities of disposing of the
product are increased, but the necessity of such disposal
outside the unit of production is also increased. It is
always the essence of industrialization that the use of
machinery and power so multiplies the effort of the producers that the unit in which production takes place can
never as a unit hope to consume directly all of the product
produced by it. It is quite out of the question to set up
a modern dairy production unit solely to supply the dairy
needs of the individuals involved in the unit itself.

    <u>Inanimate products</u>. Briefly, in connection with the
division of labor one may differentiate a second type of
raw material, namely, those that are inanimate. Here the
possibilities of self-propagation under control are generally out of the question despite a few scattered discoveries such as the possibility of "growing" crystals. In
this sphere one is confined to collection techniques
though these may vary widely. There is a difference between the ways in which the production of inanimate raw
materials may or must fit into a society and the ways in
which animate materials may or must fit. It is conceivable
that a vegetarian society making little or no use of
animal raw materials or inanimate raw materials exist. A
society similarly focused on animal products is also at
least conceivable. Similar concentration upon inanimate
raw materials is, however, quite out of the question because of the relative unavailability of inanimate raw
materials as foodstuffs. At the very outset it would seem
that inanimate raw material production must be integrated

with some system of production of animate raw materials.
It may well be that some inanimate raw materials are also
inevitably involved in any society, but the difference in
degree of preoccupation possible on a raw material level
as between animate and inanimate materials is nevertheless
significant. Hunting, fishing, agrarian, or husbandry
structures can conceivably well-nigh, if not completely,
exhaust the raw material production structures of a society. This cannot even conceivably be the case with regard
to inanimate raw material production such as mining, and
the like.

On the whole, however, some structures of production
of inanimate raw materials are usually present just as the
production of both plant and animal raw materials is the
rule rather than the exception. Heavy concentration on
animal or plant raw materials is possible whereas this is
not the case for inanimate products if a whole society is
concerned. Nevertheless, any research worker reporting on
a society would ordinarily expect to find some production
of all three sorts of raw materials. The absence of any
one or especially any two of them, while conceivable, would
certainly be sufficiently rare to receive special attention
and extremely careful checking and could hardly fail to
have special consequences for the general social structure.

With regard to the production of inanimate raw materials the distinctions between degrees and types of industrialization and nonindustrialization must also be explored.
Beyond the general remarks made above, however, nothing
more need be added here on that score.

b. Production of manufactured goods. Manufactured
goods have been defined above as all goods that are modified by human activity for human purposes from a raw
material state. Before the general category of manufactured goods is discussed a word must be said concerning
the implications of this definition for the preceding
category of raw materials. Given this definition some

element of manufacture enters the raw material picture
whenever it passes the most rudimentary collection structures. Certainly, in both cultivation and husbandry such
considerations enter, for almost at once some modification
and selection of stocks takes place. Some such elements
enter the picture to a marked degree with structures of
industrialization. In the analysis of what is done in
terms of economic production, therefore, elements of manufacture in the production of raw materials must be carefully distinguished.

Structures of production of manufactured goods obviously cannot stand alone in any society. In relation to
any manufactured good two other questions germane to economic production inevitably arise. First, there is the
question of the raw materials that are modified. What are
they? How are they produced? How do they come to the
manufacturer, etc? There must be answers to all these
questions. In the second place, there is the question of
the modification itself. What further goods and services
are required for this process? Where do they come from?
How do they get to the manufacturer, etc? It may be conceivable for a society to exist in which production is
confined to that of raw materials and the services of
allocation, but this cannot be true of societies in which
manufacture takes place. When there is manufacture, there
must be structures of production of the other two sorts as
well.

Manufacture as defined here covers such rudimentary
modifications as to make it an inevitable component of any
society. Cooked food, sharpened tools, as well as a
modern blast furnace would come under the definition of
manufactured goods used here. Virtually all raw materials
in all societies undergo some modification by human activity prior to consumption. If that is the case, why then
need manufactured goods be distinguished from raw materials? The importance of the distinction lies in the fact

that some raw materials may be directly consumed without
modification beyond the gathering of it. Wild fruit may
be consumed, for example, by the person who picks it when
and where it is picked. Such structures cannot, of course,
be the sole structures of production because of the helplessness of some of the members of a society, but they may
be present for many. As soon as the question of modification arises, however, the questions of the source and
character of the things modified and the things used to
modify them arise. These involve production beyond that
immediately being considered. Why, then, is not the concept of manufactured goods so defined as to enter the
picture only when its order of implication for social
structure is of the major sort involved in industrial societies? The answer to this question is a pragmatic one
of the type germane in the defense of any concept. To
define the concept in such a manner would involve terribly
difficult problems of distinction. The degrees and types
of modification of raw materials are subject to the widest
and most minute variations. Where and in what respects
would it be most useful to draw the line? Less difficulty,
in the judgment of the present writer, is encountered if
one draws the distinction in the relatively restricted
categories of small structural significance than if the
line is drawn elsewhere with the possibility of situations
of major structural implications of raw material modification on both sides of the line.

    To get at problems of the larger order of distinction,
the distinction between industrialized and nonindustrialized manufacture is used here. The harnessing of inanimate
sources of power and the production of machines that make
possible a multiplication of individual effort inevitably
involve rather far-reaching distinctions between raw materials and consumption of the finished product. Furthermore, at least in respect to the combination of inanimate
power sources and machines, the factors involved in the

distinction differ precisely in kind and not in degree
from other such separations of raw material production and
consumption. That distinction will differentiate what is
commonly called industrial from that which is not and in a
manner that may be capable of precise operational measurement. If animals or men furnish the power and/or if the
tools do not multiply the human effort involved, industrialization is not present. In the degree and/or kind that
inanimate power sources and multiplication of effort are
present, industrialization is present. The present stage
of knowledge makes possible rather precise distinctions
between animate and inanimate sources of power and degrees
of multiplication of effort. Furthermore, as stated previously, precise distinctions in these terms among different degrees as well as kinds of industrialization may well
be possible.

The limits on multiplication of human effort in
nonindustrial manufacture are very much more restricted
than in the case of industrial manufacture. Nevertheless,
wide differences within the nonindustrial range are possible. Hunting with bows and arrows is a great deal more
effective in many respects than hunting with sticks and
stones. The difference between such methods, however, is
certainly relatively small by comparison with the increased
range, penetration, and general effectiveness of firearms.
For these reasons the definition of manufactured goods has
been left extremely general and the range within the
definition narrowed by the use of the concept of industrialization and nonindustrialization. Still further narrowing of the range of phenomena may proceed with some precision by means of distinctions among different types and
degrees of industrialization and different types of nonindustrialization.

The general question of the types of concrete units
in which production takes place will be considered below.
Here in relation to the production of manufactured goods a

few of the many possibilities will be mentioned largely in
an effort to indicate one range of variation of major importance in these respects.

With regard to nonindustrialized production the range
of variation is in certain respects wider than in the industrialized case. The emphasis placed by the requirements
of industrialization on rationality, universalism, and
functional specificity, for example, limit the possibilities of relationships and membership units in general
quite sharply. In nonindustrial manufacture, units of the
sort commonly found in industrialized production may occur,
but also a whole range of other types of units may be of
outstanding significance. Most notably, units with predominantly particularistic criteria of membership are both
possible and practical in such situations. Indeed, units
of a predominantly universalistic sort in terms of which
production is carried out are almost certainly the exception rather than the rule in nonindustrial manufacture.
The theoretical explanation of these differences need not
divert the discussion at this point. Suffice it to say
that on general, but empirical, grounds, a strong hypothetical case for this point can be made out.

In nonindustrial manufacture predominantly particularistic units in terms of which production is carried out
vary widely as is to be expected. Some notable types are
extremely common, however. Most notable, perhaps, are
kinship units of all sorts -- clans, families, and the
like. Units based on kinship criteria are sometimes the
most important units, structurally speaking, in terms of
which production is carried out (as in the case of "traditional" China) and are perhaps never totally absent as
nonindustrial production units in any society. Units of a
guild type are also common as are units based on religious
criteria, sex role differentiations, and many other criteria. Perhaps the most general point to be kept in mind
for analysis of these phenomena is the fact that, whenever

one distinguishes units in terms of which production is
carried out, one must also distinguish the structures by
which such production is related to consumption. In any
case, the fact of variability of such units and the relation of the range of such variability to the various distinctions of industrialization and nonindustrialization
cannot be ignored in the case of any society.

     c. <u>Production of allocation</u>. Along with the dis-
tinctions between the production of raw materials and
manufactured goods, the production of actual allocation
must be mentioned. Here two categories will be distinguished. First, there is allocation in the <u>managerial</u>
<u>sense</u>, i.e., the planning and supervision of the produc-
tive processes themselves. Second, there is the <u>distribu-</u>
<u>tion</u> of the goods and services produced to the persons or
groups that will consume them. Both forms of allocation
must take place if the society is to survive. Goods and
services are not produced at random nor are they dissipated
at random. There must be structures of action, social
structures, that cover both of these problems of existence.

     At this point, it must be indicated that in the
general economic picture the question of what is production
and what is consumption is in large degree a question of
where one decides to enter the process of allocation of
goods and services. Automobiles are products of the automobile industry and consumption objects for other units
that employ them.[5] Insofar as they are used by the automobile industry itself they are objects of consumption
from that point of view too. The labels of production and
consumption do not inhere in any specific process. They
only apply to a specific process from a specific point of
view. Even the consumption of food is from one point of
view an agent in the process of production of services,

---

5. See above, pp. 61-62.

for without such consumption the human agents of production could not function at all.

These observations hold with regard to the production
of allocation as well as with regard to the production of
goods. From different points of view, allocation is at
one and the same time, or at different times, consumption
or production. Nevertheless, in this case, as in the case
of raw materials and manufactured goods, it is of extreme
importance to know from whose points of view, at what
times, and in what respects these services appear as items
of production or consumption. There is one sense in which
the production of allocation differs from the production
of raw materials or manufactured goods. In many, if not
most, cases the goods concerned are subject to deferred
consumption. The length of such possible delay is of
great importance in some economic structures and hence in
the total structure of the societies concerned, since the
economic structures are merely one aspect, analytically
distinguished, of the total concrete structural unit. The
processes of allocation are at one and the same time produced and consumed. Both types of allocative processes
share this characteristic. A given act involving allocative aspects may be only one step in a further chain of
allocation, but as it is effectuated it is consumed. The
organization of a hunting party is done when it is done.
It may stand idle for months, though organized, but it is
in essence consuming its "organization characteristic" all
the time. A good delivered to a wholesaler's warehouse
may sit there forever, but the production and consumption
of its delivery are simultaneous.

One peculiarity of the managerial form of allocation
is its possibility of being consumed indefinitely. However indestructible goods may be, they have some span of
existence as a particular type of good. This "life span"
may be one of seconds or one of decades, but it is not
indefinite. Some types of services are indefinite in

these respects. The organization of a hunting group might endure unendingly barring relevant changes in the nonhuman and human elements of its setting. In rapidly changing societies this is less likely to be the case than in others, but the possibility always exists to some degree.

A major distinction between managerial allocation and the physical distribution of the fruits of production exists with regard to their respective separability from the relevant production involved. The former is not separable and the latter is. Managerial allocation of some sort inheres in every process with a productive aspect and goes on simultaneously with it. The distribution of the fruits may be handled by separate units altogether. No factory can exist without direction either centralized or decentralized, and from the point of view of the total social system there must be actual distributive mechanisms too, but these need not be directly in terms of the factory. A private business may build automobiles, and other and quite distinct concerns, either private or state, may drive them away. The possibility of such distinctions requires that some recognition of them be taken into consideration by the observer of any society.

Finally, in regard to the production of allocation, its general relevance to the structure of political allocation must be noted briefly. Managerial allocation is, of course, inseparable from the allocation of power and responsibility in the productive processes. This type of allocation is inseparable from the control of such processes and responsibility for them. To manage these processes one must be able to influence the action of those concerned in them. Whether this is done by coercion, persuasion, or whatever other method is beside the point here. Managerial allocation cannot, therefore, be separable in any sense save the analytical from the structures of power and responsibility in the society. It is separable analytically only if one looks at it, on the one hand,

from the point of view of its relevance to the production
of goods and services and, on the other, from the point of
view of its relevance to the allocation of power and responsibility.

The actual distribution of goods and services is no
less inextricably involved with the questions of power and
responsibility, but in a different way. Here, the touch-
stone is the relevance of the actual distribution of goods
and services for the allocation of power and responsibility. Obviously, without some command over the allocation
of goods and services neither power nor responsibility
holders would be alive to carry out their roles, but the
matter goes far beyond this. The relevance of the allocation of goods and services as a tool for coercion,
persuasion, and the like, can not be overlooked. One need
not go to the extreme of holding in essence that "man
lives by bread alone" for the relevance of such factors to
be clear. It is only necessary to realize that "man lives
not by nonmaterial factors alone." There is a limit to
the degree of "other worldliness" possible in a society
even though some minimum of "other worldliness" may be
inescapable. Within that limit the allocation of goods
and services cannot fail to be relevant to the allocation
of power and responsibility. Any study of any social phenomenon that fails to disclose this relevance, however
slight, is incomplete and to some degree leaves both the
allocation of goods and services and that of power and
responsibility unintelligible.

2.   Concrete units of production

The discussion in the preceding sections has been
oriented to the question of what is produced although many
other considerations have entered peripherally. The discussion of the present section will be oriented to distinctions among the types of concrete units in terms of

which production takes place. In this discussion many
elements touched on before will be involved. There will
be four basic sections of the present treatment: the first
will concern itself with the distinction of various degrees
of self-sufficiency in the units involved; the second will
concern itself with the relationship aspects of the units;
the third will concern itself with the type of product
orientation of the unit; and the fourth will raise the
question of the predominant orientation of the unit in
terms of the analytic structural requisites of any society.

 a. <u>The degree of economic self-sufficiency of the
unit</u>. A concrete unit will be considered economically
self-sufficient to the degree and in the respects that its
membership can and does both produce and consume all of
the goods and services necessary to and resulting from the
operation of the unit. Given this definition of economic
self-sufficiency no concrete substructure of a society can
be completely self-sufficient in the economic sense though
the society itself may be. The reason for this hypothesis
is simple enough. It rests on the necessity of the integration of any single concrete unit with other concrete
units in the society. The researcher on societies is,
therefore, concerned with relative degrees and types of
economic self-sufficiency rather than absolute and complete
economic self-sufficiency.

 Although the question of self-sufficiency in relation
to consumption will be discussed below in this chapter, a
brief word in this connection is necessary in the general
remarks made here on the concept of economic self-sufficiency. Perhaps the major utility for general analysis of
the concept of economic self-sufficiency used here lies in
the fact that examination of the allocation of goods and
services from this point of view immediately brings under
attention certain minimal interrelations in economic terms
that must exist between concrete units. If complete economic self-sufficiency were possible for any specific

concrete substructure of a society, there would be no
minimal requirements for relations between that unit and
any other that could be established on economic grounds.
To the degree that self-sufficiency is incomplete, certain
minimal interrelationships with other groups are immediately indicated. This is certainly true of the production
aspect of economic structure. The members of a unit that
produces shoes but no food must have contacts with units
producing food. The importance and necessity of such
interrelationships is no less an implication of lack of
self-sufficiency in consumption. A group that cannot, for
reasons structural or otherwise, consume all that it produces must, if it is to continue as a structure, have
interrelations with other groups that can fulfill this
function of consumption, or it must accumulate endlessly
unconsumed products. Its only alternative is to cut production with the structural changes that would thereby be
involved.

What, if any, implications relative to economic
structure can application of the concept of self-sufficiency to the units in terms of which production is
carried out bring out? They are all implications for the
involvement of the members of the units concerned with
other units in the society and implications of the economic aspects of the unit concerned for other aspects of
the unit. Self-sufficiency may vary widely if not infinitely in both degree and type. This is true of both
consumption and production. Some specific formulation of
the degree and type of self-sufficiency of the units in
terms of which production is carried out is necessary in
the analysis of any society.

Self-sufficiency of a unit in terms of production
lies in two directions. First, to what extent does the
operation of the unit produce all the necessary factors
for its own production? Second, to what extent does the
operation of the unit produce the factors necessary for

the consumption of the unit apart from that involved in
the production itself? The first question is always involved in units in terms of which production takes place.
The second is only involved directly in those units in
terms of which consumption of both types takes place.
Some examples may illuminate this distinction. A typical
factory unit of a modern business concern in a highly industrialized society is oriented consumptionwise to those
materials necessary for its productive concerns. It consumes raw materials, labor, machines, power, and the like.
Its self-sufficiency is to be reckoned in those terms.
The consumption of its members, apart from factors like
the above utilized for the purpose of factory production,
is institutionally expected to be carried out in terms of
quite different units. To some extent these different
units are family units, to some extent they may be individuals or groupings on a wide variety of other bases.
The lack of self-sufficiency productionwise of these other
units is not immediately germane to the factory unit's
self-sufficiency unless this lack of self-sufficiency
interferes with the members' ability to fulfill those
roles necessary for the factory to function. Thus, housing for workers is not ordinarily a concern of the factory
unit or of the business unit that controls it. On the
other hand, if a decision is made to locate a factory in a
place such that housing is inaccessible for workers, some
provision of housing itself or of transportation of workers from available housing is directly germane to the
self-sufficiency productionwise of the factory unit.

On the other hand, if one looks at a society like
that of "traditional" China, quite a different picture
obtains. In this case the basic unit in terms of which
production is carried out is the peasant family unit.
This unit, unlike the factory unit, is, institutionally
speaking, also the unit in terms of which the consumption
of those members engaged in production is carried out.

Here, both types of considerations relative to self-sufficiency are germane, not just in special cases as above
but, institutionally speaking, in virtually every case
regardless of whether it is directly germane to the production functions involved in the unit. The "traditional"
Chinese peasant family unit lacks economic self-sufficiency, institutionally speaking, not only if it cannot
produce the tools, seeds, etc. necessary for its agrarian
production but also if it does not produce the food, clothing, shelter, and services necessary for its consumption.
As a unit it is institutionally expected to provide both
types of production.

     Certainly, the degree of economic interdependence of
units of the second type is less than in the case of the
former type if the units operate as institutionally expected. This consideration is not only of significance
when the systems concerned operate according to expectations. They are equally relevant when this fails to be the
case. Cases like that of the factory unit, for example,
require an institutionalized system of economic interdependence of far-reaching proportions. Cases like that of
the "traditional" Chinese peasant family do not and commonly lack such a system. In situations of economic failures
the problems raised in the factory case are the problems
of this institutionalized interdependence. Failure to dispose of factory products brings unemployment of factory
workers, their unemployment lowers their ability to purchase foodstuffs and the like, this in turn affects other
units of production, and, depending on the degree of interdependence, the effects of such an economic dislocation
spread widely and rapidly throughout the society and other
societies economically interdependent with it. In the
"traditional" Chinese peasant family case such spreads are
far less likely. Only conditions such as droughts, floods,
and insect scourges that wipe out simultaneously the basis
of production of large numbers of families bring widespread

economic depression. When such depressions occur and
spread, they are not basically understandable in terms of
the concatenations of the units and their interstitial
adjustments. Furthermore, the problems of relief are in a
sense complicated by the fact that ordinarily in systems
like that of "traditional" China the very units dislocated
are the standard relief units, and organization of relief
requires the erection of a system of economic interdependency of a type not previously in existence.

The implications of differences in productive self-
sufficiency as seen in their purely economic aspects may
be differentiated from their implications for other analytic structures in a society. These implications exist
for all the other analytic structural requisites, but they
are, perhaps, most obvious in the case of political allocation. Units of relatively low self-sufficiency in these
respects are especially vulnerable to control from outside
the unit proper. Any establishment of power over the
factors necessary for production carries with it the possibility of exerting control over the units requiring
those factors. Veblen in his analysis of modern industrial
economies was fond of pointing out the extreme importance
both economically and politically (in the sense of the
term used here) of "key industries." Key industries for
Veblen were industries strategic for factors of production
of other production units, and at the same time industries
in which the scale required by technological factors was
extremely large and/or which could be even larger than
necessary on "purely technological grounds." The presence
of such units and the interdependence or dependence of
other units on their products permitted, according to
Veblen, an immense amount of control quite apart from the
types of conspiracy and collusion at which the antitrust
laws of the United States were aimed. It was an indication
of Veblen's relative sophistication for his time that he
realized so clearly that in an industrial system "bigness"

per se cannot be made the focal point of attack on concentration of control via control of the "key industries."
The essence of the problem, of course, lies in the fact
that controls in highly interdependent production systems
can easily convert interdependence into rather complete
dependence productionwise. Furthermore, the control over
production in systems in which much of the consumption is
carried out in terms of units quite different from those
in which production is carried out carries with it automatically the basis for control of the units of consumption since these units do not produce directly what they
consume, or at most only a fraction of it.

In the case of highly self-sufficient production
units the problem of control by other units is more difficult. Each unit under these circumstances is as strategic
for its own control as any other. If these units are not
simultaneously the units of consumption of their members,
control of these units will still make possible the control of the consumption units as in the case just discussed
above. Commonly, however, highly self-sufficient production units are at one and the same time the consumption
units of their members. In the cases in which this is so,
centralization of power becomes most difficult, at least
when viewed from the standpoint of the economic factors
involved. Power under these circumstances, insofar as it
involves economic factors as sanctions or the like, must
be detailed and specific. Any relaxation of specific control permits of an immediate growth of decentralization.
The power systems of any society must always contain elements other than the economic as will be brought out in
the following chapter, but the importance of such elements
is rather greater in the presence of highly self-sufficient
units of production and consumption.

The implications for structures of role differentiation and solidarity are less obvious only because they
have characteristically been a source of less preoccupation

in these matters than the political implications. The
multiplication of units of production of the type implied
by lack of productive self-sufficiency need not necessarily increase the differentiated production roles though it
must increase the combinations of these roles with membership roles in different units. The same may be said of
units more or less self-sufficient in combining the two
types of production mentioned above, i.e., combining in
one unit production in general and that for the direct
consumption of the members as well. Commonly, however,
there is an absolute decrease of role differentiation on
an economic basis in the case of units of high economic
self-sufficiency. The economic self-sufficiency of units
is by no means correlated in any complete sense to the
degree of specialization possible for the members of the
units in which economic allocation takes place. Nevertheless, these factors do not vary at random relative to one
another either, and in a rough sense it is probably true
that the greater the degree of economic self-sufficiency
of the concrete structures the lower is the degree of role
differentiation on an economic basis. This is not necessarily true of the number of different economically based
roles of the average single individual. Quite the contrary is likely to be the case. The members of units of
high economic self-sufficiency are more likely to be
"jacks of all trades" than members of units of less economic self-sufficiency. The differentiation of roles as
between total individuals will, however, certainly be
greater in the latter case.

The implications of differences in type and degree of
economic self-sufficiency for structures of solidarity in
a society are, once explicitly considered, in a general
sense too obvious for prolonged discussion here. Other
things being equal, the greater the economic self-sufficiency of the units, the lower the differentiation and
proliferation of types of units. A lower number of dif-

ferent bases and types of solidarity would, of course, be concomitant with this. The question of comparative loyalty is always germane to solidarity structures, and it is not a matter of chance that societies having the widest known proliferation and differentiation of units in terms of which economic allocation takes place are also the societies in which, superficially at least, the problem of ordering one's institutionally differentiated loyalties would seem to be greatest.

From what has gone before, the relevance for social change of the type and degree of economic self-sufficiency of concrete structures is reasonably clear. In the case of societies that institutionalize highly self-sufficient units in these respects relatively slight shifts in the direction of interdependence may have extremely far-reaching consequences. Technological changes that make peasant spare-time occupations in China uneconomical not only put the products of those roles on a different basis but also affect others deeply too. They carry with them an increased need for media of exchange, an increased marketing of other family products, and a consequent loss of economic self-sufficiency that reaches far beyond the products initially affected. Professor Fei Hsiao-T'ung in one of his volumes has described the effects on village social structures of the erection of a small silk industry in a peasant village.[6] There were in this case not only rather basic changes in the position of women in the village and in their families, but also the village economy became subject to cyclical economic fluctuations in the highly industrialized western world in a manner both catastrophic and enigmatic as far as the villagers were concerned.

Highly interdependent systems are no less vulnerable

_____

6. See his Peasant Life in China, Dutton, New York, 1939.

to shifts in the direction of self-sufficiency than are
highly self-sufficient systems to shifts in the direction
of interdependence. One may illustrate these differences
with reference to modern changes in the direction of highly authoritarian regimes. As sources of power these
regimes seek increased economic efficiency and output, and
as methods of control they have almost without exception
attempted extremely close local supervision and surveillance of individuals including the attempt to minimize
geographical mobility. In China, with her widespread,
highly sedentary, and self-sufficient family units, the
change to increased local supervision is a comparatively
easy change to make. In the absence of other changes
nothing could be easier. It is changes in the direction
of interdependence that will be extremely difficult for
the Chinese and will have very far-reaching consequences.
Other types of changes will be the more difficult insofar
as complicated by shifts in the direction of greater
interdependence. Such complications are, of course, inevitable since the concentration of control inherent in an
authoritarian regime, particularly of the modern sort,
involves some major shifts in the direction of interdependence even if those are limited to changes affecting
only the centralized authorities. On the other hand, any
authoritarian regime attempting to take over the United
States would find the change to local supervision extremely difficult and directly in conflict with the former.
Surveillance and supervision are time consuming. The U.S.
economy has raised to an unusual point the emphasis on
high locational mobility in amounts, frequency, speed, etc.
Surveillance of travel of the type common in authoritarian
countries of either the extreme right or the extreme left
could only be achieved at the cost of cuts in economic
efficiency and output in such a situation. These are
elementary and all too obvious examples, but they serve to
illustrate the fact that for many problems in social change

the type and degree of economic self-sufficiency of the
concrete substructures of the society are inevitably
relevant for the analysis.

     b. <u>The relationship aspects of the unit</u>. The reader
will recall the treatment in Chapter VI of the variations
in different aspects of relationships in a society. The
units in terms of which production takes place in societies are almost never units institutionalized as having a
single member. When and if they are, the question of relationships arises in the contacts between different units.
Insofar as relationships are, if not an inevitable component of units in which production takes place, at least
a highly general feature of societies, the implications of
relationship aspects must be considered.

     It would require far too extensive a treatment to
attempt to outline in detail the varying possible implications for the production of goods and services of different combinations of the variations possible in relationship aspects. Instead, an attempt will be made to indicate
the type of relevance involved for units in terms of which
production is carried out. Future development of this
type of structural analysis will certainly produce theories
of rather wide relevance as to what combinations of these
aspects of relationships are compatible with different
types of production and consumption systems. For the
present, theories of this sort will not be presented systematically but merely raised from time to time to illustrate the relevance of these concepts in this context.
For present purposes, in order to illustrate the type and
range of implications of variations in the relationship
aspects for economic structure, and vice versa, the distinction between highly industrialized and nonindustrial
or relatively slightly industrialized societies will be
explored briefly and tentatively.

     <u>The cognitive aspects</u>. To some extent the concrete

structures in terms of which production is carried out must institutionalize rationality in cognition if the society is to persist. A sufficient degree of rationality must be involved to assure the cognitive basis for sufficient economic production to meet the minimal physical needs of a number of the members of the society sufficient to permit its persistence. Beyond this minimal emphasis extreme variations in the intrusion of nonrational factors are possible. Societies combining rational and magical actions in the field of economic production are by no means scarce. Frequently, planting techniques are accompanied by magical ritual and highly nonrational structures of other sorts as well. No society dependent upon agricultural activities can or does resort solely to magical activities for agricultural production. Incantation may accompany planting and cultivation and be regarded as not one whit less important than these other actions, but it is never considered capable of substituting entirely for these actions. A frequent occurrence in social structure is the traditionalization[7] of action that is in fact rational within a specific set of circumstances. Under these circumstances no conflict between the rational elements and the nonrational aspects of traditionalization need arise. But should the circumstances change in such a manner as to make the traditionalized practices irrational, survival may well require an abandonment of the traditional structures. Under such circumstances survival is by no means a foregone conclusion, of course, for the traditional structures may be maintained even in the face of destruction.

In the case of a highly industrialized modern economic system the emphasis placed on rationality must be extremely

---

7. See above, p. 108, for the definition of the concepts of tradition, traditional, and traditionalization as used here.

great. The high degree of interdependence, the rapidity
of technological change, the highly complex technology
involved, and the extremely widespread effects of irrational actions all combine to force such an emphasis. In
these circumstances the type of combination of tradition
and rationality mentioned above is not feasible even in
the short run because of the rapidity of the technological
changes.[8]

Societies in which the state of technology and the
circumstances of production are both stable and relatively
unchanging may combine traditional and rational action in
the units in terms of which production takes place and may
place overwhelming emphasis on the former to the degree of
seriously endangering the survival of the system in the
face of changes. Such a situation is present to a rather
high degree in nonindustrial or slightly industrialized
societies and conspicuously absent in highly industrialized
ones. To the extent that these hypotheses may be confirmed, obvious implications for possible distinctions in
the institutionalization of rationality in the economically productive aspects of action would follow. The converse
is no less likely perhaps, since, on the one hand, the
implications of the institutionalization of rationality

----

8. Given the terms as defined here, traditional action may be rational in certain circumstances, but it is
not possible to traditionalize a specific action and traditionalize (or institutionalize) rationality in the same
sphere. It is the essence of tradition that an action be
justified as "good" because it follows precedent, whereas
it is the essence of rational action that a given end be
attained by an adequate means, that precedent be followed
only if it indicates an adequate means. All other prece-
dents inject irrational or arational elements into the action. It may be possible (as the terms are used here) to
traditionalize rationality as a general matter, but especially in the face of changed (or changing) circumstances,
the use of specific traditionalized means for a given end
may well entail inadequate means and hence nonrational
action.

sans tradition, or as taking precedence over tradition,
for change at least in the spheres of action oriented to
empirical ends are so great as to be incompatible with the
heavy emphasis on a stable and unchanging technology and
circumstances of production. On the other hand, emphasis
on nonrational factors such as those involved in tradition
over and above rational ones is to a high degree incompatible with the necessity of coping with the complex and
changing technology so characteristic of highly industrialized societies.

The membership criteria aspects. The distinctions
drawn previously between predominantly universalistic and
predominantly particularistic structures are directly germane to the type of units possible for different types of
production. In systems of production in which relatively
slight differences in skills are highly relevant for the
material ends sought, the concrete structures in terms of
which production is carried out must emphasize predominantly universalistic criteria. In simple terms relevant
to present considerations, predominantly universalistic
criteria emphasize what an individual can do that is germane to the purpose for which he is being selected, i.e.,
his relevant "abilities." Predominantly particularistic
criteria emphasize "who he is." In systems of production
in which relatively slight differences in skills are highly
relevant for the empirical ends sought, particularistic
criteria may enter the situation without prejudice to the
degree of attainment of the ends sought only if the specific criteria in question have a perfect or extremely
high correlation with the differences in ability that are
relevant, or if the objective criteria for judgment of
ability in the respects relevant are so poorly developed
that selection on the particularistic basis is no less
likely to produce maximum recruitment of able persons than
is selection on the basis of universalistic criteria.

Recognizing that, while cases of the institutionali-

zation of purely particularistic and purely universalistic
criteria exist, the more ordinary case is some combination
of the two with differing emphases that permit of the use
of the terms predominantly universalistic and predominantly
particularistic, the relevance of these concepts may be
illustrated with reference to highly industrialized and
nonindustrial, or slightly industrialized, systems of production. In the case of highly industrialized societies
the multiplication of human effort via the power sources
and the machines involved is such as to make relatively
small differences in skill highly significant for the outcome of the processes concerned. Two men of slight difference in their ability to handle ordinary shovels will
not dig significantly different amounts of earth in terms
of the goals usually, if not inevitably, associated with
such production. On the other hand, in the operation of a
steam shovel that supplements exponentially the ability of
the operator or multiplies it in any of many different
ways, relatively slight differences in the skill of two
operators may make enormously significant differences in
their output. This type of relevance is not restricted to
highly complex mechanical manipulations. It may inhere in
manipulations no more complex than pushing "start" and
"stop" buttons or handling simple speed regulators. In
the case of workers operating an assembly line, for example, relatively slight differences in the reaction time
involved in pressing a "stop" button may make differences
calculable in thousands of units of production and machinery replacement or idleness when the production line is
impeded. Depending on the degree and type of multiplication involved, the relevance of differences in ability for
the attainment of the production goals sought is increased
or decreased. Other factors are also relevant in these
respects. The degree and type of interdependence of the
system in question is relevant if only because some types
of interdependence themselves multiply the effects of

differences in skill. In the United States, for example,
if one of the major automobile producers were suddenly to
be able to produce with twice the efficiency of its com-
petitors and expand rapidly enough to take over the share
of the market it could obtain by price competition on this
basis, in the short run at least, widespread economic re-
adjustments would be necessary far beyond the change in
number of cars produced and the companies which produced
them. Not only the producers of automobiles and the consumers of these would be affected, but also the bankruptcy
of other large producers made possible by such differences
in skills would affect labor and production of many sorts.
The financial market, and ultimately the economic system
of the United States as a whole and that portion of the
world's economic system involved with it in general would,
as a minimum, also be affected.

In societies with highly industrialized systems of
economic production the two conditions necessary, if predominantly particularistic criteria are not to inhibit the
production processes, are not commonly present. In the
first place, it is not true that the particularistic elements involved have either a perfect or a high correlation
with the presence of the abilities that are germane to
production. A son may occasionally be the person best
fitted to succeed to his father's managerial position, but
there is no reason to believe that this is necessarily so
or even that it will be so in a statistically large number
of cases. It is even less likely that the objective criteria for judgment of ability in the respects relevant will
be so poorly developed that recruitment on a particularistic basis is no less likely to produce a maximum selection on the basis of persons with the relevant abilities
than is selection on the basis of universalistic criteria.
In a sense the type of cognition that is involved in the
planning and execution of processes in which relatively
slight differences in skill are so important at one and

the same time gives one a basis for selection on highly
universalistic grounds. If worse comes to worst, the test
can always be made of trying out the candidates in the
production role itself and measuring the effect of one on
output as opposed to that of a competitor. One may at
least suggest that by no means all such selection on comparatively particularistic bases as does exist in highly
industrialized systems rests on the lack of objective
criteria that will give more accurate selection.

This point about particularistic elements has been
raised because particularistic elements in selection for
economic production roles are by no means eliminated in
highly industrialized systems. In some production roles
the criteria remain almost purely particularistic. Ordinarily, the roles of household production are so determined. The cooks, dishwashers, and baby tenders in families are not even in the most highly industrialized societies chosen on a universalistic basis save by that small
portion of households in which these jobs can be delegated
to servants. On the whole, such particularistic criteria
as sex, family roles (e.g., wife, father, mother, etc.),
age, and generation apply in this sphere. Ability becomes
the basis for selection only in rather extreme cases,
largely those in which the person assigned on particularistic grounds is so inept at the roles, for whatever reason,
that the stability of the unit is threatened if no substitute is found. Even in this extreme case it is by no means
certain that a substitute will be found.

Those production roles of the sort just mentioned are
not the main concern here, however. For reasons too far
afield to discuss here, it is generally not considered an
instance of the sin of nepotism for one's wife to be one's
cook even in the most highly industrialized societies.
The manner in which production is structured in units like
the family is such that, whatever the mechanical aids,
slight differences in skill are not of great importance to

the economic standing of the unit. The problems of importance here are those production roles in which slight
differences in skill are of great importance, in which
objective criteria of relevant abilities exist, and in
which particularistic elements still enter. For example,
for some jobs only men may be hired and for some only
women. For some jobs persons of one social category or
another are excluded on that basis, and so forth. Several
things may be said about the intrusion of such particularistic elements in highly industrialized systems. First,
these elements usually place limits on universalistic
selection rather than completely eliminate it. For example, only men may be hired as machinists in a plant, but
selection from among the male applicants will be solely on
the basis of the best available objective judgment of
differences in relevant abilities. Completely particularistic criteria for selection for such roles would not only
doom the system but is in fact not present for any appreciable fraction of such production roles in any known
highly industrialized system. Second, the nature of the
particularistic elements in combination with the distribution of relevant abilities in relation to role requirements
for them may be such that the particularistic elements will
not in fact interfere with the maximum recruitment of
persons of maximum ability. If, for example, five machinists are needed, if of the ten candidates five are male
and five are female but all of the males are better machinists than any of the females, the particularistic requirement that only males be hired will not prevent the same
outcome as purely universalistic criteria would procure.
This situation may obtain in greater or lesser approximation of the pure case set up as an example, and any one of
several elements may vary in these respects. The particularistic elements may coincide with the objective differences in skill. They also may not coincide, but the
differences that do not coincide may not make important

differences from the point of view of the operations in
hand. Other combinations of this sort are also possible.
Third, while the situation cited in the second case mentioned above may obtain, it frequently, if not usually,
does not, and some significant difference from the point
of view of production results. The more highly industrialized the system the greater is the likelihood that the
particularistic elements will interfere significantly.
Both the degree and type of industrialization must be
studied in these respects. The more highly specialized
and interdependent the system is, the greater is the likelihood that such elements will be significant. Unless the
situation outlined above in the second point holds true,
there will always be an economic cost of such elements,
and this cost will be reflected in the difference between
the standard of living of the members of the system and
that possible for them in the absence of such elements.
Finally, the presence of some types of particularistic
elements in such a system will always make some difference,
and for each such system there are some types and degrees
of particularistic elements the presence of which will
make impossible the operation of the system as set up.

     The situation in these respects for nonindustrialized
or relatively slightly industrialized systems is, of
course, markedly different. In such societies the differences in skill are not similarly strategic for economic
production, and insofar as economic production is relevant
for other aspects of the society, they are not so strategic
for them either. In such societies a possibility exists
that is sharply limited or nearly nonexistent in the case
of highly industrialized societies. There is the possibility of so organizing units in which economic production
takes place that they coincide with units oriented to
quite different considerations and units whose membership
is particularistically determined. This permits, of
course, a minimization of the possibilities of conflicts

in solidarities. It is, perhaps, difficult to demonstrate that in all societies there must be some concrete units recruited on a predominantly particularistic basis, but there is hardly any question that such units do exist in all known societies. In many, if not most or all, such societies, the institutionalization of some of the units organized on a predominantly particularistic basis (or a completely particularistic one) is either crucial or at least highly strategic for the structure of the society as a whole. This is true of highly industrialized societies as well as nonindustrial ones or ones with relatively little industrialization. The family structure of the United States is far less the major focus of attention of the members of the society than is the family structure of "traditional" China, but in both cases crucial institutions are involved, or at least highly strategic ones.

The fact that units of solidarity recruited[9] on a predominantly universalistic basis as well as those recruited on a predominantly particularistic basis must exist in a given society certainly complicates the problems of solidarity of that society. It is not possible here to explore the whole range of problems raised for social structure in this respect. Suffice it to say that they are numerous and that in nonindustrial or relatively slightly industrial societies this range of problems may be minimized or even eliminated altogether.

The substantive definition aspects. The concepts in terms of which the substantive definition aspects of relationships have been distinguished are those of functional specificity and functional diffuseness. From the point of

---

9. Selection on a predominantly universalistic basis, particularly when the criteria involved have not been reduced to clear-cut tests, may take place primarily through dismissal of those who prove themselves less skillful and the hiring of others, rather than by careful selection for initial employment.

view of production units the institutionalization of functionally specific relationships makes possible a maximum
precision of definition of the relationships involved and
reduces to a minimum the need of the unit concerned to
allow for unforeseen eventualities in these respects or to
divert attention to factors not directly and immediately
germane to considerations of production. To the degree
that functionally diffuse elements enter the picture these
possibilities are reduced.

Highly industrialized systems place a heavy emphasis
on functional specificity just as they do on universalistic
criteria. To some degree the necessary emphasis in such
systems on universalistic criteria is highly relevant to
the emphasis on functional specificity. ·Functionally
diffuse elements in relationships furnish one avenue
through which pressure for particularistic elements may be
exerted. Nepotism frequently has its major strength in
the fact that the functionally diffuse obligations of
family relationships involve pressure for an individual in
other roles to "take care of his own," and so forth. In
any case functionally diffuse elements in relationships
can and in many cases do seriously inhibit the freedom in
selection (including both admission to and dismissal from
roles) necessary to maintain universalistic criteria.

There are other implications of advanced industrialization that are, if anything, even more significant in
these respects. The multiplication aspect of industrialization involves greatly increased output.[10] This involves
the increase of factors processed in production as well as
an increase of the factors that must be disposed of following their production. There is hardly space in this
volume to examine in detail the relationship between

---

10. Here it will be necessary to bring in factors
from the consumption as well as the production sphere.

increases in the degree and different types of industrialization and increases in the degree and different types
of scale of economic activities,[11] but the existence of
such relationships can hardly be questioned. Given the
present state of industrial technologies, high degrees of
industrialization require large scale economic activities.
The erection of a modern automobile production unit for
operation by a single consumer, or even a small number of
consumers, to meet his needs and no others would multiply
the human effort necessary for automobile production
rather than reduce it, quite apart from the circumstance
that, given the present state of technology, automobile
production on this basis would be quite out of the question on other grounds.

It is not unreasonable on the whole, therefore, to
maintain that high levels of industrialization, as opposed
to low ones or lack of industrialization, involve enormous
differences in scale of operation. The increase of interdependency necessary for high levels of industrialization
is also germane to the problem under discussion here.
These factors taken together indicate that the number and
complexity of relationships involved in highly industrialized production systems as opposed to other systems of
production are enormously greater. Insofar as this is
true an emphasis on functionally specific relationships is
likewise enormously more eufunctional for the system. The
cognitive problems alone require such an emphasis. It is
difficult enough to plan and carry out such activities when
the obligations and rights of the various parties to the

---

11. It must be borne in mind throughout this volume
that the use of such phrases as economic activities, production and consumption units, etc., refer to analytically
distinguishable aspects of action and units and not to ones
concretely differentiated in these terms and these alone.
For concrete distinctions of this sort phrases such as
"predominantly economically oriented," "predominantly production oriented," etc., are used throughout.

action can be and are defined empirically in great detail.
If, in addition, a whole host of obligations and rights
relatively unpredictable in character and volume were involved, operation of such units would become impossible.
The volume of personnel required to keep track of such
details on a functionally specific basis is enormous. It
would be very much greater to the degree that functionally
diffuse relationships were present to increase indefinitely
the character, volume, and unpredictability of additional
considerations. The factors germane here apply no less to
production than to consumption. The scale of highly industrialized production and its inordinate productivity by
comparison with nonindustrial production require large
scale distribution to consumers as well as large scale
production of the goods themselves. It may be true that
the degree of centralization and the scale of many activities in highly industrialized societies could be cut down
to some degree without sacrifice of economic ends sought,
but the possibility of reducing them to a handful of relationships or to relatively small numbers of relationships
is quite out of the question. If one considers the number
of relationships necessary for the operation of even a
single automobile plant in a highly industrialized society, the problem involved becomes obvious. There are
thousands of workers, hundreds of managerial personnel,
hundreds of suppliers of materials, machinery, etc.,
hundreds of distributors, and so forth involved. One may
quarter the magnitudes suggested, and the problem will be
hardly less obvious.

On the other hand, production in nonindustrial contexts is not similarly complicated. If one is dealing with
a nonindustrial society or one in which only rudimentary
industrial forms exist, quite other possibilities are open.
In the case of the membership criteria aspects the inevitability of some predominantly particularistic concrete
structures has been alluded to. The same type of argument

will hold true of some predominantly functionally diffuse concrete structures. In nonindustrial societies there exists the possibility of considerably simplified solidarity structures since production units can be organized on a functionally diffuse basis and hence need not be separated from the general functionally diffuse organizations of the society. Commonly, in societies characterized by nonindustrial production, or relatively rudimentary industrialization, production units are organized after this fashion. Production on a family, clan, fraternal, club, guild, or similar basis is too familiar to require comment in this connection. Suffice it to say that all these organizations are in their characteristic forms predominantly functionally diffuse.

In conclusion of this section on the substantive definition aspects of production a general word is in order about the apparently close relation between universalism and functional specificity, on the one hand, and particularism and functional diffuseness on the other. It is not true, as has been noted above,[12] that universalism and functional diffuseness cannot be combined in a single relationship. The husband-wife relationship is almost always, if not inevitably, institutionalized as a functionally diffuse relationship, but the choice of mates is sometimes to a rather high degree carried out on a predominantly universalistic basis. Nevertheless, with a degree of frequency that argues against mere chance, concrete structures stressing universalism stress functional specificity and vice versa. The same is true relative to particularism and functional diffuseness. The following line of speculation is, therefore, advanced in these respects. In concrete structures for whose operation universalistic criteria of recruitment are highly eufunctional

---

some very specific empirical ends must be recognized explicitly. If this were not the case, the distinction of
specific abilities and the judgment of their germane
character would be out of the question. The presence of
such specific and explicitly recognized ends makes possible the limitation of the relationships concerned to precisely defined considerations. In the absence of such
explicit aims this is obviously out of the question. At
the same time, concrete structures for whose operations
functional specificity is highly eufunctional must also
have some explicitly recognized aims, and the more eufunctional is functional specificity the more explicitly
recognized must all the aims of the unit's operations be.
If the aims are thus empirical and precisely defined, the
possibility is accordingly increased that the explicit
selection of members with a view to the different abilities
of candidates in achieving the desired aims will also be
eufunctional. Finally, the presence of particularistic
elements in recruitment always opens the possibility for
functionally diffuse elements in the subsequent relationship. If members are recruited on the basis of who they
are rather than what they can do that is germane to the
purposes for which they are chosen, the possibility is
always open that the best abilities for the purposes of
the organizations will not be selected and quite other
abilities and interests will have to be catered to or at
least tolerated. This accordingly minimizes the degree to
which the relationship can be functionally specific since
it introduces automatically undefined possibilities via
the recruitment process itself. Similarly, if the substantive definition of a relationship is to a high degree
functionally diffuse, it becomes virtually impossible to
set up criteria such that universalistic selection is
possible. If functionally specific elements were completely lacking, it would be impossible to set up universalistic
criteria for selection. Thus, in a predominantly function-

ally diffuse relationship like that of husband and wife in
"traditional" China one also finds functionally specific
elements such as childbearing, housekeeping, sewing, etc.,
and it is in terms of these functionally specific elements
of the relationship that the universalistic criteria present in the selection of wives are set up.

Similar arguments for the relevance of particularism
and functional diffuseness for one another can be stated,
but they are to a high degree implicit in what has been
said above. Extensive elaboration of this subject should
rightly not confine itself merely to two aspects of relationship structures in any case[13] but should examine the
whole six for such relevant combinations. In any case the
following hypotheses may be suggested here: (1) in concrete structures for which universalistic elements are
eufunctional, functionally specific elements will be eufunctional too; (2) the correlation need not be perfect
and may vary in degree but the eufunctional or dysfunctional character of one or the other type of elements that
refer to membership criteria is never irrelevant to the
eufunctional or dysfunctional character of one or the other
type of substantive definition elements; (3) as the degree
of eufunctionality (or dysfunctionality) of universalistic
elements increases, the degree of eufunctionality (dysfunctionality) of functionally specific elements increases and
vice versa. This is true of the direction of increase if

13. For example, emphasis on rationality is very
likely to go along with emphasis on universalistic criteria
and functionally specific substantive definitions. This
is, to put it briefly, because selection on nongermane
grounds might introduce nonrational elements, and, in the
absence of rationality, functional specificity is hard to
maintain and vice versa. If such theories about clustering of these aspects of relationship patterns can be maintained, and if their relevance to a whole host of phenomena
such as that of industrialization can be developed, they
will prove extremely useful in and of themselves as well
as for the development of further theories.

not of the absolute amounts. Similarly, as the degree of
eufunctionality (or dysfunctionality) of functional diffuseness increases, the degree of dysfunctionality (or
eufunctionality) of universalistic elements is increased
and vice versa.[14] The practical implications of these
hypotheses are obvious enough. The presence of universalistic elements indicates the probability of functionally
specific elements and vice versa. The same sort of implication holds for particularism and functional diffuseness.
If in empirical situations this proves not to be the case,
the hypotheses presented here are to that extent disconfirmed, but explicit reexamination of them and their
derivation in light of the evidence should lead to new
hypotheses and more nearly valid hypotheses in these respects, and should thereby also serve the systematization
and development of research.

 The affective aspects. The general state of development of the concepts and knowledge of the affective aspects
of action in general make it exceedingly difficult to deal
with the implications of the affective aspects of relationships in production units. Depending upon the types of
production involved, however, there will be distinctions
among affective possibilities on the basis of their eufunctionality or dysfunctionality to the ends sought. Given
the general state of development of this area of analysis
it is not intended even to push hypothesis far on this
point. Researchers in social structure must certainly be
on the alert for the eufunctional or dysfunctional implications of the institutionalization of different types and
degrees of affect for the concrete structures concerned.

 Beyond the extremely general suggestion above, some
specific differentiation in terms of the avoidance and

---

14. It is not necessary to state all the possible
combinations of phrasing of this hypothesis. The two presented should be sufficient for illustrative purposes.

intimacy categories may be attempted relative to the distinction between highly industrialized and nonindustrial
production. As far as highly industrialized production is
concerned, the hypotheses may be phrased in the following
manner: the importance in general of affective elements is
the emphasis they place on the specific value of the personal relationship whatever that value may be. The eufunctionality (or dysfunctionality) of intimacy structures for
industrial production varies with the degree to which the
intimacy structures carry with them functionally diffuse
elements and the degree to which the functionally diffuse
elements are dysfunctional (or eufunctional) for the concrete structures concerned. For example, in a highly
industrialized plant it would almost certainly be highly
dysfunctional if it were institutionally expected that all
the workers be to a high degree intimate with one another
on the basis of extremely highly developed "friendship"
affects or "romantic love" affects or the like. The
affective interplay typical among close friends and lovers,
relative to one another and relative to those outside such
bonds, would make the type of cooperation necessary in
such a unit among individuals on universalistic grounds
out of the question. Avoidance affects would not carry
quite the same problems, but here again the interference
with functional specificity is the important question.
Avoidance structures that make impossible the rapidly made
and broken contacts of such workers, their interchange,
etc., would be highly dysfunctional in such a situation.
In a sense, the greater the degree of industrialization
the greater the emphasis on affective neutrality. Ideally
speaking, the affective structures must make the personal
contacts necessary for the work facile to form but not
carry them to the point at which affective considerations
can interfere with specific empirical aims of the organization.

The nonindustrial production units are even more

difficult to generalize about in these respects. There is
the obvious point that affects dysfunctional for the minimum production required cannot be institutionalized if the
society is to persist, but this, of course, holds for any
type of production unit. Other than that it is for the
present difficult to say more than that the affective
possibilities will vary with the character of the functionally diffuse elements so commonly institutionalized in
units of nonindustrial production. In contrast to the
industrial picture an emphasis on affective neutrality
would seem to be well-nigh out of the question.

The goal orientation aspects. The question of goal
orientations opens a wide variety of possibilities. With
regard to the aspects previously treated, the distinction
between industrial and nonindustrial production units
coincides with one side or the other of the aspects distinguished or at a point of neutrality. This is not true
of the distinction between individualistic and responsible
orientations. These concepts refer to the structuring of
"motivation," and possibilities in either direction are
present in either highly industrialized or nonindustrial
societies. Indeed, either type of society may conceivably
mix the two types of structuring of "motivation" in different fields of production. In a modern industrial society
such a mixture may be seen in the institutionalized distinctions between industry conducted on a private business
footing and the professions. In a nonindustrial society
such a distinction may be seen in the structures of an
individual dealing with a total stranger as opposed to
dealing with a person with whom he has an established relationship. In the one case, individualistic considerations rule; in the other, responsible ones do.

The essential factor to note here is that the industrial-nonindustrial distinction tells one nothing, on the
level of analysis applicable to any society of either type,
about the structured "motivation" in terms of the individ-

ualistic and responsible orientations. At the same time
the distinction is not irrelevant because the implications
of individualistic as opposed to responsible orientations
will vary considerably depending on whether or not the
system of production is highly industrialized. In the
case of highly industrialized production, the possibility
of dysfunctionality of individualistically structured
"motivation" lies in the extent to which it may permit
deviant action that might have extremely widespread effects
because of the interdependency of the system, economically
speaking. In the case of nonindustrial societies, the
possibility of dysfunctionality of individualistic goal
orientations is that they may lead to a disruption of the
membership units concerned. The effects on other units
need not be widespread if self-sufficiency is high, but
the membership units in terms of which production takes
place are often not predominantly economically oriented in
nonindustrial societies. The accompanying dislocation in
these noneconomic respects may, therefore, be very great
under such conditions.

Whatever the case may be for highly industrialized as
opposed to nonindustrial societies in these respects, the
question of goal orientation in the concrete structures in
terms of which production is carried out is of major
significance in seeking the interrelationships between the
economic aspects of social structure and other aspects.
This is especially true if the concrete structures in
terms of which production crucial for survival takes place
are different units than those in terms of which consumption takes place. The predominantly individualistic
orientation is most striking in these respects since persons who operate in such terms must be tied by other
orientations, or in terms of other units, to those who are
dependent upon their production for survival, if that
survival is not to be threatened. Such interrelationships
may be part of the predominantly responsible orientation

itself, particularly when the basic production units are
at one and the same time the basic consumption units of
the society.

It is questionable whether predominantly individualistic orientations can be combined in the production
sphere with units that simultaneously combine the basic
consumption and production of the society. Such units
would be to a high degree self-sufficient units like those
of the "traditional" Chinese family. In such cases individualistic orientation vis-à-vis strangers is quite possible, but responsible orientation vis-à-vis fellow unit
members is an absolute requirement, and most of one's
economic activities are with fellow unit members rather
than with strangers. In terms of this line of argument,
it may be suggested that the specialization and interdependence that go along with highly developed industrialization make possible, and necessary, the operation of
production units quite distinct from the consumption units
in terms of which individual physiological needs are met.
To this extent industrialization necessarily carries with
it a situation in which a high degree of emphasis on individualistic orientation is possible. It by no means
precludes an emphasis on the responsible orientation.
Nonindustrial societies may have both possibilities as
well, but unlike industrial societies the structural requisites for individualistically oriented members of production units are not necessarily present.

The stratification aspects. Beyond assertion of the
importance of ascertaining the nature of stratification in
production units, those aspects need not detain the treatment here at any length. Nonhierarchical arrangement of
some types of production units is by no means out of the
question. At the same time, a society with nothing but
nonhierarchically arranged production would also seem to
be out of the question. Two factors serve as inescapable
bases for hierarchies in this sphere. First, there is the

factor of differences in ability. The production sphere
is always concerned to some degree with empirical abilities. Differences in those abilities always make some
economic difference even in nonindustrial societies, and
such differences always exist. Second, there is the
managerial question, the problem of organizing production.
In the last analysis this always involves some hierarchical considerations in political terms even if those are
restricted to the control of deviant behavior among members of units ordinarily treated as equals.

Both factors must operate to some extent in all societies whether they be nonindustrial or highly industrialized. In nonindustrial societies, however primitive the
techniques of production, there are minimum differences
that must be recognized on the basis of abilities even if
that recognition is confined to the differences between
the experienced worker and the person just entering training. The nonindustrial society must also have the hierarchical factor of the political sort too in the economic
structure. Again, as a minimum it must, if it is to
survive, be able to put down deviance in production and to
avoid it in consumption too. At least to the author's
knowledge, there are no known societies in which stratification aspects of this sort are entirely lacking in the
economic structure.

At the same time, while some minimal requirements in
those respects exist for nonindustrial as well as highly
industrialized societies, the requirements in the latter
case are far more stringent. The emphasis on universalistic criteria of selection carries with it differential
ranking of individuals on the basis of skill. Job selection, promotions, etc., must be made on this basis. The
distinction between "skilled" and "unskilled" labor
achieves a general prominence and elaboration in highly
industrialized societies that is virtually unheard of in
nonindustrial societies. There develops in such societies

a hierarchy of types of occupations and a hierarchy of
individuals within a given type. The hierarchy may carry
with it a hierarchy of incomes, prestige, or whatever, but
it carries some such considerations, and their importance
is inescapable not only for an understanding of the economic aspects of action but for others as well.

The scale and interdependence of highly industrialized
production carry with them tremendously complicated managerial problems. Production is so complex that it must be
most carefully planned and directed. Power hierarchies in
the production structures cannot be confined merely to
punishing or preventing rare deviant behavior. In the
highly industrialized situation the average behavior would
be disruptive in lieu of planning and direction if only
because of the cognitive problems involved in every participant fully understanding the whole operation.

The types and degrees of hierarchies may vary widely.
The most notable distinction for general analysis is,
perhaps, that between hierarchies oriented primarily to
economic considerations and those oriented to other considerations. The concrete structures in terms of which
economic activities are carried out are by no means necessarily predominantly economically oriented structures, as
will be brought out below, and hence their hierarchies are
not necessarily so oriented. The emphasis on functional
specificity in highly industrialized societies requires
that the production unit at least of such a society, and
hence some at least of the consumption units, be predominantly economically oriented to a much higher degree than
is necessary in nonindustrial situations. The presence of
hierarchies that are not predominantly economically oriented in the economic structure, of course, opens up all
sorts of possible variations and problems. Most notably
from the economic point of view the precedence of noneconomic over economic considerations is raised. If the
hierarchies are predominantly economically oriented, how-

ever, the range of variation possible is to a corresponding
degree tightly tied to technological considerations of one
sort or another and will vary on that basis within the
range set by social structures defining the type of empirical operations possible in the economic sphere.

     c. <u>The type of product orientation of the units</u>.
The type of products of economic production have been
split up under three headings: raw materials, manufactured
goods, and allocation. It is not proposed to repeat that
discussion at this point. It is, however, necessary to
point out that considerable differences for economic structure may be reckoned in terms of the sort of products or
combinations of products with which the units of production concern themselves. Exploration of these possibilities would require a volume in and of itself. Even
exploration of the industrial-nonindustrial distinction
in this respect could not be short. Industrialization at
one and the same time makes possible extreme product differentiation and specialization and extreme combinations
of products.

     The significance of the type of product produced for
the type of unit producing it is likely to be greater for
functionally specific, predominantly economically oriented
units, but the considerations involved cannot be overlooked, however the system of production may be organized.
In examination of the economic structure of societies, the
type of product orientation, even when it is a secondary
or minor orientation, always tells the investigator something of significance for economic structure in particular
and social structure in general.

     d. <u>The analytic structural orientation of the units</u>.
There is a major and inescapable question, which has
already been alluded to above in passing on several occasions, involved in the analysis of the economic structure of any society. This is the question of whether or

not the concrete structures in terms of which production
is carried out are predominantly economically oriented or
not. It is by no means certain that any units in a society must be so oriented. It is only necessary, if a society
is to persist, that however the concrete structures be oriented, sufficient orientation to economic considerations
be present to guarantee survival.

Perhaps the main lead for analysis furnished by
pursuit of this distinction is the type and degree of
precedence, or lack of it, taken by economic considerations in the structure of the society. If the units in
terms of which production is carried out are not predominantly economically oriented, this will immediately
establish a secondary priority for economic considerations.
On the other hand, the implications of predominantly economically oriented production units are not equally clear.
Such units may themselves be subordinated to quite different considerations. In any case, careful pursuit of the
distinction furnishes insight into the role of economic
factors in the social structure.

In this connection a brief word on the relevance of
such considerations to the Marxist theory of economic
determinism is in order. Insofar as the theory maintains
that all other social variables are dependent variables of
the economic ones the picture given is clearly untenable.
One has only to look at the many examples of the precedence of other variables to see the flaw in this theory.
It is hard to conceive of any setting within which a
society is possible such that the minimal economic implications of that setting will permit of one and only one
set of social structures. Only if such a setting can be
shown to exist can a full-blown theory of economic determinism be maintained, and even then only on the basis
of the presumed continuance of a society in such a setting.
Furthermore, the discovery of such a setting would establish a theory of economic determinism only for that

particular case and not for the general case of any society, let alone the case of any social system.

On the other hand, the structure of economic allocation is an analytic structural requisite of any society,
and as such it cannot be left out of the picture either.
Part of the Marxist fallacy has lain in the confusion of
the analytic structure of economic allocation with the
concrete structures in terms of which economic allocation
is carried out. A single analytic structure in a system
cannot for obvious reasons be the single independent
variable in a system of analysis. It is always an interdependent factor. As soon as one sees the possibility and
the actual existence of societies in which the basic concrete structures in terms of which production is carried
out are not predominantly economically oriented, the whole
basis of any simple economic determinism falls to the
ground. In this case the theory fails on two grounds, the
one of theoretical impossibility and the other of empirical
contradictions to the theory.

The superficial basis for widespread plausibility of
the Marxist theory in these respects has lain in the widespread spectacle of social change and conquest, from at
least the second decade on, of the nineteenth century, by
societies that had highly developed systems of predominantly economically oriented concrete structures. For the
last century or more the world has seen a picture of the
invasion of a wide variety of societies by a group of societies possessing a more or less common economic structure
at least in the respects of rapidly increasing industrialization and a heavy emphasis on predominantly economically
oriented concrete structures of production. These societies have proved disruptive of all the societies they have
invaded either militarily or via export of their social
structures. Such a one-way picture of social conquest
could not fail to be impressive, and attention was focused
on the economic aspects not only by virtue of this fact

but also by virtue of the fact that societies originally
lacking these structures were quickly, once they had acquired the structures, shown to have some at least of the
same "advantages" as the original possessors of the structures. The tendency of this spectacle has been to obscure
the importance of other variables. The importance of the
other variables, however, comes to light at once if one
examines the differing rates at which these changes in
structures have taken place in different societies. The
contrast of China and Japan in these respects cannot fail
to be illuminating.

The possible variations in analytic structural orientations of the concrete structures in terms of which
economic production is carried out are certainly numerous.
The extent to which predominantly economically oriented
units of this sort form a special case in the general
history of the structure of societies cannot be overemphasized. Without extensive marshalling of empirical evidence
one may at least advance the hypothesis that, far from
being the general case with regard to societies, it is a
quite specific case. Furthermore, the extent to which
such units are predominantly economically oriented has
never been pushed so far as in the case of the modern industrial societies. Even in some of the modern industrial
societies, recent years have seen attempts, in the more
authoritarian societies, to make political factors the
predominant orientation in this sphere. In time of war,
with the increase in authoritarianism in ordinarily relatively nonauthoritarian societies, shifts in this direction seem to be fairly obvious.

In nonindustrial societies clear-cut cases of the
predominantly economic orientation of such units are
probably rare. There are some structural bases for this
hypothesis. The possibility of such units being institutionalized as predominantly functionally diffuse ones in
nonindustrial or relatively slightly industrial societies

is present at least in a degree out of all question in highly industrialized societies. In functionally diffuse units the clear emergence of a single predominant analytic orientation is out of the question by virtue of the very vagueness of the obligations covered by the substantive definition of the relationships involved. Under some circumstances economic considerations may be posed as the major issue, under others political or solidarity questions may occupy such a position, and so forth. The "traditional" Chinese peasant family unit is an excellent case in point. In that society the peasant family unit is, at least in the overwhelming majority of cases, the unit in terms of which both production and consumption are carried out. No understanding of the structure of that society is possible if one ignores the economic aspects of those units, but understanding is equally impossible if one assumes that the allocation of goods and services is the primary concern of such units. Solidarity considerations, role differentiation considerations, and others often take precedence over economic considerations. In fact, economic considerations take clear precedence, as it were, only when the ordinary formulations of other considerations threaten the entire future of the unit because of their economic implications. The precedence of the aged, for example, is disallowed only under such extreme conditions, and sometimes not even then, in which cases family ruin may be the result.

Furthermore, in nonindustrial or relatively little industrialized societies the possibility is present of highly self-sufficient units that not only are self-sufficient in production but also in the sense that they produce what they need for virtually all consumption purposes and consume virtually all that they produce. For reasons already discussed above this is out of the question in highly industrialized societies. Under these conditions other problems are placed in the way of a predominantly

economic orientation of these units. There are several
reasons for this. In the first place, the purely economic
issues involved in consumption by no means coincide with
those of production. More basically, however, the implications of consumption touch all of the other functional
requisites of a society more directly than do those of
production since production touches some of these only by
virtue of its provision of the materials for consumption.
Predominantly economic orientation of these units would
not only threaten the performance of these functions, it
would also be out of the question, if societies are to
persist, by virtue of the fact that, whatever they may be,
the criteria for consumption can never be purely economic
ones or even predominantly economic ones since evaluations
other than those solely in terms of goods and services
must be involved. Here again, a contradiction to the
simple theory of economic determinism is involved. Production units may be set up on a predominantly economically oriented basis if they are not to consume a major
portion of their own products, but even in this case the
criteria of consumption to which production is oriented
cannot be understood solely in economic terms.

B. THE STRUCTURE OF CONSUMPTION

Much of what has been said above of the structure of
production is relevant to the structure of consumption in
fashions too obvious to require elaboration here. Treatment of the structure of consumption, apart from introductory remarks, will be divided into two parts with relevant factors already treated above mentioned under those
headings when necessary. Those divisions will be based on
a distinction between concrete units that combine production and consumption, and those that separate them. Obviously, there is a sense in which all units performing
economic functions combine production and consumption.
Effort and materials are always consumed in production, and

in the consumption of efforts and materials the basis, at
least, for other efforts and materials is always produced.
The distinction intended here is that between units that
consume all or major proportions of their economic production and those that dispose of all or a major proportion
of their production and whose members are supplied with
consumption materials from other sources. The distinction
may be put another way. The concrete structures here
spoken of as combining production and consumption are
those whose members are institutionally expected to carry
out their consumption of goods and services largely in
terms of the units in which it is produced. The concrete
structures here spoken of as separating these aspects of
action are those in which it is institutionally expected
that the consumption of their members takes place largely
in terms of different concrete structures than those in
terms of which production is carried out. In both cases
differences in degree are possible, of course, and some
vagueness is lent the distinction by the use of the adverb
"largely." For the present, at least, it would seem best
to leave the distinction as one between relative institutional emphasis on self-sufficiency of units in all economic aspects and institutional emphasis on the interdependency of concrete structures in these respects,
recognizing that in no society is complete economic
self-sufficiency of all units possible. From the attempt
to apply the concepts suggested here to actual empirical
studies of different societies, hints at least in the
direction of useful and precise operational distinctions
of this sort should emerge more profitably than via their
treatment on the present level of abstraction.

1. General considerations of the structure of consumption

        It is via the structure of consumption that the rele-
vance of economic factors to the performance of the func-

tional requisites of a society is directly shown, for the performance of any of the functional requisites involves the dissipation of some goods and services. Here, one has a correspondence to the division of labor in production. Who consumes what and when poses the question of role differentiation on the basis of consumption. This would be a matter of vital concern in the analysis of social structure if it had no other implications than to reveal how the results of the production processes were disposed of. But it has others since to some degree there must be some basis of consumption for any other role differentiations.

In questions of role differentiation on the basis of consumption the type of goods and services consumed are not irrelevant, but the distinctions drawn in these respects relative to production are less relevant than other distinctions here. It matters whether or not the factors consumed are raw materials, manufactured goods, or allocation services, and whether or not they are produced under industrial or nonindustrial conditions, but more revealing is the manner in which the consumption implements other structures in the society. How, for example, does command over consumption implement the allocation of power and responsibility? How much and what sorts of consumption are allocated to what sorts of educational activities? The distinctions among what is produced have direct implications for how it may be produced because of the empirical nature of the processes involved. The same factors cannot be overlooked in studying the structure of consumption, but because of the type of values involved in allocation and the possibility of, say, industrially and nonindustrially produced goods serving the same consumption purposes, the purposes institutionalized become a more directly relevant part of the analysis.

There are three factors that must be considered in the analysis of any units in terms of which consumption is

carried out. First, there is the question of the source
and type of income of the unit. Second, there is the
question of how and by whom the distribution of the income
is controlled. Does it, for example, go into a common
fund or is it individually held by some or all of the
members? Is distribution controlled by all members, by a
single head, or by a selected group of members? Third,
there is the question of to whom and for what purposes it
is allocated. These questions enter any consideration of
the structure of consumption, and many of the factors
already discussed in other chapters restrict the range of
possible variations in these respects. The helplessness
of infants and role differentiation on this basis at one
and the same time precludes their service as managers and
requires that the roles of others be so differentiated as
to preserve the interests of infants. If power in a society is primarily allocated to individuals on the basis
of sex, this must be reflected in the consumption roles of
the society because of the relevance of consumption to the
allocation of power. It is beyond the scope of the present analysis to attempt to elaborate, except for purposes
of example, even the material presented here for lower
levels of generalization of the study of social structure.
The three questions raised above are raised in the belief
that in the attempt to answer these questions the answers
to those relevant in these respects on lower levels of
generalization will emerge.

Discussion of the general relevance of the distinction between self-sufficient units of consumption and
non-self-sufficient ones will be reserved for the following section of this treatment of consumption, but something must be said here of the relationship aspects of
these units. Here, the possibilities are quite different
from those present with regard to production.

It is conceivable that the processes of production be
largely or even entirely carried out in terms of inter-

mediate rather than ultimate ends and hence production
considerations can at least immediately be phrased in
terms of empirical goals. This is by no means true under
any and all circumstances, and the possibility is modified
by the type and degree of combination of production and
consumption units. The case is different for consumption,
however, if only for the reason that action oriented to
ultimate ends must also have a direct basis in consumption.
Production may take place entirely in empirical terms and
within an empirically defined framework, and nonempirical
factors may enter at a further remove in the means-end
chain. This can not be true to the same degree of consumption because in some instances the framework of ends
must be directly nonempirical. This limits markedly the
possibilities of the institutionalization of rational
cognitive criteria in consumption relationships by comparison with those of production. It is, of course, by no
means true that the institutionalization of arational
factors in consumption relationships will, in fact, always
receive greater institutional emphasis than in the case of
production relationships. It does mean that this may be
the case in some societies, and, perhaps, must be the case
in societies in which heavy institutional emphasis is
placed on rationality in the sphere of production. In the
highly industrialized societies in which rationality in
the sphere of both production and consumption is strongly
emphasized, arationality in the latter sphere is notorious-
ly more obvious and institutionally more acceptable to the
members of such societies. There is little reason to
doubt the teachings of common sense in this particular
respect. Furthermore, the arationality of consumption as
opposed to production in such societies has posed major
theoretical problems for the development of economics as a
science, and some at least of the irrationality especially,
and probably the arationality as well, that does appear in
the production sphere may be attributed to the cognitive

problems involved in making rational production decisions
oriented to distribution of goods and services for consumption in which irrational and arational actions play
such a prominent part.

In the case of production the necessity of some minimal emphasis on rational action has been pointed out. In
the case of consumption this is no less true. Some types
of production must take place to furnish the minimal consumption basis necessary for survival. Similarly, some
types of consumption must take place if that process of
survival is to be completed. The members of the society
must eat food after it has been produced. It is, perhaps,
conceivable theoretically in the case of both production
and consumption that the minimal requirements in these
respects might be carried out entirely on nonrational
grounds, that is to say, that institutionalized nonrational action would have sufficient latent (and/or UIR) functions of a type that would guarantee the minimal empirical
state of affairs necessary for survival. The theoretical
possibility, however, need not detain the student. It may
be as confidently suggested as a hypothesis that there is
no society entirely lacking institutionalized rational
elements in the sphere of consumption as the same hypothesis may be suggested relative to production. To some
degree and in some respects the relevance of workmanship
for output is always recognized. To some degree and in
some respects the relevance of empirical consumption to
survival is also always recognized.

With regard to the distinction between universalistic
and particularistic criteria for memberships in the concrete structures in terms of which consumption is carried
out, there is again a difference in the range of possible
variation open to production and consumption units. Except in those cases in which consumption is directly and
immediately oriented to production, universalistic criteria of membership in consumption units cannot play so

prominent a role as is open to them in the case of production units. Within rather wide limits differences in the ability to consume make little difference in terms of the purposes toward which much consumption is oriented. Furthermore, some of the consumption units must be predominantly functionally diffuse, and the difficulty of institutionalizing universalistic criteria under these circumstances has been pointed out above.[15]

Whatever may be said of this question on the general theoretical level attacked here, the case on more specific levels is still relatively clear. In no known society do predominantly particularistic criteria fail to figure as crucial institutions and as highly strategic ones in the consumption sphere. This is true even in highly industrialized societies in which the importance of predominantly universalistic criteria is institutionalized to a high degree in the production sphere. Much of the consumption of the members of predominantly universalistic production units is carried out in units particularistically recruited. The consumption in terms of family units is an obvious case in point.

This distinction must be kept in mind for purposes of research. It is at least a suggestive hypothesis that the lesser amenability of consumption units to predominantly universalistic recruitment may be an important factor in one phenomenon that has marked the progressive industrialization of every society that has undergone such a process. This phenomenon is the increasing distinction and separation of the concrete structures in terms of which production and consumption are carried out. In many nonindustrial or relatively slightly industrialized societies the activities involved in production and consumption are carried out to a very high degree in terms of a single

---

15. See above, pp. 434-437.

unit. In many such societies the unit of both production
and consumption is the family unit. Under these conditions the family unit may not, in some cases, consume what
it produces. It may, for example, give or "sell" its production to another family unit and buy or receive as a
gift what it consumes. Nevertheless, the members who
produce together consume together. This cannot be true of
all the units in the society, but it may be true to a very
high degree. This cannot be and is not similarly true of
highly industrialized societies in which the members of
the units of production consume in terms of quite different units.

Similar distinctions in possible variation arise for
similar reasons with respect to the substantive definition
aspects of relationships in the production and consumption
spheres. The intrusion of functionally diffuse elements
into the realm of consumption under all forms of societies
is inevitable. In the case of the highly industrialized
societies the elimination of functionally diffuse elements
from the units of consumption is never carried to the
lengths true of the units of production. In nonindustrial
societies consumption units are no less marked by functional diffuseness on the whole than are production units
when the two are separated. In highly industrialized
societies the consumption units are a great deal more so
marked than are production units. This factor is also
involved in the separation of such units that marks industrial societies.

In terms of the affective aspects, the goal orientation aspects, and the stratification aspects of consumption units similar implications for consumption units as
differentiated from production units may be traced out.
Consumption units under industrialized conditions are open
to wider possibilities of both intimacy and avoidance than
are production units, for example, and so forth. The
importance of these distinctions for isolated or compara-

tive analyses cannot be stressed too strongly, particularly in cases in which industrial elements are involved
since these elements seem to carry with them such far-reaching implications in these respects. They have their implications, for example, for extremely concrete and practical
problems. The numerous attempts to set up "company towns"
or company sponsored living quarters for workers in the
United States, for example, involve a combination or interrelationship of production and consumption units of a sort
quite distinct from those that have on the whole developed.
Even when such projects have offered substantial material
advantages to the members of the consumption units involved, they have frequently entered upon a "sea of trou-
bles" in the area of human relations. Some of the differences and distinctions touched on here may be found to
play important roles in such "problems."

2. Concrete structural distinctions

a. <u>Concrete structural units institutionally combining the consumption and production of the membership</u>. As
has been pointed out above, production and consumption are
in some respects always simultaneous. As one produces
goods and services, consumption of other goods and services
takes place; as one consumes goods and services production
of other goods and services, if only in the form of energy,
takes place. Apart from this inescapable combination of
the two activities, there is another type of combination
possible but not inevitable. This is the institutional
provision that consumption and production activities that
are capable of separation from one another be combined in
the same concrete structures. Thus, one cannot avoid the
consumption of ore in the production of steel or the production of energy potentials in the eating of food, but
the steel worker need not consume his food in terms of the
same concrete structure in terms of which he contributes

to the production of steel.

Concrete structures that combine for their membership production and consumption activities that are capable of separation open up the possibility of high degrees of economic self-sufficiency for the units concerned. A Chinese family unit that produces virtually all that it consumes and consumes virtually all that it produces is highly self-sufficient in both the production and consumption senses. This type of self-sufficiency is important for the purposes of social analysis because it has far-reaching implications for the type of social stability that is present and for the sources of social change and disruption to which the system is most vulnerable. Suggestions of this sort have already been pointed out above in the treatment of self-sufficiency in relation to concrete structures in terms of which production is carried out.[16] The implications of these suggestions for the present section are sufficiently obvious to make further elaboration of them here redundant.

A word of caution is necessary nonetheless. It has already been pointed out that this type of self-sufficiency cannot exist for all the concrete structures of society if only because some units must exist to interrelate such economically self-sufficient structures. There is, however, another possibility of variation. A combination of production and consumption spheres such as that envisaged here may take place while self-sufficiency of the units remains relatively low. Two examples of such possibilities may be cited. In the first place, there is at least one known case of a society (Trobriand society)[17] in which production and consumption are both carried out in terms of family units, but the production in substantial part of

---

16.   See pp. 412-421.

17.   See B. Malinowski, <u>Coral Gardens and their Magic</u>, American Book Co., New York, 1935, 2 vols.

one family unit is given to another family unit related to
the first one by kinship ties, and the production of still
a third family unit similarly related to the first is
given to the first unit. Another example of interdependency of units that combine both spheres is furnished by
craft production of the sort so prominent under the guild
system in preindustrial Europe or by "household industry"
in Europe. Such production was frequently carried out in
family terms, the working unit consisting of family members or of family members plus one or two outsiders
virtually assimilated to family membership, at least
temporarily. The family in this sense was also the unit
in terms of which the consumption of the members was carried out. Between production and consumption, however,
the goods and services produced were in substantial part
disposed of and exchanged directly or indirectly through
more or less complex media of exchange for the goods and
services that were consumed. In all such cases interdependency is introduced. It should be obvious from the
examples given that the type and implications of interdependency under these conditions may vary widely. For
example, in the first case cited a breakdown of the interdependency would force a reformulation of the interrelationships among family units, but it would not necessitate
far-reaching changes in the type of production carried out
by any particular family. In the second case, not only
the interrelationships among concrete structures would
have to change, but a reformulation of economic structure
internal to the concrete structures would also have to
take place. They would, for example, have to turn more
attention to direct production of food and other goods and
services formerly provided for by exchange of their own
special products.

    The brief preceding discussion of the implications of
consumption for the relationship aspects of the concrete
structures in terms of which it takes place and the longer

discussions above of these matters in relation to production should make it quite obvious that the combination of production and consumption spheres always has some implications understandable in these respects -- at least with regard to the range of variation possible within a given type of concrete structure. It is not necessary to reiterate that material here beyond emphasizing that data gathered from either of these points of view has implications for the other. If those implications are mutually inconsistent, the hypotheses advanced here or the data gathered or some combination of the two is faulty.

Before leaving the question of concrete structures combining production and consumption by the membership, the implication for the possibility of predominantly economically oriented concrete structures must be examined. Under the conditions involved here any such clear-cut predominance is virtually out of the question. The standards in terms of which consumption is allocated can never be purely economic ones to the same extent possible in the sphere of production if only because of the greater possibilities of confining the production sphere to the intermediate means-ends scheme. In such combinations the production sphere may be economically oriented to a high degree. Certainly a higher degree then is possible than is possible for the consumption sphere. But its combination in a single unit with the consumption sphere limits the variations of the production sphere itself by considerations of the general structure of the unit. In separate concrete structures of production and consumption it is easier to change the general structure of the unit of production in response to the needs of production. If one looks at empirical instances of the combination of such spheres as opposed to their separation in terms of concrete structures, one is struck at once by the quite different degree of emphasis on goods and services in and of themselves that is possible in separated production units.

The different possibilities for the institutionalization of universalistic and particularistic criteria in the two spheres should furnish some confirmation of this point.

b. Separate concrete structures of production and consumption. When the membership of concrete structures are institutionally expected to carry out the major portion of their production in units different from those in terms of which they carry out consumption, interdependency is an obvious and necessary concomitant feature. It is not necessary or even possible that these consumption oriented units involve no production. The family units in modern industrial societies are units of this sort. The major income of these family units comes from the income earned by production of the father or husband outside the family structure in the ordinary case. The production of other family members may be carried on in family terms as is the case with housekeeping and the like. Under these circumstances, though separated, the activities in the production sphere are crucially or at least more or less strategically relevant to the activities in the consumption sphere. It is in terms of the experience of social history no mean feat of highly industrialized societies that a sphere of action so important for family concerns and the concerns of other concrete structures in terms of which consumption is carried out has been so effectively and thoroughly insulated from family influences. In terms of the general features of a wide variety of societies it is not astonishing that so much nepotism and the like exists in modern industrial societies. It is astonishing that so little of it exists and that nepotism in the sphere of production could ever be institutionalized as an evil at all.

The interdependency inherent in the separation of the consumption and production units of individuals in major respects carries with it a corresponding emphasis on media

of exchange.[18] If the members of production units consume
in quite different units and characteristically consume
directly little of what they produce, there must exist
some method whereby other productive efforts may be translated into the means of consumption. In situations of
little product differentiation and relatively slight
specialization barter systems may operate effectively.
There may be direct exchange of goods and services for
others. When interdependency is high and products are
highly specialized and differentiated as is the case in
highly industrial societies, there must be highly generalized media of exchange. In the economic sphere discussed here a medium of exchange will be considered more
or less generalized to the degree that it can be used in
the exchange of goods and services in a given society.
For example, if there are two societies with monetary systems and if the goods and services that can be acquired or
transferred by the use of money are identical in both societies save for the fact that in one of them land cannot
be exchanged via the medium of money, while in the other
money can be used for these purposes, then, in the former,
money is a less generalized medium of exchange than in the
latter. Differences in generalization of media of exchange are extremely important for social structure. One
need not be an economic determinist to appreciate fully
the amount of social insight that may be acquired simply
by learning what may be exchanged for what and how in a
given society.

The highly industrialized society requires a highly
generalized medium of exchange for reasons sufficiently
obvious from what has been said before in this chapter.
It also requires that, however many different media of

---

18. There must also be an emphasis on media of exchange to the degree that the units, though combined, lack
self-sufficiency.

exchange exist, one exceed the other in generality at
least in the sense that there be one medium in terms of
which the others may be translated. Multiplication of
media of exchange may add flexibility under some circumstances, but it may restrict it too, especially if lack of
convertibility of a medium in one sphere in effect limits
the possibilities of the development of interdependency
between that sphere and others. The highly industrial
case is, of course, merely used to illustrate the more
general case of separation of production and consumption
units, because it carries that separation to such extreme
degrees.

The separation of consumption units from production
units in major respects makes the institutionalized sources
of income for the consumption unit an especially strategic
question for analysis since it singles out individuals for
production roles in a context different from their consumption roles. When this is coupled with the more generalized media of exchange generally present under such
conditions, special problems of maintaining allegiances to
specific consumption units are created by the greater
economic basis for personal independence present. One of
the major sources of social control in "traditional" China
was the high degree of inability of a rebellious family
member to cut himself off from his family and still acquire
an acceptable basis for consumption. The possibility of
employment alternative to family employment and on a relatively nonparticularistic basis has been opened there by
the relatively slight industrialization present, and its
effects on the old methods of social control have been
far-reaching. In the United States, on the other hand,
the separation of these units has been carried so far that
it is surprising that consumption units such as the family
hold together as well as they do. Under such conditions,
return to large scale highly complex family units is difficult, if not impossible, for several reasons, but one such

reason is certainly the ease with which a dissatisfied
individual in such a unit can leave it and still fulfill
his consumption goals.

Preoccupation with this separation may, however, lead
the observer astray. Such separation is never complete.
It is, perhaps, carried as far in the American family
structure as in any major concrete structure in any society. The source of income of these family units is primarily the amount of generalized medium of exchange (viz.,
money) acquired by the husband in his occupational role(s)
outside the family. The amount of production involved in
cooking, "housework," child care, etc., that takes place
in the family context is not negligible save, perhaps, in
the highest income groups. Even in the latter the managerial function in the family unit is performed to some
degree on a family basis. The importance of these combinations of production and consumption tends to escape one
because consumption of these goods and services is to such
a high degree simultaneous with their production and
because the material basis for the production involved
is to such a high degree furnished by the individual(s)
with the nonfamily occupational roles. Even when the
separation is great, therefore, one must seek out the production aspects of such consumption units.

It is not necessary here to take up in detail the
implications of the separation for the relationship aspects of the units. It is hoped that these are reasonably
clear from what has been said before in this chapter on
the relationship aspects of concrete structures viewed
from the economic standpoint. It need only be reiterated
that, when the separation exists, it is by no means true
that the consumption units must or can institutionalize
the same structures in these respects as the production
units. There is one general consideration involved, however, that should be noted. When the separation exists
and when the relationship aspects are differently institu-

tionalized in the two types of units, institutionalization must be rather delicately worked out if stability is to result. The institutionalization of these aspects in the one sphere must be such as to interfere relatively little with their different institutionalization in the other. This is especially true when training relevant in one sphere takes place in the other. Family membership is, of course, particularistically defined in the families of a highly industrialized society like the United States (as it is in all societies), and membership in the major units of production is dependent upon predominantly universalistic criteria, institutionally speaking. One is expected in the United States to love one's children because they are one's children. It is not a matter of chance, however, that the degree and kind of affection given to children is, to the high degree noted by anthropologists, psychiatrists, and others, based on competitively viewed and comparatively judged performances. Whatever sources of insecurity and future personality problems may inhere in such family practices, it is questionable whether fewer problems would be raised if the individual were totally unprepared by such treatment for the treatment on predominantly universalistic and functionally specific grounds he inevitably receives as an adult in that society.

In concluding this chapter two points must be raised. The first has to do with one limitation of the treatment here, the second with some of the implications of the approach used here for interdisciplinary cooperation with the conventionally distinguished field of economics. As regards the former, the usual cautions relative to other portions of this work will hold, but one of these needs special emphasis. Even on the level of generality attempted here by no means all of the relevant problems have been explicitly attacked. The congeries of problems centering around the concept of "property" fall into this

category. All that is hoped for the present treatment is
that investigation of a specific society in the terms
suggested here will bring to light material on those problems not explicitly treated here because of the inescapable
implications of the former for the latter. The raising of
these questions in different specific empirical contexts
should give one continually developing insight into uniformities that must be given consideration on the level
attempted here.

With regard to the interdisciplinary implications of
this treatment the considerations may be stated briefly
and simply. The theoretical structure of economics has
been based upon the consideration of the implications of
rational action within a specific set of social structures.
Theoretical development in the field of economics takes
place largely in terms of more detailed and more tenable,
logical, or mathematical development of the implications
of rational action within such a context and by variation
of the assumptions relative to that context. It is to the
latter source of development that these remarks are directed. One need not elaborate on the fact that those
assumptions in the literature of economics have often been
implicit and imprecise rather than explicit and precise,
and often quite out of conformity with the empirical state
of affairs to which the results were applied. The consideration of interest here is that changes in those assumptions have come either from arbitrarily chosen alternatives
to the prevailing ones or correction of them via empirical
research. The source of interdisciplinary cooperation
seen here bears on the process by suggesting a systematic
empirically relevant basis for developing economic theory
via variation of these assumptions, on the one hand, and,
on the other, via the use of the solutions to allocative
problems so obtained to set limits of possible variation
for other social structures.

Further development of the work attempted here should

make possible the development not only of the economic
structural requisites of any society but also of less general types of societies and of specific societies. The
range of possible variation in these respects within any
specific context should be capable of discovery. The
development of economic theory could then address itself
systematically to the exploration of the implications of
rational action oriented to the allocation of goods and
services within the different contexts of different structural requisites or different possible structural variations. Empirical difficulties in applying the theoretical
results of developments in terms of one such set of assumptions to a context in which they do not apply could thereby be systematically minimized.

On the other side, the discovery by means of developments in economic theory of the implications of such varied
contexts for economic allocation should, by virtue of the
implications of such allocation for the range of variation
of general social structures, make possible an increasing
degree of precision in the statement of the range of possible variation of those structures within any specific
context. Repetition of the process could then take place
indefinitely with gains for the development of both economics and the other social studies. Some such interdisciplinary cooperation must take place if economics,
which is at present the most highly developed theoretically of the social sciences, is to have systematic relevance
beyond a highly restricted social context of which the
limitations and exact nature are only dimly appreciated.

C H A P T E R   X

THE STRUCTURE OF POLITICAL ALLOCATION

Political allocation for the purposes of this study
has been defined above as the distribution of power over
and responsibility for the actions of the various members
of the concrete structure concerned, involving, on the one
hand, coercive sanctions, of which force is the extreme
form in one direction, and, on the other, accountability
to the members and in terms of the structure concerned, or
to the members of other concrete structures. The term
power has been defined above as the ability to exercise
authority and control over the actions of others. Responsibility has been defined as the accountability of an
individual(s) to another individual(s) or group(s) for his
own acts and/or the acts of others.

The functional requisite basis for the structural
requisite of political allocation is not difficult to
find. In the first place, there is the functional necessity of the control of disruptive forms of behavior. The
use of force for the acquisition of ends is extremely
efficient if the objectives be sufficiently limited. As
has been pointed out long ago by E. Goldhamer and E. A.
Shils, force can not be relied upon exclusively in broad
contexts. They have observed pointedly that:

> Large amounts of power cannot be exercised
> in a purely coercive fashion, for even though
> the mass of subordinated individuals do not rec-
> ognize the power holder as exercising legitimate
> power, the necessity of utilizing a large staff
> would introduce other than purely coercive power

into the total power system; for the subordinate
power-holders, who exercise dependent power and
carry out sanctions for cases of non-conformity
among the mass cannot themselves be controlled
by coercion alone.[1]

Despite the limits on the effective use of force, its
effectiveness for limited purposes is such that disruptive
behavior involving force must be curbed if the society is
to be stable or to survive. The importance of power allocations to control such outbursts as this is obvious
enough, but power allocation is no less important in the
curbing of disruptive behavior that takes other forms. If
there is to be stability, the power to curb disruptive
apathetic behavior is no less important than power to curb
the "illegitimate"[2] use of force. Between these two poles
lie unending possibilities of variations in disruptive behavior that must come under institutionalized control, if
the concrete structure concerned is not to change in the
respects in which it is defined or not to be totally dis-
rupted.

This control must be institutionalized too. Again,
the limited effectiveness of purely coercive sanctions is
germane. The question of _quis custodiet ipsos custodes_
posed by Goldhamer and Shils in the article quoted above
is always germane to power systems. Both legitimate
expectations of conformity with structures of power

---

1. See "Types of Power and Status," _Am. Jour. of
Soc._, Vol. XLV, No. 2 (Sept. 1939), pp. 171-183.

2. The terms _legitimate_ and _illegitimate_ with regard
to power and responsibility refer to the factor of institutionalization or its absence. _Legitimate_ means institutionalized; _illegitimate_ means noninstitutionalized. "Murder" as that term is generally used in the legal sense is
a noninstitutionalized killing of an individual(s) and is
illegitimate insofar as this is the case. A legal execution of a convicted kidnapper is a _legitimate_ killing in
this sense. It is in this sense that the state or nation
is often defined as having in the last analysis the monopo-
ly of the _legitimate_ use of force relative to its members.

wielding and reactions to failures in these respects must
be present to insure the stability of social systems from
this point of view. The institutionalization must cover
not only the application of power, it must also define the
contexts in which it is to be used. The functional requisite of adequate institutionalization itself requires
this. The circumstances under which power is applied and
responsibility required cannot be left socially random,
for this would not only leave the road of calculated disruptive behavior open but would also leave all other forms
of disruptive behavior open and introduce another disruptive element in the failure to exercise restraint in some
form.

The importance of elements of power and responsibility in these respects crops up in other functional requisites as well. The regulation of the choice of means and
of affective expression are cases in point. Here again,
the relevant consideration is the disruptive possibilities
opened up by failures to institutionalize structures of
political allocation. There is, however, another general
order of consideration. There is the inescapable problem
of control of those members of the society who lack the
maturity and knowledge necessary if they are to be held
effectively responsible by the members of the society.
Retarded and handicapped individuals of all sorts furnish
examples of this sort, but a far more important group in
any society is that formed by new members of the structure,
especially, of course, those introduced to the society by
birth. These individuals are always present to some degree in societies as defined here. The future existence
of the society hangs on their training in action in terms
of the structures of society. Some controls over them are
necessary if that is to be accomplished. A certain amount
of control is necessary to prevent their destruction
either from lack of comprehension of danger or inability
to cope with it. In other respects control is necessary

to insure that they receive the training necessary if the
society is to be perpetuated. This consideration involves
control not only of the infants and children themselves
but to some extent also of the adults who carry out these
operations in relation to them.

Finally, there is the general question of coordination and direction of effort. The facts of role differentiation imply also the facts of role coordination.
There are many different conditions that must be fulfilled
if a society is to survive. Not all individuals can be
completely self-sufficient in the performance of these
functional requirements. There must be some form of direction or management of the concrete unit in terms of
which this coordination is carried out. In some societies
and in some types of units the cognitive problems involved
require specific role allocations of direction and planning. Even when this is not the case, however, the
impossibility of preserving adequate operation of the
units in the absence of some elements of power and responsibility is always relevant.

In the case of the structure of political allocation
three questions must always be examined. In the first
place, there is the question of locus of power and responsibility. Who possesses the power and/or responsibility,
or how are power and responsibility allocated? Some aspects of this question have already been discussed above
in the chapter on role differentiation. In the second
place, there is the question of definition of political
allocation. What range of action is covered by power
and/or responsibility? Over what is power wielded? Relative to what is responsibility exacted? In the third
place, there is the question of procedure. How are the
applications of power and/or responsibility carried out?

The question of the locus of power and responsibility
is always a matter of the first importance in the examination of the sources of order and change in a society, i.e.,

of the problem of stability. It has been suggested above
that a generalization of an extremely high order may be
made in these terms: any concrete structure in which the
locus of power is not balanced by the locus of responsibility has inherent sources of instability. These sources
are of two sorts. First, individuals or groups who possess power without responsibility for their exercise of
that power always raise the possibility of power applications that are capricious from the point of view of the
structure concerned. They may be capricious in the sense
that they need not or do not coincide with the institutionalized power structures of the structure.[3] If they
are capricious in this sense, they need not be disruptive,
but to the extent that they are capricious, they may be
disruptive; and that is sufficient to establish a source
of instability in the structure concerned. The problem of
balancing power with responsibility is always posed in an
especially difficult and obvious form by highly autocratic
and authoritarian systems. Enforcement of responsibility
on such power holders limits the scope of their power to
some extent. The failure to do so opens the possibility
that the actions of the power holders may destroy the social structure in general and the very basis of their own
power as well. The figures, Nero and Caligula, are classic examples of this sort, although modern history has
already furnished equally clear-cut examples and seems to
promise others.

Second, responsibility that is unaccompanied by power
is no less a source of instability because of the impossibility of the effective execution of responsibility in the
face of opposition under those circumstances. If an

---

3. The sources of instability in a concrete structure with no institutionalized power structures are too
obvious to require comment here.

individual is responsible for a particular performance on
his own part or on that of others but lacks the power
necessary to ensure such performance, his responsibility,
whatever its other implications, cannot ensure that performance. Insofar as the performance involved is crucial
or more or less strategic for the structure concerned such
an imbalance opens the road to instability. No matter how
the individual concerned may be disciplined for the failure possible under these circumstances, the enforcement of
his responsibility will not accomplish the performances
sought. Insofar as failure of that performance is germane
to the stability of the structure, elements of instability
inhere in the structure. It is completely ineffective,
for example, to hold an individual responsible for housing
others if he is given no powers of requisitioning shelters
or materials for shelters or the power required to get the
objects of the housing to use it when provided.

The generalizations suggested above are not recondite
nor are they unknown. Any administrator of any experience
is fully aware of both sources of difficulty. The capricious application of power in the absence of responsibility
and the bootlessness of responsibility in the absence of
power is part of the lore and wisdom of men of all ages.
The extent to which an authentic pedigree of these generalizations can be traced in written and oral records and
testimony is almost certainly limited only by the extent
of the records and testimony themselves. The systematic
use and development of these generalizations for the
scientific analysis of social phenomena has not, however,
been forthcoming, but it cannot be avoided as an element
in the scientific analysis of society. The analysis of
order and change is always germane to social phenomena in
some sense, and the balance of loci of power and responsibility is always in some respects relevant to the problems of order and change in social phenomena.

There are two highly general types of balance of the
loci of power and responsibility. The first is of a
nonhierarchical sort, and the second is of a hierarchical
sort. The nonhierarchical balance of power and responsibility involves the same balance from the point of view of
all the parties to the relationship. This is the situation of mutually equal powers and responsibilities already
discussed in Chapter VI in relation to the hierarchical
aspects of relationships. Here, the focus of attention is,
however, exclusively on power and responsibility factors.
Friendship, as that relationship is frequently institutionalized, is a case in point. In modern western societies, for example, two friends are expected to have equal
powers over one another, and equal responsibilities to one
another to the degree that similarity of their circumstances and their degrees of friendship permit. To the
extent that these circumstances and degrees of friendship
are equal, the powers and responsibilities involved in the
relationship are equal. Furthermore, in such a relationship the responsibilities and powers are mutually owed and
held. The two friends are responsible to one another for
their acts relevant to one another, and have powers allocated and defined in a similar fashion. The relevance of
what they do in their roles as mutual friends will no
doubt have relevance for their roles in other relationships and hence power and responsibility ramifications
there too, but as far as the friendship unit is concerned
the relationship is institutionalized as a mutual one in
these respects.

But the nonhierarchical political structure can never
be the sole type of political structure in any society.
In fact, some crucial institutions and some more or less
strategic ones must institutionalize hierarchical political structures. The nonhierarchical structure represents
a balance of power such that the relationship may be
dissolved by either party. Only the desire by all the

parties to such a relationship to preserve the status quo
can keep such political systems in operation. If that
mutual desire, however "motivated," breaks down from one
side or all sides, the political picture changes radically.
Obviously, such a system is not well adapted to the curbing of disruptive behavior, for characteristic of such
behavior is the desire of some parties to restrain it and
of others to carry it through.[4] In the field of international relations the instability possible in a system of
balanced powers and responsibilities has been all too
obvious in history. The periodic collapse of such balances and the restoration of stability by the establishment of a new hierarchy by a passage of arms or a recom-
bination of nations has been seen again and again in
modern western history. The instability of a mutual
balance system internal to a society is no less obvious
and seems never to have been institutionalized for a
society as a whole. The problem of training children and
keeping them from harm would alone necessitate hierarchical elements. Complete stability is by no means always
institutionalized in a society though some, such as
Tokugawa Japan, have made rather extensive efforts in
this direction. Some societies institutionalize specific
sorts of changes as is illustrated by the phenomenon of
technological change in modern industrial societies.
Whatever the leeway of societies in this respect, some
structures of order, even of order in direction and type
of change, must be institutionalized if the society is to
persist as defined, and the institutionalization of such
order requires at some points the institutionalization of
hierarchical political structures.

On the level of generalization under analysis here
the institutionalization of hierarchical political struc-

---

4.   Hence one, at least, of the major elements of ro-
manticism in the anarchistic faiths.

tures always poses the problem of maintaining a balance of
the loci of power and responsibility. It is the essence
of such hierarchical systems that responsibility is owed
from the bottom up, from the less to the more powerful,
and that power is wielded from the top down. Another way
of putting the matter is that in a hierarchical political
structure responsibility is not owed directly to the individual or groups over whom power is wielded in the respects
in which power is wielded. If the contrary were true, a
mutual balance in these respects would exist, and the possibility of the interference with the exercise of power
would exist at every point. A military system of the
ordinary sort is, perhaps, the most clear-cut example of
such a hierarchy. Theoretically, in such organizations
the greatest power is concentrated in the highest ranking
official; the lower ranks each owe responsibility to the
ranks above and have power over the ranks below. It is
essential for the efficient operation of such systems that
the "chain of command" be clearly defined.

In these hierarchical systems there are two general
methods of maintaining the balance of power and responsibility. In neither case is the responsibility directly
owed those over whom power is wielded in the respects in
which it is wielded. One type of balance is that in which
the power holder owes responsibility directly and explicitly for the results of his exercise of power to some other
empirical individual or group. In the military forces of
the United States the balance is maintained by the institutionalization of responsibility of the highest officer
of the forces to the civilian government and of that civilian government to the population at large via elected
representatives and their appointees. The commanding
officer can not be called to account directly by his subordinates but only by his superiors, to whom the subordinates may appeal under specific rules, and in the last
analysis the commander-in-chief is a civilian official,

the president, responsible for his acts in specific ways
to the electorate.

The same sort of balance may be seen in the family
structure of the United States. A father does not owe
direct responsibility to his nonadult son for the results
of his power over that son, but the government through its
courts and law enforcement officers exacts such responsibility. The case against a father for maltreatment of his
son is not phrased "son X vs. father Y" but rather "the
state vs. father Y." Balances of this sort involve an
unending chain of powers and responsibilities. The eufunctional aspects of such a balance inhere in the fact
that, at least in theory, the method of balancing power
and responsibility is clear in any specific case at any
specific stage of its development, and that it is such
that the enforcement of responsibility does not interfere
with the manifest eufunctional aspects of the exercise of
power. This type of balance of power and responsibility
may be called an empirically oriented political hierarchy.[5]

Another type of political hierarchy may be called a
nonempirically oriented political hierarchy. In such a
hierarchy as this responsibility is balanced with power by
virtue of the power holder's faith in and allegiance to
nonempirical factors. These nonempirical factors may be
ultimate ends such as justice, honor, and the like, or
they may be nonempirical entities such as gods, the spirits
of ancestors, and the like. A clear example of this sort
of balance is that in the "traditional" Chinese family
system. A Chinese father whose male ancestors were dead

---

5. It is "empirically oriented" in the sense that
the individual(s) or groups holding power, the individ-
ual(s) or groups bearing responsibility, and those over
whom power is held and to whom responsibility is owed are
all empirically defined.

held virtually complete power over his son. Father-daughter-in-law incest was, perhaps, the only act that justified direct resistance by the son. In theory, at least, it was unfilial, the cardinal Chinese sin, for a son to resist physical abuse, and cases are cited of sons who have been beaten to death or nearly so by their fathers without a show of resistance. If the father was also the family head, no other family member was qualified to interfere with this exercise of power, and the officials of the government, not to mention one's friends and neighbors, were not expected to interfere either. The balance was maintained, ideally speaking, via the allegiance owed by the father to his ancestors and his obligation to them to ensure the maintenance of the family. It was unfilial of the father to so abuse his son or to so treat him (e.g., not provide him with a wife) as to prevent the continuity of the family. The maintenance of the balance depended upon the father's recognition of this obligation and his "motivation" in terms of it, however, and cases of fathers who ignored these obligations and ruined their families without empirical interference internal or external to the family are not difficult to find. Fortunately for the stability of "traditional" Chinese society the conformity aspects of the institutionalization of these obligations were extremely high as far as fathers were concerned.

In the type of nonempirically oriented political hierarchy cited above there is at least an indirect empirical element. The obligation that balances the loci of power and responsibility is to a group of nonempirical entities, the ancestors, but the factors covered by the obligations may be to a high degree explicitly and empirically defined. This was certainly true of the Chinese case cited. The obligations of a father to his son owed indirectly by virtue of his obligations to the ancestors involved such explicit empirical factors as the continuity of the family and, if possible, its increasing prosperity, which was also explicitly defined. There is, however, another possibility with regard to nonempirical political hierarchies. This is the case in which the balance is due to the allegiance, real or assumed, of the power holder to nonempirical factors but in which the nature of the obligations involved is not empirically defined or is so defined only by the decision of the power holder himself.[6] An example of this sort of balance is that present (or absent) in the type of power holders referred to by Max Weber as charismatic leaders. Charismatic leaders are power holders who are judged by those who believe in them to be capable of themselves defining the obligations for which they are responsible. It is true that such leaders inevitably operate within some empirical limitations, but other possibilities are left to their decision unlimited in other respects as far as the faith of their followers is concerned. Hitler, in Germany, was such a leader, and he operated in terms of a nonempirical orientation that might be phrased as the "greater glory of the German Reich."[7] Some empirical referents such as the "redress of the Treaty of Versailles" were involved, but to a large extent "the greater glory of the German Reich" was what Hitler said it was in the eyes of his devotees,[8] and he was institutionally responsible to no empirical source for his decisions. Responsibility was finally invoked in his case by outside powers, a noninstitutionalized source as

---

6. The case of empirical definition of the obligation by the nonempirical entity involved is ignored because of the impossibility of the empirical confirmation of such an "act" of definition by a nonempirical entity.

7. Its nonempirical aspects lay in its relative lack of definition until Hitler had spoken or someone spoke in his name.

8. There is some evidence that, despite the avowedly materialistic orientation of the communists, Stalin plays a similar charismatic role in the communist system.

far as the structure of his own society was concerned.

Another example of the nonempirically oriented political hierarchy in which empirical factors play a relatively minor role, even indirectly, is a phenomenon associated with the Protestant Reformation. In that period some of the members of some sects took quite literally the obligation to work out "God's Will on earth," its unknowability save in the revelation vouchsafed in the Bible, and the obligation of each individual to seek it out for himself. This made each individual in a sense his own charismatic leader and resulted on the part of some extremist sects in some of the most anarchic activity ever witnessed.[9]

The implications of nonempirical political hierarchies . for the stability of social systems in general and of societies in particular are extremely interesting. Only under very specific circumstances can the sources of instability involved be prevented from becoming a major source of change and/or disruption of the society. If the political hierarchy is nonempirically oriented in the factors to which responsibility is owed but contains empirical elements in that the obligations involved are explicit and specific empirical ones, then instability can be avoided only if the sources and methods of "motivation" of the individual concerned are such as to keep the conformity aspects of the institutionalization involved high enough to prevent structural changes that would be involved in lowered conformity aspects. In the China case cited above conformity aspects in the "traditional" period were extraordinarily high, and the implications of industrialization for the sources and methods of such "motivation" have been one of the major sources of the disruptive effects for

---

9.   See E. Belfort Bax, Rise and Fall of the Anabaptists, Macmillan Co., New York, 1903.

that social structure involved in the small degree of industrialization that has affected that society in the past
century or less.

In the second type of nonempirically oriented political hierarchy the problem of stability is even greater
than in the Chinese type. In this second type, the problem is one of "motivating" the charismatic leader in such
a way that the empirical obligations he does identify
empirically will not be disruptive of the social structure
and that he does identify those that will preserve it.
The odds are overwhelmingly against either requirement for
at least two reasons. At the present stage of knowledge
the cognitive problems involved in the rational apprecia-
tion of these factors by the charismatic leader make such
identification by him on a rational basis almost certainly
out of the question. His accurate identification of them
by nonrational means, if not out of the question, is at
least inscrutable from the scientific point of view. The
past history of charismatic leaders would not lead one to
expect long-run stability from this source since systems of
this sort have seldom lasted beyond the life of a single
individual and often the death of the charismatic leader
himself has been at least in part the result of the in-
stabilities of his system and/or the signal for its dissolution as defined.

There is yet another reason for expecting instability
under such circumstances. There is neither time nor space
here to go into the functional and structural prerequisites
of the social changes that result in such political situations. It is not unreasonable, nevertheless, to suggest
that situations of extreme tension and dissatisfaction are
involved, that a desire or readiness for social change is
an important factor "motivating" such allegiances. If
this is the case, then one of the most dysfunctional things
such leaders could do as far as their own power is concerned would be a maintenance of the status quo. Certainly

the history of such political hierarchies has always been
one of social change both during the existence of the system and in its dissolution. It is of the essence of such
political hierarchies that they are eufunctional for social change however dysfunctional they may be from other
points of view.

In the last analysis some nonempirically oriented
political hierarchies[10] must be involved in every society
if only because one of the possible ranges of variation
of human action is its orientation to ultimate ends. Furthermore, such orientation would seem to be ubiquitous in
some respects in all societies. The allocation of power
and responsibility is always germane in some respects for
any action whether directly oriented to ultimate ends or
not. If this is so, then political aspects inhere also in
action with such nonempirical orientations. If there is
to be stability in social systems from this point of view,
it will vary with the degree to which the balanced power
and responsibility involve as a minimum indirect but specific empirical definitions and the degree to which the
conformity aspects of institutionalization in these respects can be maintained at a high level.

In general, hierarchical political structures share
in common one characteristic that is eufunctional for social systems with rare exceptions, and certainly is eufunctional to some degree for any society. This is the fact
that such structures of political allocation facilitate
the wielding of power by minimizing the possibility of
interference of those over whom power is wielded. In many
situations inability to exercise power with relatively
little interference from those subjected to it would be
dysfunctional for the units concerned. At the same time
hierarchical systems of political allocation always pose

---

10. And no doubt some nonempirically oriented economic structures, solidarity structures, etc.

the problem of balancing the power of those at the top of
the power hierarchy with responsibility. The "democratic"
theory of government attempts one solution to this problem
by holding that the power holders for a society are responsible to the public at large, and various systems of
elections, etc., are present so that such responsibility
may be enforced. Authoritarian systems of political allocation institutionalize quite different structures in
these respects. In the field of international relations
the problem of this balance is raised in an acute form.
It is not difficult to devise a system for the delegation
of power to a world organization, but how can one hold it
responsible for its acts?[11] Literally hundreds of the

---

11. The technology of power wielding is relatively
well worked out, particularly with regard to the technology
of the application of force as an extreme resort. Furthermore, the results of these applications and their techniques (if not the applications and techniques themselves)
can be and are quite generally understood and appreciated
by persons whose social backgrounds show the widest diver-
gences. Thus, a bombing raid by ten thousand United Nations planes seeking to enforce a ruling of that body on a
deviant nation would be quickly understood by Americans,
Russians, French, Chinese, Israelis, Belgians, etc. The
question of the size and type of "police force" needed as
a last resort by such an international organization is
largely a technological matter. But the concepts on the
part of these diverse peoples of what would constitute
"adequate safeguards" against the "improper" use of such
power and hence the problems of holding such an organization with such powers responsible -- these are by no means
so commonly understood or appreciated. The relevant authorities in both Russia and the United States could, for
example, agree relatively quickly on what allocations of
men and material the United Nations Organization would need
in order to curb either one of them willy nilly. But, with
their differing social structures and individual "motivations," agreement on "adequate safeguards" against the misuse of such power appears to be very much more difficult,
if not impossible. Even with its extremely limited command
over actual force, this problem is acutely reflected in
the United Nations Organization in the use of the veto and
the differing attitudes toward that use. If, for example,
the authorities (and people?) of both Russia and the United

current problems of western societies and of the world in
general have this problem of balance of power and responsibility as a central concern whether it is recognized or
not. Structural analysis cannot be complete without explicit consideration of this problem, and explicit consideration of it in varying social contexts of greater and
lesser stability and of widely different types may produce
generalizations of wide practical importance in the field
of social engineering.

All social action involves some allocation of power
and responsibility just as all social action involves some
allocation of goods and services. In an attempt to answer
the three questions always posed relative to political
allocation, i.e., those of locus, definition, and procedure, the first step requires the identification of
those concrete structures that appear in a society on the
level of generalization on which that society is being
studied. Power and responsibility are, of course, always
allocated and executed in terms of concrete structures.
In terms of specific concrete structures one must, therefore, determine the type of balance (or lack of balance)
of power and responsibility and identify the distribution
of roles in this respect, the factors covered by the allocation both institutionally and otherwise, and the pro-

---

States could be convinced of the adequacy and effectiveness
of safeguards in these respects as they are of the ability
of an organization to exert pressure if it has sufficient
planes and atom bombs at its disposal, then many of the
current problems of an international organization to preserve peace would vanish. The exercise of power and the
delegation of the means of power to such an organization
is by no means simply a problem of current military logis-
tics, but, whatever these complexities may be, they are
pale, at least from the point of view of the participants,
by comparison with this problem of responsibility. It
might be added that the contributions by scientists to the
understanding of the responsibility aspect of the problem
would certainly seem to have been more modest than their
contributions to the problems of the power aspect.

cedures used to apply power and responsibility. Since all
of the concrete structures present on any level of study
of a society cannot be identical, if only because of the
necessity of some concrete structures that regulate relations among others, the political aspects of all the concrete structures can never be identical. One specific
political structure can never be the sole political structure for a society.

One type of concrete structure is, perhaps, of special
significance in these respects. That is the type that has
been referred to above as a predominantly politically oriented structure. It is by no means certain that such
concrete structures must exist in any society. It is
quite within the realm of possibility that societies carry
out political allocation in terms of structures otherwise
oriented or ones in which no particular orientation seems
predominant. On the other hand, when predominantly politically oriented structures do appear, certain implications are necessarily clear. Above all, such units must
be oriented to the regulation or supervision of relationships among other units. The only possible exception to
this implication would involve structures in which the
internal allocation of power and responsibility was an end
in itself. This is certainly not characteristically the
case. Predominantly politically oriented structures such
as governmental bodies of various sorts are inevitably
oriented to the regulation of interrelationships among
other concrete structures. Usually, such structures enforce responsibility on other structures. To the extent
that this is so another implication also follows. The
presence of such structures always limits and defines to
some degree the political allocation that takes place in
terms of other structures. Most notably, perhaps, such
structures are usually oriented, among other things, to
the control of disruptive behavior in the society.

When predominantly politically oriented structures

are present, they may be expected to furnish one of the
primary sources of balance for the allocation of power and
responsibility in a society. The effectiveness of such
structures in performing this function may be quite significant in the analysis of stability in a society. Such an
hypothesis would seem reasonable under the circumstances,
and in the event that its application be contradicted by
the data, at least the examination of the social structure
in these terms should lead to identification of those
other structures that exceed it in significance in these
respects.

In concrete structures generally, and in predominantly politically oriented ones in particular, three common
distinctions may be noted in structural examination from
the political point of view. These are the familiar distinctions between executive, legislative, and judicial
functions or structures. The term executive pertains to
the actual wielding of power or bearing of responsibility.
The term legislative pertains to the establishment of
structures defining who shall wield power and/or bear responsibility, in what respects, and how. The term judicial
pertains to the interpretation of the structures of political allocation, the judgment of what the structures
mean in specific circumstances, and when and how they
apply.

In the analysis of political structure the differentiation of executive, legislative, and judicial roles must
be discovered. The range of variation possible is extremely great. In some respects the distinctions can only
be made on an analytic basis. One of the most significant
factors to note about political structure is whether
executive, legislative, and judicial roles are distinguished from one another or whether they are combined.
Another is the degree to which they are set up in concrete
structures primarily oriented to one or the other or all
three, or whether they are set up within the general

concrete structures distinguished within a society or in predominantly politically oriented structures. In comparing concrete structures of similar types in different societies significant similarities or dissimilarities may emerge. Executive, legislative, and judicial roles are institutionalized in both the "traditional" Chinese family structure and that of the "urban middle-class" family in the United States. The systems are quite different, however, particularly with respect to the allocation of these roles and their definition. In both "traditional" China and the United States predominantly politically oriented governmental structures are institutionalized. The extent of power and responsibility of such structures, especially with reference to family structures, varies widely. Furthermore, in the case of the United States, there exist within the governmental structure sharply differentiated units predominantly oriented to executive, legislative, and judicial functions. In the Chinese case these are characteristically combined in such units as the district magistrates. Many, if not all, of the social changes in both societies, and certainly their comparative analysis, are unintelligible without reference to such factors.

The question of procedure in political structure again offers familiar aspects. The use of force is by no means the only method of procedure. It is in fact only the extreme in one direction. Again, reference may be made to the problem of who is to guard the guards themselves. Coercion can never be the sole basis of the political structure of a society. Authoritarian systems like that of the nazis in Germany carry the use of coercion to extreme lengths, but even that political structure is not comprehensible solely in these terms. Faith in Hitler as a charismatic leader was a vital element in that structure. The nazis themselves clearly understood the importance of other elements besides sheer coercion as do the authoritarian rulers of Russia today. To a very high degree both

at home and abroad the nazis of yesterday, as well as the
communists of today, relied on propaganda and education in
their peculiar "ideals" for lasting support. Coercion was
a strategic tool for ensuring the success of propaganda
and education, and for the maintenance of the "motivation"
that came from other sources to support the regime. Opposition was removed by coercion, but support was by no
means completely secured in that fashion. Had coercion
been the sole method or virtually the sole method, the
military defeat of the nazis would have eliminated at one
stroke nazi attitudes and ideals. The extent to which
these attitudes and ideals have proved more difficult to
destroy than the system of coercion itself would seem to
indicate the limited role played by coercion in even so
highly coercive a system as that one.

Coercive sanctions are never the sole political procedures in a society. At the same time their extreme
efficiency for limited ends cannot be ignored either. The
institutionalization of the use of force to secure responsibility or to eliminate disruptive elements from which
responsibility cannot be secured may be essential for the
stability of a society. It is certainly essential for
stability if conformity cannot be "motivated" in other
ways although, as stated above, conformity can never be
secured solely in this fashion.

One of the major problems facing societies that institutionalize broad tolerance of deviant political behavior is understandable in these terms. The civil liber-
ties institutionalized in the United States, for example,
furnish a basis of protection for groups that seek to
overthrow that system itself. When the system fails to
"motivate" conformity or to drain off the energies of
dissident elements in other ways, as was done in the past
to some extent by the geographical frontier, deviant
groups may arise that actually threaten to use the area
of tolerance as a basis to gather strength to overthrow

the structure within which they operate or that are conceived of as being able to do so. If the former is the
case, failure to increase coercion will result in a closure of the area of tolerance by accession of the deviant
group to power. In the latter case, whether justified
objectively or not, a closure of the area of tolerance may
occur to prevent such an overthrow. In any case, societies
institutionalizing such an area of tolerance are peculiarly liable to social change in the political realm from
real or fancied threats.

The problem of maintaining power and responsibility
structures by means other than coercive ones is very complex indeed. The whole problem of "motivation" and of the
process of inculcation of social structures, of the maintenance of social institutions, is involved. Even the
general possibilities involved cannot be treated here
largely as the result of ignorance and of the elementary
stage of development of this field and partly from lack
of space. Some elements germane to this problem are
treated in the following chapter of this volume, but in
essence that is most fragmentary. The relatively easy
observability of the applications of coercion and their
extremely dramatic character when evidenced in torture,
killings, concentration camps, jails, economic sanctions,
and the like have tended to preoccupy students of political phenomena with the question of the institutionalized
or noninstitutionalized use of force. The essence of the
problem is rather the allocation of power and responsibility in the absence of coercive sanctions. Durkheim has
pointed out that the contractual elements in contracts
would never be comprehensible without an understanding of
the noncontractual elements of contracts.[12] Something of

---

12. See Emile Durkheim, De la division du travail
social, Felix Alcan, Paris, 1932, pp. 184-197, esp. pp.
189 and 193.

the same sort applies here. The noncoercive aspects of
allocation of power and responsibility must always be analyzed if a society is to be understood, and must be analyzed even if the coercive aspects alone are to be comprehensible.

In connection with procedure in the allocation of
power and responsibility the general relevance of economic
and political allocation may be raised again. The view
taken here is that, while economic and political allocation are aspects of the same things, they are not the same
things themselves. Several propositions follow from this
position. First, although political allocation is not
necessarily determined by economic allocation or vice
versa, the two are never completely independent of one
another since some allocation of goods and services must
be involved in any allocation of power and responsibility
and vice versa. Second, for any given type of economic
structure, unless that structure is defined on the purely
descriptive level, there will be a range of variation possible in the structures of political allocation and vice
versa. Third, if the structure of economic allocation is
to remain unchanged, limits to the range of variation of
the structure of political allocation can be sought by
examining the implications of economic allocation for
political allocation. The reverse of this proposition may
also be advanced as an hypothesis.

The matter of the inescapable relevance of economic
allocation for political allocation has been raised before
in this volume. In recapitulation the matter may be put
simply. Power and responsibility cannot be exercised in
the absence of some allocation of goods and services if
only because a sufficient amount must be involved to keep
the political role holders alive to act in their political
roles. Allocation of goods and services cannot be carried
out without some allocation of power and responsibility in
that allocation even if that allocation is by mutual and

tacit consent. It is, however, no less true that role differentiations, solidarity structures, and other analytically distinguished structures are also involved in both. The mutual relevance of economic and political structure is stressed here because it always exists empirically and because it has been a matter of so much preoccupation in social analysis. The range of variation of these analytic structures relative to one another is emphasized as well. There are three reasons for this. First, it is an hypothesis of this work that this range of variation is capable of empirical demonstration. Second, emphasis on the mutual relevance of these two structures and at the same time their range of possible variation relative to one another provides a method of handling the aspects of social phenomena that have made monistic economic and political theories of social phenomena appealing, but does not fall into such monistic theories. Third, it furnishes an example of analysis of ranges of variation in terms of analytic structures and indicates that the relationship of the other analytic structural requisites have a similar type of relevance for, and possible range of variation with regard to, the two specifically taken up.

It may be suggested as one of the most general hypotheses in structural-functional requisite analysis that the analytic structural requisites of any concrete structure are always relevant to one another to some degree, but that each possesses a range of possible variation relative to any one other unless the concrete structure is defined completely on the descriptive level. Furthermore, the range of variation of any one analytic structure that is possible without some change on the level of generalization under study in the others is more limited as more of the total number of structural requisites present in the analysis are involved. For example, the minimum relevance of economic and political allocation for one another has been cited. An example of a range of possible variation

set in these respects may be cited as follows. If the
economic structure of a society is of the "capitalist" or
"business enterprise" type involving allocation via, institutionally speaking, rational attempts to maximize
income of private owners or managers of goods and services,
definite limits are placed on the degree and types of
power that can be institutionalized for predominantly politically oriented structures in the society. The range
of variation possible in the political structures is
narrowed further if one cites specific elements on the
same level of generalization in the structures of role
differentiation and solidarity.

Theoretically speaking, the structure of role differentiation, for example, has no fewer implications for the
structure of political allocation than has the structure
of economic allocation. The same is true of the structure
of solidarity and so forth. At the same time the relatively high development of economic analysis relative to
other types of social analysis, particularly with regard
to certain types of societies, along with the greater ease
of operational definitions in terms of goods and services,
make the structure of economic allocation an especially
strategic one for scientific social analysis. The theoretical advance in that field and its operational advantages make it an extremely useful starting point in the
analysis of a society in the attempt to narrow down the
range of possible variation of other structures. To a
somewhat lesser degree the same sort of thing may be said
of political structure, but these factors, though of great
pragmatic value for current social analysis, must not lead
the observer into the error of deciding that somehow economic and political structures are "more basic" than other
types as causative agents in social phenomena. As has
been pointed out above,[13] analytic structures in general

---

13. See above, pp. 95-100.

are not causative agents in any sense, though this does
not mean that knowledge of them carries no explanatory or
predictive material. Whatever their relative stage of
development and ease of use, the political and economic
structures are no more "basic" in their predictive and
explanatory value than are the other analytic structural
requisites distinguished here. Despite the temptations
for their use, a political monism or a political-economic
dualism involve all the dangers of other monisms or rigidly limited sets of variables seen as capable of total explanations.

The range of variation possible between economic and
political structures is not hard to illustrate in a rough
way. In some societies, for example in post-Meiji Japan,
economic concentration and political concentration sometimes have gone hand in hand. It has not always been so,
however, for sometimes the military clique diverged from
the zaibatsu, the great holders of economic wealth, and
subordinated the latter. In the history of India one also
sees the picture of the almost unchallenged position of
Brahmin leadership by no means highly correlated with concentration of goods and services in Brahmin hands.

Without attempting to overemphasize economic and political aspects of action as the sole or even major elements relevant to one another, some implications for
political structure contained in one distinction drawn
above in the chapter on economic structure may be examined
as an example of factors affecting these ranges of variation. The implications of the presence in a society of
concrete structures that are highly self-sufficient economically as opposed to highly interdependent ones are
extremely interesting in these respects. If the concrete
substructures of a society are highly self-sufficient economically, real limitations are placed on the political
structure and on changes in that structure. It is extremely difficult in such a society to utilize the control
of goods and services as a technique of power concentration.

Economic techniques for power concentration in such a society require either a change in the degree of economic
self-sufficiency of the units or specific control of them
one by one. The most obvious predominantly economic
technique for power concentration in such a situation lies
in concentration on those goods and services with regard
to which self-sufficiency does not exist, if those goods
and services are of a type that can be easily monopolized.
The "traditional" Chinese system presented such a picture.
The presence of government monopolies of such goods as
salt was extremely significant for that society. Furthermore, the economic self-sufficiency of family units made
tax and rent collections a matter that had to be carried
to individual families directly, and failure to do this
was always marked by the maximum evasion possible.

But even in this situation, noneconomic aspects of
action can rather easily be shown to play a direct role.
The solidarity structures of "traditional" China concentrated overwhelmingly on the family. Family loyalty took
precedence over loyalty to the state. This, coupled with
a high degree of family economic self-sufficiency, ensured
maximum difficulty in control of the family by the state
through predominantly economic means and evasion by the
family wherever possible of the obligation to furnish the
economic basis of power in the imperial structure. It is
not difficult to see why under these conditions Chinese
history should furnish unending examples of Chinese families that knew virtually no governmental restraint or of
cases of firm governmental control of an area being made
the occasion of collecting taxes as much as several decades in advance.

On the other hand, in pre-Meiji Japan, especially
under the Tokugawa, the picture was quite different despite the fact that the degree of economic self-sufficiency of the concrete structures was hardly less. But
in the Japanese case the solidarity structures were quite

different. Family loyalty was important, but loyalty to
the feudal hierarchy was even more important. The economic self-sufficiency of the units would have created the
same difficulties for political allocation by economic
techniques. They did not, however, exist to the same degree among the peasants at least,[14] and the reasons for
that situation must be sought outside the aspects of action
of economic self-sufficiency, just as noneconomic aspects
of action are relevant in the Chinese case. The relevance
of the noneconomic aspects of action in either case ceases
to be obscure when such a comparison is made.

Highly developed economic interdependence in a society greatly facilitates the use of predominantly economic
aspects of action for political allocation. In a society
like that in the modern United States complete control of
rather restricted goods and/or services could carry with
it nearly complete control or nearly complete disruption
of the whole society. Ruthless control of the barge system servicing New York City, for example, could make that
area capitulate or become uninhabitable, and the same is
true, say, of the water supply. In such social systems
the way is open and easy for the use of economic aspects
of action for their political implications. That is to
say, it is open and easy in the sense that under such conditions the coercive possibilities of the manipulation of
economic aspects of action are extremely great, but this
is not by any means the whole of the story. The degree
and type of interdependency place limiting factors on the
use of predominantly economic means for political allocation too. It is true that this situation opens the way
for such manipulation, but it also places a price on it.

---

14. There was, of course, considerable difficulty
with the feudal lords in the matter of taxation, but this
went hand in hand with a breakdown in the power aspects of
the central government.

Systems of high interdependency are often, if not inevitably, rather delicately balanced systems, and manipulation
of the economic aspects of such systems for political ends
can interfere substantially with the other functions produced by the operation of the system. Manipulations of
this sort might increase, decrease, or maintain the economic efficiency of the system. Regardless of what effect
it might have, the cognitive problems alone in the rational
use of such techniques are enormous. Furthermore, processes in such a system may be irreversible, and "mistakes"
once made may be irretrievable from everyone's point of
view. There is now a considerable body of recent historical experience in these respects. The rapid industrialization of Japan and Germany, the relatively ineffective
industrialization of China, the switch to extremely authoritarian regimes in Germany and Italy and to a modern
form of authoritarian regime in Russia, and finally some
of the experience of military government efforts following
the last war are all cases in which these particular factors have, perhaps, played major roles. Such considerations are germane in any case, but in some cases like those
cited they may well be especially revealing lines of investigation.

It is not necessary in the present chapter to examine
in detail the implications of possible variations in the
relationship aspects of concrete structures. Much of the
material that has already been gone into in Chapters VI
and IX is germane of course, and the major differences
that would arise would find their source in examination of
the same material from the political rather than another
point of view. At least one general principle is fairly
clear. All concrete structures have political aspects,
and therefore, for example, nonpolitical considerations
requiring the institutionalization of predominantly universalistic recruitment can not be contradicted by the
political structures involved if stability is to result.

The same sort of observation may be made about political
aspects of concrete structures that regulate other concrete structures. The institutional requirements of relationship structures are to an extremely high degree
interdependent factors. Many of the pressing practical
problems on which the comparative analysis of institutions
may throw some light are in major respects understandable
in these terms. To what degree can authoritarian regimes
be combined with highly industrialized ones with stable
results? Where and in what respects are stresses and
strains likely to appear in systems that attempt such combinations? What sorts of increases or decreases of freedom from control are likely to be irreversible changes in
an industrialized society, and so forth? The relationship
requirements in concrete structures viewed from the political point of view are not necessarily the same as those
viewed from the economic point of view. The one does not
completely determine the other, but they are never irrelevant for one another either.

     One distinction that is always observable relative to
concrete structures, if their members are in contact with
the members of other concrete structures, is the distinction
between political allocation "internal" to the structure
and those "external" to it. In modern nationalistic terms
this distinction takes the form of the distinction between
the "domestic" and "foreign" realms. The phrase, internal
to the structure, indicates those considerations or structures that relate the members of the structural unit to
one another in terms of the unit concerned. The phrase,
external to the structure, indicates those considerations
or structures that relate the members of one concrete
structure to the members of another as unit to unit or as
individuals of one unit to another unit. The political
structures relating the United States to the United Nations
Organization are external aspects of the United States'
social structure in this sense of the term. The relations

between the Federal Bureau of Investigation and a citizen
who has broken the law are internal aspects of political
allocation from the point of view of the United States
social structure. The distinction between internal and
external aspects is only precise in terms of specific
units, of course, and aspects that are internal from the
point of view of one concrete structure may be external
from the point of view of another.

The distinction focuses attention on two factors: the
first is that of the sources of stability or change within
the structure concerned insofar as political allocations
are germane; the second is that of the relationship of a
specific concrete structure to other concrete structures
with which it is in contact. The obvious relevance of
political considerations for general questions of order
and change makes this a fruitful line to take in tracing
the part played by a specific type of concrete structure
in the total structure of a society. A third element may
arise from the use of this distinction; it may well be
that the specific formulation of a concrete structure is
not comprehensible save in terms of its external relationships. An obvious case in point is that of the urban
middle-class American family, the survival of which is
simply incomprehensible without understanding of the way
in which the husband and father member fits into the
general occupational role structure of the society.

A somewhat more subtle case of this sort of problem
seen from the political point of view is furnished by the
"traditional" Chinese family. One would expect external
relations to have a minimal significance given such highly
self-sufficient, self-oriented structures. That is true
in many respects, but it is not true if one asks the question, How are the political allocations internal to the
family maintained? It is not proposed here to argue the
question of the relative security or insecurity of Chinese
individuals and those in other societies. Suffice it to

say as a hypothesis that those in the roles of son, daughter-in-law, and wife were often subjected to extreme strains, and yet the degree of stability in the face of these strains has been so marked as to lead many observers to doubt the existence of these strains altogether. One of the factors of great structural importance in this picture has been the fact that in the "traditional" situation the possibility of setting up an acceptable alternative economic basis for existence was virtually out of the question. External relations were conducted to a high degree in family terms. A person unfilial enough to revolt from his family cut himself off automatically from the major possibility of establishing himself directly or indirectly in economic roles alternative to those that came to him automatically in his own family. The structure of external relations of family units was such that a rebel had almost no prospects of bettering his lot by running away. Suicide was cut off as an alternative in most cases by other structures, and internal family revolt was cut off not only by the full force of training but also by virtue of the fact that such unfilial conduct internal to the family could be "set to rights" by appeals to the clan or to the district magistrate units. Some confirmation of the importance of these factors of external relations is to be found in the fact that even the slight intrusion of modern industrial structures found in China provided directly and indirectly for an increased possibility of alternative employment on a nonfamily basis and that the effect of this possibility on family political structures has apparently been explosive. In the parts of China where these possibilities exist, the treatment of sons, daughters-in-law, and wives must be tempered if stability is to be maintained. Particularly in the case of sons, failure to temper their treatment has been met by revolt through flight, and self-conscious use of the threat of flight has been reported.[15]

The internal and external structures when the latter
are relevant, of political allocation must reinforce one
another to a large extent if there is to be stability in
the situation. The power of fathers over sons necessary
to make a given type of family organization work cannot be
maintained if contradicted by certain types of state organizations, or if it can be maintained, the state organizations in question cannot operate. Perhaps the most
strategic line of reinforcement to investigate in these
respects is that which has to do with the maintenance of
the balance of power and responsibility. Quite often in
hierarchical political structures the balance of power and
responsibility of those at the top of the hierarchy is
maintained by the external relations of the unit concerned.
For example, in the United States the state and local
governments enforce, when necessary, certain minimal responsibilities of parents for their children.

The balance of power and responsibility via external
relations of the concrete substructures of a society is
one of the reasons why changes in one type of concrete
structure may have far-reaching consequences for others.
This phenomenon is marked when viewed in terms of economic
interdependency. It is no less marked in terms of political interdependency. One may speak of concrete structures
that are politically highly self-sufficient and politically highly interdependent just as one may speak of structures in this manner in economic terms. In the political
sense the reference is made to the degree of balance of
power and responsibility internal to the unit as opposed
to relevant structures external to the unit. As in the
case of economic allocation complete political self-suffi-

---

15. See Olga Lang, Chinese Family and Society, Yale,
New Haven, 1946, p. 261.

ciency for all the concrete substructures of a society is
out of the question, but the range of variation possible
is nonetheless enormous. In these respects as in economic
respects the "traditional" Chinese family is to a very
high degree politically self-sufficient despite its essential interdependencies noted above in the case of deviant
activities. The balance of power and responsibility internal to the family via nonempirical orientations of the
family head has also been cited briefly above. At that
point the importance of specific empirical referents of
this nonempirical orientation was suggested as an important element in the balance of power and responsibility.
Here, the emphasis is on the fact that the balance as far
as the family head is concerned depends primarily on factors internal to the family. The family head in "traditional" China, who was not sufficiently curbed by these
structures, could and did sometimes destroy his family
organization. In the United States the role played by
predominantly politically oriented public structures is
much greater, and in this respect, at least, the family
system of the United States is less self-sufficient.

As in the case of economic interdependency, political
interdependency at one and the same time makes changes
easier and more precarious. A highly interdependent balance is easier to upset, but the odds are overwhelming
that the direction and character of the changes will be
far more difficult to control rationally. These are questions that merit careful consideration from those social
engineers interested in planned social change. The action
of such people is, of course, manifestly dysfunctional to
the system they seek to change. It is highly important
that such individuals examine the possible latent dysfunctions of the changes they propose as well as the manifest
dysfunctions they seek. For example, it is often proposed
in modern industrial societies that the upper income
groups be made or encouraged to increase their birth rate

markedly or that the family system be changed in the direction of a return to larger family units of greater
solidarity such as a patriarchal, patrilineal, patrilocal
family unit. The manifest dysfunctions (from the point of
view of the prevailing system) of increasing the use of
educational opportunities, reducing certain types of stress,
etc., are easy enough to discern in these measures. On
the other hand, persons advocating these changes do not
usually seek to change the system of allocation of occupational roles on a predominantly universalistic basis or to
decrease the level of material productivity of their societies, and both eventualities may be shown to be possible, if not highly probable, latent dysfunctions (from the
point of view of the prevailing system) of such reform
measures.

In closing this chapter as in the case of the preceding one, a few suggestions as to the possible development of the branch of social science explicitly concerned
with the political aspects of phenomena may be made. An
attempt has been made here to develop and illustrate certain political structural requisites of any society, and
to indicate broad ranges of variation in these respects.
Again, it may be observed that much systematic development
of political science might proceed in terms of the development of the implications of these factors for lower levels
of generalization. One of the most pressing current
practical problems in this respect is the range of variation in the structure of political allocation possible in
highly industrialized societies. There are reasons, too
complex and ill-developed to present here, to believe that
highly authoritarian political developments are both en-
gendered by and at the same time, in the long run at least,
highly dysfunctional to such societies. Development of the
political structural requisites of any highly industrialized society would illuminate this problem.

The use of such a system of analysis as the present

one is not confined to the development of the political
structural requisites of societies. Other types of concrete structures can be analyzed by essentially the same
methods. Here again the current practical implications
are great. What are the political structural requisites,
for example, of an international organization capable of
preventing international wars? Such knowledge would
immensely facilitate the erection of such an organization
or at least forestall a waste of effort should it prove
impossible.

Finally, as in the case of economics cited in the
preceding chapter, systematic development of political
science within such a framework as the present one would
eliminate the development of that branch of knowledge in
isolation from those studying other aspects of social
phenomena. The fallacies of misplaced concreteness and
unjustified generalizations that are so common in the
isolated development of theories about analytically distinguished aspects of phenomena could, perhaps, be modified to some degree by such a procedure. The procedure
would certainly clarify many of the statements of problems
in this field. If that clarification did no more than
prove some other explicit procedure necessary, it would
have served some scientific purpose.

C H A P T E R   XI

THE STRUCTURE OF INTEGRATION AND EXPRESSION

The structure of integration and expression remains
at the present state of development of this work in essence
a residual category. Some attempt will be made to be explicit about this concept, or congeries of concepts, but
nothing like even the moderate degree of clarity or explicitness obtainable in the preceding four analytic structures is attainable here at the present stage of development. The present chapter does not attempt any radical
departures in this sphere. It merely seeks to state as
clearly as possible those elements of the conceptual scheme
and theoretical system presented here that remain, from the
author's point of view at least, in a most unsatisfactory
stage of development. This is stated explicitly lest failure to do so convey a false sense of security in the usefulness of these concepts or the assurance with which they
are advanced to other students in this field.

The concept of _integration_ used here denotes eufunctional adaptation to a concrete structure. The analytic
structure of integration in a society or other concrete
structure consists of those structures the operations of
which make for the eufunctional adaptation of the members
and/or members-to-be of the structure to the structure
concerned.[1] The matter is not a simple one, unfortunately.

---

1. The structure of integration is thus a portion of
the general structure of eustructures in a society.

Few, if any, structures are perfectly integrative, that is,
give rise to no dysfunctions whether latent, manifest, UIR,
or IUR. Therefore, specific structures spoken of as integrative often have malintegrative aspects too, that is to
say their operation results in dysfunctions as well as eufunctions. A structure will be considered predominantly
integrative if on the whole the results of its operation
are more eufunctional than dysfunctional. The difficulties
of measurement are too obvious to require comment here.
Suffice it to say for the present that those integrative
structures that are structural requisites must be predominantly integrative ones if the concrete structure of which
they are structural requisites is capable of stability at
all. It must always be borne in mind that by no means all
concrete structures are capable of stability. Integrative
structures are classified as analytic structures for the
same reason that the other analytic structures are so
classified. They are relatively stable aspects analytically distinguished in concrete actions. Just as no allocation of goods and services takes place that does not
involve some role differentiation, some solidarity structures, some political allocations, and so forth, so no
integration occurs in connection with which no economic
allocation, no political allocation, no role differentiation, and so forth, is discernible. In the study of integration one is again concerned with an analytically
distinguishable aspect of concrete actions and not with
concrete actions themselves.

The concept of expression used here denotes the type
and limits of reaction, symbolic or otherwise, on the part
of individuals or groups to the various phenomena with
which they come into contact. The analytic structure of
expression in a society or other concrete structure consists of those structures that define the type and limits
of reaction, symbolic or otherwise, on the part of individuals or groups to the various phenomena with which they

come into contact. One of the most notable types of reaction to phenomena is that type spoken of previously as
affective. It is primarily to that type that the present
treatment will be oriented. Here, one is involved again
in the difficulties presented by the unsatisfactory state
of the concept of affects. Suffice it to say that, in
concrete actions, structures of affective expression are
discernible. Under some circumstances in all societies
some types of affective expression are considered appropriate and others inappropriate. In the United States it
is considered "bad" for men to weep under conditions that
Frenchmen consider quite appropriate. The Japanese repress overt expressions of affect in situations in which
such repression would be considered most "unnatural" in
other societies, and so forth. The structures in these
respects are analytically distinguished just as are those
of integration and the others treated here.

The question may be raised as to the advisability of
combining the concepts of integration and expression in
one category. With further development it certainly may
prove inadvisable, but at the present stage of development
both categories are residual in so many respects that little effect seems to be gained by their separation. Furthermore, in their present formulations they are so difficult to separate, even analytically, that relatively
little would be gained by their separation. Finally, on
the basis of what is no more than intuition, it may be
suggested that further development in this field may find
it most useful to develop the structures of expression as
subcategories of integration.

With regard to the structure of integration and expression two initial distinctions may be made. First,
what are the structures whereby the socialization of new
members of the society is attained, and what are the
structures whereby the general inculcation and maintenance
of the values, attitudes, and procedures of a society are

carried out?   Second, how are the expressions of the members of a society defined and limited, institutionally
speaking?

Perhaps the most easily distinguished structure under
the first heading is that of _education_. All societies
must have methods whereby the new members of the society
are taught its structures. Here, the problem is twofold.
First, there is the problem of new members recruited by
birth. A newborn infant is presumably completely ignorant
of the social structure of the society into whose membership he is born. At least, one may advance this as a
hypothesis in the absence of evidence to the contrary. In
terms of the factors of human heredity and nonhuman environment about all that can be said of the newborn, without raising a storm of controversy, is that they are
capable of learning over a period of time a wide range of
structures and that the variation in what they are capable
of learning is enormous. Furthermore, if they survive,
some such learning is inescapable for them. The very
attention from others necessary for their survival has
effects in this respect upon the recipients of it. If a
society is to persist, the infants must, as they develop,
not only learn something, but a very large proportion of
them must also learn those things that will permit them to
replace the other society members who have previously
acted in terms of the crucial and more or less strategic
institutions of the society.

The problem presented by infants is not the only educational problem. There may be also the problem posed by
new members recruited by means other than birth. In some
societies such recruitment of new members may be totally
lacking, but whenever it is not, the educational problem
exists. The problem of these new members is quite different from that of infants for in this case not only the
learning of new structures is involved but also the "un-
learning" of old ones is necessary, at least insofar as the

old and the new conflict.

Education is not confined to the early stages of the individual's development even when the individual is "born into" a society. The rate of education during the periods of infancy and childhood are almost certainly greater than at any other periods, but insofar as differentiation of roles on bases beyond these two age periods takes place, some education must be carried out at later stages. The periods of development in which education of the individual are concentrated and the variations possible in these respects are important bases for distinctions among societies.

General analysis of the educational structure of a society is too broad and complex a matter to treat here, but three things must always be determined about any particular system of education: (1) the content of education, i.e., what is taught, (2) the educational procedure, i.e., what are the methods by which the content is taught, and (3) who, and under what conditions, have the roles of students and teachers. Obviously, none of these factors can be left random in a society, and, equally obviously, they are closely related to other aspects of social action. For example, the allocation of power and responsibility in the educational sphere is of great importance. To some degree in all societies the roles of teacher and student can not be combined in all respects in a single individual if only because of the obvious limitations posed by infancy. On the other hand, in many, if not all, societies some aspects of education are left entirely to the individual: that is, he combines the roles of teacher and student in those respects. The more highly mobile and less traditionalized are the structures of a society, the greater is the likelihood of such a combination of roles, but in all societies education of this sort can take place only on an educational foundation in which these roles are separated.

The integrative aspects of educational structures are not difficult to see. If conformity with the structures of a society is not automatic on bases explicable solely in terms of human heredity and nonhuman environment, then structures of inculcation of these structures must exist if the society is to exist. The structures whose operations result in eufunctions must be learned if there is to be any integration at all unless that integration is explicable in nonsocial terms. The functional requisite of adequate socialization is obviously germane here, but so in a sense are all other functional requisites. There is no functional requisite in which education does not play some role. Communication is an example; some common learning of some symbols must be present if there is to be any communication at all. Education is as a minimum always relevant to the cognitive element in action, and some element of cognition is always involved in social action. It is bootless to ask the question of what sort of cognition would be present in a human raised in complete isolation from others. The conditions would preclude survival. The relevant question is, "What sorts of cognition must arise under specific social conditions if stability is or is not to result?" Education is the technique of giving rise to that cognition.

The structure of <u>motivation</u> is another subcategory of the general structure of integration and expression. The structure of education answers the problem of inculcation of cognitive and other elements. <u>Motivation</u> is concerned with the establishment of the ends of action whether these be empirical or nonempirical, intermediate or ultimate. How are individuals brought to desire or seek those ends that will permit the maintenance of a society, or of the dissolution or change of one for that matter? A structure of "motivation" that results in dysfunctional action is malintegrative, and one that results in eufunctional action is integrative. Quite commonly, the structure of

"motivation" contains elements of both sorts. Just as in
the case of cognition, "motivation" in societies is not
apparently solely explicable in terms of human heredity
and nonhuman environment. Limits of variation in this
respect may be explicable in these nonsocial terms, but
specific solutions are not. The apparent "desire" of infants and even adults for food may be explained in nonsocial terms, but the specific gratification within a range
of possible gratification even of infants is not solely
explicable in these terms, and certainly such gratifications are capable of relatively easy manipulations within
certain ranges. Adults, at least under the influence of
other "motivations," would even seem in some extreme cases
to be capable of suppressing such "physiological motivations" altogether, as is witnessed by some of the more
bizarre forms of suicide.

Consideration of the structures of economic and political allocation raises an interesting problem in relation to "motivation." The impossibility of economic
allocation that does not involve some general evaluative
standards beyond the allocation of goods and services and
the impossibility of political allocation based solely on
coercion have been discussed in preceding chapters. These
hypotheses are illustrations of the fact that the structure of "motivation" in a society cannot proceed solely in
terms of the intermediate means-ends schema. For "motivation" to exist within the intermediate means-ends schema
relative to economic allocation in society some ultimate
ends to which the allocation of goods and services is
relevant must be involved. For allocations of power and
responsibility to exist in a society some elements of
noncoerced allegiance must be present, and again that
cannot be solely in terms of the intermediate means-ends
scheme relevant to political allocation. These factors
would seem to indicate that the methods of institutionalization of the ultimate goals that are present in a society

and the nature of these goals is always essential for social analysis. How is "motivation" relative to such goals
inculcated on the members of the society? Apparently, one
of the ranges of action open to humans in terms of their
hereditary constitution and their nonhuman environment is
that of orienting their action to such ultimate ends. The
question here is not an ontological one. This study is not
concerned with whether or not such ends are "real" or have
"true existence or significance." This study is concerned
only with the fact that humans everywhere seem to conceive
of such ends and to orient their action to such ends. For
present purposes it makes little difference whether these
conceptions of ultimate ends are illusory or not. The
fact that men orient their actions to them makes their
conceptions of them important data for social analysis in
general and that of "motivation" in particular.

Discussion of ultimate ends in their relation to the
structure of "motivation" takes the discussion into the
realm of religious activity. Religion for the purposes of
the present study has been defined as aspects of action
directly oriented to ultimate ends. This definition is
both broader and narrower than many of the definitions
commonly in use. It is narrower in the sense that it does
not include many of the aspects of action in the intermediate means-ends schema that are commonly called religious activity, and it does not include those aspects of
action that are methodologically alogical. It covers
only those aspects of action of an ultimately alogical
sort in which the nonempirical ends are also ultimate
ends. It is broader than the usual connotations of the
term in that it is not confined to systems of belief involving supernatural entities but includes those in
which the ultimate nonempirical orientation is purely
evaluative or ethical. Given the definition of religion
used here, religious elements appear in all societies and
are strategic for analysis if only because of their rele-

vance to the general framework of "motivation."

Religious systems in societies may be roughly divided
into two sorts. All religious systems involve ultimate
values, but some orient to such values directly and some
through orientation to one or more supernatural entities,
orientation to or belief in whom involves ultimate values.
The first of these two will be called the ethical religions
and the second will be called the supernatural religions.
The distinction used here is not intended to convey that
one type is "better" than another. They have empirical
differences. By any particular standard of values either
type of religion may be judged "good," "bad," or "indifferent." On this question pure science is purely agnostic.
Epicureanism and Humanism in some of their forms are examples of ethical religions. Buddhism, Christianity,
Mohammedanism, etc., are examples of supernatural religions.
For reasons at present unknown, but of great interest as
far as questions of social analysis in general and of social change in particular are concerned, the supernatural
religions have been far more common as the major religious
elements in societies than the ethical religions. There
would also seem to be a tendency for ethical religions to
take on supernatural elements in societies in which they
predominate or form important elements. The current intrusion of supernatural elements into the communist religion in the form of doctrines of leader infallibility
(sic, the apparent deification of Stalin) and the like is
interesting in these respects. The extreme prominence of
supernatural religious systems and the tendency of supernatural elements to invade ethical religions, if these can
be verified, would seem to suggest that one highly general
characteristic of human beings is that ultimate value
orientations are more easily maintained and inculcated if
they involve supernatural entities. It is further interesting to observe that these supernatural entities frequently, if not invariably, involve anthropomorphic

features or at least features understandable by reference
to empirical phenomena. In the case of anthropomorphic
deities the anthropomorphic features are limited by
qualities that permit an answer to such problems as that
of "evil" in the world, meaning, origins, etc. Frequently,
for example, the deity is conceived as quite human in many
respects but possessed of omnipotence, omniscience, and the
like. A striking example of this sort of religious formulation is that of the Greek pantheon the members of which
are probably as anthropomorphic in detail as any deities
ever conceived.

Concrete structures predominantly oriented to religious action will be called <u>predominantly religious struc-</u>
<u>tures</u>. Predominantly religious structures are not neces-
sarily present in any society since these activities may
be carried out in terms of other concrete structures by no
means predominantly oriented to religious action in any
obvious sense. However, it may again be noted that the
presence of some predominantly religious structures would
seem to be the rule rather than the exception for societies. Although the matter is by no means clear in these
respects, it would seem that the presence of some predominantly religious structures is necessary for the maintenance of stability in religious structures. If this is
so, it may well be due to the possibility, if not the
probability, of other considerations in concrete structures
taking precedence over religious ones and hence widely
modifying the religious structures. Even in the case of
Confucianism in China, a religious system carried out to
a very high degree in terms of family units, there existed
concrete structures predominantly oriented to Confucianism
outside the family.

There is another distinction relative to religious
systems that is of far-reaching importance for an understanding of social structure. This is the distinction
between <u>exclusive</u> and <u>nonexclusive</u> religions. <u>Exclusive</u>

<u>religions</u> are those that are institutionalized in such a fashion that an individual may, institutionally speaking, be oriented to one and only one religious system at any one time. <u>Nonexclusive religions</u> are those that are institutionalized in such a fashion that an individual may, institutionally speaking, be oriented to more than one religious system at any one time. The Occidental religious systems, such as Judaism and Christianity, are thoroughly exclusive religions. The same is true of Mohammedanism. One may not, institutionally speaking, be both a Christian and a Jew simultaneously. One may not be a Mohammedan and a Christian simultaneously. The exclusive character of these religions is carried even into their various subdivisions. One may not be both an Orthodox and a Reform Jew. One may not be both a Catholic and a Baptist. Not only may one not be a member of two exclusive religions at one and the same time, but also, from the point of view of a true believer in an exclusive religion, one may not simultaneously believe in an exclusive religion and a nonexclusive one.

On the other hand, many of the Oriental religious systems such as Confucianism, Taoism, Buddhism, systems of folk gods, etc., are nonexclusive. In "traditional" China many, if not most, persons oriented their actions to all four of these, and as far as they were concerned there was no difficulty in adding one or more exclusive religions to the list, though the exclusive aspect was hardly meaningful to them. Missionaries for exclusive religions have found this a major problem in the Far East. It is not difficult to get many Orientals to take up a new religion, but it is extremely difficult to get them to adhere to it exclusively. The history of Christianity in China furnishes one especially clear-cut case of this. Catholicism under the Jesuits in China made considerable headway at one time. Part of its success was made via a compromise of the exclusive character of Catholicism whereby ancestor

worship (Confucianism) was permitted to Catholic converts.
A Church directive forbidding this practice brought an
almost immediate halt to the success of Catholicism in
China at that time.

In terms of stability and change in societies the
institutionalization of exclusive or nonexclusive religions
has interesting implications. The institutionalization of
a single exclusive religion has certain obvious advantages
from the point of view of stability. It permits all or
none answers to problems affecting the broadest framework
of "motivation" since competing institutionalized ultimate
ends are eliminated. As such it tends also to freeze the
structures of intermediate "motivation," at least insofar
as they are relevant to the ultimate structures. On the
other hand, such a system may be highly dysfunctional to a
society that institutionalizes a particular sort of change,
such as technological change.

Perhaps the major source of instability involved with
exclusive religions in a society arises, however, in those
societies in which more than one exclusive religion exists.
Here, conflicts among the adherents of the different systems is very much in the realm of possibility if not
probability. The history of western and near eastern
societies has shown many such conflicts. There is also
another potential source of conflict given exclusive religious systems in a society. There may be latent as well
as manifest religious systems in a society. Often ethical
religions are latent in a society. In the modern western
world nationalism has something of this character though
in many respects it is to an increasing degree a manifest
religious system, and in many other parts of the world
nationalism plays an increasingly prominent role.

The essence of nationalism as a religion in the sense
used here is the ethical tenet summed up in American experience by the tenet, "Our Country! In her intercourse
with foreign nations may she always be in the right; but

our country, right or wrong" (Stephen Decatur, Toast
given at Norfolk, April 1916). When predominantly religious structures of a nonnational character or of an
international character exist in a society that institutionalizes nationalism, the possibility of conflict exists.
The same is true of other broad ethical religious orientations vis-à-vis the exclusive religions unless the values
involved in both types of religious systems happen to
coincide. Ethical religions may also be exclusive ones,
and in religious terms it is nationalism rather than other
religious systems that has perhaps proved to be the major
bulwark so far against a highly centralized Russian communism and threatens that system most in the future.

The nonexclusive religions do not serve as a source
of potential instability by virtue of the possibility of
conflicts carried out in religious terms. The religious
conflicts of the Orient, for example, have been understandable precisely in terms of the increase of exclusive
elements in the religious systems there or in rather
self-conscious attempts of rulers to use predominantly
religious structures for political purposes. On the other
hand, the presence of nonexclusive religions in a society
makes the inculcation and maintenance of the basic value
structure of the society, and hence its structure of
"motivation," somewhat more vulnerable to change than is
the case with exclusive religions. Extreme caution is due
in the use of such hypotheses, however. Only in the last
century of a two-thousand-year period has China, a society
institutionalizing nonexclusive religions, shown marked
revolutionary tendencies as far as its most general social
structure is concerned. The West, on the other hand, has
institutionalized highly exclusive religions and has shown
far more marked revolutions in basic social structure in
that period. Other societies with nonexclusive religious
systems such as Japan have shown considerable structural
fluctuations, and other societies with exclusive religions

such as some of the Mohammedan ones have shown little
fluctuation. The implications of exclusivism and nonex-
clusivism in religion for stability and change cannot be
ignored, but they by no means furnish the grounds for a
religious monism either.

In the discussion of "motivation" in relation to
ultimate nonempirical ends, one peculiarity of the social
situation must be brought out. If these ends are to have
any effect on social action, they must to some degree involve empirical referents. Either there must be some
tendency to equate empirical action or states with the
nonempirical referent itself or at least some specific
forms of action must be seen as conducive to these nonempirical ends. Even if in fact the ends are believed to be
completely inscrutable from the point of view of the actor,
some latent empirical elements are involved since only
inaction or relatively unstructured action could result
from "motivation" to completely inscrutable ends. The
concept of Nirvana in Oriental religions is as thoroughly
nonempirical an end as any, perhaps, and yet certain empirical factors came to be clearly identified with it.
Most notably in that case action is oriented to as little
involvement with the empirical factors of ordinary life as
is possible. From the point of view of general empirical
concerns the result in the case of the true believer is as
close an approach to pure apathy as is conceivable, culmi-
nating in periods of complete avoidance of, and withdrawal
by means of trances from, empirical factors including
other humans. Ascetic Taoism has similar implications,
and yet in both cases elaborate empirical actions were
sometimes developed on the theory that they were conducive
to such complete escape from empirical concerns. Elaborate
systems of physical exercise, retreat in isolation into
uninhabited regions, and similar techniques are common in
such cases. Obviously, such empirical identifications of
nonempirical ends, if widely adhered to, are not compatible

with the existence of a society. In essence rigorous
adherence to them withdraws the practitioners rather effectively from a society, although it does not necessarily
relieve other members of the society of the necessity of
dealing with them.

The phenomenon of Protestantism previously referred
to is also revealing in this respect. The original Protestant injunction to work out God's Will on earth coupled
with the assumption that His Will was inscrutable save for
the Revelation found in the Bible left the range of empirical identification of the nonempirical end of "God's
Will on earth" open to wide interpretation. As mentioned
above, some of the new faithful took the injunctions quite
literally, and each on his own responsibility sought out
the empirical means to such an end, sometimes with the
most unstructured and disruptive results. For the bulk of
the faithful, however, more systematic empirical identifications of the nonempirical end were discovered, most
particularly, if one is to believe Max Weber, in the
attempt at ascetic mastery over empirical phenomena, rather
than avoidance of them, and in the typical "business" forms
of economic aspects of action. At any rate, for the bulk
of the adherents, God's Will remained inscrutable only in
part, and a wide range of empirical acts were rather explicitly believed to be a part of "His Will on earth."

The case of charismatic leaders already discussed
briefly above in connection with political allocation is
another case of this sort. The tremendous impact of such
leaders on social structure comes as a result of the fact
that in the eyes of their believers they are specifically
the individuals qualified to identify infallibly certain
empirical actions as conducive to nonempirical ends. Thus,
a Hitler can tell the nazi faithful what new actions are
conducive to the "greater glory of the German Reich," be
it a compact with the previously hated Russians or the
invasion of some new area. Stalin has apparently acquired

or achieved a similar role in Russia, and his position as
a charismatic leader gives that system a certain empirical
flexibility that is required to shift with ease and rapidity among actions that appear radically incompatible to the
nonbeliever.

But in all these cases the degree of actual nonempirical content of the ends accounts only for a flexibility of action in terms of them or for an apathetic reaction.
Manifestly structured action always involves some identification of empirical actions with nonempirical ends. Why
this "doubling" of ends takes place is an interesting
problem. Whether it should or should not be eliminated
as far as possible is no scientific question. For science
the relevant fact is that men behave in such a fashion,
and therefore, if their action and its results are to be
studied scientifically, recognition must be given to such
factors and their effects on action. Furthermore, there
is another problem involved. The range of variation of
action possible within the limits set by human heredity
and nonhuman environment is so broad that, unless knowledge is forthcoming that proves empirically a far more
narrow possible range of variation than presently seems
to hold, it is difficult to conceive of any method by
which men may order possible empirical choices save by
virtue of orientation to some nonempirical standards with
which subsequent, concurrent, or even previous empirical
choices are identified. Even if it becomes possible to
demonstrate in terms of the factors of human heredity and
nonhuman environment that a large proportion of, or all
members of, the species involved strive for survival of
themselves as individuals and their species as a type, the
range of possible paths to such a survival will still require some nonempirical standards of choice with which
empirical choices can be identified. This will continue
to be the case, at least in theory, until such time as all
of what are now conceived to be decisions among possible

choices of action can be shown to be determined explicitly in terms of species heredity and nonspecies environment.
At present no such biologistic determinism is possible on
purely scientific grounds, and the actions of men are intelligible in terms of concepts such as faith in the
nonempirical ends of action and identification of empirical
ends with them. Furthermore, knowledge of the type of
orientation to nonempirical ends and the type of nonempirical ends involved is relevant to the range of possible
empirical identifications with such ends. As long as
these theories are not disconfirmed, orientation to nonempirical concepts in general, and religious structures
specifically, must continue to play a vital role in the
analysis of the structure of "motivation" in societies.

By no means all of the "motivational" structure of a
society is phrased in terms of ultimate ends. The structure of ultimate ends furnishes a framework within which
social action takes place. "Motivation" in terms of
intermediate ends is no less strategic for social structure than "motivation" in terms of ultimate ends. The
structure of intermediate ends is to a high degree capable
of definition in empirical terms, and classification of
the structures inculcating such "motivation" as rational
or nonrational is quite within the realm of possibility.
From the point of view of order and change one of the most
significant features of "motivation" in terms of intermediate ends is that it must to a rather high degree be
carried out on a voluntary basis. The use of coercive
sanctions to maintain "motivation" in the intermediate
realm is always an indication of malintegration, in that
some individuals are acting or are presumed to be acting
in dysfunctional fashions. Furthermore, as pointed out
before, the use of pure coercion is always limited in societies. In essence, only those uses of coercion that
will "motivate" subsequent voluntary conformity will contribute to the integration of a society, and the limita-

tions on the use of coercion even for these purposes is
considerable. If spanking a child for bullying others
will stop that action and convince the child that it
should not be done regardless of whether subsequent spanking will ensue, it will make for the child's integration
in a society in which bullying is denigrated, provided, of
course, that the latent effects of such discipline are not
such as to result in malintegration on other scores.

The problem of intermediate "motivation" is a ticklish
one since "motivations" in terms of the various concrete
structures of a society cannot be mutually incompatible if
stability is to result, and most probably must to a high
degree be mutually reinforced if any considerable degree
of stability is to be attained. The more highly involved
and complex is the development of differentiated concrete
structures, the more highly involved and complex must be
the structure of "motivation." For all the complexity of
"traditional" China in many respects it was relatively
simple in this respect. Two types of concrete structures
were of overwhelming importance: the family structure on
the one hand and the imperial bureaucracy on the other.
The family units were to a high degree self-sufficient.
Hence "motivation" of the individual to serve family ends
sufficed for an enormous proportion of the average individual's activities. Most of the average individual's
concrete actions were carried out in terms of his family
structure, and family "motivation" applied, therefore, to
most of the economic, political, and other aspects of his
action. The imperial bureaucracy, to which, perhaps,
should be added concrete neighborhood structures and clan
structures, performed most of the functions having to do
with interfamilial relationships in the society. The
great problem of "motivation" in "traditional" China as
far as social stability was concerned was to ensure that
a situation would exist such that family interest would
dictate conformity of family members to the institutional-

ized structures of interfamilial and nonfamilial relationships. This problem was in turn simplified by the relatively small number of interfamily activities, nonfamily
activities, or activities relating families and other
concrete structures made possible by the high degree of
family self-sufficiency. It matters relatively little
that a son will not inform on his father's criminal activities or testify against his father, if fathers sufficiently family oriented to train their sons can be counted
on by virtue of that same family orientation to refrain
from criminal activities lest their apprehension threaten
the whole family fortune.

Compare the Chinese situation in these respects,
however, to a society of many different types of highly
interdependent concrete structures. Many of these concrete structures, though specifically insulated from one
another, are crucial for one another. Membership in such
concrete structures is highly mobile both ideally and
actually, and in many of them orientation to specific
types of concrete structures is to a high degree detailed
and limited. Modern industrial societies are of this
type. In such societies the problem of intermediate
"motivation" is highly complex by comparison with that of
"traditional" China. Concentration on family loyalties
would introduce nepotistic factors dysfunctional to the
predominantly economically oriented structures of such
societies; concentration on individual mobility necessary
for industrial recruitment requires highly mobile family
units that have apparently substantial sources of instability, if the divorce rate in such societies is any
indication of family instability. Inculcation on children
of belief in universalistic criteria for all sorts of
selections including affection and intimacy prepares them
for the occupational world but makes family units highly
fragile, and so it goes. To the extent that the intermediate means-end range of action is complicated, the

intermediate "motivational" structure is also complicated.

One of the problems of societies with highly complicated intermediate means-ends ranges of action is the
direct relevance and effectiveness of ultimate ends.
Here, the question of indeterminacy in goal orientations
and hence in the structure of "motivation" must be raised
again. A completely institutionalized system of goals to
cover all possible contingencies facing individuals is
quite out of the question for even the simplest societies.
The cognitive problems alone would make such a state of
affairs impossible. Even if the cognitive problems were
not of such an order, the slightest changes in the setting
factors of the society would require complete reformulation of the "motivational" system, and temporarily at
least a chaotic state would result. To a high degree in
all societies stability of the social structure depends
on "motivation" of individuals in more or less general
terms and a general structuring of action such that maintenance of the crucial or more or less strategic structures will serve different ends within this range of
indeterminacy. Thus, profit seeking in predominantly
economically oriented structures in the United States may
serve such diverse further ends as money for consumption
goals and leisure expenditures, money for philanthropic
purposes, capital for further expansion of production, the
economic requirements for increased power over others, and
so forth. Regardless of which one, or which combination
of such ends, a businessman may have in that society his
actions in his role as executive in a business firm in the
face of different market situations may very well be
identical. Similarly, two physicians, one with an "altruistic" love of his fellow man, and another seeking only
his personal advancement in the field, may both be led to
act identically in emergency situations. These are both
examples in which the goals intermediate to a diversity of
further goals require the same means regardless of which

of the further goals the actor may seek. The instability
that might otherwise result from the indeterminacy about
the further goals is in situations like these mitigated
at least by the structured uniformity of the situation.

The types of indeterminacy in the "motivational"
structure that can be tolerated without change in a society are of great significance in understanding sources
of order and change in the society. A modern industrial
society, for example, can tolerate considerable indeterminacy and variation in "motivation" as to how increases
in material productivity are to be utilized, but they are
not nearly so flexible with regard to the question of
whether or not increases in material productivity should
be sought at all. For many problems of social analysis
the factors relative to which explicit "motivational"
structures are lacking are quite as significant as those
factors relative to which such structures are present.

Before leaving the general subject of integration a
few notes on the question of uncertainty and certainty in
social systems are necessary. A tremendous amount of
social science literature has in the past concerned itself
with social structures that serve the function of ac-
climating or reconciling individuals to situations of
uncertainty. The phenomenon of magic as discussed by
Malinowski[2] is, perhaps, the classic example of this sort
of concern. Malinowski discovered a great deal of magical
activity among the Trobriand Islanders. Magical activity,
as the term is used here, involves the use of nonempirical
means for empirical ends. Malinowski found activity of
this sort in many areas, but the clue to the function of
such structures relative to uncertainty emerged when he
compared deep-sea fishing with lagoon fishing. In the

---

2. B. Malinowski, Magic, Science, and Religion and
Other Essays, The Free Press, Glencoe, Ill., 1948, pp. 11-
16.

latter, yield was relatively assured in relation to effort,
danger was almost nonexistent, and the relevant empirical
factors were either clearly understood or relatively invariant. In deep-sea fishing, yield was uncertain, danger
was often great, and the empirical factors involved were
neither clearly understood nor relatively invariant.
Malinowski reported no magical action relative to lagoon
fishing and a great deal relative to deep-sea fishing.
He also found that in relation to deep-sea fishing a clear
line between "bad" magic and "bad" workmanship was drawn.
Disaster from a storm was the result of "bad" magic, failure as the result of a poorly made canoe was "bad" workmanship, and so forth. In other applications of magic
Malinowski and others inevitably found elements of uncertainty, and came to the conclusion that explanation of
success or failure in uncertainty situations via nonempirical agencies somehow provided for men the reassurance
necessary for them to continue the activities.

Another form of activity highly relevant to uncertainty situations[3] is that which may be described as
faddism. Faddism may be defined as the relatively rapid
and intense alteration and application of means for relatively fixed ends. This type of action may fall into any
of the rational or nonrational categories. The rapid
alteration of fashions in clothing in many societies, of
some of the techniques of therapy in modern medical practice, of recreational forms, and the like, are all examples of this phenomenon. Uncertainty elements are
usually marked in the situations in which fads operate.
The element of novelty is of the essence of fads, and
integration to uncertainty is in terms of the faith that
the new method may serve to secure or maintain the old
end.

---

3. And also to certainty ones: see immediately below.

Integration to certainty situations is also a phenomenon of social systems. The problem of certainty in
social systems has been more neglected than that of uncertainty, perhaps because the latter has been more intriguing by virtue of its frequent dramatic aspects. The
problem of certainty has not been totally ignored, of
course. Thomas and Znaniecki treat of it explicitly via
their concept of the desire for new experience.[4] Nevertheless the phenomenon of boredom in societies has not
been extensively treated by social scientists despite the
fact of the existence of several types of activity that
may be interpreted rather obviously in these terms. Most
notable, perhaps, is the phenomenon of gambling which in
one form or another is almost universally reported as a
feature of societies. A major aspect of gambling lies in
the creation of uncertainty where it was previously absent.
The outcome of a horse race is uncertain in itself. Bet-
ting money on a horse race ties an economic allocation to
this uncertainty. The uncertainties of gambling create
the possibility, at least in the mind of the gambler, that
windfall gains may accrue to him even though it is certain that they will not come from other sources. The
frequent association of magical action with gambling also
argues for the uncertainty element involved in gambling
itself.

Faddism has been mentioned above as a technique of
integration to uncertainty. It may also integrate to
certainty by destroying the certainty. The essence of
faddism is novelty and the essence of certainty is the
absence of novelty. The functions to be served by fads
in situations of boredom (i.e., malintegration because of
certainty) are patent enough. In the case of fads both
certainty and uncertainty factors may operate simultaneous-

---

4. W. I. Thomas and F. Znaniecki, The Polish Peasant
in Europe and America, Boston, 1918, Vol. I, p. 73.

ly. In modern medical practice, for example, the certainty that established techniques will be of little use and
the uncertainty attendant on doing nothing may both serve
as stimuli to faddish activity.[5]

Whatever the case may be for the specific suggestions
made here, integration to both uncertainty and certainty
situations are often, if not inevitably, crucial in societies. Individuals seem to be frequently upset by both
conditions of certainty and uncertainty. The results of
such disturbances may have far-reaching consequences.
Magic, faddism, and gambling cover the range of different
types of situations involving empirical certainty or uncertainty.[6] Magic apparently integrates individuals well
to uncertainty situations. Fads apparently may serve the
same functions relative to certainty or uncertainty situations. Gambling is admirably suited for integration to
certainty situations. The apparent ubiquity, or at least
the frequency of appearance, of all three types of phenomena in all societies is surely not a matter of chance.
Certainly, ranges of variation relative to certainty must
exist in all societies. The problem posed by such phenomena as magic, fads, gambling, and the like, as far as
social stability is concerned, is whether or not the eufunctional aspects of such phenomena are equaled or offset
by dysfunctional aspects. Social engineers concerned with
alterations in such structures might be well advised to
investigate such problems carefully and thoroughly or have
them investigated by others before attempting changes in
them.

---

5. In unpublished lectures delivered at Harvard on
the medical profession, Parsons has presented an extensive
discussion of medical fads in much the same terms as those
used here. The present material on medical fads rests
on those lectures.

6. Religious action as defined here covers the range
of problems concerned with certainty and uncertainty about
nonempirical ends.

In the general area of expression the residual elements make analysis as much of a problem as that of integration. All action has expressive aspects as well as
integrative (or malintegrative) ones, economic ones, and
so forth. Some of the primary concerns touched on briefly
elsewhere in this volume are roughly lumped together under
the present heading. These include such forms of expression as recreation, artistic activities, and "other emotional reactions." The lines dividing such distinctions
are extremely difficult to draw. Artistic endeavor may be
recreation, and so forth.

Recreational activities as the term is used here
covers those activities viewed by the individuals concerned as furnishing relaxation and release from the usual
duties and concerns of daily life. Games, gossip, dancing,
reading, drinking, feasting, vacationing, and a variety
of similar phenomena fall under this general heading. One
of the most obvious eufunctional aspects of such activities is the release from the tensions and strains of
everyday life that they afford.

With respect to recreational activities one of the
most general distinctions that can be raised is that between societies or portions of societies in which recreational activities are combined simultaneously with the
usual duties and concerns of everyday life and those in
which the two are sharply separated from one another. The
contrast between relatively nonindustrialized societies
and highly industrialized ones is marked in these respects.
In recent years a song[7] of brief but intense popularity in
the United States put the distinction well by stating the
point of view of a member of a hypothetical nonliterate
unindustrialized society. This "savage" states that he

---

7. See Civilization (Bongo, Bongo, Bongo), words and
music by Bob Hilliard and Carl Sigman, Edwin H. Morris and
Co., New York, 1947.

has no desire to seek the delights of "civilization" since
the people already enjoying those delights seem to him to
suffer most of the year in order to practice for two weeks
the delights he pursues day in and day out. The song no
doubt distorts both the pictures of nonindustrial and
highly industrial social life, but there can hardly be any
doubt that, especially with regard to the structure of
occupational roles, the daily routine in highly industrialized societies is something to be escaped from in a
sense that it is certainly not in many nonindustrialized
or little industrialized situations. The phenomenon of
vacations (with pay) in which the individual seeks to
differentiate his activities as much as possible from his
usual ones may not be entirely absent from nonindustrial
societies, but it is certainly not the center of emphasis
in any of them that it is in highly industrialized societies, and it is often absent altogether.

It cannot be emphasized too strongly that the essence
of recreation is not the absence of expenditure of energy.
Many of the most highly prized forms of recreation, notably
games, amateur sports, and the like, are often extremely
rigorous physical expressions. The essence of the difference lies rather in the fact that to be worn out by a day
at the office is considered highly unpleasant and sometimes even productive of sleepless nights whereas physical
exhaustion resultant from a day's recreation is usually
considered both pleasant and productive of a "good night's
sleep."

The distinction is not an idle one. Recreation, as
the referent of that term is conceived here, serves the
function of integrating the individual to the usual duties
and concerns of daily life. To the extent that it is
"built in," as it were, those duties and concerns themselves, it bolsters the "motivational" structure necessary
to maintain them. To the extent that it is sharply differentiated it may fail to do so. If the distinction

reaches the point at which the individual conceives himself as "living" only in relatively restricted recreational periods, much of the "motivational" structure for the
other periods may hang solely on making that recreation
possible. Such a situation makes the predominantly recrea-
tionally oriented concrete structures immensely important
from the point of view of the total social system.

Such a situation has apparently already been approximated in some highly industrialized situations. The requirements of operation of mechanized mass production and
many attendant occupations such as secretarial work are
such as to require unremitting attention and effort. Even
such activities as conversation with fellow workers may be
highly disruptive to efficiency under such conditions. It
is not a matter of accident that cliques and small personal
freedoms are so jealously guarded by and play so important
a role in the morale of industrial workers.[8] It is also
not an accident that recent years have witnessed so many
different attempts to provide recreation on the job in
such situations via musical programs, production contests,
and the like. The mark of success of such attempts is the
discovery of a form of recreation that will be enjoyed and
not interfere with production or, if possible, even increase production.

Closely connected with the question of whether or not
or in what respects recreational aspects of action are
tied in with the everyday routines of existence or separated sharply from them is the question of the character
of the recreational aspect itself. In this respect a
distinction may be drawn between escapist and nonescapist
recreational structures. The distinguishing mark of
escapist recreational structure as the concept is used

---

8. The pioneering work of F. J. Roethlisberger and
W. J. Dickson and the subsequent work of many others is
illustrative of this point.

here lies in the element of "nonreality" involved in the
structures concerned. The recreational aspects of action
may be considered escapist to the extent and in the manner
that the recreational value of an activity for the individuals concerned inheres either manifestly or latently in
the fact that the action concerned permits the individual
to identify himself in part or in whole with a state of
affairs in fact not his or to lose all sense of contact
with his own state of affairs. Some illustrations of the
application of this concept come easily to hand. Using
this definition of escapist recreational structures, some
of the use of drugs and alchohol is an example of almost
purely escapist recreational structures. The action of
these substances is sometimes such as to take the user out
of effectual contact with the empirical world as far as
his own consciousness is concerned and give him at least
temporarily a feeling of ease and content in which the
actual empirical state of his affairs, aside from the
taking of the drug or alchohol itself, plays an extremely
restricted role if any. In fact, the role played by his
actual empirical condition is likely to have its most
important effect by way of defining, at least negatively,
the ideal state to which the action of these substances
gives access, at least on an imaginative level.[9] These
substances may also be escapist in a more negative sense
in that their use may bring unconsciousness and a loss of

_____

9. One of the most prominent features of drug addiction, of course, is the increasing difficulty of attaining
such a state and the increasing dependence on the drug to
maintain an "even keel," let alone reach the escapist
stage. For such addicts the escapist aspect of the use of
drugs may be reduced solely to the avoidance of the "withdrawal symptoms" felt by the addict in the absence of
drugs. It is by no means intended to imply that the uses
and effects of drugs and alchohol are identical. On the
subject of opiates see, A. R. Lindesmith, Opiate Addiction,
Principia Press, Bloomington, Ind., 1947.

all awareness, imaginative or otherwise.

Amateur participation in competetive sports is, on the other hand, to a high degree nonescapist as a recreational structure. Such sports activities may or may not be directly tied into or strictly separated from the usual duties and concerns of everyday life, but the essence of its nonescapist character, as that concept is used here, lies in the emphasis that such activities place on the actual abilities of the individual and his relative standing vis-à-vis others in these respects. Actual participation in competitive sports emphasizes quite definite empirical aspects of the individual, and at least some of the recreational value of such activities lies not in its difference from the actual state of affairs but rather in its emphasis on the actual state in these respects.

Spectator forms of recreation, on the other hand, open up the possibility of escapist elements. By no means all of the recreational aspects of spectator actions are escapist, but many of them often are. Spectators at sports events, at least in many cases, would appear to gain a considerable amount of relaxation and enjoyment from vicarious participation in the events they witness.[10] The motion picture as a recreational instrument in the United States is a marked example of a spectator form of recreation containing major escapist elements. The tendency of American motion pictures to present idealized rather than highly realistic reflections of daily life is too obvious to require comment. This has been the basis of much adverse aesthetic criticism of the motion pictures, but from the standpoint of their eufunctional or dysfunctional results in the society these escapist aspects may

------

10. In some forms of recreation usually considered extreme and often classified as pathological in some societies this vicarious participation is virtually the whole of the phenomenon. Voyeurism is one of the most obvious examples of this sort of activity.

be of the greatest significance. Persistent repetition
of the theme of the "poor but honest and good" girl who
marries the wealthy exemplary young man may be dysfunctional in that it increases the dissatisfaction of the
average "poor but honest and good" girl with her actual
lot. It almost certainly has eufunctional aspects too,
however, in that at least for a period of an hour or so
the average "poor but honest and good" girl may enjoy
vicariously things as they "should" be from her point of
view. Adventure tales in which virtue always triumphs
over evil contain similar elements.

There are rather interestingly different implications
of escapist and nonescapist recreational structures as far
as social stability is concerned. Nonescapist structures
hold out signal possibilities for reinforcing directly the
structures of daily routines at the same time that relaxation from them is afforded. Participation in competitive
sports, for example, in the United States clearly emphasizes universalistic criteria of selection and many other
standards that are of crucial institutional significance
in other social areas. In fact, childhood participation
in such activities is almost certainly one of the most
important educational elements in that society. Starting
at a very early age it inculcates an understanding and
faith in universalistic criteria, for example, that tempers
the highly particularistic treatment of the child as a
family member, and prepares him in part for the increasingly great emphasis that others with whom he comes into
contact as he matures are likely to place on such criteria
in selecting or rejecting him for an extremely wide range
of relationships. It may be suggested, therefore, that
nonescapist recreational structures may play vital educational and other directly integrative roles in many other
spheres of activity.

Escapist structures, on the other hand, do not promise
such reinforcement of structures in other realms. The

eufunctional implications of purely escapist structures
inhere in the fact that they remove the individual at
least temporarily from the whole realm in which tensions
and conflicts arise. As far as dysfunctional results are
concerned, escapist structures open two possibilities at
least. The first is negative and relative because the
operation of such structures may be dysfunctional in that,
by comparison with others, they fail to buttress requisite
structures in other social actions. The other is more
directly observable. If the stresses and strains of everyday life are great and if highly effective purely escapist
structures are available, they may become a goal of such
primacy that the individual no longer operates effectively
in his other roles with dysfunctional results that will
vary in type and degree with the variation of his other
roles and their significance in the society as a whole and
its component concrete structures. Alchoholism is sometimes a clear-cut case of this sort.

Recreational structures that combine escapist and
nonescapist elements may, of course, combine the eufunctional and dysfunctional possibilities of both. The most
romantic motion pictures may picture more or less correctly the ideal structures of a society while at the same
time they distort its actual structures. They may thus
at one and the same time reinforce the ideal structures
and offer the spectator escape into that fairyland in
which the degree of conformity with those structures is
so much greater than it is in actual experience. The extremely complex possibilities in these respects are again
no argument against social engineering, but argue merely
that in this field too the cognitive problems of social
engineering are by no means simple. It is not possible on
a priori grounds to assume that, since recreational structures are often not judged the legitimate forms of serious
preoccupation for mature individuals, they are somehow
less significant as far as social structure is concerned

than structures that are regarded as a legitimate focus
of serious preoccupation for mature individuals.

The question of _artistic_ structures is closely related to that of recreation specifically and of integration and expression in general. _Artistic_ structures as
the term is used here have reference to the structures
that prevail in such fields as plastic, graphic, literary,
musical, and dramatic expression. Action in terms of
artistic structures, particularly in the case of the enjoyment of the results of things produced in terms of such
structures, contains major recreational elements. Relaxation and pleasure and release from the usual duties and
concerns of everyday life are certainly involved, but the
activities usually classified as predominantly artistic
place a special emphasis on other factors as well. Most
notably, perhaps, the emphasis is placed on skill of
execution within the medium chosen and the ability of the
chosen medium to stimulate the observer emotionally
through the observer's reception of the results of the
process rather than his participation in it. With regard
to artistic structures the distinctions made with respect
to recreation in general may be observed. Artistic structures integrally built into daily activities and ones
sharply separated from them may be observed in different
societies or even within a single society. Escapist and
nonescapist forms may be distinguished, and the implications of these distinctions may be sought.

There is, however, an added distinction of considerable general relevance in this sphere. Emphasizing as
they do skill of execution and the ability to produce
emotional response in the observer, artistic structures
usually focus on the element of "creativity" of the artist
or artists. What special quality do these men add to what
they do, whether they add it in a spectacularly individualistic fashion or in an anonymous group? It is in terms
of this factor of "creativity" that the distinction invoked

here arises. The distinction has to do with the range of
creativity. Does it operate within a highly institutionalized rigidly defined framework with a consequently narrowed range of departures in expressive technique or does
it operate with wide latitude in these respects? The
range open to the creativity of the Chinese landscape
painters at some periods in Chinese history fell into the
first category. Modern painting in the twentieth century
falls into the latter. This distinction, sometimes referred to as that between highly formalized art and its
opposite, may be of some significance in the analysis of
order and change in societies. The restricted range of
creativity is likely to be eufunctional unless certain
types of change are institutionalized in the society and
unless the range of possible artistic variations is in
that society relevant to such changes.

The category of "other emotional reactions" includes
the structures of expression of such states as "anger,"
"grief," "love," "pleasure," "hate," "pity," and the like.
As has been pointed out above in Chapter IV, the state of
definition and analysis of the whole range of aspects of
phenomena classified as "affective" or "emotional" is
extremely unsatisfactory. No attempt will be made here to
attack this truly formidable problem in any basic manner.
All that will be attempted here are some distinctions
among types of structures of affective expression.

In Chapter IV the importance of the regulation of
affective expression was discussed, and some attempt was
made to show that some state of regulation of affective
expression is a functional requisite for any society.
Here, a polar distinction between complete repression of
affective expression and complete freedom of affective
expression may be drawn. Obviously, neither pole may be
realized for any society as a whole though either may be
realized in some respects at some times relative to some
parts of a society. For societies as a whole it is, of

course, a matter of differing emphases.

In some societies overt affective expression is repressed to an extreme degree. In such there must be
highly institutionalized structures of interrelationships
worked out in great detail and carried to very low levels
of generalization. If overt affective expression is to be
highly repressed, there must exist a highly elaborate
rigidly defined set of structures that will cover action
in situations likely to have strong affective effects.
Failure to develop such elaborate and rigid institutions
runs the risk of leaving elements of the situation undefined in the affective aspects of action. It is not
enough merely to interdict certain forms of overt affective expression if affective expression is to be highly
repressed. Problems of interpretation would be much too
great to list in detail all forms of affective expression
that must or could be repressed. In such societies elaborate systems of overt affective expression in relationships must be institutionalized regardless of whether
these particular ones are in any specific case sincerely
felt or not. The elaborate systems of honorific modes of
address in Tokugawa Japan is an indication of this sort of
situation. The very habits of speech formalize overt
affective expression. In such systems relatively slight
breakdowns in conformity are highly noticeable, and such
systems may be very precariously balanced. Whether or not
a "hydraulic theory" of affective phenomena, i.e., that
affects repressed must find some outlet sooner or later,
is tenable, it would at least seem tenable to hold that
not all forms of affective expression can be so rigidly
defined in a society. In such tightly defined systems
there are usually some specific phenomena that can be interpreted as outlets. The release afforded Japanese
peasants by drinking and dancing bouts at parties of the
sort cited by Embree[11] has inescapable overtones of this

---

11. John Embree, Suye Mura, University of Chicago
Press, Chicago, 1939, pp. 99-104.

sort. Moreover, in modern Japan the sentimental weeping
of Japanese of both sexes in darkened cinema houses is in
marked contrast with their impassive reaction to the varying experiences of everyday life in the presence of others.
It is reasonable to suspect that such outlets will exist
in such tightly defined systems, and insofar as they do
changes affecting the outlets may have dramatic consequences for other apparently unrelated ranges of action.

Another interesting aspect of societies in which
overt affective expression is minutely defined institutionally is that the members of such societies are radically cut loose from affective regulations if placed in situations to which their habitual institutions have little or
no reference. Again Japan may afford examples. The rape
of Nanking by Japanese soldiers must certainly have contained elements of this sort. The type of affective display in the non-Japanese setting of Nanking would have
been out of the question in Japan itself. In Japan proper,
crimes involving personal violence are far more rare than
in the United States, but although violent displays by
American soldiers in the last war were by no means absent,
no such mass berserk phenomena seem to have been recorded
for them. The structures of affective expression in the
United States permit more markedly violent affective displays in daily life than do the structures of Japan.
Nevertheless, via the institutionalization of predominantly universalistic rather than particularistic standards
in these respects, the affective structures of the United
States leave no social situations so thoroughly undefined
as in the case of the Japanese structures.

In marked contrast with the case of extreme repression
of affective expression is that of relative freedom in
these respects. Of course, freedom can never be complete
if there is to be stability because of the extremely disruptive implications of unregulated affective expression.
The problem posed for social stability by such a system as

this is not the problem of maintaining outlets for affective expression as in the previous case but rather the
problem of controlling outlets. One of the interesting
hypotheses that may be advanced has to do with the contrast between predominantly particularistic and predominantly universalistic standards of affective expression.
In highly repressive systems the importance of tight
positive definitions of affective expression tends to
emphasize particularistic standards in these respects.
Affective expression is a reaction to what is done. Restrictions on it in terms of who a person is makes possible the institutionalization of specific forms of affective expression regardless of circumstances. Universalistic standards, emphasizing as they do what is done, tie
affective expression to variations in what is done. Since
the range of variation of action open to a person is
always greater than the range of variation of the ideal
definitions of his roles, the flexibility of universalistic standards is much greater than that of particularistic ones in this respect.

    The usual situation in societies is one of an ex-
tremely complicated mixture of repressions and freedoms in
affective expression. A society may repress displays of
"anger," encourage expressions of "love," and formalize
expressions of "grief." Variation follows at least four
major criteria. In the first place, there is variation in
what affects may or must be more or less freely expressed
or repressed. In the second place, there is variation in
who may express them. In the third place, there is variation in what is considered a legitimate stimulus for
affective expression. Finally, there is a range of variation in the socially acceptable procedure of expressing
affective reactions. In future development in this field
classification and analysis of societies in terms of
development of these four criteria are likely to be more
fruitful than a simple polar distinction such as that

between repressed and free expression. In further development of this fourfold scheme application of such distinctions as those between repressive and nonrepressive,
universalistic and particularistic, and the like, may be
given a precision of use which they currently lack so
conspicuously in the realm of affective expression.

Perhaps the major reason for devoting space at even
this stage of development to such structures as those of
integration and expression is the implication of such
concepts even in a primitive and rather inchoate state
for other structures rather easier to deal with. The
various solutions presented to the possible range of variation in the structures of integration and expression
are directly germane to other structures. Freedom in
expression of the affect of "romantic love" is almost
certain to be functionally incompatible with the usual
systems of arranged marriages and undoubtedly is functionally incompatible with arranged marriages on a highly
particularistic basis such as a cross-cousin system. Furthermore, free expression of "romantic love" is likely to
be functionally incompatible with the factors of selection
that must necessarily be involved in large scale family
units and may well be functionally incompatible with any
type of family unit that is not highly vulnerable to
disruption via divorce or desertion. Societies requiring
highly universalistic criteria for economic role selection
can hardly carry out the educational aspects of action
largely in highly particularistic family terms. Other-
worldly religious orientations are functionally incompatible with the material preoccupations that must prevail in modern industrial societies. Grievous errors
can be made by singling out a single analytically distinguished aspect of action of this sort, examining its implications for other aspects, and then attributing causal
significance to the original aspect in relation to its
implications. This, however, is the pitfall inherent

in any use of analytic as opposed to concrete structures
for purposes of scientific study. At the same time, to
ignore the inescapable relevance of the structures whose
operations affect one aspect of action for those whose
operations affect another is no less grievous an error.
For all the difficulties presented by the concepts of
integration and expression they can no more be left out
of such analysis than the other analytic structures treated
here. Explicit recognition of their inchoate almost wholly
residual category is a present expedient for the avoidance
of both these extremes.

EXPANDED OUTLINE

This expanded table of contents including most of the definitions of the various concepts used in the text is appended here for the convenience of the reader. Its various subdivisions are more detailed than those that appear as headings in the text, and hence the lettering and numbering system used does not always coincide with that of the text. The page numbers of the passages referred to by these categories are given directly after each item, however, in order that the relevant passages may be located quickly and the difficulties raised by this inconsistency thereby minimized.

CHAPTER I

INTRODUCTION

2) Definition of a strategic institution, 106
A given institution is more or less strategic to the extent that: it is the institutionalized form of all or a portion of a structural requisite (the substantive aspect); and the pattern concerned may (or may not) be altered without destroying the structural requisite involved (critical aspect).
e. The concept of tradition, 108
1) Definition of tradition
A tradition is an institution whose perpetuation is institutionalized.
2) Degree of traditionalization
An institution will be considered more or less traditionalized to the extent that its perpetuation is institutionalized without regard to changes in functional implications of its operations, whether these be eufunctional or dysfunctional implications.

CHAPTER III

THE CONCEPT OF SOCIETY

A. Introduction and definition, 111
1. Introduction, 111
2. Definition of society, 113
A society is a system of action in operation which: (a) involves a plurality of interacting individuals of a given species (or group of species) whose actions are primarily oriented to the system concerned and who are recruited at least in part by the sexual reproduction of members of the plurality involved; (b) is at least in theory self-sufficient for the action of this plurality; and (c) is capable of existing longer than the life span of an individual of the type (or types) involved.
3. Identity and continuity of a society, 116
B. Discussion of the concept of society, 122
1. Membership of the system, 122
a. Definition of members of a society, 122
The members of a society are the plurality of interacting individuals who are involved in a system of action of the type defined here by virtue of the fact that their action is primarily oriented to the system concerned.
1) By primarily oriented is meant that the action of the individual proceeds more in terms of the structures in general, but of the highly strategic and crucial institutions in particular, of one such system than of any other, 123
b. Degree of integration of member, 123
An individual is a more or less well-integrated member of a society to the extent that he accepts and orients his action without conflict to the structures in general, but particularly to the strategic and crucial institutions, of that society.
c. Distinction between ideal and actual structures, 123
1) Definition of utopian structures
A utopian structure is an ideal structure of a sort with which general conformity is not even expected.
d. Distinction between genuine and expedient members, 126
2. Sexual recruitment of the system, 127
a. Two implications of the phrase, 127
1) A society must have a bisexual membership.
2) Recruitment must result at least in part from heterosexual activities.
b. Categories of social systems excluded, 127
1) Systems with members of one sex only
2) Systems with bisexual membership which forbid heterosexual contacts
3) Systems with bisexual membership permitting heterosexual contacts but which are not necessarily recruited in part by such contacts
3. Theoretical self-sufficiency of the system, 129

a. Definition of self-sufficiency, 130

A system of action in operation is in theory self-sufficient only if it is in theory capable of furnishing structures covering all of the functional requisites of the system.

b. Implications of requirement of self-sufficiency, 130

1) In relation of unit to setting, 130

2) In the definition of the unit and the level of generality of the definition, 131

4. Duration of the system, 134

C. Termination and change of a society, 137

1. Four conditions for termination of society, 137

a. Biological extinction or dispersion of the members, 137

b. Apathy of members, 139

1) Definition of apathy, 139

Apathy is the cessation of individual "motivation."

c. The war of all against all, 139

1) Definition, 139

This condition is considered present if the members of an aggregate pursue their ends by means selected only on the basis of instrumental effeciency.

d. Absorption of the society into another society, 140

2. Usefulness of the four conditions in determining the functional requisites of a society, 141

3. Social change, 142

a. Usefulness of the four conditions, 142

b. Definition, note 32, 142

Social change is any alteration which occurs in a system of action of a given species and which is not subject to explanation solely in terms of heredity of that species and its nonspecies environment.

c. Importance of level of generality of definition of unit, 142

D. The concept of culture, 144

1. Definition of culture, 146

A culture is the system of action of a society considered apart from its involvement of a "plurality of interacting individuals...," apart from its operation.

2. Distinctions between society and culture, 146

CHAPTER IV

THE FUNCTIONAL REQUISITES OF ANY SOCIETY

A. Introduction, 149

1. Brief definition of functional requisite, 149

A given function is a requisite of any society if in its absence the relationship between the unit under discussion and its setting in the most general terms can be shown to be such that one or some combination of the four conditions for the termination of a society would result.

2. Tentative nature of any list of functional requisites, 150

3. Analytical distinctness of present list, 150

B. List of functional requisites, 151

1. Provision for an adequate physiological relationship to the setting and for sexual recruitment, 151

a. Aspects of this requisite, 152

1) Maintenance of a sufficient number and kind of the members if the society at an adequate level of functioning, 152

2) Dealing with the implications of the setting for the existence of the unit concerned in a manner that permits of the biological persistence of the membership, 154

3) Structuring of heterosexual relationships to insure opportunities and "motivation" for a sufficient rate of reproduction, 155
2. Role differentiation and role assignment, 157
  a. Introduction and basic definitions, 157
    1) Definition of role, 159
    Role is any position differentiated in terms of a given social structure whether the position be institutionalized or not.
      a) An ideal role is an institutionalized role, 159
      b) An actual role is the position in fact occupied by an individual, 159
    2) Definition of status, 160
    Status is the sum total of an individual's (or group's) ideal or institutionalized roles.
    3) Definition of social standing, 160
    A person's social standing is the sum total of all his roles both ideal and actual.
      a) Definition of actual social standing: the sum total of an individual's actual roles, 160
      b) Definition of ideal social standing, i.e., status: the sum total of an individual's ideal roles, 160
    4) Definition of office (by reference to K. Davis; see note 19), 160
    5) Definition of station, 160
    Station is a cluster of roles which may be combined in one individual and recognized as so combined in a great many cases.
    6) Definition of stratum, 160
    Stratum is a mass of persons in a given society enjoying roughly the same station.
  b. Definitions of role differentiation and role assignment as functions, 161
    1) Role differentiation is that state of affairs in which the roles involved are heterogeneous.
    2) Role assignment is that state of affairs that exists when the obligations, rights, and expected performances involved in roles are taught and allocated to an individual or individuals.
  c. Basis for classification of role differentiation and role assignment as a functional requisite of any society, 161
  d. Definition of stratification, 164
    Stratification is the particular type of role differentiation that differentiates higher and lower standings in terms of one or more criteria.
3. Communication, 166
  a. Definition of communication, 166
    Communication is the activity or process whereby one (or more individuals) of a given species infers from the behavior (whether language of both oral and written types, gesture, or posture) of another individual (or group of individuals) of the same or different species an idea or feeling or state of affairs that the other individual(s) is trying to convey.
  b. Basis for classification of communication as a functional requisite of any society, 167
4. Shared cognitive orientations, 168
  a. Definition of cognition, 168
    Cognition is knowledge or understanding of a situation or phenomenon (empirical or nonempirical).
  b. Basis for classification of shared cognitive orientations as a functional requisite of any society, 169
  c. Classification of cognitive orientations, 171
    1) Basic cognitive orientations, 171
    Definition: those elements of cognition in a society that must be institutionalized for every member of the society at some stage of his or her development

if the society is to persist as defined.
2) Intermediate cognitive orientations, 171
   Definition: all cognitive orientations other than the basic ones in a society.
   a) Institutionalized
   b) Noninstitutionalized
   c) Application of concepts _crucial_ and _strategic_ (and its qualifying aspects)
      to cognitive orientations, 172
5. A shared articulated set of goals, 173
   a. Definition of goal, 173
      A goal is a state of affairs deemed desirable by the actors concerned.
   b. Basis for classification of a shared articulated set of goals as a functional
      requisite of any society, 173
   c. Classification of goals, 174
      1) Basic value orientations, 175
         The basic value orientations of a society are those goals that are such that
         the members of that society must hold them sufficiently in common to "moti-
         vate" the performance of the functional requisites of that society and that
         are such that the holding of them is institutionalized for each member of the
         society at some stage of his development.
      2) Intermediate value orientations, or intermediate goals, 175
         a) Institutionalized
         b) Noninstitutionalized
   d. Possibility of mutually incompatible goals, or goals with dysfunctional aspects,
      177
   e. Empirical and nonempirical goals, 179
   f. Indeterminacy of goal systems, 180
      Definition: indeterminate goal systems are goal systems that do not identify all
      possible goals in the actions of the members of the society.
6. The regulation of the choice of means, 182
   a. Definition: the prescription of means for attaining the socially formulated goals
      of a society and its substructures, 182
   b. Basis for classification of the regulation of the choice of means as a functional
      requisite of any society, 182
7. The regulation of affective expression, 183
   a. Definition of affect, 183
      The term affect includes components of pleasurable or painful significance to the
      actor, and of approval or disapproval of the object or state which occasions the
      reaction, and those reactions to stimuli which are commonly catalogued under the
      term "emotions," i.e., "anger," "hate," "fear," "love," "pity," etc.
   b. Basis for classification of the regulation of affective expression as a function-
      al requisite for any society, 183
      1) Aspects of the regulation of affective expression, 183
         a) Comprehensibility of affective states, 183
         b) Suppression of certain affects, 185
         c) Production of certain affects, 186
         d) Regulation of lengths to which affective expression is carried, 186
8. Adequate socialization, 187
   a. Definition of socialization, 187
      Socialization is the inculcation of the structure of action of a society on an
      individual (or group).
      1) Adequate socialization of an individual, 187
         An individual is adequately socialized if he has been inculcated with a suffi-
         cient portion of the structures of action of his society to permit the ef-
         fective performance of his roles in the society.
      2) Adequate socialization in a society, 187
         There is adequate socialization in a society if there is a sufficient number

CHAPTER V

SOME METHODOLOGICAL PROBLEMS

CHAPTER VI

THE ANALYTIC ASPECTS OF RELATIONSHIP STRUCTURES

CHAPTER VII

THE STRUCTURE OF ROLE DIFFERENTIATION

A. Introduction, 299

 1. Definition, 299

The analytic structure of role differentiation in any social system is defined as the structures of distribution of the members of the system among the various posi-

CHAPTER VIII

THE STRUCTURE OF SOLIDARITY

CHAPTER IX

THE STRUCTURE OF ECONOMIC ALLOCATION

a. Degree of economic self-sufficiency of the unit, 412
   1) Definition, 412
     A concrete unit will be considered economically self-sufficient to the degree
     and in the respects that its membership can and does both produce and consume
     all of the goods and services necessary to and resulting from the operation
     of the unit.
   2) Implications of economic self-sufficiency for interrelationships between
     concrete units, 412
   3) Variation in degree and type of self-sufficiency, 413
     a) Extent of production by unit of factors needed for its own production
     b) Extent of production by unit of factors needed for consumption by unit
       apart from that involved in the production itself
       (1) Examples: factory unit of modern business concern and family unit in
          "traditional" China, 414
   4) Implications of productive self-sufficiency for other analytic structures in
     society, 416
     a) For political allocation: difference in ease of control from outside unit,
       416
     b) For role differentiation and solidarity, 417
   5) Relevance of degree and type of economic self-sufficiency for social change,
     418
b. The relationship aspects of the unit: with respect to distinction between industrialized and nonindustrialized societies, 421
   1) The cognitive aspects, 421
     a) Industrial society requires rationality
     b) Nonindustrial societies usually "traditional"
   2) The membership criteria aspects, 424
     a) Industrialized societies: requires predominantly universalistic criteria
       (1) Intrusion of particularistic elements, 428
     b) Nonindustrial societies: usually predominantly particularistic, 429
   3) The substantive definition aspects, 430
     a) Industrialized systems: requires functional specificity, 431
     b) Nonindustrialized systems: usually functionally diffuse, 433
     c) Close relation between particularism and functional specificity, 434
   4) The affective aspects, 437
     a) Industrialized systems: eufunctionality of intimacy structures varies with
       degree to which they carry with them functionally diffuse elements, 438
     b) Nonindustrialized societies: will vary with the character of the func-
       tionally diffuse elements, 438
   5) The goal orientation aspects, 439
     a) Both industrialized and nonindustrialized societies may mix individual-
       istic and responsible orientations, 439
     b) Possibility of dysfunctionality of individualistic orientation in highly
       industrialized societies, 440
     c) Implication of goal orientation aspect in productive unit for interrela-
       tionship between economic and other aspects of social structure, 440
     d) Difficulty of individualistic orientations in units combining basic pro-
       duction and consumption, 441
   6) The stratification aspect, 441
     a) Production units in both types of societies must, in some at least, be
       hierarchically arranged
       (1) Difference in ability
       (2) Managerial requirement
     b) Types and degrees of hierarchies, 443
c. The type of product orientation of the unit, 444
   1) Raw materials

CHAPTER X

THE STRUCTURE OF POLITICAL ALLOCATION

CHAPTER XI

THE STRUCTURE OF INTEGRATION AND EXPRESSION

A. Introduction, 504
   1. A residual category, 504
   2. Integration, 504
      a. Integration denotes eufunctional adaptation to a concrete structure, 504
      b. The analytical structure of integration in a concrete structure consists of
         those structures the operation of which makes for the eufunctional adaptation
         of the members and/or members to be of the structure to the structure concerned.
      c. Few patterns which are entirely integrative, 505
         1) A predominantly integrative structure is one which on the whole has more
            eufunctional than dysfunctional results from its operations.
   3. Expression, 505
      a. Expression denotes the type and limits of reaction, symbolic or otherwise, on
         the part of individuals or groups to the various phenomena with which they come
         in contact.
      b. The analytic structure of expression in a society or other concrete structure
         consists of those structures that define the type and limits of reaction,
         symbolic or otherwise, on the part of individuals or groups to the various
         phenomena with which they come into contact.
      c. Main reaction here is affective
B. Integration: what are the structures whereby the socialization of new members of the
   society is attained, and what are the structures whereby the general inculcation and
   maintenance of the values, attitudes, and procedures of a society are carried out?,
   506
   1. Education, 507
      a. Requisite basis, 507
         1) Problem of new members recruited by birth, 507
         2) Problem of other new members, 507
         3) Education at later stages of development, 508
      b. Factors to be determined about any particular system of education, 508
         1) Content of education
         2) Educational procedure
         3) Who, and under what conditions, have the roles of students and teachers?
      c. Integrative aspects of educational structures, 509
   2. Structure of "motivation," 509
      a. "Motivation" is concerned with the establishment of the ends of action whether
         these be empirical or nonempirical, intermediate or ultimate.
      b. "Motivation" to ultimate values, 510
         1) Religion, 511
            a) Definition (see expanded outline, p. 557)
            b) Two sorts, 512
               (1) Ethical religions are religions which orient to ultimate values
                   directly.
               (2) Supernatural religions are religions which orient to ultimate values
                   through orientation to one or more supernatural entities.
            c) Predominantly religious structures (see expanded outline, p. 557), 513
            d) Distinction between exclusive and nonexclusive religions, 513
               (1) Exclusive religions are those that are institutionalized in such
                   fashion that an individual may, institutionally speaking, be oriented
                   to one and only one religious system at one time, 514
               (2) Nonexclusive religions are those that are institutionalized in such
                   fashion that an individual may, institutionally speaking, be oriented
                   to more than one religious system at any one time, 514